Wendy Wong

Grassroots for Hire

Although "grassroots" conjures up images of independent citizen organiz-ing, much mass participation today is sponsored by elite consultants work-ing for corporations and powerful interest groups. This book pulls back the curtain to reveal a lucrative industry of consulting firms that incentivize public activism as a marketable service. Edward Walker illustrates how, spurred by the post-1960s advocacy explosion and rising business political engagement, elite consultants have deployed new technologies to commerci-alize mass participation. Using evidence from interviews, surveys, and public records, *Grassroots for Hire* paints a detailed portrait of these con-sultants and their clients. Today, *Fortune* 500 firms hire them to counter-mobilize against regulation, protest, or controversy. Ironically, some advo-cacy groups now outsource organizing to them. Walker also finds that consultants are reshaping both participation and policymaking, but uneth-ical "astroturf" strategies are often ineffective. This path-breaking book calls for a rethinking of interactions between corporations, advocacy groups, and elites in politics.

EDWARD T. WALKER is Assistant Professor in the Department of Sociology at the University of California, Los Angeles.

Grassroots for Hire

Public Affairs Consultants in American Democracy

EDWARD T. WALKER
University of California, Los Angeles

CAMBRIDGE
UNIVERSITY PRESS

University Printing House, Cambridge CB2 8BS, United Kingdom

Published in the United States of America by Cambridge University Press, New York

Cambridge University Press is part of the University of Cambridge.

It furthers the University's mission by disseminating knowledge in the pursuit of education, learning, and research at the highest international levels of excellence.

www.cambridge.org
Information on this title: www.cambridge.org/9781107619012

© Edward T. Walker 2014

First published 2014

Printed in the United Kingdom by Clays, St Ives plc

A catalogue record for this publication is available from the British Library

Library of Congress Cataloguing in Publication data
Walker, Edward T.
Grassroots for hire : public affairs consultants in American democracy / Edward T. Walker.
    pages   cm. – (Business and public policy)
Includes bibliographical references and index.
ISBN 978-1-107-02136-5 (hardback)
1. Public interest lobbying – United States.   2. Community organization – United States.   3. Business and politics – United States.   4. Industrial policy – United States.   5. Democracy – United States.   I. Title.
JK1118.W346   2014
322′.30973–dc23

2013046196

ISBN 978-1-107-02136-5 Hardback
ISBN 978-1-107-61901-2 Paperback

For Evelyn

Contents

Figures

Tables

Acknowledgements

Studying how organizations mobilize political participation has instilled in me a deep appreciation of how individual and group actions are made possible by particular social contexts. Intellectual production is no different, as ideas about how best to understand social life require a fertile context in which to take root. Accordingly, this study would not have been possible without the support of those colleagues, students, research collaborators, family, and friends who helped me as I over-hauled what started as a dissertation into a finished book.

First, I thank the public affairs consultants who took the time to sit for an interview with me, respond to my survey, and/or provide feedback on the project. Although our confidentiality agreements do not, of course, permit me to offer personal thanks here to the many who took time out of their (often incredibly) busy schedules to participate, I hope all of my interviewees and respondents know how much I value their support of this research.

This work was made possible with the support of a number of grants and fellowships. As a doctoral dissertation, this research was awarded a Doctoral Dissertation Improvement Grant from the National Science Foundation (#SES-0527344). This grant was used to collect the baseline data on the population of consultants. In order to assess which of these consulting firms survived, I received a small seed grant from the University of Vermont College of Arts and Sciences. This allowed me to write the grant proposal for the surveys and interviews of the firms that survived, which, in turn, was funded jointly by the NSF's Sociology and Political Science programs (#SES-0851153). Support through the Robert Wood Johnson Foundation's (RWJF) Scholars in Health Policy Research program provided me with a leave from teaching and time to complete this book. Of course, although I am exceedingly grateful for support from these funders, they bear no responsibility for the analyses reported here.

I was also fortunate enough to receive thoughtful questions and feedback on various portions of this project during talks at Harvard

Business School, New York University, the Ohio State University, Pennsylvania State University, Institut d'études politiques de Paris (Sciences-Po), University of Connecticut, University of North Carolina-Chapel Hill, University of California-Los Angeles, University of California-San Diego, University of Michigan, University of Vermont, and the University of Western Ontario's Ivey School of Business.

This project would not have been possible without the hard work of a number of research assistants and peers at Penn State, Vermont, and Michigan who helped with data collection, including Simon Boehme, Benjamin Dube, Heather Ellis, Dara Ewing, Rebecca Falkenstern, Jasmine Fledderjohann, Katie Johnson, Kirstin Kapustik, Marie Krouse, Kathryn Lindenmuth, Daniele Loprieno, Leslie MacConnell, Jennifer Matson, Jessica Pavel, Heather Seitz, Coryn Shiflet, and Rachel Smith.

Colleagues at each of my institutional homes since this project began have helped in some fashion. At Penn State, the dissertation committee who helped me to launch this project deserves particular thanks: John McCarthy, Alan Sica, Lee Ann Banaszak, Roger Finke, and Nancy Love. Alan's unrivaled knowledge of the history of sociological thought continues to serve as an excellent resource for his students. In John I found perhaps the best intellectual mentor that a junior scholar could be so fortunate to find. His commitment to rigorous, systematic, and yet creative forms of sociological inquiry are an inspiration, and his model as a careful mentor of graduate student research is one that I can only hope to emulate in some small part with my own students.

A number of peers at Penn State also read drafts, provided feedback, and offered moral support during the project's early stages: Amy Adamczyk, Latrica Best, Amber Boydstun, Cassie Dorius, Shawn Dorius, Dan Hawkins, Nathan Hess, Jacob Hibel, Kelly Innes, Erik Johnson, Andrew Lindner, Andrew Martin, Nivi Menon, Pat Rafail, Phil Schwadel, and Michael Stout. Frank Baumgartner also provided helpful resources as the project developed, both in our collaborative work and in his suggestions about this book. I am also grateful for his willingness to share data that he and John McCarthy collected from the *Encyclopedia of Associations* (used in Chapter 6).

The University of Vermont's sociology department served as a stimulating and collegial context during this project's adolescent stage. I received useful feedback on this project throughout my time there. Beth

Mintz read what became Chapter 6 carefully and made excellent suggestions. I also benefited from discussions about Chapter 3 and the broader project with Nick Danigelis, Alice Fothergill, Kathy Fox, Anthony Gierzynski, Lutz Kaelber, Nikki Khanna, Tom Streeter, and Rick Vanden Bergh.

My time as an RWJF Scholar in Health Policy Research provided access to what is perhaps the most fertile scholarly environment in the social sciences. Through this fellowship, I received feedback on portions of this book, especially the introductory chapters and Chapters 4–7, from Megan Andrew, Graeme Boushey, Seth Freedman, Alice Goffman, Rick Hall, Hahrie Han, Paula Lantz, Trevon Logan, Hans Noel, Edward Norton, Brendan Nyhan, Fabio Rojas, Kevin Stange, and Patty Strach. While at Michigan, I also received excellent suggestions from scholars outside the RWJF program including Elizabeth Armstrong, Jerry Davis, Liz Gerber, Michael Heaney, Rob Jansen, Sandy Levitsky, Mark Mizruchi, and Kiyo Tsutsui. Most of all, I was lucky enough to have Mayer Zald as a regular lunch date and reviewer of my work during those years, as Mayer's ideas helped to inspire and motivate this research. His passing in 2012 was a great personal and collective loss.

UCLA has served as an ideal intellectual home since my arrival here in 2011, and my thinking about public participation and advocacy has evolved based on exchanges with Josh Bloom, Rogers Brubaker, Zeke Hasenfeld, Hannah Landecker, Ching Kwan Lee, Michael Mann, Chris Rea, Gabriel Rossman, Bill Roy, Abigail Saguy, Stefan Timmermans, Roger Waldinger, Andreas Wimmer, and Lynne Zucker. I also thank Alan Fiske and Mark Peterson for help navigating the institution during my transition to the university and in the final months of completing this book.

Beyond my various institutional homes, a number of scholars have read, commented on, or discussed chapters of this book, and deserve particular thanks: Forrest Briscoe, Matt Desmond, Marc Dixon, Jonathan Doh, Craig Jenkins, Colin Jerolmack, Brayden King, Jeff Manza, David Meyer, Sarah Soule, Steve Vallas, David Vogel, Tim Werner, and Lori Qingyuan Yue. Doug McAdam has also provided support for my scholarly development during my time writing this book. Caroline Lee and Michael McQuarrie, my collaborators on a broader project about the link between public participation and inequality, have served as important sources of ideas throughout my time working on this project. I also thank Vincent Roscigno and Randy Hodson, who offered thorough feedback in their role as editors of the *American Sociological Review* when my article – the major findings of which are reproduced in Chapter 3 – appeared in 2009. Additionally, thanks are due to those who have supported my efforts to publicize this research, including former *Contexts* editors Doug Hartmann and Chris Uggen and also Sewell Chan at the *New York Times*.

My survey would not have been possible without the support of Penn State's Survey Research Center, especially Brian Sonak for his careful attention to programming details. I also received essential feedback on survey drafts from Frank Baumgartner, Daniel Kreiss, Michael Lord, John McCarthy, Beth Mintz, and Patty Strach.

Moving further into the past, I would like to thank those advisors who inspired my initial interest in sociology. Doug Porpora's love of ideas is contagious, and I know that I'm not the only one of his former students who credits their continuing excitement about sociology, in part, to those famous multi-hour conversations in his office. I also owe much to the early mentorship of Bob Brulle, Dave Kutzik, and Wes Shumar.

My particular thanks go to Business and Public Policy series editor Aseem Prakash, to John Haslam at Cambridge University Press, and to editorial board members Sarah Soule and David Vogel. Both Aseem and John have made considerable efforts to improve this manuscript and bring it into print. Additionally, I thank Aseem for hosting a thought-provoking session at the International Studies Association meetings in San Diego in 2012, highlighting recent or forthcoming books in the Business and Public Policy series.

Lastly, I would like to thank my family for their strong support during the writing of this book. My parents and brother – respectively, Joan, Edward, and Daniel Walker – were careful listeners and offered excellent suggestions for how to help the work reach a broader audience. Most of all, I thank Lauren Kusiv for her crucial support of me and of this project from the very start. Lauren has read draft chapters, helped me think through decisions along the way, and talked with me endlessly about the changing nature of public participation and advocacy. She has also been an exceedingly patient, supportive, and caring partner throughout multiple moves and during times when finishing this book and presenting its findings kept me away from home.

This book is dedicated to our daughter, Evelyn Rose Walker.

PART I

Sources

1 | *Grassroots from the top down*

The front stage of public participation

In 2010, a wave of student activism was under way on the campuses of for-profit colleges and universities across the US. Recognizing that new federal rules could effectively make many such institutions close their doors to the diverse non-traditional enrollees that call such schools home, students began to organize to make their case against the new regulations. Called the "gainful employment" rule, regulations proposed by the US Department of Education would cut off the flow of federal student loans and Pell grants to institutions in which a majority of students graduate with higher monthly student loan payments than they could be expected to comfortably repay in their selected profession.[1] Given that student loans are the lifeblood of higher education, many students felt threatened that they would no longer be able to attend their school of choice. Indeed, the way the regulation was written, a logical interpretation for many was not that the Department of Education wanted to reform the *practices of these institutions*, but instead that regulators wanted to take away *students' access to loans*.

One such student was Dawn Connor of Globe University in Eau Claire, Wisconsin. At the start of 2010, Dawn was just a regular college student, taking night courses to become a veterinary technician, while working during the day at a local shelter spaying and neutering dogs

---

[1] More specifically, the original rules proposed by the Department of Education in January 2010 would have required that "a majority of [an institution's] graduates' annual student loan payments under a 10-year repayment plan must be no more than eight percent of the incomes of those in the lowest quarter of their respective professions"; earnings data would come from the Bureau of Labor Statistics (Gorski, 2010). This was later revised such that programs had to meet one of three criteria in order to maintain eligibility for student aid: at least 35 percent of graduates must be successfully repaying their loans, students' estimated annual loan payments must not exceed 12 percent of projected earnings, or payments must not exceed 30 percent of discretionary income (Lewin, 2012).

and cats.[2] She had been active in a variety of leadership roles around the university, including serving as student ambassador for the Veterinary Technology program, president of the Veterinary Technology club, and playing a role in meeting and welcoming new students to campus. She had graduated from high school early, then drifted from one traditional college to another, ultimately changing majors a few times and making progress without earning a degree. Globe University, a for-profit institution with eight branches throughout Wisconsin, Minnesota, and South Dakota, turned out to be a great fit for Connor. Despite the substantial tuition for a vocational degree – the two-year associate's degree in veterinary technology runs to over $44,000 plus lab fees and book expenses – the school had the advantage of being located in Connor's hometown and fit her other priorities. She especially liked that she was able to maintain a conventional job during the day while working toward her degree through night classes.

Catching wind of the Department of Education's proposed regulations, Dawn was happy to visit Washington to lobby on behalf of students at for-profit institutions in March 2010. She felt so strongly about her institution, in fact, that she became a force in helping to propel a national student campaign against the regulations, through an organization called Students for Academic Choice (SAC). The group, which described itself as an association of "proud students and graduates of private, post-secondary career-oriented institutions,"[3] was focused on ensuring "access to a quality education" and recognizing the value that "non-traditional learners" bring to the workforce. More specifically, the organization focused on the fear among many students at for-profit schools that they would lose access to the funding they need to pursue their education.

Only a few months later, SAC had an estimated 150 leaders and was working with a lawyer to gain official nonprofit status. The group was a co-sponsor of a rally in Washington that claimed to have assembled over two thousand students of private sector colleges to voice their opposition to the gainful employment rule.[4] More significantly, SAC became active in organizing college students across the entire for-profit university system, ultimately assembling some 32,000 signatures on a petition asking that the Department of Education avoid enacting the

[2] The following builds largely from Gorski (2010).
[3] Students for Academic Choice (2012).   [4] States News Service (2010).

What is at stake, then, is the very means by which we, as a society, connect with one another in order to bring about change on those issues that matter most to us.

The argument: consultants and top-down participation

Cases like the one described above, while striking in many ways, will not surprise long-time scholars of mass mobilization, as theorists from Gramsci to Schumpeter were well aware of the means by which elites mobilize popular participation in order to enhance their standing, promote their agendas, and win contentious disputes.[21] As Gramsci once argued in his *Prison Notebooks*, "the superstructures of civil society are like the trench-systems of modern warfare."[22] Indeed, a mainstay in modern political research is the notion that grassroots lobbying tactics are central to interest groups' repertoires for gaining influence.[23] Similarly, scholars of social movements recognized a generation ago the tendency toward the professionalization of advocacy,[24] which is manifested today in the growing number of "associations without members" such as think tanks, policy institutes, and other largely staff-driven advocacy groups that tend to mobilize members and funds from the top down. Some worry that there has been a growth of advocacy without a corresponding expansion of citizen engagement.[25]

What *is* new, I will argue, is the extent to which public affairs campaigns are being used to commercialize and further professionalize popular participation, thereby borrowing the repertoire of grassroots mobilization and, in turn, offering this repertoire as a service to organizational clients like corporations, industry associations, government agencies, and even the very advocacy organizations from whom these tactics were learned in the first place.[26] As David Meyer and Sidney Tarrow have argued, grassroots advocacy repertoires are employed not only by those excluded from routine channels of political authority, but

---

[21] Gramsci (1959); Schumpeter (1942).   [22] Gramsci (1971: 235).

[23] Goldstein (1999); Kollman (1998); Caldeira and Wright (1998); Schlozman and Tierney (1986).

[24] McCarthy and Zald (1977); Jenkins and Eckert (1986).

[25] Skocpol (1999, 2003); Walker, McCarthy, and Baumgartner (2011); Jordan and Maloney (1997).

[26] On organizational repertoires, see Clemens (1993, 1997).

also by elites for their own purposes.[27] Repertoires of grassroots participation, originally developed by citizen advocacy organizations, have been adapted into the standard practices of a field of organizations that offer contracted advocacy services on the commercial market to a variety of organized interests.

The growth and institutionalization of the field of public affairs consultants makes possible, then, an increasingly *subsidized public*. Corporations, trade associations, wealthy advocacy organizations, and campaign groups utilize the services of public affairs consultants to lower the costs of participation for targeted activist groups. Organized interests have always sought to facilitate popular participation through offering publics various types of incentives to get involved.[28] But new communications technologies, professional practices for popular mobilization, and a changed field of advocacy organizations have combined to make it much easier for elites to recruit citizen activists.

The notion of a subsidized public differs, then, from what communications scholar Philip Howard describes as a public of "managed citizens,"[29] in that much of what public affairs consultants do is not so much to exercise strong control over participants, but instead to encourage only select groups of citizens to voice their opinions. Further, grassroots participation consultants often support and augment the activism of many who *would have been active in the policy process to begin with*, such as when they work with existing community-based organizations in order to broaden their issue advocacy coalition. Consultants bring their considerable financial and technical resources to bear in employing innovative methods for targeting and recruiting activists for their client's cause; the resources, and, to a lesser extent, professionalism that participatory consultants employ is what differentiates them from other types of grassroots advocacy campaigns by, for example, community organizations. Although the work of consultants on behalf of their clients does, at times, meet the definition of "astroturf" (i.e., is heavily incentivized, involves dishonest or fraudulent claims-making, or is less than fully transparent about its patrons), the main effect of consultants' practices on democracy lies in the selective targeting of citizens for their recruitment requests. As

[27] Meyer and Tarrow (1998).   [28] Clark and Wilson (1961).
[29] Howard (2006).

I make clear especially in Chapter 7, consultants' requests for citizen engagement are targeted primarily at pre-existing political activists, strong political partisans, likely voters, and the college educated; these tendencies exacerbate participatory inequalities.

While sociologists tend to think of mass participation as an antidote to elite- and expert-driven politics, the model of the subsidized public proposed here holds that mass participation is today used as a form of elite legitimation,[30] going beyond elite competition over votes or the endorsements of influential interest groups. Campaigns orchestrated by public affairs consultants, in fact, represent only one manifestation of the modern subsidized public. Although beyond the scope of this book, observers of contemporary institutional domains as diverse as public sector governance,[31] worker participation in flexible production regimes,[32] international aid, development, and micro-finance[33] have called attention to the increasing interest of elites in facilitating popular participation to suit elite agendas in a context of neoliberalism.

Habermas, in his classic *Structural Transformation of the Public Sphere*,[34] outlined a theory of public life dominated by the interests of state administration and market accumulation, an argument echoed and augmented by theorists in the years since its English-language publication, and further elaborated in the second volume of his *Theory of Communicative Action* in his discussion of system and life-world.[35] However, unlike the late modern public sphere described by Habermas, the "subsidized public" described here posits a model of citizenship that allows for a greater degree of citizen agency.

Those who are called upon by consultants to participate are typically not – although, as I make clear, there are certainly exceptions to this – duped, manipulated, or tricked into participation. Many readers of this book, I am sure, have signed a form letter, called a representative, or written a letter to the editor using talking points that were suggested by some sort of organized interest, and likely still agreed strongly with the issue position they were personally expressing therein. The aggregate influence of public affairs consultants on participation, similarly, is of a more subtle nature: although participants may fully agree with the

[30] On elite-driven collective action more broadly, see Aguirre (1984).
[31] Bingham, Nabatchi, and O'Leary (2005).   [32] Vallas (2003).
[33] Fisher (1997).   [34] Habermas (1987, 1989).
[35] See, for example, Calhoun (1992); Mansbridge (2012).

message they are communicating, only certain individuals will be called upon to participate in the first place. Many would not have even thought of the issue as one of concern to them if they weren't the subject of a targeted request.[36] Overall, the subsidized public involves an increasing number of citizens having the chance to "have their say," but, even if diverse citizens are recruited, only those who are seen as worthy targets by a paying client will have their participation targeted and subsidized at all.[37]

interesting

The goal of the book, then, is to illustrate the causes and consequences of the adoption of grassroots participation repertoires by a field of organizations that sell public advocacy services on the commercial market to organized interests. They sell these services not only to groups like corporations that usually lack inherent capacities for mobilizing stakeholders, but also to the very citizen organizations from whom they borrowed these tactics, and who themselves now contract with consultants for support in motivating popular activism on issues of their policy interest.

In the process, I examine not only how this field got off the ground and running, but also how consultants are linked to certain sets of clients, how they target activists and deploy technologies to advocate their cause, and the ways that they incentivize citizens to take action and shape policy formation. I also explain in some depth the effects that these consultant-backed campaigns are having both on public participation and on the policy effectiveness of firms' clients. In particular, the book shows that campaigns that engage in so-called "astroturf" strategies – especially by being less than transparent – are not only unethical but also ineffective. Consultants are influencing civil society, yet are still limited by the force of contending civic and political interests. Like other organized advocates, consultants must navigate complex policy environments, study their opposition, and mobilize resources and allies to get behind their cause.

More broadly, the book tells a story of how the professionalization and commercialization of popular advocacy is changing the contours of democracy and the role of civil society in contemporary politics. To the extent that campaigns engage in selective targeting of citizens through carefully targeted appeals via mailing lists, television advertisements,

---

[36] Brady, Schlozman, and Verba (1999); Verba, Schlozman, and Brady (1995); Walker (2008); Jordan and Maloney (1997).
[37] See Schier (2000); Crenson and Ginsberg (2004).

or social networking sites, participatory inequalities may be exacer-
bated. The strategic mobilization of those already likely to say "yes"
to requests for participation appears to make our democracy both more
partisan and more unequal.

Yet this need not mean that we should simply accept the critiques of
those who cast aside every campaign that involves the support of
political professionals or the resources of an external patron as mere
"astroturf," or fake grassroots mobilization. Consultants disproportionately, but not exclusively, target more advantaged citizens; thus,
their campaigns do at times help to expand democratic engagement.
Further, campaigns that do not develop the genuine support of an
independent constituency are, as I argue in Chapter 7, often likely to
fail. The most effective public affairs campaigns are those that make
coalition with existing civil society groups who have a genuine and
independent interest in the client's cause. Additionally, as the arguments
in this book reveal, there are many continuities between the grassroots
practices of public affairs consultants and those of grassroots organizers
of other stripes. Finally, as resource mobilization approaches to social
movements have long made clear, grassroots organizations of all types
tend to require the patronage of outside elites and other resource
providers.[38]

Approach

An emerging body of scholarship integrates insights from research on
advocacy by scholars of social movements / collective behavior, political
sociology, organizational theory, political science, and nonprofit studies. While scholars in these varied traditions often talk past one another
when describing fundamentally similar phenomena, there is much to be
learned by building from these diverse intellectual traditions. Toward a
further integration of these approaches, I adopt throughout the book
the innovative understanding of advocacy suggested by sociologists
Kenneth Andrews and Bob Edwards.[39] Andrews and Edwards encourage a broad focus on all groups engaged in "either promoting or

---

[38] McCarthy and Zald (1973, 1977); Walker (1991); for a contrasting perspective,
    see Ganz (2000).
[39] Andrews and Edwards (2004: 485).

consultants I spoke with were selected in order to represent a diverse cross section of firm sizes, client types, partisan affiliations, locations, and mobilization methods. I spoke with representatives of firms ranging from small boutique operations to those that are part of powerful multinational public affairs practices, and from those that work with *Fortune* 500 companies to those that help plan out the mass mobilization strategies of advocacy groups.

Although it would have been ideal to carry out an even greater number of interviews, public affairs consulting firms are often hesitant to talk with academics or journalists about their operations. As in the account given at the outset of this chapter, most public affairs professionals would prefer to remain back stage without drawing attention to their role in facilitating front-stage public participation. Nonetheless, in these interviews I promised not to provide identifying details about these consultants or their firms, and I was successful in obtaining quite detailed information about these firms. These interviews, then, offer insights into what goes on inside these elite firms, and they help to flesh out the findings of the quantitative analyses in the book.

Lastly, I made substantial efforts to uncover the client lists, partisanship, and staff profiles of consultants by examining and collecting data from their websites. This is referred to as the *website data* (Appendix 3), which includes all of the firms in the survey sample. I also collected further information on the corporations, advocacy groups, and trade associations that appear on their client lists, using corporate and associational databases (see, respectively, Appendices 5–7). In two chapters, I examine the factors that lead some individual corporations to hire public affairs consultants, as well as what influences associations to do so. These client lists help the book to offer a systematic account of which organizations find it necessary to mobilize a professional grassroots campaign with the help of a consultant, and how these patterns vary by sector and other characteristics of the client organization.

Plan of the book

In the chapters that follow, I make use of these several data sources to develop a systematic portrait of the field of public affairs consultants. Chapter 2 provides a more thorough introduction by defining the field of public affairs consulting and outlining the implications of this new domain for our understanding of modern democratic engagement. This chapter makes clear that although these consulting shops have a professional staff, they share many characteristics with other professionals involved in grassroots advocacy. It further explains that consultants engage in strategic supply-side recruitment of activists. This chapter also identifies the book's contribution to sociological debates about the commercialization of democracy, the political role of elites, the encounter between social movements and organizational theory, and renewed understandings of social capital and participatory repertoires.

Then, taking a step back, Chapter 3 examines the historical context that allowed the industry of public affairs consulting to get off the ground. After offering a brief prehistory of the field, it follows the major social changes that helped to give rise to it. In particular, Chapter 3 describes how the "explosion" of organized advocacy in the late 1970s and early 1980s, along with the increasing political mobilization of business and widening political partisanship, provided fertile conditions for such political entrepreneurship. These firms began to appear in response to the changing political and media environment that valorized public participation while redefining lobbying for the modern era of seemingly more transparent American politics.

Following this, Chapter 4 considers what these firms do now that the field is established. It unpacks the strategies that consultants employ on behalf of their clients and considers how they are related to the organizational characteristics of the consulting firms. It shows that nearly half of firms are non- or bipartisan, and that the remaining firms in the field are about evenly split between those affiliated with the Democrats and those that are Republican. It also illustrates how public affairs consultants attempt to influence the public using a plethora of tactics and technologies in order to mobilize action. They provide services ranging from direct mail to door-to-door canvassing, from signature gathering to scheduling lobbying days, and from internet-based mobilization to "intercept" communications with policymakers.[43]

---

[43] An "intercept" is an effort by a constituent – particularly one with a previous connection to a policymaker – to lobby that policymaker in an informal, person-to-person setting. A goal of such communications is to appear unplanned and spontaneous, and public affairs consultants often seek out those with personal (e.g., family, friend, community) ties to policymakers in order to execute intercepts. In fact, one firm I interviewed provides elaborate technologies that help corporations and associations to identify ties to policymakers among their employees and other stakeholders.

Chapter 5 investigates the particular use that corporations make of public affairs consultants in their efforts to mobilize stakeholder groups, showing that corporate influence in public life goes much deeper than the new forms of covert corporate political spending made possible by the Supreme Court's 2010 decision in *Citizens United v. Federal Election Commission*. The chapter finds that those firms that face major public controversies, reputational problems, or operate in a heavily regulated industry are among the most likely to incentivize grassroots participation. Chapter 6, by contrast, looks at how citizen advocacy groups make use of these firms; the largest, most profession-alized, and most well-resourced groups are among the most likely to "outsource" some portion of their grassroots campaigns to participa-tion consultants. This chapter also finds evidence that these firms are integrated into both the contemporary conservative and progressive movements.

Chapter 7 examines the outcomes of consultant-driven campaigns, both in terms of meeting the client's desired goals and in shaping policy processes more broadly. Evidence from the survey and inter-view data reveals that consultants are often effective in shaping both public participation and policy outcomes. Regarding participation, this chapter reveals that consultants, on the one hand, increase par-ticipatory inequality in the US by focusing their recruitment efforts on those most likely to say yes, who tend to be the more educated and those with a history of political activism. Yet they also seek out constituencies who appear to be independent of elite consultants' paying clients (and, indeed, the consultants themselves), and these tend to be those from more disadvantaged backgrounds. On balance, consulting firms appear to be increasing participatory inequality more than they are working against it; evidence from the survey data reveals that consultants tend to see the recruitment of, for example, minority groups as only a secondary priority in their campaigns. Regarding policy outcomes, Chapter 7 compares a consultant-driven grassroots campaign by Wal-Mart with another by Canadian National to illustrate that campaigns that are authentic, transparent, and able to generate independent support in civil society are among the most likely to generate real policy change.

Chapter 8 concludes the book by highlighting the implications of this study for our understanding of public participation in a context of substantial business participation in the public sphere, advanced communications technologies, and professionalized advocacy organizations. Building from the insights of the previous chapter, the conclusion highlights that although "grassroots for hire" campaigns are indeed commercializing participation, their influence is limited by the independent power of organized civil society. Campaigns that seek to "fake" the support of broad coalitions behind a paying client's interests through "astroturfing" or "sock puppeting" are of only limited effectiveness. Instead, public affairs campaigns tend to be more effective when consultants can help to facilitate the participation of genuine supporters who may not have been aware of the issue in question. Thus, although consultants are reshaping participation, they still must play by the same rules as community organizations, social movements, and other organized advocates in civil society.

2 | Defining the field and its implications

Introduction

The term "grassroots" calls to mind an image of citizen politics rooted in local community. For most, the term conjures up images of local residents joining together to pressure the mayor to support urban redevelopment and affordable housing, citizens in New England getting together on Town Meeting Day to hammer out their local budget, or neighborhood activists mobilizing local parents against undesirable changes to school district policies. Grassroots participation is often seen as a populist response to the failures of markets and ineffective bureaucracies.[1] All of these images hold in common the notion of citizen participation independent of the interests of elites, whether those elites are in government, industry, or powerful civic organizations like foundations or policy institutes. "Grassroots," then, carries with it an air of authenticity. To be truly "grassroots" is to be taken as legitimate in our democratic system. As the late *New York Times* columnist William Safire once put it in his well-known *Political Dictionary*,[2] the grassroots are "the ultimate source of power, usually patronized, occasionally feared." It carries an "up-from-the-people" meaning that is deeply rooted in American politics and culture, in which the porousness of the American state and rich traditions of civic organizing continually reaffirm the value of public engagement independent of the state and the marketplace.

But that image of grassroots is today – and, to some extent, always has been – more of an ideal than a reality. Consider, for example, the fact that community organizations with greater resources and the public support of local elites are significantly more likely to survive over the long term.[3] Much of the canvassing work done today on behalf of environmental and other public causes is carried out by

---

[1] Boyte (1980). [2] Safire (1978: 289). [3] Walker and McCarthy (2010).

paid, semi-professional canvassers.[4] Social movements, interest groups, and other forms of citizen political activism tend to require the sponsorship, resources, and/or political support of elite patrons.[5] However, throughout the literature on social movements and civic participation, the assumption remains that grassroots activism is predominantly a weapon of the weak, or a populist tool for everyday citizens to challenge the power of states, corporations, and other powerful organizations that make the decisions that affect their lives.

Grassroots participation is not, however, simply a tactic employed by those who are marginalized and refused a hearing. For many policy matters on which elite actors perceive themselves to be at a political disadvantage and which are amenable to framing as issues of broad popular concern, they too will adopt a populist posture and seek to mobilize mass publics.[6] This book examines the role of a field of consulting firms that offer what I call "grassroots for hire," or paid services to mobilize public participation on behalf of a business, industry group, professional association, labor union, government agency, or citizen advocacy organization. These firms provide a wide range of services to their clients to help them to improve their social and political standing, as well as to help them win legislative battles and influence the decisions of government agencies. And their activities are wide-ranging: they help sports teams to mobilize fans to fight new ticket taxes in the state legislature; they help telecommunications firms to fight unfavorable FCC decisions by recruiting community advocates; they work, on behalf of pharmaceutical manufacturers, with local community-based organizations to highlight the low-cost medicines that drug-makers make available to low-income communities; they help advocacy groups activate untapped sources of public support; they coach citizens on how to make their point to policymakers more effectively.

This book explores the work of these professional service firms from multiple angles, examining their client bases, the ways they target citizens for participation, and the effects these campaigns are having on civic and political life across the nation. In the process, this book tells

---

[4] Fisher (2006).
[5] McCarthy and Zald (1973, 1977); Walker (1991); Jenkins (2006).
[6] On the differentiation between such issues, see Schattschneider's (1960) classic statement, as well as Baumgartner (1989: 45–46); Culpepper (2011); Smith (2000); Walker (2010).

a story about an overlooked aspect of how American civic and political
life has changed since the 1970s.

Grassroots participation is no longer, if it ever truly was, an *exclusive*
weapon of the weak; we now have an increasingly *subsidized public* in
which select citizens are targeted and trained for participation.
Although advocacy organizations of all stripes have long been recognized for their inherent capacity to train and educate citizens in the skills
of democratic participation,[7] members of the narrowly subsidized public tend to be mobilized instead in a more ad hoc fashion in order to help
elites win legislative, administrative, and other policy issues, thus challenging the notion that participation and social capital – that is, citizens'
democratic norms, social networks, and feelings of trust in institutions[8] – go hand in hand.

Indeed, the model I develop of the subsidized public suggests that
social capital and participation have become, to some extent,
decoupled. The paid consultants in this study, in most cases, facilitate
participation in letter-writing, fundraising, and viral political marketing
campaigns that do not build new political networks among participants. These are not, then, unlike participation in what Robert
Putnam calls "tertiary associations," in which individuals share support
for the same cause without developing links or bonds to one another; as
he puts it, this form of engagement is less like a gardening club and more
like being a fan of the Boston Red Sox or Honda automobiles.[9] While
the present case warrants a more measured description – especially
because many campaigns involve co-opting pre-existing social networks in the interest of winning a particular issue – much of the activism
facilitated by participation consultants fits this broader model.

In this chapter, I begin by defining and explaining the characteristics
of a public affairs consulting firm, including their degree of professionalism, client base, targeting strategies, methods for the recruitment of
activists, means of incentivizing participation, and use of communications technologies. I then elaborate the significance of firms' practices
for our understanding of commercial interests in public participation,
the role of elites in contemporary society and politics, the interaction
between social movements and organizations, and the implications of

---

[7] de Tocqueville (1839); Almond and Verba (1963); Verba, Schlozman, and Brady
(1995).
[8] Putnam (1995, 2000).   [9] Putnam (1995: 71).

the study for our understanding of social capital and participatory repertoires.

Defining the field of public affairs consulting

What are the key characteristics of the firms that are active in public affairs consulting? I begin with a definition of a public affairs consultancy, which I then unpack and elaborate:

A public affairs consultancy is a *professional service firm* that contracts with an *organizational client* in order to *manage the client's political and social environment strategically* through *campaigns* that *mobilize public participation*, often in coordination with traditional forms of lobbying ("government affairs"). As such, public affairs consultancies develop and execute issue campaigns that involve the *selective targeting* of *stakeholder groups* in order to achieve the client organization's *goals*, often using *information and communications technologies* (ICTs) both in how they *recruit activists* and in *incentivizing their engagement.*

Professional service firms

As Weber argued in his famous essay on "Politics as a Vocation," "politics, just as economic pursuits, may be a man's avocation or his vocation."[10] Although Weber's distinction between these two forms of engagement in political life was not, strictly speaking, a categorical and exclusive one, he maintained, "He who strives to make politics a permanent *source of income* lives 'off' politics as a vocation, whereas he who does not do this lives 'for' politics."[11] In modern capitalist societies, then, the capacity to live "for" politics is conditioned on attaining a certain wealth or status that allows for such independent engagement. At the same time, Weber expected that the growth of formal democratic institutions, suffrage, and modern party organizations would necessitate the expansion in number and power of a class of political professionals. Among these professionals, Weber referred primarily to latter-day professional politicians ("political officials") and functionaries ("administrative officials") and their historical antecedents in positions of religious, educational, judicial, and legal authority; however, he acknowledged that the domain of professionalism in

---

[10] Weber (1946: 83).   [11] Ibid.: 84. Emphasis in original.

politics would continue to be reconfigured as those with political talents would choose between overlapping professional domains of journalism, political staffing, and interest group politics.[12] His argument prefigures the ways in which the professionalization of politics would become increasingly pervasive and, perhaps more importantly, would extend well beyond electoral and administrative politics.

Politics, then, is increasingly a vocation for many, and the public affairs consultancies that seek influence for their clients in civil society represent one distinct niche among the diverse class of modern paid political operatives. At least since McCarthy and Zald's classic statement on the mobilization of resources in protest movements and advocacy politics,[13] scholars have recognized the particular role of professionals and civic entrepreneurs in issue advocacy. The late 1970s and early 1980s saw a massive expansion in the number of citizen advocacy groups in the US,[14] and with this came new and bright possibilities for careers in activism: from canvassing and fundraising to staff-driven political research institutes. And, as expected by McCarthy and Zald,[15] the skills developed by individuals in careers in advocacy, nonprofit, and social movement organizations are, at times, transferable to careers in professional advocacy consulting. The increasing formal organization of US national civic and political life helped to encourage the development of public affairs consultancies in the first place, as businesses and associations came to rely upon them for support in stirring up distant public participation.

Public affairs consulting can be differentiated from electoral *campaign consulting* in that although many public affairs consultants have campaign clients (approximately 26 percent of public affairs consultants' aggregate client base is comprised of candidate campaigns) and often complement a campaign's media strategy by providing paid Get-Out-The-Vote (GOTV) services, grassroots public affairs consultants also provide services beyond winning elections. Further, as I explain in Chapter 3, although many consultants in this field started out as electoral consultants, they often found that they needed other revenue sources to smooth out their uneven revenue between election cycles.

They also stand out from traditional *lobbyists* or "government relations" consultants in that they seek to gain influence through mobilizing

[12] Ibid.: 114.   [13] McCarthy and Zald (1977).
[14] Berry (1977); Walker (1991); Andrews and Edwards (2004).
[15] McCarthy and Zald (1977: 1235).

the public rather than limiting their political strategies to direct contacts with policymakers.[16] Further, they are distinct from *public relations* firms, who tend to be more involved in managing communication and messaging rather than seeking to mobilize public participation or build coalitions. Lastly, they stand out from specific *vendors* of services in advertising, political marketing, and polling/research, who more often assist in learning about, locating, and communicating with a target demographic group, but are also less likely to directly subsidize the activism of stakeholders or the broader public.[17] Despite these considerations, public affairs consultancies often overlap with the work of professionals in related sectors: campaign consultants often take up corporate public affairs during political off-seasons, public relations firms may contract with public affairs consultants when their client faces an outpouring of protest in a local community, and public affairs consultants often rely on political advertising firms in their efforts to get the message out to would-be citizen activists for their cause.

Public affairs firms represent a unique niche among political operatives and professional service firms more broadly. As the Public Affairs Council, the leading association for corporate public affairs professionals defines the practice, it "combines government relations, communications, issues management, and corporate citizenship strategies to influence public policy, build a strong reputation, and find common ground with stakeholders," all in the interest of assisting organizations in their attempts to "monitor and manage" their external environments.[18] Still, although grassroots public affairs consulting is professionalized in the sense used by scholars of advocacy, the field, of course, lacks the more complete professionalization of fields such as law or medicine. For a more detailed discussion on this point, see Appendix 8.

Organizational clients

These professional service firms can also be recognized by the presence of organizational clients, including individual corporations, trade associations, advocacy organizations, labor unions, government agencies,

---

[16] On the difference between these two forms of political action, most often distinguished between "inside" and "outside" lobbying, see Kollman (1998) and Goldstein (1999).

[17] However, vendors are included in the baseline data described in Appendix 1.

[18] Public Affairs Council (2010a).

and political parties. They work on behalf of these clients in a fashion similar to other professional service firms, which, as organizational theorists have recognized, have diffuse authority structures, do knowledge-intensive work, and trade on their "intellectual capital and expertise."[19] Having diverse clients, professional service firms generally need to maintain a degree of flexibility in their client portfolio, and to be ready to adapt to changing environments and diverse needs.[20]

A plurality of firms' aggregate client base includes individual corporations and trade associations, reflecting the fact that other organizations – such as citizen interest groups and labor unions – have a member base that they can, more often, mobilize by using their internal organizational mechanisms, thus negating the need to contract with a consultant. Thus, despite the fact that grassroots advocacy techniques tend to be employed at an overall higher rate by citizen groups,[21] the clients of public affairs consultants are disproportionately for-profit organizations. However, a wide range of large and influential citizen interest groups also contract with public affairs consultants, especially when they need to mobilize participation outside their membership base and in the general public.

As consultants, the principals of public affairs firms must gain the confidence of new clients, whether that client is a multinational corporation targeting federal legislation or a regional water district seeking to mobilize local residents for greater state-level utility subsidies. Unlike an organization's in-house public affairs professionals, those who work in stand-alone consulting shops must work to build and maintain the trust of the organizations they aspire to represent. In this sense, they share key characteristics with other types of consultants.[22] They, like management consultants, public relations specialists, lobbying specialists, and others who provide confidential counsel to organizations, help to standardize and routinize technical knowledge about best practices; given that the consultants in this study assist in mobilizing public participation, the institutionalization of this field represents a new and important

[19] Greenwood, Suddaby, and McDougald (2006).
[20] Malhotra, Morris, and Hinings (2006).   [21] Kollman (1998).
[22] As Pieczka (2002: 322) puts it, consultancies hold "expertise which is distinctive yet flexible enough to be applicable across a wide field, replicable, routinized as schemes and available for hire . . . an outside agent who must, at least partly, interact with clients by re-interpreting their needs in ways malleable to professional expertise."

development in the further professionalization of public participation. Similar to the development and adaptation of participatory repertoires by turn-of-the-century interest groups as identified by Elisabeth Clemens,[23] public affairs consultants have adapted and commercialized the repertoire of citizen participation. I develop this argument further when describing the broader implications of this study at the end of this chapter.

Client goals and policy targets

Before deciding which citizens' participation to incentivize (or how they will do so), consultants need to determine precisely what the client's goals are. Such goals may range from the development of an ad hoc coalition to gain influence quickly, through an outpouring of support or dissent, to long-term strategies for building public and political support across a broad base.[24] Analysts and practitioners increasingly encourage, as a best practice for corporations and associations, the continuous development of constituency networks as a means of managing an organization's institutional environment.[25] Whether the campaign is part of a short-term or long-term strategy, clients must, like organizers for social change in general,[26] identify a policy target. Public affairs consultants advocate for their clients in six major domains: *legislative, administrative, electoral campaigns, ballot measures, public opinion, and non-state organizations' policies*.[27] An advantage of this perspective is that it moves beyond the over-emphasis on legislative lobbying, which continues to be dominant in the scholarly research on advocacy.[28]

This is not to say, of course, that the emphasis on federal *legislative* campaigns is unwarranted, as many of the most prominent and resource-intensive grassroots campaigns involve major federal

---

[23] Clemens (1993, 1997).   [24] Lerbinger (2006: 254–255).
[25] See, for example, Hillman and Hitt (1999); Lord (2001).
[26] Walker, Martin, and McCarthy (2008).
[27] A smaller set of campaigns also engages in electoral activity, particularly in Get-Out-The-Vote (GOTV) efforts and canvassing on behalf of candidates for elected office. Grassroots lobbying campaigns also play a role in shaping the judiciary, although indirectly through campaigns to influence Congressional confirmation or rejection for Supreme Court nominees (Caldeira and Wright, 1998).
[28] Hojnacki et al. (2012: 385).

legislative issues in policy domains such as energy, health, and environmental policy. Firms in the manufacturing sector in particular are quite
active in supporting grassroots activism on federal legislative issues.
Such was the strategy of health insurers, pharmaceutical manufacturers,
medical device manufacturers, and other health industries in the run-up
to the Patient Protection and Affordable Care Act of 2010,[29] just as
health industry grassroots mobilization was prevalent during the failure
of health reform legislation in 1993–1994.[30]

Public affairs consultants also often take on campaigns for clients that
seek to influence *administrative* policy, such as in the for-profit colleges
case that was described in the introduction. As Daniel Carpenter and
colleagues argue,[31] although "agencies are lobbied with every bit the
intensity that legislators are," there has been a "failure of interest-group
scholars to study patterns of executive and administrative lobbying."[32]
This distinctive understanding of the difference between forms of influence directed at legislatures and those directed at agencies is also found
in the law, as the definition in the IRS tax code of "grassroots lobbying"
(as it applies to nonprofits) excludes organizations' efforts to pressure
an executive branch agency like the EPA.[33]

Grassroots consultants are also at times hired by electoral campaigns
to influence *voters* through canvassing and Get-Out-The-Vote work. As
I describe in Chapter 3, campaign consulting is the most common prior
occupation of the consultants in this study. Although none of the
consultants in this study work exclusively with electoral campaigns,
nonetheless some firms do help campaigns to identify and target voters,
manage their "ground game," and craft a compelling message for
generating support. Note that although I describe grassroots consultants' electoral work briefly in Chapters 4 and 7, consultants' role in
candidate campaigns has been very well studied already and such work
is generally beyond the scope of this book.[34]

Clients with an interest in *ballot measures*, especially in states like
California, Oregon, Colorado, and Arizona, also represent a sizable
portion of the market for public affairs consultants. Particularly in these

---

[29] Walker (2010).
[30] Goldstein (1999); Skocpol (1997: Ch. 5); Quadagno (2005).
[31] Carpenter, Esterling, and Lazer (1998: 425).
[32] A prominent exception, they note, is Peterson (1992).
[33] Vernick (1999: 1426); see also Berry and Arons (2003: 151–154).
[34] See, for example, Kreiss (2012); Nielsen (2012); Lathrop (2003).

states, a number of public affairs consultants help organizations register voters, gather signatures, gain the endorsements of noteworthy elites, and activate key opinion leaders in local communities in order to help their clients win in the realm of direct democracy. Political marketing firms in California have come to play a central role in the initiative and referendum process, as early progressive reforms in the structure of primary elections weakened the power of the state's political parties and offered greater autonomy to those public affairs consultants working on ballot measures.[35] For example, a firm I interviewed called Valley Signature Gatherers[36] claims to have gathered over one million signatures on a 2004 California ballot measure, adding to its significant history of petitioning efforts in states including Michigan, Ohio, Indiana, Florida, and Nevada. The essential role of public affairs specialists on ballot measures has been the subject of critique and debate from a variety of sources, including journalists, political scientists, and practitioners.[37]

Public affairs consultants also often seek to shape *public opinion* through mobilizing participation. One organization interviewed for this study, for example, reported coordinating product release events for a major auto manufacturer. As one senior consultant said to me about these events, "We need [interested consumers of the client's products] to show up to events on a Saturday, to take time out of their schedule to participate ... there's certainly participation involved there," even if not *political* participation. Another senior consultant with the same firm jumped in on this point and added, "once we've got them involved, we've *got them*" and can rely on them politically at a later point as part of a long-term strategy.[38]

Lastly, and perhaps least commonly, the consultants in this study occasionally engage in campaigns to influence the *policies of a non-state organization*, such as a corporation, educational institution, religious order, professional association, or other nonprofit organization. While

---

[35] Bowler, Donovan, and Fernandez (1996: 174–175).   [36] A pseudonym.

[37] Broder (2000); Johnson (2002).

[38] Although beyond the scope of this book, I acknowledge that consultants' recruitment efforts may also, in fact, encourage recruited citizens to be more active in other, more independent, forms of grassroots participation in the future. Historical research has pointed out how elite-facilitated mobilizations may ultimately come to challenge those very elites (Markoff, 1997). I thank William Roy for calling my attention to this point.

campaigns targeting non-state organizations are generally outside the scope of this book, it bears mentioning that such strategies are somewhat common in contentious contract negotiations between firms, such as those between cable companies and content providers, as well as between health insurers and hospital systems. Prominent examples include a 2009 dispute between Time Warner Cable and Fox Broadcasting and a battle in 2000 between Blue Cross / Blue Shield of California and Sutter Health.[39] Public affairs consultants in these campaigns generally encourage the public to lobby their opponents through their respective customer service offices.

Supply-side recruitment of activists

Analysts of social movements and other, more institutionalized forms of advocacy have called attention to the usage of "supply-side recruitment" strategies, in which appeals for public participation are targeted at those most likely to say yes to a particular request for participation.[40] Like social movements' need to build "consensus mobilization" (i.e., distributing the cause's messages in the public sphere) prior to "action mobilization" (i.e., mobilizing the cause's supporters to take action), participation consultants need to frame the message in a way that not only resonates with certain segments of the public but also galvanizes supporters into action.[41] As Alan Schussman and Sarah Soule note, activists' pre-existing ties to advocacy organizations highlight their "structural availability" to recruiters.[42]

While it's undoubtedly true that organized advocates will be strategic and selective in targeting new members or donors and also in how they frame the issue in question, supply-side recruitment allows for the professional micro-targeting of activists that fit highly specific demographic profiles. As Ronald Shaiko points out, such efforts make it possible to target those who are, for example, white female homeowning Democrats who wear glasses, read *Newsweek*, and drive a foreign car.[43] The professional grassroots recruiters in this study represent the formalization and increasing commercialization of supply-side

---

[39] See, respectively, Collins (2010); Koenig (2009).
[40] Jordan and Maloney (1997); Bosso (2005); Brady, Schlozman, and Verba (1999).
[41] Klandermans (1984).   [42] Schussman and Soule (2005).
[43] Shaiko (1999: 184).

recruitment, building upon but also going beyond advocacy organizations' own professional mobilization strategies. Indeed, even when the consultants in this study seek to activate an existing community organization or group of opinion leaders in a community – through what is known in the field as "grasstops" recruiting – they are highly strategic and instrumental in which potential allies they select.

Once an organizational client has sought out the services of a public affairs firm for assistance in a campaign – a "campaign" being any sustained effort to provide assistance to clients through encouraging public participation – the next step is to decide whose activism would be most advisable to encourage. For example, when a firm needs to gain popular support for a client active in seeking media reform, they might activate representatives of small record labels, musicians, sympathetic academics, and certain small business owners who are worried about the effects of media consolidation. When working on behalf of a major environmental interest, however, they might mobilize ties to state-level environmental organizations, popular liberal blogs, and local opinion leaders. Public affairs consultants like to point out that every campaign faces a set of unique circumstances, and therefore must be tailored rather than standardized in order to have the best chances of success.

Some analysts have described an increasing trend among advocacy organizations in turning to "targeted activation" strategies in place of broad-based member mobilization,[44] and public affairs consultancies are specialists in activating a target constituency. Considering this, however, there still remains the decision as to which constituency to mobilize. A proprietary survey of in-house public affairs representatives, for example, recently found that businesses most often seek to mobilize their employees (among them, management is the most common), and, to a lesser extent, their retirees, customers, local community members, allied interest groups, suppliers, and shareholders in grassroots participatory programs; associations, on the other hand, tend to mobilize their members and allied interest groups.[45] I explore this further in Chapter 7.

Regardless of which particular stakeholder groups are activated in a campaign, public affairs consultancies recognize the value of building a constituency, a strategy that business has increasingly borrowed from

---

[44] Schier (2000); Crenson and Ginsberg (2004).
[45] Public Affairs Council (2008: 26–27).

civic and political organizations.[46] Of course, as will be described in detail later, there are essential differences between client types in which forms of constituency-building they demand: for instance, member-based civic organizations have less of a need to build a constituency (their members and patrons, in most cases, serve this role well already), while the structure of corporations more often necessitates efforts to build and activate a constituency among their diverse stakeholder groups and, at times, the general public.

Management scholar Michael Lord, for example, argues that there is particular value in constituency-building for corporate actors seeking to influence public policy.[47] In contrast to other ways in which business may seek to gain political influence (e.g., lobbying, litigation), Lord argues that "some of the most effective corporate grassroots efforts are those that cost relatively little; instead, they are creatively and effectively organized to tap into the energy and influence of a diverse universe of sincere and committed corporate stakeholders." In contrast to the notion that corporate public participation programs tend toward inauthenticity, Lord further argues that the quality of communications sent to officials tends to be more influential than their quantity, and that "Astroturf efforts have quite a negative effect [in that] they degrade the credibility and reputation of those who engage in them,"[48] an argument consistent with the findings of Chapter 7 in this book.

A subsidized public or a manufactured one?
The question of "astroturf"

Perhaps more pointedly than any other fictional account, director Barry Levinson's 1998 film *Wag the Dog* – adapted from Larry Beinhart's novel *American Hero* – depicts a nightmare scenario of media manipulation and the manufacture of populist authenticity. The film tells the story of a Washington public relations and media consultant who, in an effort to deflect public attention away from a series of scandals inside the president's administration, creates a media campaign about a fake war against Albania. In the process, the consultants orchestrate a national campaign to bring home a fictional soldier left behind during the alleged conflict, who gains national sympathy. The fabricated soldier, Lieutenant Schurman (nicknamed "old shoe") is valorized in songs

[46] Lord (2000a, 2000b, 2003).   [47] Lord (2001).   [48] Ibid.: 11.

that get regular radio airplay, while also becoming the subject of a national outcry for his safe return, thereby averting the reputational crisis the president would have otherwise faced.

As unrealistic as this example is, it speaks to popular concerns that public affairs campaigns are "astroturf" efforts to subvert democracy by manufacturing grassroots engagement in support of elite interests. The term has been used widely since being coined by former senator and US Treasury Secretary Lloyd Bentsen in 1985 to distinguish between "generated mail" (in his case facilitated by the insurance industry) and communications that represent the authentic and unprompted views of the mass citizenry.[49] Today, the label "astroturf" often becomes a political Rorschach test applied to one's opponents to delegitimate their claims on the basis of inauthenticity, dishonesty, and/or misinformation.[50]

Analysts and commentators often use the term "astroturf" quite broadly to refer to forms of public participation that are considered illegitimate for one or more of the following reasons:

1. *Incentivized:* Participants are offered incentives for their engagement or threatened with negative consequences if they do not take part.
2. *Fraudulent:* Participants either do not believe or do not fully comprehend the claims they are making (or, worse, campaign organizers engage in fraud by attributing claims to individuals that were never actually made). Participants take part despite these limitations because they are either incentivized or threatened (see #1).
3. *Masquerading:* The campaign has covert elite sponsorship and is masquerading as a movement with a broad base of non-elite support.[51]

---

[49] Zellner (2010: 362).   [50] Walker (2010).

[51] Most definitions highlight the third characteristic. Zellner (2010: 361), for example, says that astroturf is an effort by "paid lobbyists to conduct a political or public relations campaign on behalf of a client, typically an interest group, designed in such a way as to mask its origins and create the impression that it is spur-of-the-moment grassroots behavior" (see also McNutt and Boland, 2007). Similarly, Lyon and Maxwell (2004: 561) argue that astroturf is when a business "covertly subsidizes a group with similar views to lobby when it normally would not," thus emphasizing the third characteristic but also implying the first (i.e., incentives). Popular commentators often use the term to refer to fraud (cf. Sager, 2009), and this meaning was highlighted by the consultants I interviewed (see Chapter 4).

The work of grassroots public affairs consultants does, at times, meet one or more of these criteria, but not all of these features clearly differentiate consultant-backed campaigns from the work of most advocacy organizations, particularly regarding the use of incentives. I consider each of these features in turn.

First, on *incentives*, it is of course true that consultants offer incentives to would-be participants to encourage them to become involved, and they also highlight that negative policy consequences may follow if citizens fail to take action. But, with some exceptions (including one I describe below), consultants prefer not to offer financial incentives, which run the risk of delegitimizing their entire campaign.[52] What they offer instead are incentives that are similar to those employed by other kinds of advocacy campaigns, such as informational incentives (educating the public about how and why to participate), incentives based on one's professional or workplace identity, offering networking and socialization opportunities, or giving participants the chance to feel they are a meaningful player in policymaking.[53] Thus, although a primary activity of public affairs consultants is incentivizing participation, most of their campaigns are no more "astroturf" on this count than the work of most advocacy organizations, which also rely upon selective incentives to overcome the collective action dilemmas identified long ago by Mancur Olson.[54] Just like interest groups work to motivate the participation of their members and political parties act to lower the "cost" of voting by providing citizens cues for understanding which candidate is closest to their preference,[55] public affairs

---

[52] For example, the online marketing forum *ReveNews* reported in 2008 that members of MyPoints, a consumer rewards program, were contacted with messages asking that they "Tell Congress to Protect Seniors' Medical Benefits," and offering them five "points" for visiting the website of the AMA Patients' Action Network, or 50 "points" for emailing Congress (Allen, 2008). These points could then be used to secure discounted products and offers from retailers (ibid.).

[53] In the interest of space, this large literature on participatory incentives is not reviewed here. However, the broadest and most influential categorization of incentive systems goes back to Clark and Wilson (1961; see also Zald and Ash, 1966; Knoke, 1988), who distinguished between material incentives (money, goods, services), solidary incentives (intangible rewards that derive from the act of association), and purposive incentives (also intangible, but derive from the goal rather than the means of participation, such as the desire for policy change).

[54] Olson (1965). For a more recent application, see Prakash and Gugerty (2010).

[55] Downs (1957).

consultants have multiple means of making it easier for citizens to take part in the political process (albeit in a narrowly targeted fashion aligned with their clients' interests).

Second, regarding outright *fraud* or misrepresentation by elite recruiters or their agents, these practices do take place but are accompanied by more severe risks. The discovery of communications that are forged or otherwise misrepresent an individual citizen's issue position can be quite costly to both the firm and the client(s) it represents. In 2009, for instance, a Congressional subcommittee opened hearings on the practice of paid public affairs work after it was revealed that an employee of a prominent public affairs firm, working on behalf of a client in the energy industry, sent forged constituent letters to a Virginia representative urging him not to support proposed climate change legislation. These letters brought considerable and unwelcome scrutiny not only to this particular consultant, but also to the entire consultant industry. That it did so at all also calls attention to a second reason why fraud is risky: the ubiquity of the internet and new communications technologies makes it much easier for advocacy groups and the media to locate the source of manufactured communications. New technologies have made it possible, for example, to reveal evidence of how many fake computer-generated Twitter followers a political leader or advocacy organization has, through the "truthy" project at Indiana University.[56] Watchdog groups like the Center for Media and Democracy have also made it a priority to call attention to covert public affairs strategies.

Setting aside concerns of fraud, consider the more commonplace worry that public affairs campaigns stimulate the participation of those who either do not believe or do not fully understand the issue. A recent report, for instance, described how Gotham Public Affairs recruited paid protestors on behalf of the television network Ovation against Time Warner Cable's decision to cut the network from its channel lineup, all under the guise of a group called "Citizens for Access to the Arts."[57] As an online ad recruiting participants described,

... this is a very easy and quick job. This client pays $20 an hour for a little less than an hour. All you really have to do is show up and support our rally. We ask that you DO NOT under any circumstances talk to the press or media on

---

[56] Ratkiewicz et al. (2011).   [57] Gittlitz (2013).

our behalf or discuss anything about your attendance or compensation with them.[58]

Strategies like these are indeed deployed by public affairs consultants with some regularity. Nonetheless, given that their disclosure makes such events (or broader campaigns) relatively easy to discredit, consultants have a strong interest in avoiding their usage, especially on high-stakes policy debates.

The subsidized public may be one in which elites have become more dominant players, but this need not entail the assumption that incentivized activists are disingenuous. Even if the outcome of their activism is to support the preferences of consultants' elite clients, this does not necessarily mean that activists are dishonest about their own preferences. Consultants' goals, instead, are often (although not always) to identify and make alliance with those who have an authentic interest in the cause.

But we must also acknowledge that political recruiters tend to exercise a more subtle form of power over those they request to become engaged. It is not uncommon, for instance, for consultants to help employers recruit their employees to participate in political activism on behalf of the firm, although a number of states explicitly prohibit employer coercion in this process.[59] Similarly, trade associations have organized protest events that recruit employees from member firms to speak out on behalf of industry, such as in the American Petroleum Institute's "Energy Citizens" rallies against climate legislation in the summer of 2009.[60] Or in other cases where public affairs consultants engage in forms of "bloc recruitment"[61] – what consultants call "grasstops" – rank-and-file members may feel pressured to join the campaign because their leadership is already on board. In all of these instances, activists may fear that remaining inactive could indirectly result in either personal harm or unwanted policy consequences.

Third, on the issue of undisclosed elite support (*masquerading*), consultants' record is more equivocal. Consultants do, at times, create

---

[58] Ibid.

[59] On employers pressuring employees to lobby on behalf of their firm, see Keim (2005); Heath, Douglas, and Russell (1995). Regarding state restrictions against such practices, see Volokh (2012: 315–318). California law, for example, states that employers may not engage in "controlling or directing, or tending to control or direct, the political activities or affiliations of employees" (ibid.: 315).

[60] Snyder and Brush (2009).   [61] Oberschall (1973).

front groups through which elite interests masquerade as citizen groups, such as how gambling interests created Citizens for Riverboat Gambling in Iowa in the early 1990s, or how consultants fabricated the pro-Gulf War campaign called Citizens for a Free Kuwait.[62] Many of the consultants I interviewed contend that if the participants they sponsor have a genuine belief in the cause, that fact alone is sufficient to defend the campaign's legitimacy. They also regularly pointed out, correctly, that advocacy organizations are not required by federal law to disclose their donors, and thus can be charged with engaging in "astroturf" just as easily as campaigns organized by consultants. Nonetheless, it remains true that consultants often fail to disclose information about the identity of the client, the role of the consultant, and/or which other funding sources are being applied to the campaign.

For example, campaigns may misrepresent the breadth of their funding sources when they are heavily dependent on a single patron. This was the case for Working Families for Wal-Mart, which I describe in greater depth in Chapter 7; the campaign initially claimed that Wal-Mart was *only one* of the (presumably numerous) funders of the campaign, although it was later revealed that Wal-Mart was its *sole* funder. Similarly, in a groundbreaking series about covert lobbying by the manufacturers of flame-retardant chemicals done by the *Chicago Tribune*, journalists revealed that these firms worked through a front group called Citizens for Fire Safety to create the appearance of broad community support in favor of flame-retardant chemicals being used in furniture, claiming to include fire marshals, scientists, and representatives of low-income and minority communities.[63] Record labels at times organize "phoner" campaigns to request spins of sponsored songs and make it appear that these songs are more broadly popular.[64] A lack of disclosure about the funding of these campaigns makes it difficult for citizens to interpret consultants' mobilization requests.

Taking these considerations as a whole, then, consultants' record is somewhat mixed. Their use of incentives is generally not very different from what most advocacy organizations do in their own mobilization of resources. Some consultants do engage in fraud and/or misrepresentation, although this is a risky strategy (and, as I show in Chapter 7, one that is likely to be ineffective). And there is a general lack of

---

[62] Bodensteiner (1997); Fitzpatrick and Palenchar (2006: 208).
[63] *Chicago Tribune* (2012).   [64] Rossman (2012: 34).

transparency in the field, both regarding the role of the consultant and the client.

Nonetheless, consultants still are not in a position to truly "manufacture" real civic and political participation out of whole cloth. Consultants help to locate and target would-be activists, offer them (usually non-monetary) incentives for participation, and provide information about venues in which to become active. They also work heavily with existing civic and political organizations, thus transplanting, if you will, already grown grassroots to new issue environments. And, in these efforts, they hope that their campaign will independently take root in its new locale, even if only for a short time.

For these reasons, perhaps a better metaphor for most consultant-backed organizing work would be the planting of sod rather than laying astroturf. That is, consultants seek to borrow grassroots that were grown for other purposes and put them to use for those of their clients. In so doing, they generally hope that roots will grow in this new environment. I return to this point in Chapter 8.

Communications technologies and the means of participatory production

Finally, public affairs consultancies are defined by their employment of communications technologies in facilitating popular activism. Since the early 1970s, participation consultants have capitalized on the availability of a low-cost long-distance phone service, faxing technologies, direct mail, and demographic mapping and targeting services in order to stir up the grassroots and help their clients win issues. Today, this repertoire has expanded considerably, as micro-targeted email campaigns are increasingly supplemented by web technologies, robocalls, texting, and social networking sites like Facebook and Twitter. This has caused the volume of communications citizens send to Congress to increase in exponential terms,[65] and there is also evidence that administrative agencies are coping with an excess of standardized form letters sent their way.[66] On the other hand, at the same time that these new technologies have engendered an age of mechanical reproduction of political messages, public affairs consultants seek to make their

---

[65] Fitch and Goldschmidt (2005).   [66] Shulman (2006).

campaigns stand out by incentivizing citizens to offer their unique perspectives.

Using these technologies, public affairs consultants request a wide range of participatory activities of those they target for engagement, although they face a consistent trade-off between encouraging high-cost, low-tech forms of participation that only the most committed of participants will take up (for example, flying to Washington to meet with their representative about an issue) versus low-cost forms of participation that policymakers can more easily ignore (such as signing one's name at the bottom of a mass-emailed form letter). In fact, it may be the case that the more standardized the letter, the less likely policymakers are to take the communication seriously.[67]

Public affairs consultants attempt to find the best match between the client's goals, the stakeholder groups targeted, and the type of participation to request. Sometimes a broad-based strategy using multiple tactics is called for that mobilizes diverse stakeholder groups alongside receptive members of the broader public; on high-stakes issues that can be cast in more ideological terms, firms may go beyond their natural constituency and mobilize the mass public through web, television, or newspaper ads (this has been a common strategy adopted by health insurance and banking firms during periods of proposed regulatory reform). At other times more narrowly focused or even one-on-one strategies are more appropriate: for instance, modern campaigns often employ an "intercept" strategy, which involves the staging of a seemingly unplanned encounter between a prominent constituent and a policymaker in order to attain a deeper level of person-to-person influence.[68]

Implications of professional public affairs

Having considered what it is that defines this organizational field, what are the implications of the activities of participation consultants for how best to understand participation in contemporary democracy, the political role of elites, and how social movements interact with organizations?

---

[67] Silverstein (1998); Browne (1995); Fitch and Goldschmidt (2005).
[68] Jalonick (2003).

Commercialized democracy

Scholars of American political development have called attention to how, since the 1960s, a more activist state encouraged the growth of both service-providing and advocacy-oriented nonprofit organizations.[69] To the extent that these organizations were oriented toward patronage by external grant-makers, their operations tended to be more professionalized.[70] Many of these organizations began to contract with government agencies in order to provide services, in line with the devolution of federal authority to the states and outsourcing of services to the nonprofit sector.[71]

But professionalization is only one part of the picture, as advocacy has been not only professionalized but also *commercialized*. A perhaps even more significant part of the story, then, has been overlooked: how the growth of formal organizations active in public advocacy, along with the expansion of business political mobilization, created a new demand for mobilizing grassroots constituents in the political marketplace. While grassroots lobbying tactics by well-heeled organizations are hardly new to the American political scene,[72] the extent to which services for galvanizing public support or opposition on a particular issue have been packaged and sold to paying clients is a rather novel development.

Consider, for example, how Grassroots Enterprise (a Washington, DC consulting shop owned by PR conglomerate Edelman, with a predominantly trade association clientele) describes its services in promotional materials, and how it merges techniques from advertising, political organizing, and electoral campaign strategies to help its clients win. This firm claims to:

- Help the client to create and delineate specific end goals, and develop a plan to get there that includes analysis of the key decision-makers, strategies for messaging, design of promotional materials, and background research on the issue
- Help create and carry out web-based programs that encourage targeted participants to join the campaign (through paid ad spots, efforts to build "buzz," and viral marketing)

---

[69] Skocpol (2007); see also Minkoff (1995).   [70] Minkoff and Powell (2006).
[71] Marwell (2004).   [72] Kollman (1998); Goldstein (1999).

- Provide clients access to their pre-existing national network of influential opinion leaders, who can be activated to leverage support for the client
- Offer services to develop a database of in-depth profiles of the behaviors of each stakeholder, as well as to identify which of these stakeholders are mavens or opinion leaders on whom others rely for key decision-making information[73]
- Measure the participation of stakeholders in real time, thereby allowing clients to make crucial adjustments during the course of the campaign

Thus, the participation of citizens is not only organized on behalf of paying clients, but micro-targeted and monitored by the public affairs firm charged with facilitating it. "Citizens" have been turned into "stakeholders," and efforts to mobilize participation have been restructured into advertised appeals. This would, to say the least, seem to augur poorly for the possibility of a public sphere which is relatively free of the communicative distortions introduced by media technologies, corporate influence over civil society, and the power of experts relative to the lay public.[74]

Despite these substantial concerns, this particular form of commercialized advocacy is not, strictly speaking, replacing the activism of grassroots citizens' groups. Often, in fact, many citizen advocates turn to public affairs consultants in order to improve their own operations. For example, consultants like Crossroads Campaign Solutions, the Richard Norman Company, and Shirley & Banister Public Affairs, which I discuss in Chapter 6, all focus on improving the efforts of pre-existing advocacy organizations by helping them both to conduct more effective outreach into the broader public and also to make more effective use of their existing members and resources. *Thus, on its own, it's unclear whether the participatory commercialization that public affairs consultants represent is harming public engagement writ large; on the other hand, the selective targeting of activists by well-resourced interests can, as we will see, exacerbate participatory inequalities.*

---

[73] On opinion leaders, see the classic work by Katz and Lazarsfeld (1955) and contemporary critiques by Watts and Dodds (2007) and Rossman (2012). For a popular application, see Gladwell (2000: 19).

[74] See Habermas (1989); Calhoun (1992).

A renewed understanding of the political role of elites

Grassroots public affairs consultants are political elites who, in their work through professional service firms, mobilize mass participation for a living. They possess expertise in facilitating public engagement, which they draw from diverse sources such as electoral campaigning, grassroots organizing, lobbying, public relations, and advertising. As Steven Brint has argued, the post-1960s era in the US brought with it massive growth in the ranks of expert professionals, who can be characterized as those who convert professional knowledge into marketable resources.[75]

The role of elites in society is a topic that is returning to the center of sociological investigation due to a variety of factors, including vastly widening income inequality in the US since the 1970s, new technologies in network analysis for modeling relations among elites, and the increased popularity of the work of Pierre Bourdieu (especially in how his work illuminates elite cultural capital and how it may be converted into other forms of capital).[76] In addition, organizational theorists are finding that a renewed interest in elites and power dynamics in organizational fields helps to correct some of the well-recognized limitations of institutional theory in its understanding of interests, agency, and strategic action.[77]

Mayer Zald and Michael Lounsbury, for instance, argue in a seminal article that the transition from the "old institutionalism" of scholars like Philip Selznick and toward the "new" institutionalism replaced a focus on actors within organizations with an emphasis on more generalized culture and cognition, thus shifting the focus away from strategic decision-making and the political power of elites.[78] Returning to insights from C. Wright Mills, they argue that it is important for organizational analysts to understand how contemporary elites occupy "command posts" which are "centers of societal power ... that regulate, oversee, and aim to maintain social order in society and economy, both at regional, nation-state and inter-state levels."[79] Importantly, command posts are not only those positions within political parties, bureaucracies, or elected offices that offer access to the levers of political power, but they argue that positions of power in other societal

---

[75] Brint (1994: 204).   [76] Khan (2012).
[77] Walker (2012b: 584–587); Roscigno (2011).
[78] Zald and Lounsbury (2010).   [79] Ibid.: 964; Mills (1956).

institutions and broader organizational fields are also worthy of the label. Thus, they maintain, command posts also include what Stephen Barley has called the "asteroid belt" of actors surrounding the state, including "varied elites and experts often connected to large corporations, sundry lobbyist organizations, law firms, social movement organizations, NGOs, etc."[80]

Professional service firms like the consultants in this book are an important yet under-investigated command post for the contemporary elite, serving as a mediator between corporations, organized interests, and the state.[81] What this study contributes is evidence of how such elites play a part in the framing of political issues (often in a quite populist fashion), targeting of political messages to particular audiences, and in the management of the political environment for paying organizational clients. Especially in offering citizens ready-made templates for participation – a more dramatic version of what Paul Lichterman refers to as "plug-in" volunteering, which takes place "under the direction of a professional who defines the tasks" for participants[82] – elite consultants help to shape both the form and the content of much mass participation today.

The practices of public affairs consultants also bear on broader questions of the influence of elites in society, hearkening back both to the classic Dewey-Lippmann debate over the potential for an informed and meaningful democracy given the problems of a mass public, as well as the more general debate between elitists and pluralists in political sociology and political science.[83] Fundamentally a question of the extent to which equality in representation and policymaking is possible in advanced democracies, elite theorists generally expect that a privileged minority have outsized political influence, whereas pluralists contend that competition among opposing interests helps to (imperfectly)

---

[80] Zald and Lounsbury (2010: 965); see Greenwood (2008), as well as Barley (2007, 2010). Think tanks should also be added to this list, given their position within elite policy networks; for an investigation into whether think tanks fit the expectations of elite theorists, see Medvetz (2012).

[81] Greenwood (2008: 155).   [82] Lichterman (2006: 540).

[83] Lippmann (1922); Dewey (1922); Whipple (2005). The sociology and political science literatures on the elitism–pluralism debate are vast and reviewing them lies beyond the scope of this book. However, for reviews, see Kahn (2012) and McFarland (2007). For a systematic recent application of these ideas to questions of public participation and political inequality, see Schlozman, Verba, and Brady (2012).

level the playing field between the desires of the privileged against those who lack access to power and resources.

On the one hand, the practices of public affairs consultants would seem to offer strong evidence in support of an elitist view of politics, and some popular commentators see this as a particularly worrisome role in which elite interests masquerade through seemingly broad-based, popular mobilization.[84] After all, as I show in Chapter 5, nearly 40 percent of the massive corporations in the *Fortune 500* appear as the clients of these consultants, and in Chapter 6 I show that the advocacy organizations that hire consultants tend to have budgets that are around fourteen times larger than those groups that do not. As E. E. Schattschneider once argued, "the flaw in the pluralist heaven is that the heavenly chorus sings with a strong upper class accent," and it might be said that public affairs consultants offer those upper class voices a bullhorn. Indeed, a case could be made that consultant-backed campaigns are primarily efforts by elites to engage in a sort of pluralist window-dressing in which elite interests are falsely made to appear representative of the broader public interest. Especially when they fail to disclose their (or their client's) role through such actions as creating "third party" or "front" groups, they work against the plural-ist goal of a more transparent, open society in which political battles are won on the basis of the honest competition among interest groups for support. This is undoubtedly true for some of the campaigns described in this book.

However, an elitist approach seems to go too far in the suggestion that popular influence can simply be "bought" by hiring a consultant. While I acknowledge, in agreement with a number of contemporary analysts,[85] that the US system of advocacy organizations is systemati-cally biased toward representing the interests of the affluent and edu-cated, it is equally important to recognize that consultants' campaigns for their clients must contend with competing interests and existing preferences in public opinion. In addition, like other kinds of political organizers, they must study the opposition, craft a message that reso-nates with the public, and seek out policy targets that offer them an opening for generating real change. And they must do so, as I show in Chapter 7, in a way that connects with constituencies that have an

---

[84] Stauber and Rampton (1995); Beder (1998).
[85] For example, Schlozman, Verba, and Brady (2012); Skocpol (2003).

authentic interest in the cause, one that is *independent* of the interests of the paying sponsor. Try as they might to manufacture a base of support for a paying client, campaigns that fail to connect with an authentic base of supporters are likely to fail. Thus, the efforts of these elite consultants are, to some extent, limited by the independent force of existing preferences and organized interests, thus providing some pluralist counterbalance to elite influence.

Social movements and organizational theory

Scholars have shown that organizations outside the state – such as corporations, educational institutions, trade or professional associations – are regularly targets of popular contention, and that the character of challenges to these organizations is often fundamentally different from protests against government agencies or officials.[86] Organizations can be seen as polities in their own right, having their own internal politics, covert power struggles, and ways of managing uprisings within their ranks.[87] Social movement actors, for their part, seek out vulnerabilities and opportunities for change which are based on activists' understanding of the unique configuration of organizational decision-making found in an organization or in a broader field.[88]

Consistent with the expectations of neo-institutionalism – which emphasizes how organizations respond to the coercive, mimetic, and normative pressures they face in their environments – a variety of studies emphasize how public contention against non-state organizations leads targeted organizations to take steps to signal their alignment with the demands of secondary stakeholders like protest groups. This has led, for example, to new forms of self-regulation such as those in forestry and apparel manufacturing, certification systems for dolphin-free tuna, and various fair trade standards.[89] Others have shown that after facing protests, individual companies make efforts to signal their social responsibility through philanthropy and other practices.[90]

This study contributes to the broader discussion of how social movements shape organizational practices on a number of levels. First and

---

[86] Walker, Martin, and McCarthy (2008); Armstrong and Bernstein (2008); Soule (2009).
[87] Zald and Berger (1978). [88] Weber, Rao, and Thomas (2009).
[89] E.g., Bartley (2007). [90] Ingram, Yue, and Rao (2010).

foremost, I show that the mobilization of grassroots campaigns is an important yet under-investigated response to public contention that corporations often take. As I show in Chapter 5, corporations seek to mobilize their own grassroots activism when faced with protest or controversy, and this is especially prevalent among low-reputation firms. Responses such as these help to illustrate the importance of strategic action in response to external pressures and also to better understand the political character of contemporary corporations.[91] Second, this study illuminates how consultants serve as an important mediator in managing contention. Like other professional service firms, public affairs consultants play a needed boundary-spanning function between an organization and its environment. I return to this point in Chapter 4. Lastly, I make clear in Chapter 3 that the founding of new advocacy organizations helped to support the early development of grassroots public affairs consultants, thus showing how advocacy may support the development of new industries.[92]

In responding to contention, organizations work with consultants to mobilize support that appears to be authentic and genuine. Organizational theorists have shown the particular value of authenticity in organizational fields, in applications ranging from microbrews to handicrafts.[93] Authenticity is essential to the reception of grassroots participation, as audiences are likely to discredit participation that appears to be incentivized or staged on behalf of an outside interest. As Robert Fishkin once argued, echoing Habermas, political engagement must be unmanipulated to be taken as legitimate.[94] This is why, as I describe in Chapter 7, it is particularly crucial for consultant-driven campaigns to connect with those who have an independent interest in the issue that is an arm's length removed from the sponsor.

Implications for social capital

The observation that America is in a state of civic decline is, ironically, a near constant in the nation's history. As Michael Schudson points out in his highly regarded history of American citizenship,[95] the theme of civic privatism and individualism run amok has been found throughout our intellectual discourse in works going back to Tocqueville and

---

[91] See Oliver (1991).   [92] Rao (2008).   [93] E.g., Carroll and Wheaton (2009).
[94] Fishkin (1992: 159).   [95] Schudson (1998: Ch. 7).

continuing into the thought of Lippmann, Riesman, Bellah, and, today, Putnam.[96] In more recent years, the "civic decline" discourse has continued apace, with considerable debate over whether we are seeing a civic "decline" or instead simply a shift into new, more flexible forms of association.[97]

The practice of professional public affairs consulting fits into this story in that paid, professional mobilization of public participation both reflects and reinforces the changing structure of association in our society. It reflects civic change in that advocacy organizations have shifted toward more professionalized activities that rely on policy research, litigation, polling, and fundraising rather than general member mobilization.[98] The grassroots lobbying services that consultants provide complement and reinforce this organizational shift, in that they provide their organizational clients – who are, not coincidentally, often more professionalized advocacy groups, as I show in Chapter 6 – with the best available means of targeting the right segments of the public for participatory incentives.

On the other hand, there is reason to believe that the work of these consultants is not so much leading to a decline in Americans' stock of social capital, but is instead encouraging the further development of a new and different form of it. Indeed, I will argue that the targeted activation of specific citizens, or what I refer to as the growth of the narrowly *subsidized public*, need not displace citizens from taking action in other sorts of community engagement. The concern, then, is not that those who are targeted decide no longer to remain involved in other aspects of civic and political life; instead, it is those who are already involved that are among the most likely to be targeted. Thus, a larger degree of political inequality may be between those who are associational "joiners" and those who are unengaged; political recruiters, as discussed earlier, often engage in supply-side recruitment

---

[96] Lippmann (1922); Riesman, Glazer, and Denney (1950); Bellah et al. (1985); Putnam (1995, 2000). For a more sweeping historical perspective, see Sennett (1977).

[97] Wuthnow (2002).

[98] This need not, however, entail the *replacement* of member-based organizations with staff-driven non-membership groups, as membership organizations and non-membership groups tend to rely on one another for mutual support (Walker, McCarthy, and Baumgartner 2011).

with a disproportionate emphasis on turning known activists onto their cause. To the extent that participants tend to be more privileged than the general populace, targeting joiners may be a source of increasing political inequalities.

Adapting repertoires: decoupling the toolkit from the toolmaker

Scholars of social movements and organized advocacy often argue that despite the myriad ways in which those seeking change might make claims in the public sphere, only a limited number of strategies are "thinkable" to actors in a given moment.[99] Organized advocates, like other types of social actors, possess a toolkit for taking action that both enables and constrains effective action.[100] The sum total of tactics that are culturally available to actors at a given moment can be thought of as a "tactical repertoire,"[101] from which actors select on the basis of shared cultural assumptions and bounded rational calculation. Importantly, repertoires are flexible and may be readily adapted to new circumstances, or, importantly, diffused to new actors other than those who created them; this can be thought of, in Tarrow's terms, as a modular repertoire.[102]

The latter concept is relevant here, as public affairs consultants adapted the repertoire of organized advocacy to the changed political and civic environment of US political life starting in the 1970s. This environment was characterized by a massive expansion of citizen advocacy organizations (and their increasing professionalization), the decentralization of power in Congress, declining trust in government, intensification of political partisanship, and the availability of new communications technologies that allowed for weak-tie mobilization of low-cost participation. Under these circumstances, participation consulting emerged to offer professionalized civic groups and politicized business groups a way to mobilize public participation in novel ways. In the fashion of the bricoleur – one who creatively assembles a new organizational practice out of diverse existing cultural contents[103] – public affairs consultants adapted certain parts of the repertoire of

---

[99] Perrin (2006).   [100] Swidler (1986); Clemens (1993, 1997).
[101] Tilly (1995).   [102] Tarrow (1993).   [103] Douglas (1986).

citizen participation to the commercial purveyance of participatory services. In this interaction, certain groups competing for power gain strategic advantages by developing new tactics, while other contenders respond and adapt to those innovations.[104]

In adapting the tactics of citizen advocacy for commercial purposes, part of this repertoire was kept intact, but other parts were cast aside or only partially adapted. Like the Naderite and Public Interest Movement advocates of the late 1960s and early 1970s,[105] public affairs consultants found new ways to exploit the media and communications technologies to get people involved in the political process. On the other hand, consultants can only do so much to build organizational infrastructure on their own, and so they instead learned to rely on the existing capacities of other organizations, developing a productive division of labor between consultants' professionalism and grassroots organizations' thick network ties; this can be seen today in how public affairs consultants build coalitions and mobilize opinion leaders through "grasstops" lobbying. As I show in Chapter 7, consultants' top priority when targeting organizational stakeholders is to mobilize pre-existing opinion leaders, thus utilizing the existing infrastructure of civil society to meet their clients' ends.

What we learn from this account is that repertoires of action often diffuse across institutional boundaries, including between their civic origins and ultimate commercial uses. Marketers, for example, increasingly employ viral techniques that build upon individuals' social networks in order to sell products and services. Political activists, in turn, have used many of the same techniques to "market" their issue or cause.[106] In this case, the growth of citizen advocacy organizations and increasingly activist orientation of business made it possible for activist tactics to be employed by paid professional consultants. The blurring of boundaries between states, markets, and civil societies has made the spread of repertoires across societal sectors much easier to facilitate.

---

[104] McAdam (1983). Also, numerous manuals and how-to books offer suggestions for how corporations and interest groups can win in public relations battles against activists seeking regulation, accountability, or Not-In-My-Back-Yard legislation (e.g., Deegan, 2001; Harrison, 1993; Grefe and Linsky, 1995; Wittenberg and Wittenberg, 1989).
[105] Lazarus (1974).   [106] Bosso (2005).

Conclusion

In this chapter, I introduced the field of public affairs consulting, high-lighting its qualified professionalism, use of incentives, employment of supply-side recruitment strategies, set of organizational clients, and ultimate policy targets for their campaigns. I also noted that the development of this organizational population represents not only the next step in the professionalization of advocacy, but its commercialization as a service sold in the political marketplace. Although consultants have borrowed from the repertoire of citizen participation in crafting their methods, professional public affairs consulting does not appear to be *replacing* traditional forms of grassroots advocacy. Yet, on the other hand, the selective targeting of activists may be exacerbating political inequalities.

Having defined the field of public affairs consulting and considered its implications for our understanding of modern civic and political life, we now take one step backward in order to consider how the growth of this organizational population was shaped by the changing structure of civic life starting in the late 1960s and early 1970s. In so doing, we see that public affairs consultants are both shaping and shaped by the changing structure of American civil society.

3 | *The formation of a grassroots industry*

Introduction

Public affairs consultants have risen to prominence in recent years, but their very existence is a relatively new development, as this population of organizations developed largely in the 1970s and 1980s and has become institutionalized as a regular element of the political system in the years since. This chapter examines how it was that "grassroots" went from being predominantly a characteristic of advocacy organizations and local citizens' groups to a tactic also employed by elite actors when seeking popular support.

It does so by calling attention to the major restructuring of American civic life following after the protest movements of the late 1960s and early 1970s, in which the increased activism of American government in new regulatory and social domains led to both an expansion of citizen engagement and, later, a heightened degree of political activism by businesses and industry groups. Those new organizations, many of which were groups with a professional staff and direct-mail fundraising operations, and which were often reliant on the backing of powerful external patrons (both in foundation grants and in direct corporate support), illustrated the power of harnessing new communications technologies to mobilize citizens as lobbyists. Making use of the increased availability of new communications technologies, consultants – many of whom had personally cut their teeth in the fields of citizen advocacy, corporate lobbying, and especially electoral strategy before opening up their own shops – were more than happy to apply those technologies and skills on behalf of the new population of would-be clients.

The chapter begins by offering a prehistory of public affairs consulting, describing work by earlier political and PR consultants that paved the way for the industry. Next, I trace the career paths of consultants into the profession, finding that electoral consulting was consultants' most common prior occupation. I then describe how the transformation of organized advocacy starting in the late 1960s, as well as the expansion of corporate trade associations starting in the following decade, offered fertile territory for participation consulting. Following this, I describe the emergence of the field itself and then provide the results of a statistical analysis of the founding of consulting firms between 1972 and 2002. The results of these analyses make clear that the most powerful influences on the founding of consulting firms were the growth of new civic organizations and trade associations, even after accounting for the influence of changes in Americans' political attitudes, levels of political participation, partisanship, and economic conditions.

A brief prehistory of public affairs consulting

Although it wouldn't be until the 1970s that the grassroots consulting field would truly get off the ground, the idea to generate grassroots support on behalf of elite interests was hardly new at that point. Indeed, there is a long prehistory to the rise of grassroots consulting that reaches back into antiquity; even in Shakespeare's *Julius Caesar*, Cassius played a consultant-like intermediary role in Brutus's murder of Caesar by writing fake letters "in several hands ... as if they came from several citizens."[1] In the late nineteenth century, employers developed their own public relations messages to counter the threat of the "union menace."[2] And in the twentieth century, the field had precursors in the related domains of advertising and public relations, public opinion polling, campaign consulting, and professional lobbying. In many ways, the development of grassroots consulting represents the next step in the evolution of a mass public that has come to know itself through the lens of social science research, put to work on behalf of organized advocacy.[3]

The early public relations practitioner and consultant Edward Bernays, a nephew of Sigmund Freud, can be seen as a forerunner of the contemporary consulting field in its various guises.[4] Called the "Father of Public Relations" in his *New York Times* obituary after living to the age of 103, Bernays was known for his efforts to expand the idea of public relations well beyond mere communications and into

---

[1] Sager (2009).   [2] Haydu (1999).   [3] See Igo (2007).
[4] See, e.g., Ewen (1996); Friedenberg (1997: 16).

the territory of molding popular preferences and actions.[5] Building upon social science techniques including polling and experiments, his work sought both to understand public opinion and also to find ways of reshaping it to suit his clients' preferences. One such technique, for instance, was to gain the endorsement of elite experts or others seen as influential in a peer community – thus building on the public's trust in independent experts and civic leaders – which continues today in the practice of "grasstops" mobilization strategies used by grassroots public affairs consultants. Bernays was perhaps best known for his campaign to encourage smoking among women on behalf of the American Tobacco Company's Lucky Strike brand, in which a number of young suffragettes were persuaded to march down New York's Fifth Avenue smoking cigarettes prominently; the campaign framed cigarettes as "Torches of Freedom" with the goal that smoking would become a "gesture of freedom and demand for equality among young women."[6] Bernays would lay out these principles in works including *Crystallizing Public Opinion* (1923), *Propaganda* (1928), and his (in)famous essay on the "Engineering of Consent" (1947).

Although first put into practice by Bernays and his contemporary Ivy Lee, it wasn't until 1933 that the first professional political consulting firm in the US would be founded. The firm, Campaigns, Inc., was established by Clem Whitaker and Leone Smith Baxter in California.[7] Whitaker was previously the owner of a political news service that provided reports from the state capital to eighty small-town and weekly newspapers throughout California, while also serving from time to time as a lobbyist in Sacramento. In fact, Whitaker's earlier lobbying emphasized the grassroots approach of "lobbying influential people in legislators' districts rather than the legislators themselves."[8] Baxter was formerly a corporate publicist and manager of the Redding, California Chamber of Commerce.[9] Notably, Baxter's key role in the firm illustrated the important role of women in the field of PR consultants.[10] The pair would become not only consulting partners, but life partners in that they eventually married five years after starting the

---

[5] Ewen (1996).   [6] Evans (2010).
[7] Campaigns, Inc. is widely recognized as the first political consulting firm in the US (e.g., Friedenberg, 1997; Lathrop, 2003; Magleby and Patterson, 1998; Kelley, 1956).
[8] Pitchell (1958: 279–280).   [9] Pitchell (1958: 287).   [10] Donato (1990: 143).

firm.[11] Thus, in the first political consulting firm, the lead consultants brought together hybrid knowledge about the media, the politics of industry, and indirect lobbying through opinion leaders.

California has long contended with Washington, DC as a center of professional lobbying, and the state continues to be a dominant locale for the grassroots consultants who would emerge in the 1970s and thereafter.[12] Given the state's long-standing tradition of direct democracy through the initiative and referendum process, consultants have played an important role in the state's unique policy environment around issues such as property taxes, insurance regulation, same-sex marriage, and the environmental impacts of land development.[13] California was also marked by a rather weak party system and widely dispersed population growth, which encouraged the use of mass media for statewide communications.[14] Perhaps, then, it should not be surprising that a form of consulting that brought together electoral strategies, advertising, polling, and organizing was first found in California's distinct political ecology.

Beyond this regional effect, the context of the 1930s also proved to be fecund for Whitaker and Baxter and their followers thereafter, as it was at this point that opinion polling emerged as a political tool, and one marked with the imprimatur of science.[15] Worries about how practices of political polling distort democracy and limit the development of a more deliberative and open public sphere worried such analysts as Jürgen Habermas (and, for different reasons, Pierre Bourdieu),[16] but these techniques generated usable social knowledge and offered a political opportunity for those called to consulting. The previously undifferentiated mass public could be sliced and diced into segmented audiences, and communications could begin to be targeted at those narrower audiences in order to gain influence and generate political support. Elites, then, could use firms like Campaigns, Inc. to deploy new media technologies of radio and distributed film shorts to make their case in broader public policy battles.

And that is precisely what followed in a variety of efforts organized by Campaigns, Inc., including some seventy-five campaigns they

[11] Lepore (2012). [12] See Table A1 in Walker (2009: 102).
[13] E.g., Magleby and Patterson (1998); Eckholm (2012).
[14] Lathrop (2003: 16). [15] Igo (2007); Lathrop (2003: 15).
[16] Habermas (1989); see also Bourdieu (1979).

organized between 1933 and 1955.[17] During those years, the firm morphed from a scrappy start-up working on a shoestring budget to a trusted and wildly lucrative business servicing such dominant firms as Pacific Telegraph, Standard Oil, Pacific Gas & Electric, and Southern Pacific, and a variety of prominent Republican candidates for office in the Golden State.[18] Famed novelist and California gubernatorial candidate Upton Sinclair complained in 1934 that he lost that year's election in part because of the "lie factory" of PR efforts that falsely attributed statements by the fictional characters in his novels to Sinclair himself; evidence suggests that Whitaker and Baxter were the ones feeding these false claims to the media.[19]

Their victories included campaigns such as an initiative backed by railroad firms, a salary negotiation campaign for the California Teachers Association, and, famously, work on behalf of the American Medical Association against President Truman's proposal for national health insurance.[20] As health policy expert James Morone describes the latter,

Clem Whitaker and Leone Baxter's organization, Campaigns, Inc., did a legendary job. Thirty-seven PR agents found all kinds of creative ways to shout "socialism!" at the start of the Red Scare. Their propaganda campaign has become legendary. In an inspired move, Whitaker and Baxter lined up hundreds of groups (1,829 by one count) and scripted their indignation over socialized medicine. The Truman administration archives bulge with letters, memorials, and petitions from local chapters of the Veterans of Foreign Wars and Chambers of Commerce expressing outrage, all worded suspiciously alike.[21]

By 1958, Campaigns, Inc. was such a powerful force that one political scientist would proclaim that Whitaker and Baxter "have become the giants of the industry, the most successful practitioners of the art of campaign management and the model by which all other firms may be measured."[22]

And their work helped to inspire – and, indeed train – the next generation of political consultants.[23] In fact, Pat Samuels,[24] one of the most prominent public affairs consultants in the field since the 1970s,

---

[17] Pitchell (1958: 282).   [18] Ibid.: 287.   [19] Lepore (2012).
[20] Ibid.; Morone (2011: 375–376).
[21] Morone (2011: 376); see also Starr (1982: 282–285).
[22] Pitchell (1958: 286).   [23] Harvey (1970: 41).   [24] A pseudonym.

told me in an interview that he studied the campaigns of Whitaker and Baxter as he was founding one of the first grassroots consulting firms.

Still, the work they helped to inspire was mostly in the realm of campaign consulting. By the early 1960s, political consulting started to move beyond the services of particular firms and became a budding industry,[25] but the majority of outfits were primarily those involved in consulting for electoral campaigns.[26] As Robert Friedenberg has argued, the development of campaign consulting required a number of preconditions: relatively closely contested elections, a candidate seeking office in an active (rather than passive) fashion, a large constituency, and a combination of funds, campaign organizers, and communications technologies.[27] These consultants tended to focus more on the "air game" of messaging through the media instead of the "ground game" of grassroots organizing. The *Campaigns & Elections* "Political Pages" directory today shows that traditional campaign consultants continue to make up a far greater share of the political consulting field than grassroots public affairs consultants do.[28]

Thus, it would not be until the early 1970s that the industry of grassroots public affairs consulting – differentiated by these consultants' efforts to mobilize groundswells of public participation on behalf of their paying clients – would really get off the ground.[29] It wasn't until that later point that a vastly expanded interest group field (following the 1960s-era social movements), the political mobilization of business, and the widening partisan gap would all come together to support this burgeoning field.

Paths into the industry

The consultants who heeded the call to start new consulting firms hailed from a variety of backgrounds, although my interviews with a number

---

[25] Medvic (2003: 33).   [26] Dulio (2003: 19).   [27] Friedenberg (1997: 5).

[28] See Appendix 1 on using *Campaigns & Elections* as a data source.

[29] However, note that there were precursors to grassroots public affairs consulting firms in the work of certain "full service" electoral consultants that offered not only more established services like media training, speech preparation, fundraising solicitations, and the like, but also grassroots services such as canvassing, facilitating town hall meetings and other public dialogues, etc. Republican strategist Stuart Spencer's firm Spencer-Roberts was an early practitioner of this model, identified both in research (Ginsberg, 1984: 169) and in some of my interviews with contemporary firms.

of long-standing consultants revealed a few consistent pathways from previous careers into the field of grassroots public affairs consulting. These previous lines of work include positions as electoral candidates or their staffers, electoral consultants, in-house corporate public affairs officers, public opinion researchers, or work in grassroots organizing on behalf of social movement organizations and other advocacy groups. The field is generally characterized by a heterogeneous set of career backgrounds. Many consultants, like Whitaker and Baxter long before them, bring together hybrid careers themselves, often finding that grassroots consulting allows them to bricolage diverse skills accrued across varied occupations. One prominent consultant, for example, worked previously as both a campaign staffer for electoral campaigns and as a technical specialist for a telecom firm; he discusses his grassroots consulting work as the application of his technical skills to issue campaigns. Similarly, many other consultants found that the expertise they developed in electoral campaign organizing could easily transfer to work on behalf of corporate clients.

Figure 3.1 illustrates the career backgrounds of consulting firm founders, and does so using data from consultants' websites (see Appendix 3). Biographical statements for the firm's founding partners are a staple of consultants' websites, and these typically provide useful information on consultants' previous occupations prior to starting their public affairs shop. These founding consultants are almost entirely male, as only 11.2 percent of founders are women; despite women's important role in public relations more broadly,[30] women were only rarely the entrepreneurs behind these grassroots consulting firms.

What Figure 3.1 shows most clearly is that when taken as a whole, a plurality of the founders of grassroots consulting firms come from some other kind of consulting work (a combined 44.3 percent), whether it be consulting for electoral campaigns (26 percent), working for a PR or advertising shop (9.9 percent), traditional inside lobbying firm (2.3 percent), or another grassroots public affairs consultancy (6.1 percent).[31] The second cluster of career backgrounds includes those who cut their teeth in electoral politics in some way

[30] Donato (1990).
[31] Those founders who claimed to have worked for another grassroots public affairs consulting firm were concentrated within firms established more recently.

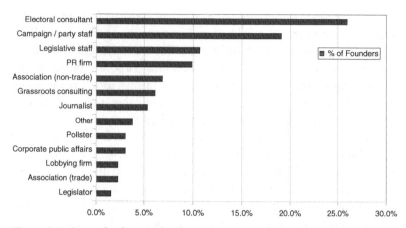

Figure 3.1 Career backgrounds of grassroots consulting firm founders

other than consulting (a combined 31.3 percent), either as campaign or party staff (19.1 percent), staff for an elected legislator (10.7 percent), or as a legislator themselves (1.5 percent).[32] Work as a leader of an advocacy organization (6.9 percent) or trade association (2.3 percent) represents a smaller third cluster. Lastly, it was much less common for firm founders to have backgrounds doing in-house corporate public affairs work (3.1 percent), journalism (5.3 percent), taking polls (3.1 percent), or other occupations such as law, government agency staffing, research, or corporate management (combined 3.8 percent). These findings square with the arguments of David Farrell and colleagues, who argue that while "early [political] consultants tended to originate in the commercial world," today "the routes of entry appear quite different, with many consultants being trained by the political parties and increasingly in specialist courses at universities across the United States."[33]

In my interviews with consultants, I heard accounts that provided further depth on how those who founded these consulting operations built upon these heterogeneous careers and also how they were responding to broader forces in the political environment.

---

[32] This low proportion of founders who were previous legislators contradicts the expectation of a "revolving door" between lobbyists and legislators (see, e.g., Salisbury et al., 1989). Grassroots public affairs consulting, by contrast, builds upon skill sets developed through electoral campaign work.

[33] Farrell, Kolodny, and Medvic (2001: 13).

Perhaps the most common story of all was that those who founded these firms were working in the burgeoning sector of electoral campaign consulting firms established in the wake of Whitaker and Baxter, and who found themselves needing more stable sources of revenue between election years. They found in the 1970s and 1980s that although electoral revenue is full of sharp peaks and valleys, corporations were increasingly finding themselves on the receiving end of both unwelcome regulation and popular controversies, and the ballooning interest group sector also needed to mobilize untapped sources of support among the mass public. And as the public became increasingly partisan, consultants found that audiences were becoming more receptive to polarizing messages about issues like the environment, taxation, and government regulation of business.

The story of how Toledo Alvarez founded his firm Toledo Alvarez Associates is, in many ways, prototypical.[34] He explained to me that the firm started out doing electoral consulting, and that he also had personal experience working as a campaign staffer, primarily on the Democratic side. He elaborated:

I come out of doing [electoral] campaigns on the East Coast, to the West Coast, to forming an organization, doing it professionally, and so on and so forth. At some point we transitioned and took the tools, which are very similar in terms of who you're communicating with. We took those tools and we applied them to [helping] individual companies who needed to navigate the political waters, if you will [...] Our business started in the 80s. We shifted it more in the 90s away from the electoral side, and I probably haven't run [an electoral] campaign in 8–10 years.

I heard a very similar account from Roger Dylan Hess, founder of the prominent West Coast public affairs consulting firm Roger Hess Advocacy:[35]

We were doing [electoral] campaigns when I started ... But mostly [in this state] we have state primaries in June and we have November elections for the most part [...] So that's about five months a year no matter what you charge. And I didn't ever believe you could charge enough in those five months to have a vacation paid for the other seven, so I tried to diversify immediately. That was the strategy and a purpose, and [we wanted] to have people [think that] if

---

[34] These are pseudonyms.   [35] Pseudonyms.

they worked for us, they'd have a job. You know, it didn't go away because election day passed. That's what we tried to follow.

Lastly, as Bill Hoover of Field Engagement, Inc.[36] described to me about his more recently founded firm, he and his co-founder had previously

worked on political campaigns; we looked around and we said, OK, you can hire just about every type of consultant imaginable. You can hire a pollster, you can hire a media consultant, you can hire a direct mail consultant, you can hire a general consultant, a finance consultant, on and on and on and on. But when it actually came to getting more people involved in [an issue] campaign, there is no outside expertise . . .

My business partner and I, when we were both doing jobs in the legislative world and I was working for [a legislator in my home state] and he was working for a member of Congress in DC. We made a similar observation that if you were an advocacy organization trying to affect change you could hire lobbyists or communications professionals, but there was no outside expertise on building a broader stakeholder base. Those were our two ideas around which we founded the company.

Perhaps most straightforward of all was what I heard from one of the most prominent firms on the West Coast, regarding why they diversified beyond candidate campaigns. When I asked why his firm shifted from working for candidates to working for corporate clients, he responded curtly that they did it simply to "make money and have year-round business."

Working as a legislative staffer was a learning experience for some consultants, showing in clear terms how constituent messages are received by policymakers. For example, Phil Frederick (whom I profile in greater detail in the next chapter)[37] noted that his work as a legislative assistant to a former senator from a large mid-Atlantic state showed him that grassroots constituent communication is effective. Similar to how one of Ken Kollman's informants in his study of grassroots lobbying said that "politicians use grass-roots contacts as a sort of hyper-concentrated version of what people are thinking back home,"[38] Phil told me that

the key is when the door is cold and it's [the senator and me] sitting in there and he's letting his hair down and talking about how he's going to determine his vote on a particular thing. Two things become blazingly true. One is that

---

[36] These are pseudonyms.   [37] A pseudonym.   [38] Kollman (1998: 155).

democracy works; [elected officials are] generally responsive. But, two: there is nothing more effective than a face-to-face meeting for an elected official.

In sum, then, the pre-existing base of political professionals active in communicating about politics to mass audiences, who learned their organizing skills in electoral campaigns and legislative work, seems to have been crucial for opening these new grassroots public affairs consultancies. But the supply of these skills is only one factor, as this also required demand from corporations and advocacy organizations. And it was not until the 1970s and 1980s that those two trends came together to produce a wave of demand for professional advocacy services.

As Pat Samuels, one of the first grassroots public affairs consultants in the US, described to me in an interview, the field took off because both corporations and consultants were independently reaching out to one another. He continued,

You know, as things change and as the politics change, more people are exposed. You know ... there were two major issues early on that were probably driving this movement [among consultants] more than any. And one was tobacco,[39] and the other was electricity: the nuke plants in the 1970s. It was major. It was major. So, they were the two industries [that] were the major drivers of the development of [corporate-backed] grassroots or public participation [...] And, you know, after the 60s, corporate interests saw the effectiveness of group participation. And they said, "Well, if they can do it ..." [...] And so, corporate and business interests said, "Well, why not. Let's go out and buy it."[40]

From streets to suites

It was in the 1970s and 1980s that these entrepreneurs found that the territory was fertile for professionals in grassroots politics. A major part of

---

[39] For a useful case study of grassroots mobilization by tobacco firms, see Givel (2007).
[40] Further highlighting the role of elite interests in sponsoring industry-backed campaigns in defense of tobacco and nuclear industries, David Meyer and Suzanne Staggenborg (1996: 1643) have pointed out that "both the nuclear power and tobacco industries in the United States determined that there were advantages to the social movement form and initiated countermovement organizations" in response to contentious challenges.

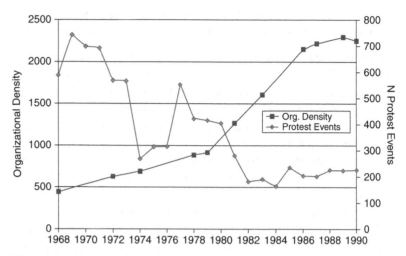

Figure 3.2 From movements to interest groups, 1968–1990

that story can be linked back to the growth in government activity in the 1960s and early 1970s, which inspired the Public Interest Movement and myriad citizen groups to be founded in the following decade.[41] Further, the wave of popular activism of the "long sixties" eventually made its way into the interest group sector, with new groups becoming professional advocates for their causes.[42] As illustrated in Figure 3.2, which compares the number of public protest events reported in the *New York Times* with the total number of generalist advocacy organizations listed in the *Encyclopedia of Associations* from 1968 to 1990, the overall volume of public protest declined significantly, while the number of advocacy organizations active in public affairs ballooned in dramatic fashion thereafter.[43] As a growing consensus of scholars in sociology and political science argue, the end of the "long sixties" protest wave brought with it a significant change in the character of advocacy: from operating outside institutions to making change on the inside, or, in Bayard Rustin's knowing phrase, from protest to politics.[44] A key element of this "institutionalization" of

---

[41] Vogel (1989); Berry (1997); Walker (1991); Skocpol (2007).
[42] Minkoff (1997).
[43] These data on protest events reported in the *New York Times* come from McAdam et al. (2009).
[44] Meyer and Tarrow (1998).

protest is the professionalization of social movement organizations, such that the boundary between the latter and formal "interest groups" becomes increasingly blurred.[45]

The organizations that sprouted up in the wake of this major cycle of contention were largely middle class, relied upon external patrons, and lobbied most often on single issues ranging from gender discrimination to the influence of business in politics. They were influential well beyond reforming policy; as political scientist Jeffrey Berry notes,[46] lobbying groups in the 1970s changed the *very context* of policymaking, in that a variety of new constituencies became aware of their ability to generate bad publicity, file lawsuits, and reshape public opinion.

Perhaps the most significant consequence of the group "explosion" was that associations blazed new trails in the strategic, targeted mobilization of citizens through media technologies.[47] It is also not coincidental that their expansion in this period followed the passage of the "Sunshine Laws" that decentralized power within Congress,[48] which were designed to make the policy process more transparent to citizens.

It therefore appears that the rise in citizen advocacy helped to support the development of the organizational field of public affairs consulting. Practitioners of public affairs consulting have, in fact, noted an association between the founding of new civic organizations with the development of their own field. For example, corporate grassroots gurus Edward Grefe and Marty Linsky argue that public affairs consulting represents the marriage of "communication and information technology with the [*sic*] 1960s grassroots organizing techniques," and they even claim heritage in the community organizing of Saul Alinsky.[49] Further, as a leading public affairs consultant argued in a statement to the *New York Times*, public affairs consultants took their cues from professionalized advocacy groups. When asked if consultants are having ill effects on American democracy, he responded: "Give me a break ... most communications to the White House or the Hill are prompted. Whether by the Sierra Club, the National Rifle Association, or the American Association of Retired People is not the point."[50]

---

[45] Burstein (1998); Andrews and Edwards (2004).   [46] Berry (1977: 289).
[47] Schier (2000); Crenson and Ginsberg (2004).
[48] Heitshusen (2000); Oppenheimer (1980).   [49] Grefe and Linsky (1995: xi).
[50] Engelberg (1993: A17).

Business gets organized

But, despite the mass mobilization of citizens' groups in response to the more activist state, business did not simply stand idly by. Far from it, as the late-1970s era brought with it a considerable borrowing of interest group methods by business lobbies, as the formalization of grassroots mobilization tactics became a service that lobbying firms and political consultants began to offer to paying clients. Indeed, as one journalist reported in the *New York Times* in 1978, new grassroots mobilization tactics appeared

... to reflect and contribute to fundamental changes in how government now works, to shifts in power relationships, and to a decline in the authority of the Presidency and Congressional leadership ... It also appears to reflect an aggressive and determined effort by industry and business to increase its direct political action, as well as a growing ability of business leaders to submerge their differences and agree on cooperative action under common tactics and strategy.[51]

Although, as David Vogel notes, the unity of business interests that characterized the late 1970s would not last,[52] public mobilization tactics came to be an institutionalized element of the tactical repertoire of industry thereafter.

The mid 1970s marked the start of a period in which business began once again to assert its power in Washington.[53] Perhaps ironically, the rise of citizen activism appears to have encouraged the adoption of civic tactics by businesses. In fact, industry was not getting results because it failed to recognize that

public policy was no longer being made in private negotiations between Washington insiders and a handful of strategically placed representatives and senators. Power within Congress had become more decentralized, the number of interest groups represented in Washington had increased, the role of the media in defining the political agenda and the terms of political debate had expanded, the importance of political parties had declined, and the courts had begun to play a much more active role in making regulatory policy.[54]

Similarly, journalist and popular commentator William Greider argues that there existed a direct relationship between the transformed

[51] Mohr (1978: D7).   [52] Vogel (1989).
[53] Vogel (1989); Peschek (1987); Plotke (1992).   [54] Vogel (1989: 10).

regulatory environment, the growth of associations, and private incentives for public participation:

The origins of information-driven politics are, ironically, traceable to progressive reform as much as to large corporations or wealth. Middle-class and liberal-minded reformers, trying to free government decisions from the crude embrace of the powerful, emphasized a politics based on facts and analysis as their goal. They assumed that forcing "substance" into the political debate, supported by disinterested policy analysis, would help overcome the natural advantages of wealth and entrenched power. But information is never neutral and, in time, every interest recognized the usefulness of buying or producing its own facts.[55]

Accordingly, businesses felt relatively weak vis-à-vis the largely liberal set of new advocacy organizations and realized that they should imitate the strategies of those who were working against them. It took about a half-dozen years for industry to respond.[56]

Public affairs consulting came about in part as a result of business mobilization in politics, beginning in the mid 1970s and accelerating immediately thereafter.[57] Because of the threat posed by regulation and citizen organizing, corporations became more sophisticated in politics. While business feared the consequences of throwing around its political weight in the 1960s, the period after the 1974 elections saw the rise of industry activism against perceived over-regulation.[58] This led to a form of class consciousness among businesses that, although fleeting, supported the development of a long-term corporate presence in paid lobbying, public relations, and policy-planning organizations.[59] In addition, in this new regulatory environment, corporations also began to place heavier emphasis on public transparency and accountability, stakeholder opinion, and philanthropic programs; many corporations also instituted in-house public affairs departments.[60] These developments were indirectly tied to the protest wave of the long 1960s, argue French sociologists Luc Boltanski and Eve Chiapello, in that protests encouraged corporations to adopt a "new spirit of capitalism" in which flexible and often participatory organizational practices were adopted, in part, in order to defuse outside criticism.[61]

---

[55] Greider (1992: 46).   [56] Vogel (1989).
[57] Faucheux (1995); Stone (1994); Vogel (1989).   [58] Pertschuk (1982).
[59] Peschek (1987).   [60] Schlozman and Tierney (1986).
[61] Boltanski and Chiapello (2005).

Thus, corporate groups developed their own forms of grassroots organization in order to shape both public opinion and to mobilize the public as a force in molding legislative decisions. The population of industry groups grew in line with increased business mobilization in politics in the late 1970s,[62] following the oil embargo, stagflation, and other economic instabilities of the middle of that decade. Business's political power was growing not just because it could hire lobbyists in Washington and contribute large sums to political campaigns, but because it was often able to show its support among the public. Whereas in earlier years grassroots campaigns were a last-ditch effort or "last line of defense, called in when other lobbying, advertising, and public relations efforts had been exhausted,"[63] today professional grassroots consultants represent an integral part of a corporation's public and political existence.

New communications technologies

New communications technologies gave participation consultants a broad new arsenal of methods for mobilizing participation. While this is not entirely new, the lowering of the costs of collective action – due in large part to the increased availability of communications technologies – opened up a variety of new possibilities. By as early as 1948, political commentators were arguing that "the system of deluging Congress with thousands of communications obtained by 'pressing a button' and giving the signal to the 'faithful' back home to write or telegraph (without their knowing necessarily what the facts and issues are) is a comparatively recent development ... yet, in the opinion of many, this technique is *already outdated* and has lost much of its effectiveness."[64] As the advocacy field was increasingly professionalized and dominated by the voices of business interests, new technologies were put to use in their service. These included low-cost long-distance phone calling, direct mail using computerized lists of likely activists (often provided by specialized vendors), and, today, web, email, and social networking technologies.

The availability of these technologies made it possible for consultants to adopt the techniques that citizens' and business groups were using to

---

[62] Akard (1992).   [63] Stone (1994: 754).
[64] LaFollette (1948: 54), emphasis added.

mobilize political action. Consider, for example, the following journal-istic account of a typical patch-through calling campaign coordinated by a public affairs consulting firm in the early 1990s:

Say, for example, the National Organization for Women opposes a nomina-tion to the Supreme Court because the candidate has an equivocal record on abortion rights. [A consultant] will take the membership rolls of the group, and match names to the phone numbers. It might also use its computer to cross-reference magazine subscriptions, data on personal purchasing habits, and precincts with particular voting and income profiles to come up with a bigger list of sympathetic people. At the company's phone bank [office], a computer dials the numbers. When someone answers, an operator comes on the line and explains NOW's position, offering to transfer the caller, at no charge, to the White House switchboard or local member of Congress.[65]

Gathering steam in the 1970s with the use of direct mail (especially by conservative entrepreneurs like Richard Viguerie), public affairs con-sulting operations began to offer to their clients technological services for mobilizing participation.[66] And, although during that period many corporations started their own in-house public affairs operations, many in the field came to recognize the importance of relying on stand-alone organizations specialized in activating the grassroots. As Kevin B. Fitzgerald of Legislative Demographic Services argued,

More associations, corporations, and unions are building grassroots lobbying operations in-house. A stark reality for many of these new departments is the complexity and multiple disciplines required for an effective grassroots oper-ation. Expertise in ... strategy development, communications, technology, event planning and public relations ... often overwhelms staff. Most organ-izations do outsource some or all of their technical and data needs to consultants.[67]

Similarly, consultant Wayne Blanchard argued,

Why not rely on experts that perform these services every day, where com-munications technology has been developed and is currently in place, and where sufficient resources are available and trained to build the support teams and mechanisms needed in a grassroots campaign? [...] There are well-organized firms that specialize in services ... such as "Direct Connect," a

---

[65] Engelberg (1993: A17).
[66] On the rise of political consulting more broadly, see Sabato (1981).
[67] Jalonick (2003: 48).

seamless transfer of constituent calls to their state or federal legislator's office and at no cost to the constituent; combined data collection or information dissemination through Web site interfaces with associated software tools and toll-free inbound lines; automated celebrity outbound communications; creative message design with targeted direct mail; and the "Blended Call" to maximize file penetration and constituent contact rates.[68]

A market for mobilization services develops

Professional lobbying of the public began with a number of boutique outlets as side projects of major PR firms, but successes by certain early boutiques made this practice appealing to those who would start independent firms.[69] Some began as direct mail outlets in the 1970s, as noted by Republican strategists like Richard Viguerie.[70] As groups began to "contract out the direct-mail and phone bank components of their grassroots operations," so "an ancillary industry has arisen to meet the demand for the new technology."[71] As early as 1978, commentators were noticing that, "especially in the business and industrial community, there has been a major increase in the use – and apparent effectiveness – of so-called indirect lobbying," activating key community leaders, mass telephone calls, and computerized lists (often matched to Congressional districts of targeted representatives).[72]

In 1993 and 1994, *Campaigns & Elections* magazine estimated, grassroots public affairs services represented an $800 million industry, not counting additional advertisement purchases from other vendors.[73] By 1998, the industry was in full bloom: "Creating citizens' movements, or the semblance of citizens' movements on demand ... has become big business. Public relations firms and boutique shops advertise such arcane-sounding specialties as 'development of third-party allies,' or 'grassroots recruitment and mobilization,' or 'grass-tops lobbying.' The goal of these campaigns is to persuade ordinary voters to serve as the front-line advocates for the paying clients."[74] By 2009, public affairs firms had learned to leverage social networking sites like Facebook and Twitter, both of which are well suited to incentivizing low-cost participation on behalf of a paying client. As one of the public affairs

---

[68] Ibid.: 48–49. [69] Stone (1994: 755). [70] Viguerie (1981).
[71] Cigler and Loomis (1995: 396). [72] Mohr (1978). [73] Ibid.
[74] Mitchell (1998: A14).

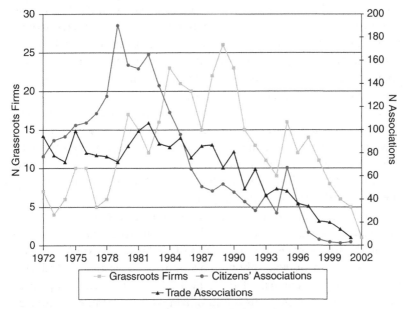

Figure 3.3 Founding patterns of organizational populations

consultants I interviewed argued, "everyone is thinking about what the next Facebook is going to be. We're a sound-bite nation, but I think this goes in pendulum swings [from mass media sources to trusted, local sources]. We're going back to the traditional sources right now, like family, friends, neighbors, etc. We grow bored with sources quickly."

Figure 3.3 illustrates the founding patterns of consulting firms, advocacy organizations, and trade associations, showing a clear pattern by which consulting firms followed after the development of citizen and, later, industry groups. Figure 3.3 maps the aggregate founding patterns of consulting firms (from the baseline data) against membership organizations listed in the *Encyclopedia of Associations* and the trade association data. This figure illustrates that the peak founding periods for both public interest groups and trade associations occurred prior to most founding events of consulting shops. However, it appears that business mobilization in industry associations had two peak years: 1975 (during which industry started to become more politically active), and 1982, following the election of Ronald Reagan. While both fields underwent substantial growth throughout the 1970s, grassroots consulting did not expand dramatically as a field until the mid-to-late 1980s, at the same time that the founding of new citizen associations went into decline. This figure presents initial evidence that business actors learned the power of the citizen organizing, which, in turn, spurred the development of participation-subsidizing organizations to adopt the tactics of public interest groups.

Assisted by the growth of communications technologies that allowed for the mass contacting of political officials with relatively low costs on the part of the participant (little effort needed to make the contact, and a ready-made message), grassroots consulting grew at a dramatic rate beginning in the late 1970s and increased steadily throughout the 1980s. Business groups found in these firms a means of expanding their lobbying operations to relevant publics as a political force. Indeed, a number of the large political consulting and public relations firms active on behalf of business expanded their operations into outside lobbying around the same time.[75] Industry groups made similar use of these firms. Public interest groups also began to employ these firms for mobilizing distant members, supporters, and donors.

A statistical model of firm formation

Given the above factors that appear to have had an effect on the formation of participation consulting firms, to which explanation should we give the most weight? The statistical models that follow allow one to determine which of these explanations hold the greatest merit, while also accounting for the confounding explanations that changes in public attitudes or engagement in civic and political life might have been more influential.

As Figure 3.3 illustrated, the field of professional public affairs consulting expanded dramatically between the early 1970s and the opening years of the new century. To understand this in greater depth, I examine patterns of consulting firm founding between 1972 and 2002, broken down across eleven regions of the country. These include the nine regions determined by the US Census Bureau, plus additional regions

---

[75] Faucheux (1995).

separated out for Washington, DC and Virginia (where, of course, a quite disproportionate share of political consultants are located) and California (where many consultants are located that specialize in petition drives and ballot measures). Then, I estimate how the number of civic organizations, industry associations, and a variety of other social and political variables – within each region in the prior year – influenced the founding of public affairs consulting firms. A full description of the measures and statistical methodology employed in these analyses is found in the article from which these findings are adapted.[76]

Table 3.1 presents the findings of the statistical model. The primary conclusion to be derived from Table 3.1 is that the expansion of advocacy organizations and the increase of business trade groups both had a significant influence on the founding of new public affairs consulting firms, even after holding a variety of other factors constant. Substantively, both of these measures also have positive and highly significant marginal effects on firm founding, as associational founding increases the mean count of consulting firms founded by, on average, 2.4 percent; the comparable increase for each additional business group is 4.9 percent. Therefore, these analyses suggest that civic and business organization founding events were highly consequential in shaping the patterns of consulting firm founding, although it is worth noting that the coefficients for business mobilization are consistently greater in magnitude. I therefore find strong support for the primary argument that heightened formal organization and business presence in civil society has encouraged the development of this new organizational population.

Importantly, the statistical models provide little support for the expectation that public affairs firms have arisen in response to the declining political participation of Americans. Similarly, Americans' level of trust in government, feelings of political efficacy, or changing levels of interest in public affairs had no significant effect on the founding of new organizations.

However, certain political factors did have strong and significant effects on the formation of firms; in particular, the increased partisanship of the American populace and the expansion of Republican Party

---

[76] Walker (2009: 91–95; 101–102).

Table 3.1 *Random effects Poisson GEE regression analyses of the founding of public affairs consulting firms, 1972–2002*

Independent variables	Coef.	Robust S.E.
Public affairs associations		
Membership organizations founded (count)	0.02***	(0.01)
Business associations		
Trade associations founded (count)	0.05***	(0.01)
Participation		
Attended a political meeting (%)	–0.02	(0.03)
Cognitive measures		
Trust in government (%)	–0.01	(0.01)
Interest in public affairs (%)	–0.02	(0.01)
Political efficacy (%)	0.00	(0.01)
Party decline		
Party workers (%)	0.08[+]	(0.04)
Republican control		
Mean governorships held by Republicans (proportion)	0.37*	(0.16)
Political partisanship		
Strong party identification (%)	0.05**	(0.02)
Economic conditions		
State corporate taxes (thousands of 2002 dollars per estab.)	0.04	(0.08)
Total non-farm employment (per thousand capita)	0.00	(0.00)
Year[1]		
Year is 1972–1974	–0.66	(0.51)
Year is 1975–1979	–0.52	(0.41)
Year is 1980–1984	–0.31	(0.30)
Year is 1990–1994	–0.10	(0.26)
Year is 1995–2002	–0.46	(0.32)
Exposure measures		
Regional population (millions)	–0.01	(0.01)
Constant	–2.96[+]	(170)
N	341	
Wald Chi-square	275.86***	
Estimated R^2	.471	

[1] The reference category for year includes 1985–1989.
Semi-robust standard errors appear in parentheses. All analyses specify an autoregressive (AR[1]) error structure.
Significance levels: $^+ p \le .10$; $^* p \le .05$; $^{**} p \le .01$; $^{***} p \le .001$

control of state governments both had noteworthy positive effects on firm founding. More specifically, each additional percentage point increase in the strong partisanship of the US citizenry was associated with a 5.2 percent increase in the mean number of firms founded, and that region-years in which Republicans control all regional governorships relate to a 44 percent increase in consulting firm founding.[77] These findings indicate that a more partisan populace, governed by the Republican Party, played a positive role in supporting consulting firm founding.

Finally, the statistical models show that economic conditions and corporate taxation had little effect on public affairs consulting firm founding,[78] and there is not much support for the notion that firms arose in order to compensate political party decline. In fact, the models show modest support for the *opposite* argument: that the presence of party workers makes it *more* likely that a firm will be founded. This finding, consistent with the evidence from consultants' career backgrounds in Figure 3.1, supports the notion that firms were often founded by former party activists, and in those locations populated by such individuals. Thus, even though aggregate national patterns of party activism were mainly in decline during the years of this analysis, pockets of greater party activism supported the development of consulting shops. Each additional percentage point increase in party activists is associated with an increase of 8 percent in the mean number of firms founded.

Making sense of the statistical findings

How might we understand the increasing prevalence of public affairs consulting firms in the US in recent decades? The findings of the above analyses suggest, interestingly, that expanding civic and business associational populations facilitated their rise. These elite consultants who mobilize public action grew in number and power as US civil society saw a

---

[77] However, these results should be interpreted with some caution, as additional analyses (not shown) indicate that Republican House seats had no significant influence on founding events, and Republican Senate seats had a slightly significant ($p < .10$) negative influence. When all three measures are included, the effect of Republican governorships remains positive and significant.

[78] This runs counter to Akard's (1992) suggestion that corporate taxation spurred business activism.

number of broad transformations. The legitimation of this new organizational field was driven by civic *organizational change* rather than the decline of individual participation. Without such changes having taken place, then, it would have been unlikely that organizations engaged in targeted mobilization of the public would have emerged.

The above analyses indicate that the central factor shaping the organizational dynamics of these private firms was the rise of business trade associations. The founding of trade associations, as organizations that are coalitions of firms or businesspersons which serve as "focal points for diverse interests,"[79] may be taken as an indicator of business recognizing its shared and collective interests. As business became more aware of its political interests – especially in response to the crisis of corporate legitimacy starting in the late 1960s[80] – industry groups utilized the services of grassroots firms in order to connect with the broader public and activate their stakeholders. Business engagement in politics, overlooked in scholarship on civic engagement, appears to be a primary support for firms that incentivize public participation.

Second, advocacy groups were only slightly less consequential in facilitating the founding of public affairs consulting firms. The "interest group explosion" assisted in the expansion of a separate, ancillary field of organizations that stir up the grassroots. It is interesting, therefore, that grassroots firms and citizen groups appear to support rather than compete with one another. It seems, then, that these consultants have not *replaced* the activism of public advocacy groups, but instead complement them. I return to this point in Chapter 6.

A noteworthy additional finding of the present analyses is that lower rates of political participation appear to have little association with the founding of participation consulting shops. Thus, although one might expect that in contexts of declining participation it might behoove businesses and interest groups to hire professional firms, there is little evidence to support this notion. On the other hand, it remains possible that specific grassroots *campaigns* occur in response to citizen participation targeted against the particular client of a consulting firm, a possibility that I explore in some detail in Chapters 5 and 7.

The disconnection and alienation of citizens from government does not show any clear effect on the likelihood of grassroots lobbying firm

---

[79] Staber and Aldrich (1982: 163).   [80] Vogel (1975).

founding. Additionally, rather than competing with political parties for resources and constituent mobilization, public affairs firms may see party members as a base for staff and executive recruitment. Indeed, as illustrated earlier, many principal lobbyists started out as electoral campaign consultants. Finally, the model suggests an important secondary conclusion: that a more partisan public, alongside a more Republican government, appears to have supported the rise of public affairs consulting as a regular part of civic and political life in the US.

Conclusion

By analyzing the founding patterns of consulting firms, this chapter provides leverage in understanding the broader civic transformations that, since the 1970s, helped paid mobilization of public participation to become a regular part of the American public sphere. Although research on civic engagement and political participation has made much ado about whether changing patterns of participation are shaped more by a generational decline in democratic norms, social networks, and generalized trust,[81] or, alternatively, by the vitiated supply side of opportunities for participation,[82] extant research has downplayed the mobilization of citizens by paid consulting operations. In addition, by analyzing two prominent organizational changes in civic life – the growth of business trade associations and the dramatic increase in advocacy groups – this chapter considered in further detail the under-examined *consequences* of these civic changes. While the effects of business mobilization on government have been well studied,[83] comparatively little work has been done on how industry activism shapes civil society.[84]

Before moving on to the next chapter, it is worth asking a key question: How can we explain the scholarly neglect of business influence on civic life and public participation? It appears that, as in classical political economy models, scholars continue to assume that a permeable but nonetheless enduring boundary tends to be maintained between the public and private spheres. Similarly, it is common to neglect the

---

[81] Putnam (1995, 2000).   [82] Skocpol (2003).
[83] See, for example, Hillman, Keim, and Schuler (2004); Plotke (1992).
[84] But see Vogel (1989).

porousness of the tripartite scheme of markets, states, and civil societies; as scholars of the nonprofit sector, for example, illustrate, it is often quite misleading to conceptualize civil society as fully independent of the state and market.[85] Although much recent work in social and political theory has emphasized the increasing encroachment on the public sphere by private interests – especially since the English-language publication of Habermas's *Structural Transformation of the Public Sphere*[86] – the influence of business on the dynamics of civil society has remained a somewhat shadowy realm for researchers of civic engagement. This chapter, in particular, suggests that a greater integration of insights from the literature on the "privatization of the public sphere" would benefit future empirical research on participation. Those studies that call attention to the increasing "sidelining" of the public represent a worthwhile first step in this direction.[87]

Additional insights from this chapter are applicable to the dynamics of legitimation in new organizational fields. Although the development of new organizational forms often jeopardizes existing interests,[88] these outfits were successful in showing how public-oriented campaigns can promote civic engagement on behalf of their organizational clients; this was mainly because these growing organizational fields presented a demand for new, low-cost communications technologies to influence an increasingly decentralized government.

Having reviewed the *sources* of participation consulting as a field, the discussion now turns to understanding the *structure* and *consequences* of these firms' practices.

---

[85] Frumkin (2002: 12); see also Friedland and Alford (1991).
[86] Habermas (1989).
[87] See, for example, Crenson and Ginsberg (2004); Schier (2000).   [88] Rao (1998).

PART II

Structure

4 | *Methods for mobilizing the public*

Introduction

We saw in the previous chapter how the field of public affairs firms was established, and how the development of these firms was in part a response to the expanded market demand for public mobilization services following the expansion of civic and business trade groups in the 1970s and 1980s. The present chapter examines how these consulting firms develop strategy in order to help their organizational clients manage their sociopolitical environments.

This chapter therefore examines organization–environment relationships on two levels.

On one level, public affairs consultants *play a mediating role* in helping their clients to manage public policy issues and respond to challenges that arise in their sociopolitical environments. They serve what organizational theorists refer to as a "boundary-spanning" function, connecting the organization to authorities and other core audiences on which the organization depends in order to sustain itself.[1]
They are therefore similar in many ways to other types of professional service firms (e.g., law firms, advertising companies, accountants, management consultants) in this general sense. However, they differ from most other professional service firms which do more to help their clients to comply with the demands of their legal, market, and/or institutional environments.[2] It is in this respect that sociologists often find that legal compliance regimes are endogenous to organizational practices.[3] While part of what public affairs consultants do is to help their clients conform

---

[1] Aldrich and Herker (1977).
[2] To be sure, as the case of Crosstown Strategists below makes clear, part of what grassroots consultants do for their clients also at times involves compliance matters.
[3] E.g., Edelman, Uggen, and Erlanger (1999); Dobbin and Kelly (2007).

to institutional pressures, they also help clients make strategic efforts to reshape those environments and resist such pressures.

On another level, consulting firms *themselves are organizations* that face inter-organizational pressures, requirements to uphold their standing and legitimacy among core audiences, and need to maintain resources in order to survive. Sociopolitical legitimacy pressures are particularly acute because consultants' role in organizing grassroots support for their clients is, at times, less than fully transparent. Although consultants regularly note that their campaigns are not illegitimate because recruited participants are voicing their honest and authentic views to policymakers, consultant-driven campaigns nonetheless often downplay or conceal their own role in facilitating such participation. A well-executed campaign should, of course, keep the consultant back stage and draw more attention to salient public opinion on an issue rather than the role of a consulting firm in amplifying it. More specifically, consultants must contend with popular mistrust of commercial efforts to incentivize public participation, which, as I described in Chapter 2, is often discredited as "fake" grassroots or "astroturf." As this chapter makes clear, the public acceptability of commercially mobilized public participation is a topic very much on the minds of consulting firms.

The chapter begins by describing two firms in detail: Frederick Partners and Williamson Strategists.[4] Both firms have a predominantly corporate and trade association client base, but both also do business on behalf of a variety of nonprofit organizations. Like many consulting firms, both got their start in political campaign consulting before shifting their attention toward organizing paid grassroots campaigns. Both play a mediating role between their client firms and clients' sociopolitical environments, often helping to buffer their clients from the considerable demands of organizing a broad-based advocacy campaign. The firms differ in that Frederick Partners focuses on brokering face-to-face contacts between leaders of pre-existing civic organizations and policymakers, whereas Williamson Strategists offers a broader menu of services including the creation of third-party organizations, organizing protests/rallies, and spreading their client's message through blogs. Williamson is also significantly more active in providing high-tech data management services and making use of social media technologies

[4] These are pseudonyms.

in their campaigns; they are also, as many of the consulting firms in this study are, more closely tied into the shift toward "big data," analytics, and the statistically driven targeting strategies that are currently revolutionizing electoral campaign strategy.[5] This difference in focus reflects both the varying skill sets of each organization's founding teams and their understanding of which services will be most effective in meeting the demands of the political marketplace.

After describing the organizational processes and institutional contexts of these two consulting firms, the remainder of the chapter uses data from my survey of consulting firms in order to discuss how firms like Frederick Partners and Williamson Strategists fit into the bigger picture of commercialized public participation through "grassroots for hire."

Mobilizing opinion leaders: Frederick Partners

Frederick Partners was founded in the 1980s and is headquartered in Washington, DC. The firm's charismatic founder, Phil Frederick, was a pioneer in this field and made Frederick Partners one of the most successful firms in the grassroots mobilization industry.[6] I interviewed Phil and his assistant in his office in the summer of 2010.

Frederick himself got his start doing public relations work for a local government office, followed by positions with the Republican Party and working as a staffer for a US senator. Despite his partisan personal background, Phil promotes the firm as a nonpartisan consultancy. He explains further that the firm doesn't do any electoral campaign work. As he sees it, for those other firms who are partisan, this allegiance naturally engenders a certain amount of trust and access with allied policymakers ("the upside is that they have these *personal* relationships ... [partisan consultants] can get through to those people where others might not"), but the risk is that being partisan limits a firm's ability to negotiate with political opponents. Further, partisan consultants have fewer options when a client needs the consultant to broker a constituency with a member of the opposite party. Such suggestions are consistent with research in political science on relations of trust between clients and political consultants.[7] As I describe later in this chapter,

---

[5] Kreiss (2012); Issenberg (2012).
[6] The consultant's name is also a pseudonym.   [7] E.g., Kolodny (2000: 116–117).

firms with a predominantly corporate client base are most likely to be nonpartisan in affiliation.

Frederick Partners has worked on behalf of a large number of *Fortune* 500 firms, trade associations, and, to a lesser extent, large national interest groups outside the corporate realm. Major campaigns for the firm include work on behalf of a large healthcare provider firm seeking to increase doctors' reimbursement rates through Medicare, a large-scale campaign to raise awareness about the Medicare prescription drug benefit on behalf of a leading global pharmaceutical firm, and efforts to help a massive defense contractor lobby against cuts to the Pentagon budget by Congress. The firm has also carried out full-scale campaigns on behalf of utility companies, trade groups for energy interests, and telecom firms.

The consultancy's dominant strategy for mobilizing stakeholders was, during the early portion of the organization's lifespan, the use of paid phone banks. But the firm now employs a much broader range of services, de-emphasizing phones. Phil suggests that this was done, in part, out of necessity as a survival strategy, implying that firms need to diversify their strategies if they are to continue to exist despite changing technologies and fluctuating issue agendas for firms and policymakers. Phil explains that during the time since the firm's founding nearly thirty years ago, "we've changed more, refined, reinvented, [and] done all the stuff you need to do to survive ... and we moved years ago away from phones." Part of this change in strategy reflects the firm's calculations about the trade-off between high-cost forms of issue mobilization (e.g., fly-ins, face-to-face meetings) and low-cost but high-volume forms (see Figure 7.4). When asked about this trade-off, Frederick suggests that although mass mobilization remains effective in some cases, the firm has adopted a sort of "back to basics" strategy, emphasizing quality over quantity.

Going back to basics has meant that the firm has shifted its efforts into two stakeholder mobilization strategies beyond phones. First and foremost, Phil suggests that the firm has moved "solidly ... to dealing with third-party groups, heads of organizations, [and] those sorts of people." The firm has become known for its abilities to mobilize leaders at the "grasstops," a term of art for those who are opinion leaders through their position in civic groups, political organizations, religious groups, workplaces, and in other types of organizations.[8] As is common

---

[8] On opinion leadership, see Katz and Lazarsfeld (1955).

in commercialized grassroots mobilization practices, they build upon and co-opt the existing structures of organized civil society.[9]

Phil indicated that the firm does, in fact, maintain a list of community organizations and interest groups and their leaders, to which the firm can turn when a client indicates that they need community support on a particular issue or in a specific congressional district. These relationships need to be cultivated over a long period in which trust is established and maintained. He suggests, "what has always been the case is [that] you have to be able to go back to them when it's something that's credible [and] that they would have an interest in." But in so doing, Phil suggests that it's in the consultant's interest to be extremely selective in targeting the right audience for mobilization. Doing otherwise could, in fact, damage relationships with those stakeholders and make future appeals less effective. But some of the best targets for mobilization, he argues, are those who are civically active but have previously had little contact with their member of Congress; the opportunity for such individuals to have a say, especially in an in-person meeting with a member of Congress, is likely to generate a lot of excitement. In other words, these individuals are especially receptive to lobbying incentives.[10] Such outreach can be beneficial to the consultant in the future, to the extent that

they had a good experience on the last issue and saw that their voice was heard. And quite frankly, the good experience ... comes back to the face-to-face meeting and all that. If they get to sit with their member of Congress or the chief of staff to the member or somebody that matters, and they really feel they've been listened to, that's good [. . .] Even if it doesn't ultimately work out perfectly, they feel that it was worth their time.

Second, Frederick now places more emphasis on general public affairs work, or "changing perceptions of different clients and issues ... reputational work." A key service in this portfolio is crisis management. Importantly, and connected with the discussion that will follow in Chapter 5, Phil Frederick sees the work that he does as closely connected to how firms manage public controversies and other uncertainties in their relationships with public audiences. Mentioning the 2010 Deepwater Horizon oil spill and the crisis this entailed for BP (formerly British Petroleum), he suggested that the work of consultants needs to

---

[9] Walker (2010).   [10] On lobbying incentives, see Knoke (1988: 323–325).

go beyond mere public relations efforts that are only cosmetic, as these may do little to protect a firm during a crisis period. He suggests that consultants often help companies to prepare for such circumstances, to the extent possible, by charting out a plan for a crisis and building support in a community of stakeholders. Importantly, he sees a corporate client's efforts to be a good citizen as integral to its ability to manage crises and protect its reputation. To that end, Frederick argues that his client firms should engage in a proactive process of

game playing different scenarios, so at least you have your internal stuff ready to move. And you have to move real time in [the] news cycle. The next thing is [that if] you have built up credibility ... versus a "surface" or advertising credibility, then you may be able to control it more. If you've worked with community organizations, for example. And [the public should] really understand what you do, the added value to the community; it's not only just the jobs and you're a good corporate citizen, but are you [supporting] scholarship? Are you somebody that cares about the community? You know, you're doing good deeds.

One of the central issues that public affairs consultants face about their own participation in politics regards the legitimacy of mobilizing participation on behalf of paying clients. This issue is often framed through the distinction between traditional forms of citizen organizing and social movement activities coded as "grassroots," in contrast to organizing that is not rooted in a genuine community and involves small, elite interest masquerading as a broad-based movement. As described in Chapter 2, the latter is often referred to as "astroturf," or fake grassroots, with troubling implications for democracy. Thus, consultants regularly face concerns that they are harming the democratic process by creating a semblance of mass support for issues that only have a narrow, often elite constituency that would stand to benefit from such engagement. How do consulting firms justify their role in such campaigns?

Phil of Frederick Partners, voicing a consistent theme in my interviews with firms like his, suggests that it's not so much the distinction between "grassroots" and "astroturf" that matters in determining the legitimacy of participation, but instead the distinction between campaigns that resonate with mediating publics versus those that do not. In his view, consultants cannot truly "manufacture" displays of public support or opposition to a public policy any more than other types of interest groups can. The support in society either exists or it doesn't, and it is the job of the organizer to do as much as possible to amplify supportive voices. In addition, the costs of engaging in a fraudulent campaign can be high for the consulting firms that misrepresent or fabricate citizen communications. Echoing the ideas of famed community organizer Saul Alinsky – similar to what others have said about the "new corporate activism"[11] – Frederick suggested that self-interest is crucial to all campaigns, and that campaigns that misrepresent popular opinion are likely to fail. When I ask him about the distinction that some make between "astroturf" and "grassroots" public participation, he responds,

I think it's bullshit. And the reason why I think it's bullshit is what matters is [whether] the person who comes forward [has] a legitimate, credible interest of why, say, farmers would care about this issue . . . And if they can articulate that in a credible way, then it's a credible issue. Whether they found out about that issue from the back of a box of Rice Krispies or an article in the newspaper or somebody like me contacting them, I really . . . I don't know that it matters so much as whether it's their legitimate opinion.

But there are other points to consider that suggest focusing on self-interest and the honesty of a recruited citizen's opinion may not be the whole story in evaluating the legitimacy of elite-driven public participation. Although such practices are not a specialty of Frederick Partners, other consultants in my study reported providing the entire organizational backbone – the writing of bylaws, renting of office space, hiring of staff, crafting of websites and press releases, and recruitment of members – on behalf of a paying client. They not only lower the costs of engaging in collective action (as described in Chapter 2), but they often go further by building up organizational infrastructure for what may become an autonomous organization.[12] This sponsoring role may *or may not* be disclosed to the public. Although all of those who participate in such an organization or cause may, in fact, genuinely support the goals of the campaign, not disclosing that a campaign may be funded by a major corporation, industry group, or other interest group suggests that public trust may be exploited by organizations purporting to support a general public interest. Similar to questions

---

[11] Grefe and Linsky (1995).
[12] Such was the goal of Students for Academic Choice, described in Chapter 1.

that have been raised about how patient advocacy organizations in the health sector often fail to disclose the major funding they receive from the pharmaceutical industry, consulting firms at times exploit public trust in apparently disinterested citizen advocacy groups.[13]

Integrated political services: Williamson Strategists

Williamson Strategists was founded in the 1980s as an organization specializing in voter demographic data, which were used predominantly by electoral campaigns and also by fundraising and grassroots mobilization efforts by companies, unions, nonprofits, and other civic and political organizations. In the years since, the firm expanded into new service areas including websites for Political Action Committee (PAC) fundraising, and, importantly, services for facilitating grassroots mobilization. Today, the firm represents a variety of clients using its grassroots services, including energy firms, food manufacturers, hospitals, financial services firms, and pharmaceutical companies. The firm is nonpartisan in both its grassroots issue campaigns and also in that it provides data services to both Republican and Democratic candidates. Williamson Strategists has also been heavily involved in a variety of international electoral campaigns. I interviewed Janice Kennedy, the firm's senior VP for public affairs, and her assistant Graham McNary, in Washington in October 2010.[14]

In contrast to Frederick Partners' more traditional strategy of mobilizing pre-existing civic groups, Williamson takes more of an "all of the above" strategy for mobilizing stakeholder support on key issues of interest to their clients. The firm provides a full range of services from website development and online recruitment to mobilizing participants to attend rallies and demonstrations targeted at the district offices of key Congressional leaders. The imprint of the firm's founding as a keeper of extensive data files on the political behaviors of Americans is present in its contemporary grassroots strategies. Janice suggested that these strengths are part of the initial conversation the firm has with a typical client:

For any client, [we ask] what are your goals? [We start by] developing a plan on how to achieve those goals, and it could be anything from writing the

---

[13] Rothman et al. (2011).   [14] All names are pseudonyms.

content for a website, writing the action alerts, writing blogs, ghostwriting blogs [...] op-eds, letters to the editor.

[We] keep contacts programmed where we identify people through the voter file on who votes, how often do they vote, [and] do they give? Those would be the top people you'd think would be engaged. We have that because, remember, going back to the '80s they developed this. They had that technology. We can, for a client, extrapolate that and know who our targets are, then go out and ask them to be involved, and then we train them ... we write training packets for them. [We also train them in] public speaking and [do] role-playing to teach them how to talk to a member of Congress. What are the legislative issues, how you do this ... everything.

When I asked Janice and Graham about how they draw the boundary between legitimate and illegitimate campaigns, they expressed the concern that regardless of the legitimacy of *consultants* being involved in campaigns, the rise of email and web-based *communications* has led to a greater level of popular mistrust among policymakers. This sentiment echoes broader findings in political research.[15] It also challenges the suggestion from one particularly well-known article by political scientist Bruce Bimber, which argues that even if the rise of networked communications technologies neither facilitates community-building nor simply empowers elites and interest groups, it leads to a more "fluid" and fragmented style of politics.[16] While the latter may be true for the online campaigns organized by citizen associations, mass communications facilitated by consultants have led to a degree of political standardization and also a worry among policymakers that apparent constituent communications might, at times, be fraudulent. As the costs of sending a message to a policymaker approach zero, many who participate may not even remember taking such an action. Referring to a widely circulated report by the Congressional Management Foundation,[17] Graham elaborated this thought further:

The problem wasn't that people were behaving badly. The problem was that people on the Hill who had to read the emails had ... gone from email not existing to being inundated with hundreds of thousands of emails. And the attitude on the Hill was basically "if it's an email, it's astroturfing ... dump it."

---

[15] Zavestoski, Shulman, and Schlosberg (2006).   [16] Bimber (1998).
[17] Goldschmidt and Ochreiter (2008).

And so there was this feeling that it was a legitimate form of communication for citizens to use, but . . . it [was] *form* email in most cases. And the people on the Hill were sort of ignoring it as illegitimate. And then . . . this technology allowed people to read a blurb, click a button, and send an email with their name on it to the Hill. Six weeks later . . . somebody at the [Congressional] office would call or send them an email [to confirm], and they'd be like "I didn't do that."

[This] created the impression of fraud [. . .] The dichotomy that was created: the industry saying "it's now easier for people to express their opinion on a wide variety of issues than it ever has been before." And people on the Hill saying, "Yeah, but those opinions aren't real, and we're not gonna accept those."

As Graham describes it, web-based communications technologies generated vast new volumes of standardized messages and engendered increasing mistrust of the public among policymakers. The implication of this is that although consultants are encouraging such communications, their actions coincide with a substantial increase in communications driven by other interest groups, trade associations, unions, and the like.

When I pressed Janice and Graham further on the proper role of a consultant in mobilizing displays of popular support or opposition to a policy, Graham acknowledged the ambiguity inherent in the consultant's role. Considering the boundary between amplifying pre-existing popular support and creating the appearance of broad support for an unpopular issue, Graham suggested that firms' campaigns "touch that line a little bit . . . it doesn't mean that every public affairs firm hasn't [at some point]." Still, Graham and Janice both suggested that the campaigns that are more likely to run the risk of fraud are those that a company or trade association runs internally without the help of a consultant:

Graham: In a lot of these [trade] associations, there's a 23-year-old kid who's responsible for writing these things up, and that's where a lot of the trouble starts. It's relatively young people in an association who have a junior position in the government relations department who are pushing emails out to the members . . . A lot of times they don't necessarily know that you need to include the name of the organization, that you need to be factual . . .

Janice: But it's our job to teach them that.

Graham: It is, but we don't always get the chance … [There are] all
            kinds of associations out there that have the technology but
            don't have the experience, knowledge, or consulting to teach
            them that.

Janice also made clear that the field of public affairs is not professionalized in the sense of requiring formal training in order to practice (see
Appendix 8). As she sees it, the skills that might make someone a
successful traditional lobbyist may not be all that helpful when seeking
to mobilize popular participation:

People in government affairs are hired to lobby, and so you have your
lobbyists who have come [from] the Hill and are well versed in this policy
issue or the other as well …

   But can they write in a way that's on a 6th-grade level so that their
constituents, so to speak, can understand it? Usually not. Can they recruit?
Do they have that marketing ability to then recruit? I mean, you're talking
about so many different skill sets that someone off the Hill oftentimes doesn't
have. Very few and far between [do they] have the skill sets to understand the
policy, yet can market, yet can do the advertising, and come up with a
campaign and can implement it, and can fundraise … And can build in
compliance …

Public affairs consultants require a huge amount of trust between consultant and client, and contracts are typically written in a very open-
ended fashion. A consultant cannot guarantee a particular policy result
for their client, only that they will do their best to obtain a desirable (or
at least less undesirable) result. When asked about what a contract with
a client typically looks like, Graham explains,

Graham: In those type of contracts our goal … is to build public
            support, build membership for your organization, generate
            communications to Capitol Hill – all those kinds of things.
            [If] we get too specific with that, [then] we're suddenly just
            checking boxes, and we don't usually get hired to check
            boxes. Usually, we're hired to actually see results. And … we
            always have opposition. We're never working in a vacuum
            where it's just us out there, so we have to be able to be
            flexible enough to respond to those results, those
            reactions …

If we're getting letters to the Hill and that's our tactic, but the legislation changes in a way that makes all of those letters we've already gotten irrelevant, but we've only got a couple of weeks before the bill's out of committee, letters don't make sense anymore. So if it's in the contract that we're gonna get letters, we're now ...

Edward: In a corner?

Graham: Yeah. And most of the people – corporations, trade associations, nonprofits who work in this field – get that. They understand that you've got to be able to pivot very, very rapidly. So ... the scope of work is usually much more broad ... [that] we'll hit certain milestones, you know.

This strategy may also promote transparency and reduce incentives for corruption. For example, one report by the Public Affairs Council on corporate lobbying in Brazil notes that firms there may be paid on the basis of "success fees," thus encouraging firms to win campaigns for their clients through whatever means necessary. Billing by the hour rather than by the outcome would seem to reduce these pressures.[18]

In sum, my interview with Janice and Graham and broader investigation into the clients and strategies of Williamson Strategists suggests that public affairs consultants help their organizational clients to manage their external environment through facilitating public participation, and they do so in a fashion that maintains a degree of flexibility both for the consultant and for the client. These elite consultants seek to be responsive to changes in the environment while maintaining compliance with lobbying regulations and contract specifications.

Interestingly, however, firms like Williamson Strategists both reduce the risk of "astroturfing" public participation by their clients while engaging directly in such strategies in other ways. The risk is reduced in that the consultant tends to be careful not to engage in fraudulent communications, yet the consultant also helps to create third-party or "front" organizations and also engages in controversial strategies like ghostwriting blog posts to support their client's issue positions. Thus, like many other firms in the field, Williamson walks a careful boundary between mobilizing authentic participation and creating a false front

---

[18] Public Affairs Council (2012: 17).

through which narrow elite interests masquerade as broad public constituencies.

Public affairs consultants in broader context

How do firms like Frederick Partners and Williamson Strategists compare to the broader field of public affairs consultants across the US? Using data from the survey of public affairs consulting firms across the US and also data from their websites (see Appendices 2 and 3), I now describe the consultants' client bases, partisanship, services provided, strategies, targets, staffing, and revenues. These findings highlight how such firms help their clients to engage in the strategic management of public issues on behalf of their corporate, advocacy, and other organizational clients. I describe how the specific services of these consulting firms relate to the needs of their varying organizational clients in Chapters 5 and 6. However, an important first step is to describe the overall client bases of public affairs consultants. I turn to that task now.

Organizational clients

Using the website data, I determined that the median public affairs consulting firm has thirty-six clients. Given that the survey data reveal that the median firm has seven staff, this translates to a ratio of approximately five clients per full-time staff member. Largely consistent with my earlier research – with certain caveats[19] – and also consistent with the case descriptions of Frederick Partners and Williamson Strategists, Figure 4.1 shows that a plurality of the average firm's clients come from the private sector (38.2 percent), as 28.6 percent of clients are individual corporations and an additional 9.6 percent of clients are trade

---

[19] See Walker (2009: 91). These differences exist because the earlier study built upon client lists culled from the full baseline data. Those data include many vendor firms that only provide a single technical service (e.g., voter mapping) and also include firms that were active *at any point* between 1990 and 2004 (many of which became defunct). In addition, however, there are differences due to the somewhat more refined set of organizational categories used in Figure 4.1; parties, campaigns, and ballot measure coalitions are disaggregated in this figure, as are types of advocacy organizations. As noted in Chapter 1 and further detailed in Appendix 3, the website data include only the subset of those organizations who provide broad-based grassroots mobilization services and continued to be active as of 2009.

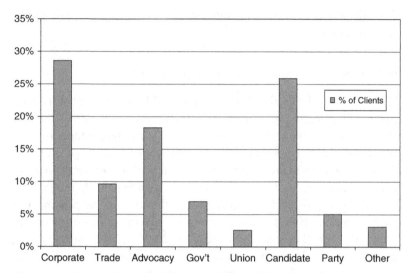

Figure 4.1 Clients of public affairs consultants (website data)

associations. This finding also squares well with other studies of American politics which have shown a predominant presence of business over other types of actors in political lobbying, and also that firms tend to lobby individually more than they do collectively.[20] The data also illustrate that advocacy groups of various types are well represented, including general advocacy organizations (18.2 percent) and, to a much lesser extent, labor unions (2.5 percent). Electoral campaigns and political party organizations comprise the bulk of other clients, such that individual candidates' campaigns represent 25.9 percent of clients and party organizations make up 5.1 percent.[21] Although public affairs consultants emphasize grassroots mobilization (rather than just the "air game" and technical services for which electoral consultants are often known[22]), recall that Chapter 3 showed that most grassroots consulting firms were founded by individuals with a background in electoral consulting. Even if these consultants have diversified in the years since, the legacy of their previous occupations,

---

[20] E.g., Hart (2004); Baumgartner and Leech (2001: 1195–1196).
[21] Among party organizations, there is an approximately even split between party groups on the Democratic side (47.9%), and those on the Republican side (47.4%). The remaining 4.7% are minor political parties.
[22] Farrell, Kolodny, and Medvic (2001: 15).

it would appear, translates to a continuing presence of electoral campaign clients on their rosters.

Lastly, government agencies appear less often but still have a notable presence (7.1 percent). The government clients of grassroots consultants tend to be local water districts, transportation or port authorities, and school districts (often lobbying for bond issues in states such as California, Illinois, and Kansas, which require voter approval of such bonds). There are particular state regulations on issue advocacy by governments, so consultants are at times limited in precisely how they can engage in grassroots on behalf of such agencies. One consultant in a large Midwestern state described to me how school districts, for example, will set up ad hoc PACs which, in turn, hire consultants to lobby on property tax levies to fund schools; school districts themselves are prohibited by that state from engaging in such activity directly. Another prominent consultant in a large Western state told me that he will often work on behalf of state government agencies to "educate" the public on particular issues of concern to those agencies, but this typically needs to stop short of "advocacy" due to concerns about the propriety and legality of so-called "taxpayer-funded lobbying."

Partisanship

Firms such as Frederick Partners and Williamson Strategists both expressed concerns about partisanship and the limits it may impose upon the business of public affairs consulting. Being too closely allied with one side or the other may limit political options for firms, although being nonpartisan may constrain trust between consultants and ideologically motivated clients. Using the website data (see Appendix 3), I determined that the field breaks down such that 27.5 percent of firms are affiliated with the Democratic Party, 25.7 percent are closer to the Republicans, and 46.8 percent of firms are either non- or bi-partisan. Thus, although Democratic firms are slightly better represented, firms are affiliated with both parties rather evenly (and a large plurality of firms do not favor one party over another).

Table 4.1 makes further use of the website data to break down the proportional representation of firms within party affiliation by primary client type. Note that because the measure relies upon the *primary* (i.e., modal) client type for each organization, these figures do not perfectly

Table 4.1 *Partisanship by primary client type (website data)*

Primary client	Democratic (%)	Republican (%)	Non- or bipartisan (%)	Total (%)
Corporate / Trade	29.8	29.5	71.6	47.5
Associations	25.5	11.4	11.9	15.8
Campaigns	44.7	59.1	10.4	34.2
Government	0.0	0.0	6.0	2.5
Total	100.00	100.00	100.00	100.00

match the distribution presented in the earlier breakdown of client types.

Table 4.1 makes clear, first and foremost, that corporate clients are most likely to be represented by non- or bipartisan firms. This finding suggests that businesses tend to be ideological in some respects but mostly avoid strong partisan affiliations in their ties to consulting firms.[23] I find that nearly 72 percent of non- or bipartisan firms, like the two described at the start of this chapter, have a predominantly corporate client base. I also find relatively little difference between Democratic- and Republican-affiliated firms in terms of their likelihood of representing a primarily corporate client base; 29.8 percent of Democratic firms have mainly corporate clients, whereas 29.5 percent of Republican-affiliated firms do.

Table 4.1 also shows that Democratic-affiliated firms are among the most likely to represent advocacy organizations (nearly 26 percent of Democratic consultants' client base), whereas only around 11 percent of Republican firms have primarily associations as clients. The Republican firms in the website data are predominantly those linked to electoral politics, such that 59 percent of such firms have a predominantly electoral client base. This finding suggests that grassroots mobilization firms are more closely tied to Republican paid Get-Out-The-Vote efforts, despite suggestions in previous research that Republicans –

---

[23] This need not rule out that certain business sectors are quite ideological in their selection of issues on which to organize grassroots campaigns, as well as in their PAC contributions and other forms of political engagement (e.g., Clawson and Neustadtl, 1989).

being more rooted in faith communities – should be less likely than
Democrats to outsource their grassroots voter mobilization efforts to
paid consultants.[24] Lastly, those few consulting firms with a predominantly government agency client base are, as one might expect,
nonpartisan.

Services

Which services do public affairs consultants provide to their clients in
order to help them to manage their environment? The cases of Frederick
Partners and Williamson Strategists both suggest that consultants tailor
their strategies to the organizational client in question and their client's
policy target, and that firms vary in their degree of specialization in a
subset of services they offer to clients.

Table 4.2 uses the data from the SPAPCO survey to present a list of
the twenty-eight possible services that public affairs consultants could
provide to their clients. Respondents were asked, to "identify the services that your firm has provided in at least one campaign in the past year
(check all that apply)." Respondents were also given detailed instructions on how a "campaign" should be defined (see Appendix 2.3).

What Table 4.2 shows quite clearly is that even when involved in
campaigns to mobilize public participation, consultants most often
provide general consulting services (68 percent) or public relations
services (55 percent). They also quite often provide services for placing
electronic media ads (45 percent), maintaining databases or lists of
potential activists (42 percent), or focusing their mobilization efforts
on pre-existing opinion leaders (42 percent). Importantly, only 26
percent of consultants also reported engaging in traditional or
"inside" lobbying activity in the past year. Although most other
services were used a moderate amount (such as field operations, or
canvassing, as well as managing public events or lobbying days), a
number of the more technologically oriented services that were used in
the 1980s and 1990s have fallen out of favor – in what is
territory ceded to more specialized firms or no longer used – such as
fax broadcasting (6 percent), satellite broadcasting (3 percent), and
developing software or technological applications for participation

---

[24] Fisher (2006).

Table 4.2 *Services provided by consultants (survey data)*

Service	%
General consulting	68
Public relations	55
Electronic media ads	45
Database / list management	42
Internet, email, or electronic comm. services	42
Grasstops / mobilize opinion leaders	42
Community coalition-building	39
News or print media advertising	39
Voter mobilization / GOTV	39
Demographic targeting	35
Direct mail	35
Ballot / initiative / referendum	35
Field operations	32
Television advertising	32
Media training / speech support	32
Polling / focus groups	32
General electoral campaign support	32
Event mgmt. / scheduling lobby days	32
Phone banking	29
Petition mgmt. / signature gathering	26
General media advertising (multiple media)	26
Inside lobbying / gov't affairs	26
Fundraising	26
Fax broadcasting	6
Other	6
Litigation / legal support	3
Satellite broadcasting	3
Software and tech. for participation	0

(0 percent). Only 3 percent of public affairs consultants reported engaging in litigation or legal support.

Considering the breadth of a firm's service offerings, the median firm provides eight such services in a given year. The survey also asked which services each firm tends to think of as its area of greatest expertise; Table 4.3 displays the distribution of these top service areas. Consistent

Table 4.3 *Primary service provided by consultants (survey data)*

Service	%
General consulting	19
Public relations	15
Polling / focus groups	15
Petition mgmt. / signature gathering	7
Direct mail	7
Inside lobbying / gov't affairs	7
Field operations	4
Phone banking	4
Television advertising	4
General media advertising (multiple media)	4
Internet, email, or electronic comm. services	4
Grasstops / mobilize opinion leaders	4
Fundraising	4
Ballot / initiative / referendum	4

with the top areas of service for the field as a whole, the leading areas of expertise are also general public affairs consulting (19 percent) and public relations (15 percent). However, a substantial proportion of consultants specialize in polling/focus groups (15 percent), petition management (7 percent), direct mail (7 percent), and inside/traditional lobbying (7 percent). Other firms specialize in particular advertising media, particular grassroots strategies, or particular technologies.

Strategies and ultimate targets

How do consultants go about getting members of the public involved in their campaigns to generate policy change? Consulting firms, like other kinds of political organizations, face a trade-off between mobilizing high-cost but potentially more effective forms of activity versus stimulating low-cost but high-volume actions. My interviews with Frederick Partners and with Williamson Strategists both suggested that this trade-off is a regular part of the decision-making of both consultants and their clients. Further, this trade-off varies depending on the ultimate target of a campaign; for example, motivating activists to help shoot down an unfavorable executive agency decision is likely to look considerably

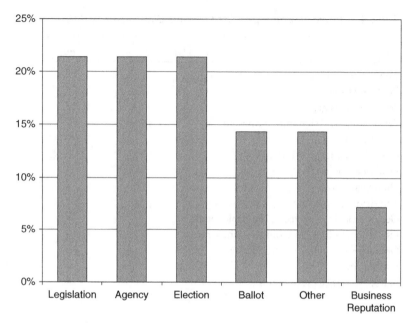

Figure 4.2 Policy target of a consultant's primary campaign (survey data)

different than if the target is a piece of legislation before Congress. Although I develop a more detailed analysis of campaigns' effectiveness in mobilizing citizen participation in Chapter 7, some initial discussion of consultants' strategies for mobilizing participation is fitting here.

Considering this, the survey asked consultants, for each of their three most prominent campaigns over the past six years, which activities they were most active in encouraging among recruited activists. I also asked what the client's ultimate policy target was for this campaign. Figure 4.2 displays the distribution of ultimate policy targets for the *most prominent campaign* of each consulting firm. Respondents were allowed to select more than one outcome, although they were also asked to identify which one was their "top priority" for the campaign.

What Figure 4.2 shows most clearly is that there are four dominant targets for policy change by public affairs consultants: legislation, agency decisions, electoral outcomes, and ballot measures. In fact, these four types combine to comprise the primary targets in the leading campaigns of almost 80 percent of the surveyed firms. The remaining approximately 20 percent of firms focused their efforts on improving the reputation of a business client[25] or meeting some other goal (e.g., the election of multiple candidates rather than one individual candidate). Thus, the grassroots mobilization services provided by these consultants serve to meet a diverse range of policy needs in an organization's institutional environment. I return to the question of the effectiveness of various strategies in Chapter 7.

One consistent finding in my interviews is that strategies for mobilizing the public must be tailored to meeting the policy goal of the client; consultants often make remarks similar to how social movement organizers describe the development of strategy.[26] Accordingly, the results from the survey show that:

1. Campaigns focused on shaping *legislation* emphasize especially in-person visits with public officials, as well as hard-copy letters, phone calls, emails, and faxes sent to their offices. In addition, consultants do their part to facilitate the writing of op-eds to newspapers, the spread of information via social networking websites like Facebook and Twitter, and often encourage electoral campaign contributions or petition signatures. Consulting firms only infrequently encourage the use of public protest tactics (regardless of their ultimate target).

2. Campaigns that seek change in the decision of an executive *agency* are somewhat less likely to encourage in-person visits with public officials, although such visits are still often encouraged by consultants. They do, however, often facilitate attendance at public forums (during public comment periods on agency decisions). Letter-writing and other mediated communications with policymakers are also a common focus, although slightly less so than in legislative campaigns that involve elections rather than appointments to hold office. They also, like campaigns directed at legislators, create opportunities for social networking activism and the writing of op-eds to shape popular opinion on the issue.

---

[25] One might expect that managing business reputations would be a more central focus for these consultants. My interviews with these consultants suggested that a division of labor exists in which more of that work goes to generalist PR firms, and not grassroots public affairs / grassroots lobbying firms, especially since such work is more likely to involve advertising and not necessarily the mobilization of activism.

[26] See, e.g., Jasper (2006).

3. Efforts by consultants to shape *electoral* outcomes are, naturally, inclined to emphasize voting as a key strategy. The primary service that public affairs consultants offer in electoral politics is to supplement the ground strategy and Get-Out-The-Vote efforts of candidates and their parties.[27] However, driving up attendance at public forums, communicating about the candidate through social networks, and generating favorable editorials are also common strategies. They also engage in substantial fundraising efforts for their candidate or party.

4. Lastly, campaigns that seek the passage or defeat of a *ballot measure* are, of course, most heavily involved in signature gathering; some grassroots consulting firms are signature-gathering outfits that also help their clients develop strategy.[28] But more broadly, the mobilizing strategies of consultants on ballot campaigns merge features of their legislative and electoral siblings. They encourage monetary contributions to support the campaign, efforts to gain popular support through media and social networking sites, and, of course, they require both a large-scale signature-gathering effort and, if the measure is eventually qualified, a substantial Get-Out-The-Vote and voter education operation.

Revenues and staffing

The survey results show that public affairs consulting firms tend to be boutique operations that operate as small businesses with relatively tiny staffs (mean staff = 12.5, median staff = 7), but with median annual revenues of approximately $375,000 (mean $2.31 million). Thus, these firms have notably higher average revenues than other firms in the same industry (NAICS #541820, Lobbying services and PR agencies), which have mean revenue per establishment of $1.2 million.[29]

The survey also asked how much revenue firms tend to generate from each campaign, for the top three campaigns to which the firm devoted the greatest effort over the past six years (see Appendix 2.3). The

[27] On campaigns' ground game strategies, with some discussion of consultants' role therein, see Nielsen (2012).

[28] Magleby and Patterson (1998).   [29] Census Bureau (2007).

median firm generated approximately \$175,000 in revenue from its top campaign over the past six years (mean = \$327,431), and generated median revenues of \$100,000 for its second and third most prominent campaigns. The highest campaign revenue figure reported by any of the firms was \$1.5 million, for a major corporate coalition mobilizing in support of the 2009 Patient Protection and Affordable Care Act. In that case, the corporate coalition hired one of the consultants in this study to build community coalitions around the issue, communicate by phone with concerned stakeholders, target specific demographic groups, send direct mail, place print advertisements, and provide general support in the campaign.

Unsurprisingly, the consultants I spoke with were often not comfortable talking about their salaries or, if they bill hourly, what those hourly rates are. But a few of the consultants helped to contextualize their firm's revenue situation. For example, Michael Craigs of the long-standing West Coast firm Hearts & Minds Strategists told me that how much they charge a client is determined entirely on a project-specific basis.[30] Two other consultants I talked with said the same. As Michael elaborated,

Michael: There's no one formula. Depends on the size of the project, the duration, how much manpower, how difficult the project is, what's the regulatory [situation] or the pathway to get [legislation] approved, or not approved, or whatever. And it depends on what level of government you're dealing with. Everything. We have prices all over the [place] but we do have an hourly rate. If some people hire us for an hourly basis they pay the straight hourly rate.

Edward: Do you mind telling me what that is? Or if you'd prefer not to, that's OK.

Michael: Yeah, I mean, I get \$400 an hour, and then it goes down to like \$125 and \$100 to some of our younger people ... it's not one rate.

Or, if a client signs a monthly retainer with Hearts & Minds,

That'll vary from \$5,000 a month to \$20,000, \$25,000, \$30,000 a month depending, again, on how big the problem is, what geographical footprint it's

---

[30] These are pseudonyms.

involved in, how [much] complexity, [and] how long it's gonna take to do whatever it is we have to do.

Other consultants I spoke with typically mentioned hourly rates in the range of $150–$400 per hour for senior consultants, often with a series of hourly tranches for less senior consultants, and monthly retainer fees toward the lower end of the distribution mentioned by Hearts & Minds. A report, for example, was released in 2011 that showed that the prominent firm Davies Public Affairs was requesting a contract with the Marina Coast Water Agency in Monterey County, California – apparently to help manage a public dispute over a water desalination plant – which would charge $375 per hour against a $5,000 weekly retainer (capped at $100,000 total).[31]

Similarly, Toledo Alvarez put his firm's revenue in the following context:

I have competitors that probably won't touch things for under $25,000 a month. Now, if you're doing $25,000 a month you're probably representing a *Fortune* 500 type company, but that's sort of the range. We are by no means the cheapest. I have a competitor who I've hired to help me on a project. I think we're paying him $5,000 a month. So he's less than we are [at $8,000 per month]. So it fluctuates. We ... have clients [that are each on retainer for] between $5,000 and $20,000 a month, depending on the service.

However, not all firms I talked with did hourly billing; some rely more on a fee-for-service structure or take very little hourly revenue but instead depend on a win bonus (or a bonus of a long-term retainer after a success which, it is agreed informally, will require very little work from the consultant). One consultant I interviewed mentioned that a competitor firm had recently commanded a win bonus (a "success" or "contingency fee") payment of $100,000; such payments are allowed for federal lobbying under certain conditions but are prohibited by law when lobbying at the state level (at least in forty-three of the states).[32]

Others reject hourly billing in favor of only working with clients on medium- to long-term retainer. As Owen Taylor, founder and CEO of Taylor Advocacy,[33] put it, for his firm

---

[31] *Monterey County Herald* (2011).   [32] NCSL (2013).
[33] These are pseudonyms.

everything is a retainer. I track hours internally here ... and just make sure we're charging the right amount of money [in retainer fees]. But I can't charge per hour for what I do. So, I mean, I have seventeen people who work for me, but I can do something in five minutes that it might take somebody else a week to do. So, you know, how do you [do that]? So you don't bill hourly [...] And people say to us, "Well, can't you do it hourly?" I tell them, that's why I'm not a lawyer anymore. I didn't want to bill hours.

Revenues by client type

To dig a bit deeper into firms' sources of revenue, Figure 4.3 displays the proportion of each type of client represented by the consulting firms in the survey (from the website data, as illustrated in Figure 4.1 earlier), and compares these figures to the proportion of their revenue generated by each type of client (from the survey data). In general, Figure 4.3 makes clear that the top sources of revenue for consultants are generally very closely proportional to their client share, as corporations, trade groups, advocacy organizations, and electoral campaigns serve also as dominant revenue sources. Political party organizations and other organizations (e.g., universities) appear as clients infrequently, and provide only a small amount of revenue. In general, Figure 4.3 shows

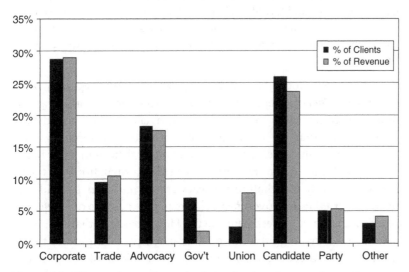

Figure 4.3 Clients of consultants (website data) and mean share of revenue provided by each client type (survey data)

that corporations, trade associations, labor unions, and political party organizations tend to pay firms somewhat more on average, while government, candidate campaigns, and advocacy organizations are less lucrative.

Importantly, these data show two exceptions to this rough proportionality: government agencies and labor unions. Government agencies comprise about 7 percent of the mean consulting firm's clients, yet provide less than 2 percent of the mean firm's revenue. By contrast, labor unions make up 2.5 percent of clients but provide almost 8 percent of revenue. How should we understand the disproportional revenues associated with these client types?

Data from my interviews with consultants, as well as additional data collected about firms' clients – described in greater detail in the next two chapters – help to illuminate these findings. I interviewed a number of consultants who either currently or previously worked with government clients, and their most common gripe was the difficulty associated with responding to government Requests for Proposals (RFPs) and the competitive bidding process necessary to win a contract. As Owen Taylor told me,

The only time we really work for government is when we're asked to do it. It's not something that I really like to do because you can't really make enough money doing it, and if you work for government you're always gonna get your name in the paper and [people will find out] how much you're making, even though you're working way under market. People are always going to think it's too much money ... plus, I don't like to – I really don't like to – compete for RFPs.

By comparison, Roger Hess Advocacy, which works regularly with government agency clients, was naturally somewhat more sanguine about the firm's work on behalf of such clients, but nonetheless acknowledged that the more stringent accounting required by such contracts generally forces the firm to hold down their number of billed hours. And John Crate of Emmitt Strategies[34] – a small firm that today works exclusively on behalf of advocacy groups and unions – said that he no longer takes on government clients in part because of a negative experience with a government client. He elaborated that Emmitt's government work required not only an extensive RFP process to get approved, but afterward the firm wasn't even paid until about a year

---

[34] These are pseudonyms.

later. Considering all of this evidence, it is not surprising that the average firm's government contracts are much less lucrative on a per-client basis.

Why, then, are unions a relatively more well-paying client type? Unions, other studies have found, tend to be even more active in using their own mechanisms of grassroots mobilization than other kinds of public interest groups.[35] Unions regularly mobilize mass participation, although their ability to do so has been weakened along with dwindling union density and broader political challenges to the union movement.[36]

Some evidence for why unions tend to be more lucrative clients, then, is that their campaigns tend to be much more large scale than the consultant-backed mobilization efforts carried out on behalf of other types of clients. For example, using data from the *Encyclopedia of Associations* (see Appendix 6), I find that the general advocacy organizations who hire public affairs consultants tend to be exceptionally large (with a median membership of 23,000), but the unions who hire these consultants tend to be larger still, and by an order of magnitude (with a median 250,000 members). Thus, although unions hire consultants much less frequently than other kinds of advocacy organizations do, the services they require tend to be much more large scale. Further, although the advocacy organizations and labor unions that do not hire consultants have approximately similar median budgets (respectively, $350,000 and $358,000), the labor unions who hire consultants tend to have vastly higher median budgets than their general advocacy counterparts ($30 million compared to $5 million).

It would appear, then, that despite how very active labor unions tend to be in mobilizing grassroots participation, they generally only turn to public affairs consultants when they require the development of broad support beyond their own in-house capacities for generating participation. As one consultant put it in an interview, unions often have a more extensive "volunteer apparatus" than many advocacy groups, and so they typically come to consultants for services that cross the high bar that exceeds their volunteer capacity. For a consultant, this means that a relatively small share of union clients may offer outsized returns, but the consultant will likely be working quite hard on large-scale campaigns to earn that revenue.

[35] Kollman (1998: 18, 94–95).   [36] E.g., Clawson and Clawson (1999).

Conclusions

The cases of Frederick Partners and Williamson Strategists both revealed how firms who provide "grassroots for hire" manage institutional pressures for their organizational clients and also how they themselves face (and respond to) pressures in their environment. Most significantly, consulting firms need to maintain revenues and provide effective policy representation to their clients. They do so by tailoring their strategies to the client in question and providing boundary-spanning services for galvanizing popular activism.

The chapter further showed that firms vary considerably depending on their political partisanship and the diversity of services they offer. Firms with predominantly corporate clients, such as Frederick Partners and Williamson Strategists, tend to avoid partisan affiliations for fear of foreclosing certain key business opportunities. Corporate clients, for their part, may prefer not to be publicly linked to actors who help to stimulate popular activism on polarizing issues. An important additional finding is that Democratic- and Republican-affiliated firms have an approximately equal representation of corporate clients, despite Republicans' reputation as the party that favors the interests of industry (and the findings of Chapter 3). The major difference between the two sets of partisan firms is that Republican firms do significantly more work on electoral campaigns, whereas Democratic firms are more likely to run grassroots campaigns for public advocacy groups.

Further, Chapter 4 made clear that consulting firms, as organizations themselves, face their own set of pressures. The median firm has a relatively small staff of seven professionals and annual revenues that are slightly higher than their organizational peers in other sectors of the lobbying and public relations industries; still, many firms command substantial resources through high hourly rates and considerable retainer fees. The median firm offers eight specific services in support of mobilizing public activism, and the major sub-specialties are providing general counsel to clients, engaging in public relations, research, signature gathering, direct mail, and linking grassroots efforts with traditional "inside" lobbying. In addition, as the cases of Frederick Partners and Williamson Strategists both indicate, the consultant industry faces substantial popular mistrust about their role in stimulating public participation. Consultants tend to respond to this concern with the counter that those who participate in such campaigns have done so voluntarily and with a genuine interest in communicating with policymakers. However, the role that consultants are playing in facilitating popular activism is often less than fully transparent.

In the next chapter, I describe in detail the particular strategies that consultants provide in supporting corporations in their grassroots campaigns, as well as the factors that lead some firms to engage in such grassroots strategies (while others choose not to).

5 | Corporate grassroots

Introduction

Individual corporations are the leading source of business for public affairs consultants, both in terms of their overall revenue and also as a share of their aggregate client base. The expansion of business political mobilization starting in the 1970s made possible the development of the field of grassroots public affairs consulting, and corporations have, in turn, remained a lucrative source of revenue for consultants. While corporate political activism has become a more common topic of popular discussion since the Supreme Court's 2010 ruling in *Citizens United v. Federal Election Commission* (described in greater detail in Chapter 8), corporations have been engaged in political activity far beyond insider lobbying and funding Political Action Committees (PACs) for many years prior to this decision.

But unlike advocacy organizations, which are generally structured for mobilizing the participation of their members – whether through face-to-face organizing or through mediated forms like mass email or other types of "clicktivism" – corporations do not typically possess in-house structures and routines for generating mass political activism on their behalf. Although it's undoubtedly true that the in-house public affairs function at many firms has become much more encompassing in recent decades and firms do at times use these offices to facilitate activism by employees, shareholders, suppliers, distributors, and/or executives,[1] the services of one or more consulting firms are often necessary when a company seeks to mount a large-scale grassroots effort.

Organizing a pro-corporate grassroots campaign is not usually – to consultants' great chagrin – a company's first line of defense when facing a threat. Companies generally need to be pressured into action by external forces, such as corporate controversies, to do so. Oftentimes

---

[1] Meznar and Nigh (1995).

these circumstances represent threats to a company's reputation, bottom line, and/or ability to operate in certain markets. The initiators of such challenges tend to include protest groups, community activists, policymakers threatening regulation or legislation, or difficult negotiations with other organizations. Indeed, if companies could resolve a controversy or becalm an anti-corporate protest group by increasing their philanthropy or co-opting opponents, this would make for a much more desirable alternative. And many companies today are doing precisely that.[2] But certain circumstances call for a more extensive and full-throated response.

This chapter, then, examines precisely which factors lead companies to mount grassroots campaigns by enlisting the support of public affairs consultants. Using public records of consultant–client relationships published on public affairs consultants' websites, this chapter examines which *Fortune 500* firms appeared on their client lists and which did not. Studying this relationship further, the chapter examines how hiring a consultant is related to the controversies and protest faced by a firm, and its reputation, financial characteristics, and other types of political engagement.

Above all else, this chapter shows that controversies and protest are key influences on consultant-backed engagement in grassroots campaigns by the largest corporations in the United States. Although these firms undoubtedly wield considerable power and influence, facing contentious claims-makers or the negative publicity associated with a controversy can lead even these powerful firms to adopt the posture of an outsider in need of mass support.

However, a secondary finding of this investigation is that these influences are moderated by corporate reputations. Reputations are understood to be those "central, enduring, and distinctive attributes that distinguish a focal organization from other members of a shared social category," which are reflected in judgments about a firm's standing relative to its peers.[3] On a practical level, I find that although both high-reputation and low-reputation companies hire public affairs consultants, only low-reputation firms tend to do so in response to controversies or protest. High-reputation firms, by contrast, appear to be less threatened by such public challenges, yet are still likely to hire such a

---

[2] Galaskiewicz and Colman (2006).
[3] See, respectively, King and Whetten (2008: 199); Love and Kraatz (2009: 314).

consultant, especially if they operate in certain highly regulated industries. Although recent research has shown that firms with stronger reputations tend to attract more protest[4] – in part because a firm's high standing both makes protests against such firms more noticeable and also because negative claims are incongruent with audience perceptions of those firms – high-status actors tend to be more aware that their responses are being observed closely. Thus, even though the data assembled here also confirm that high-reputation firms are more likely to face contentious challenges, their responses to protest should be less likely to involve grassroots mobilization on behalf of the firm.

I begin by comparing accounts of two corporations that have faced major controversies: Kimberly-Clark and Wal-Mart. While Kimberly-Clark responded to negative claims made by protest groups and policy-makers mainly by increasing its Corporate Social Responsibility (CSR) commitments, Wal-Mart responded to its challenges by hiring a public affairs consultant and organizing a grassroots campaign in addition to making CSR efforts. How can we understand these divergent trajectories?

This chapter helps to draw attention to the diversity of outcomes that follow from contention directed against corporations. Scholars working in the tradition of the "new institutionalism" in organizational theory applied their insights to understanding pressures on corporations to change their practices, highlighting how activists are often effective in generating changes in corporate practices which ultimately lead other companies to adopt similar practices. These pressures may lead companies to imitate one another by incorporating similar pro-social practices to other influential companies.[5] However, although we know that anti-corporate protest and controversy may make companies more socially responsible, we know much less about the full range of strategic options available to firms when faced with contentious claims-makers. These less-explored corporate tactics include lawsuits filed against activists,[6] soft repression of activism through counter-information or PR campaigns against corporate challengers,[7] or efforts to co-opt or partner with protest groups.[8] What

---

[4] King and McDonnell (2012).   [5] E.g., Briscoe and Safford (2008).
[6] Pring and Canan (1996).   [7] E.g., Aldrich (2010: 179).
[8] Galaskiewicz and Colman (2006); Yaziji and Doh (2009).

this chapter shows is that pro-corporate grassroots campaigning is one very important yet often overlooked consequence of contentious challenges directed against firms.

Kimberly-Clark and Greenpeace

As one of the largest paper companies in the US (second only to International Paper)[9] and the largest manufacturer of tissue products, the practices of Kimberly-Clark are highly significant and have a considerable environmental impact. It is also the largest toilet paper manufacturer in the world. Importantly, Kimberly-Clark is also seen as a relatively high-reputation firm, as *Fortune* magazine in 2009 scored the company similarly to field-leaders International Paper and Weyerhaeuser. Combined, these factors make the company a highly appealing protest target: as a large firm, bringing about changes to its practices would stand to have a powerful impact on improving environmental quality; as a high-reputation firm to which other firms look for signals of best practices, the ability to change the company's practices could lead to mimetic changes in other companies. Social movement groups often conceptualize institutional change in a fashion similar to neo-institutional theorists of social organization, hoping that changes to the field-leading firms will lead to imitation by lower-status firms.

In November 2004, Kimberly-Clark was faced with a Greenpeace-sponsored campaign called "Kleercut." The name of the campaign was a play on Kimberly-Clark's signature brand name Kleenex, implying that these tissues come from timber harvested using the controversial practice of "clear cutting" swaths of forest and leaving no remaining canopy cover. The goal of Greenpeace's campaign, in its own words, was to

help protect ancient forests in Canada and globally [apply] pressure on the company via the marketplace and its large [base of] customers and consumers. In order to highlight the issue, hundreds of protests took place globally, resulting in more than 50 activists arrested in acts of peaceful civil disobedience. Scientific and exposé reports, media mobilization and shareholder engagement were also an important part of the campaign.[10]

---

[9] See PriceWaterhouseCoopers (2009).   [10] Greenpeace (2011).

The campaign began with the announcement in November 2004 that Greenpeace, partnering with the Natural Resources Defense Council, would be pressing for the use of more recycled paper and for the company to reduce its reliance on virgin timber from the North American Boreal forest. The campaign against Kimberly-Clark followed after a year of unproductive discussions between activists and the company.[11] Although the company had a strong pre-existing commitment to harvesting wood in the most sustainable fashion and also claimed to have a policy that "prohibits the use of any wood from virgin rain forests or significant old-growth forests," a spokesman from the company acknowledged that the company did use some virgin pulp from the Boreal forest in Canada.[12] Greenpeace claimed that less than 19 percent of the company's pulp came from recycled sources, and that "the rest comes directly from clear-cutting ancient forests like Canada's Boreal, where trees range in age from 70 to 160 years old."[13]

Greenpeace's strategy was to call for consumers to boycott all Kimberly-Clark products until the company ceased, in their words, destroying ancient forests. These products included not only Kleenex, but also Scott, Viva, Cottonelle, and other brands owned by the company; because the company's products were so well known, Greenpeace sought to turn this into a vulnerability. As Greenpeace put it,

the fact that Kimberly-Clark products are sold so widely makes the company an easy target for grassroots campaigning. Because Kimberly-Clark products are sold at most grocery stores across North America and Europe, there is always an opportunity to target Kimberly-Clark products in your local community, whether you live in a small town or a big city.[14]

Greenpeace adopted a broad-based strategy to encourage the boycott to have an impact, but its focus was more on institutional buyers (retail stores) than individual consumers. Given that the campaign was mainly about the Canadian Boreal forest, the campaign placed greater emphasis on Montreal, Vancouver, and Toronto, but also had an active presence in the US. The campaign encouraged activists to visit their website (kleercut.net) and to connect with other activists who would also be willing to "adopt a grocery store" to target. Accordingly,

---

[11] Hopey (2004).   [12] Brown (2004).   [13] Greenpeace (2008).   [14] Ibid.

activists would identify a grocery store that sold Kimberly-Clark products, hold events consistently at the store including demonstrations, rallies, street theater, or picketing, and pressure the store to discontinue selling the company's products. Activists were prodded to develop relationships with store managers, distribute information packets, or even to "get the code to the store's intercom" to make announcements that Kleenex are made from ancient-growth forests.[15] Greenpeace also held events that declared the Kimberly-Clark corporate headquarters a forest "crime scene," converted a Greenpeace truck into an oversized Kleenex box marked "Kleercut," and provided activists with templates for conversations with media and retail store representatives.

The company reiterated throughout the campaign that most of its pulp comes from sawdust and chips from lumber production; they also issued statements reminding the media that they were chosen as the 2006 "sustainable leader" in the personal products sector of the Dow Jones Sustainability World Indexes.[16] Later in the campaign, the company claimed that it had reduced its use of Boreal fiber by 30 percent,[17] and the company's spokesman also said that Kimberly-Clark "has one of the most progressive fiber policies in the tissue industry."

As a high-reputation firm, Kimberly-Clark not only attracted social movement attention, but also found itself in a situation where it needed to protect its position among peer organizations as protests intensified. Although the Kleercut campaign attracted national and international attention, certain strategic options appeared to be less appealing (or perhaps even unthinkable): repressing the activists in the campaign, seeking to routinize the movement, or, importantly, the seemingly outlandish option of facilitating a counter-movement of loggers and other stakeholders who favored clear-cutting the Boreal (an activity that the company itself was against; it did so only out of an apparent lack of alternatives and a perceived consumer preference for the softer tissue of virgin pulp).[18]

The company's response, then, was to highlight its commitment to CSR and sustainability, and it brought about a series of corporate policy

[15] Ibid.   [16] Ferrar (2006).   [17] Giasone (2008).
[18] It is worth noting, however, that corporate-backed campaigns have mobilized loggers against environmentalists in the past. See Sanchez (2001).

changes that led Greenpeace to end its campaign in 2009. The company said that it would, by 2011, increase its use of recycled or Forest Stewardship Council-certified sources to 40 percent in its North American Division.[19] The new agreement also ensured that the company would no longer purchase pulp from the Kenogami and Ogoki Forests in northern Ontario unless "strict ecological criteria are met." The company also set a goal that it would move toward more sustainable sourcing of 100 percent of its fiber. Greenpeace described the campaign as a major victory and hailed Kimberly-Clark as a worthy partner after the campaign concluded in 2009.

Wal-Mart and local community groups

In contrast to Kimberly-Clark's response to Greenpeace, Wal-Mart has taken quite a different approach in its response to community activists and local political leaders who have been resisting the chain's expansion into certain major metropolitan areas where no Wal-Mart stores currently exist (such as New York City and Washington, DC), and other metro areas where proposals for new retail operations have met organized local resistance (such as Chicago, Salt Lake City, Houston, and Apple Valley, CA). Instead of focusing primarily on CSR efforts – although philanthropic giving and partnerships are clearly part of their concurrent efforts – Wal-Mart has organized a national grassroots mobilization program called the Wal-Mart Community Action Network (CAN), with branch operations in a variety of localities where the chain has met resistance to expansion. Consistent with the expectation that companies facing serious controversies while also having major reputational concerns are most likely to take an "activist" approach to handling public issues, Wal-Mart's facilitation of pro-corporate social movement activity has offered the company new strategic options that go beyond their CSR engagement.

The campaign began in late 2008 with the registration of the walmartcommunity.com domain, and by April 2009 the company was encouraging receptive members of the public to join local networks in three California communities (Chico, Merced, and Van Nuys), a regional Wal-Mart New England network, and three local networks in the Mid-Atlantic (New York City, Long Island, and one for six

---

[19] *New York Times* (2009).

locations in Pennsylvania where new stores were being proposed). A few months later (June 2009), the High Desert (Apple Valley) and Poway, California networks were established, as well as a blanket network for California.[20] As of this writing, there are fifteen local, state, and regional Wal-Mart CAN networks across the US, in addition to the overall national network. As early as 2009, the company could claim that the national networks had over 60,000 members in total.[21]

The focus of Wal-Mart's Network is mainly on the mobilization of consumers and local opinion leaders (on the use of these groups as corporate stakeholders, see Figure 7.2). As Aaron Bernstein, the firm's senior manager for advocacy and outreach puts it, "We wanted to tap into the loyalty that customers have for their (local) store . . . We needed to deliver clear and powerful voices from our customers. We wanted to provide them with a platform where they could go to learn about the issues, and then to take action."[22] The site included not only information about the firm's positions on such issues as the Employee Free Choice Act, health reform, and organized retail crime, but also offered numerous ways to take action. With the support of consulting firms including Alexandria, Virginia-based DDC Advocacy (which hosts portions of the site), the page also offers ways to join the Network for updates, places to "share your story" about the effect Wal-Mart has had on one's community, and more. As the Network advises readers of its website, "By joining CAN, you're adding your voice to the voices of other advocates across the nation who want to help build better, stronger communities. Your participation in CAN, combined with the actions of people like you, can help make a difference at home and across America."[23]

The CAN campaign followed on the heels of Working Families for Wal-Mart, a campaign I describe in depth in Chapter 7. While this earlier campaign emphasized pressuring suppliers, signing up consumers who visited Wal-Mart stores, and offering incentives for those who joined, CAN is primarily focused on web-based organizing. The CAN campaign helps the company as it seeks to expand into urban areas where they face not only community and labor opposition, but where they also often face political pushback on store openings unless

[20] Internet Archive (2011). [21] Painter (2009).
[22] Public Affairs Council (2010b). [23] Wal-Mart (2011a).

the company promises to pay a wage well beyond the federally mandated minimum.[24]

In order to understand this broader campaign in greater depth, consider the following case of contentious Wal-Mart store proposals in New York City.

Wal-Mart's grassroots campaign to enter the New York City market

Wal-Mart has faced consistent problems and setbacks in its efforts to open a new retail store in one of the five boroughs of New York City, and, although it has campaigned earnestly to open a store there since at least 2004, no such store has been approved or opened as of this writing.[25] Wal-Mart's first major attempt was to seek approval for a store in Queens, but neighborhood, labor, environmental, and local small business groups organized to express strong opposition to the proposed 132,000-square-foot store as part of a larger development by Vornado Realty Trust.[26] The company then floated a proposal to open a store in Staten Island,[27] only to find that despite the support of the borough president, the company would have to scrap the plan due not only to community opposition but also to the necessity of a costly environmental cleanup at the proposed retail site.[28]

Importantly, the company had sought to gain community support during these earlier campaigns, as the Queens campaign involved the hiring of public affairs firm The Marino Organization.[29] Marino is a firm known for its campaigns in support of real estate and land development clients, and its website provides illustrative case studies of their work on behalf of clients ranging from Home Depot to the Real Estate Board of New York. Marino helped this campaign with a major advertising push in newspapers and on the radio, as well as by commissioning a poll to show that 62 percent of New Yorkers supported Wal-Mart's efforts to enter the city.[30] The company also sought to gain the support of community and civic leaders.[31]

In 2010, Wal-Mart began to move ahead on its third attempt at a New York site, this time in the East New York section of Brooklyn. By

[24] Heller (2010).   [25] Lefkowitz (2011).   [26] Greenhouse (2005a).
[27] Greenhouse (2005b).   [28] Greenhouse (2006c).   [29] Woodberry (2005).
[30] Heilemann (2005).   [31] Frank (2005).

this time, the company had established its national Community Action Network to enlist the support of consumers and local leaders as allies and coalition partners. Although the Community Action Network had listed a state-level branch in 2009, it only registered www.walmartnyc .com in the summer of 2010, at the same time that the company was gearing up to campaign for the East New York site. In late 2010, the company hired New York City mayor Michael Bloomberg's former campaign manager to help the company's grassroots operation, while also announcing that it would consider moving into sites much smaller than a typical 150,000-square-foot supercenter. Wal-Mart sought locations where real estate prices were relatively low and that were currently underserved by local supermarkets, making the argument that stores were planned for areas that were "supermarket deserts." In East New York in particular, the company sought to reach out to leaders of the local African-American and Latino communities to help support their argument that the company has a focus on underserved populations.[32]

The company's grassroots strategy involved a combination of recruiting petition signers, partnering with local community organizations, and issuing publications, flyers, and leaflets in order to enlist members of the public to contact local officials. As one commentator put it, "their ground campaign is going into neighborhoods and trying to basically win endorsements of noted leaders."[33] And they won certain key endorsements. For instance, Wal-Mart's New York City network claims the support of representatives of the New York City Housing Authority Tenants Association, the Real Estate Board of New York, and local racial/ethnic organizations. The president of the New York State NAACP conference says, "We need jobs in our communities. We need affordable places to shop close to home. We need partners to support our neighborhood charities. And we want our voices to be heard by decision makers who claim to represent us. We welcome Walmart in New York City because they are willing to be part of the solution. It is time we support solutions and stop turning businesses away."[34] The CAN also mailed glossy brochures to thousands of New York residents, stating, "You don't ask the special interests or the political insiders for permission to watch TV. So why should they decide where you're allowed to shop?"[35] The CAN campaign in New York

[32] Otis and Cahalan (2010). [33] Harris (2011a). [34] Wal-Mart (2011b).
[35] Harris (2011).

was sophisticated enough that one city council member compared it to a major candidate campaign leading up to election day.[36]

Wal-Mart's grassroots efforts went beyond enlisting community support, and also promoted local protest events, such as a pro-Wal-Mart rally held at City Hall on December 14, 2010. Clad in blue shirts with yellow print reading "New Yorkers Want Walmart!" on the front, and "Jobs! Affordable Groceries! In Our Neighborhood!" on the back, a small rally of predominantly African-American residents promoted the company on the grounds that it would provide economic stimulus and create new jobs. For example, Divine Pryor of Medgar Evers College, City University of New York, argued that "Jobs equal public safety. Jobs equal public health. Jobs equal economic stimulus. I think we owe them a chance to sit down and come up with some reasonable negotiations and dialogue about how that can be possible."[37]

The campaign also took a multi-pronged strategy, seeking to illustrate local support for a new Wal-Mart store on YouTube, Facebook, and Twitter. On the campaign's YouTube page, the company has been issuing regular "Wal-Mart Reports," which involve man-on-the-street interviews with local residents who support the company's expansion efforts, "news" segments that define a "food desert" and explain how a new store would offer a remedy, and telling success stories of employees who were able to rise up the ranks of the company.

Importantly, this grassroots effort was not seen as a replacement for the company's CSR strategy (or a contradiction to it); instead, its CSR efforts were built directly into the campaign. For instance, Wal-Mart recently made a $4 million donation to a New York City youth empowerment program aimed at providing summer jobs to young people.[38] New York City mayor Michael Bloomberg, in a press conference after the donation was announced, called Wal-Mart "one of the great corporate citizens in this country."[39] Although the company made efforts to argue that the donation was part of its national effort to empower youth and not linked to its market interest in expanding into the New York area, in other places the company has explicitly connected its political campaign for a store opening with its philanthropy. For example, on the New York City CAN's Facebook page, Wal-Mart PR staff highlighted the following response to the donation as a "Comment of the Week" from a CAN member:

[36] Ibid.   [37] Wal-Mart (2011c).   [38] Hernandez (2011).   [39] Ibid.

This is great news! But, if Walmart [is] being so generous with it's [*sic*] money, how can we deny them the right to open stores here? If they open stores in New York – this will equal more summer and permanent jobs for New Yorkers.

The opposition the company faced included not only their traditional opponents in community organizations, labor, and small business, but also involved professionalized organizations and new coalitions created for the purpose of opposing the company's expansion. For example, PR firms were also active on behalf of the opposition, as Gotham Government Relations was enlisted to help form an anti-Wal-Mart coalition organization known as the New York Neighborhood Alliance.[40] A partner in the firm argued that "Wal-Mart will destroy how we live our lives and disrupt our daily routines [. . .] Residents will undoubtedly completely change their shopping habits, and in turn would force the closure of countless neighborhood shops – some of which have been around for decades and were passed down through generations." There also recently emerged another network of anti-Wal-Mart groups for the city, known as Wal-Mart-Free NYC.[41]

As of this writing, the campaign has not made major progress in opening a store in the NYC area, but the company did earlier reach an "agreement in principle" that local construction unions would build any new locations,[42] and an independent poll by Quinnipiac University showed that 57 percent of New Yorkers believed that politicians should not block the opening of a Wal-Mart (and 74 percent said that their low prices would benefit local residents).[43] However, the broader context remains hostile to the company's efforts, as NYC city council hearings in early 2011 were boycotted by the company, which thought it was being unfairly singled out among other big-box retailers.

Why go grassroots?

Why is it the case that when certain companies are faced with protest, they promote or augment their commitment to CSR, whereas other companies will *additionally* attempt to mobilize grassroots support in opposition? The comparison between Kimberly-Clark and Wal-Mart is

[40] PR Newswire (2011). [41] Lefkowitz (2011). [42] Naziri (2011).
[43] See Boyle (2011).

instructive for what it reveals about how a firm's reputation moderates the relationship between challenges to the firm and the decision to organize grassroots support using consultants.[44]

First and foremost, Wal-Mart is a company that has had considerable reputational challenges in the past through concerns about its union practices, environmental sustainability, and strained relationships with local community members.[45] As a company with major reputational concerns and a history of contentious protest targeted against it, the company had a much freer hand in mobilizing grassroots support in its favor. Indeed, the Community Action Networks the company created across the country were not the first time the company had engaged in political organizing, as it had earlier created the Working Families for Wal-Mart coalition with the help of a public affairs consulting firm (see Chapter 7). If the company were in a stronger reputational position, it would have been able to exercise the symbolic capital of a strong reputation and would not have been as likely to take such a full-throated strategy in response to controversy.

The case of Kimberly-Clark and Greenpeace shows what a high-reputation firm is likely to do when faced with protest. Instead of

---

[44] This is not to deny that other factors inherent in a corporation's culture may also play a role in its decision to mobilize grassroots support in response to contentious challenges. Wal-Mart's executives, for instance, have long argued that their company's success in business is directly linked to improving the quality of life for working Americans through providing access to jobs and low-cost goods (e.g., Fishman, 2006a). Kimberly-Clark's executives may indeed have a more environmentalist ethos, which, independent of reputation, may have predisposed them against organizing a grassroots campaign to counter Greenpeace. Nonetheless, there is reason to conclude that the effects of reputation continue to play a significant role even after accounting for such factors associated with corporate culture. Avery Dennison, for instance, is a paper products firm without the strong reputation of Kimberly-Clark, but which also has a notable commitment to sustainability, as evidenced in a variety of company characteristics (including an internal sustainability steering committee, a corporate leadership team for sustainability, and diverse partnerships with environmental NGOs and participation in environmental certification regimes; see Avery Dennison, 2010). While high-reputation Kimberly-Clark does not appear as the client of any public affairs consultant in my data (described below and in Appendix 5), Avery Dennison appears as the client of three consulting firms.

[45] See, for example, Ingram, Yue, and Rao (2010).

organizing a coalition in favor of the company's environmental practices, the firm wanted to appear accountable and receptive to the claims of secondary stakeholder groups. Further, it was in no position to defend a practice that it had already recanted. As the world's leading tissue manufacturer and one of the most respected firms in the forestry and paper industry, the company was a magnet for protest but also had few options for how to respond to negative claims. In the end, given the high pressure and widespread media coverage of the Greenpeace campaign, the company was pressured to concede to many of the demands of the protestors. Doing so helped Kimberly-Clark to reaffirm its position as a leader on environmental practices, as well as to gain the added legitimacy of having Greenpeace's endorsement for its sustainability.

The link between corporate responses to protest and a company's CSR practices warrants further comment. Importantly, the outcomes of both of these campaigns represented somewhat natural extensions of each firm's existing CSR. In the case of Wal-Mart, the talking points used by the Community Action Networks highlighted how new urban stores would promote the creation of new jobs (although many dispute this), and the company's philanthropic donations to support youth summer jobs were largely consistent with the campaign's argument. Further, Wal-Mart has recently focused its CSR efforts on issues of access to food, and a key argument for why the company should be permitted to open a New York store is that the proposed sites are in areas that would otherwise be "supermarket deserts." The pro-Wal-Mart rallies that the firm orchestrated also highlighted the company's support in low-income African-American communities using a jobs and economic recovery frame. Importantly, Kimberly-Clark's response was also consistent with its previous commitments, although these commitments also served as a restraint upon the firm's options for response; for example, the company could not appear to be allied with the logging companies and others who would stand to benefit from the continuation of unsustainable practices.

Importantly, both of these campaigns were not simply "private politics" in which firms were targeted *instead* of the state. In each case, activists targeted both the firm directly as well as the state, pressing for new regulations that would affect the firm and force corporate change through legal rather than voluntary mechanisms. Another similarity is that it was within each firm's power to stop the protests through its own actions: for Wal-Mart, they could shelve their plans to open in NYC; for

Kimberly-Clark, they could agree to stop using pulp from endangered forests. However, in the Wal-Mart case, the regulatory threat was more significant than the concern that consumers would respond negatively to their actions; in fact, Wal-Mart knew and highlighted the fact that a majority of New Yorkers said, in independent surveys, that they were in favor of allowing the company to open a store in one of the boroughs. The larger problem would be that city council and local regulators would block the company's expansion plans. This ongoing legislative and regulatory opposition also, it appears, facilitated a particularly *political* strategy in the company's response to protest. The relatively remote regulatory threat that Kimberly-Clark faced may have also made a heavy-handed stakeholder mobilization response less desirable, while at the same time facilitating more engagement in private regulation.[46]

These two campaigns, while insightful and illustrative, tell only a portion of the story about what leads a company to mobilize stakeholder support through working with a public affairs consultant. I now turn to a broader statistical analysis of why companies generate such displays of public support.

A statistical model of corporate grassroots activity

Background

In order to understand corporate grassroots campaigns more broadly, I estimate a statistical model of the factors that lead firms in the *Fortune* 500 to hire a grassroots public affairs consultant. Given that very few companies possess the in-house capacities needed to launch a full-scale campaign, companies generally outsource such efforts to consulting firms when they seek to employ this strategy. Using data from a variety of sources, I estimate how protest, controversies, political contexts, and other factors shape a company's likelihood to hire a consultant to organize a campaign, as well as how reputations buffer companies against controversies and protest.

Details about the data collection and measurement of variables are available in Appendix 5.

---

[46] See Bartley (2007).

Analysis

Which factors lead companies to hire public affairs consultants to mobilize their stakeholders in corporate grassroots campaigns? I conduct a series of negative binomial regression models of *Fortune* 500 firms' count of public affairs consultants hired as of 2010; a negative binomial model is appropriate to a count-based dependent variable that is over-dispersed (mean of .93 with a variance of 3.28).[47]

Results are displayed in Table 5.1. The first model, labeled "All firms," shows the effects of reputation, consumer and labor protest, stakeholder relations, political context, other types of corporate political activity, industry, revenue, and structural characteristics on the count of consultants retained for all included *Fortune* 500 firms. The second model examines the same relationships among firms at or below the median reputational score provided from *Fortune*'s "Most Admired Companies" list. The third model does the same for firms above the median in reputation. The comparison of the second and third models with the first allows one to evaluate the extent to which reputation moderates the relationship between firms' stakeholder relations and their grassroots activities.

First, it should be noted that nearly 40 percent of the *Fortune* 500 appear as the client of a public affairs consultant, and this includes over 67 percent of *Fortune* 100 members. Thus, regardless of the corporate–community relations and protest faced by these prominent firms, grassroots practices have become, by the early years of the twenty-first century, rather well institutionalized. Corporate constituency-building efforts are now a rather mainstream practice.[48]

Looking at the first (leftmost) model, the results suggest that high-reputation firms are very slightly less likely to hire public affairs consultants. At the bivariate level (not shown), in fact, I found that 56.8 percent of firms in the top reputation quartile appear as the client of at least one grassroots lobbyist (whereas only 22.5 percent of firms in the lowest reputation quartile appear as a client), but it is also clear that the highest-reputation firms tend to be those that have the highest revenues,

---

[47] In additional models (not shown), I also specified a binary dependent variable and entered the same independent variables into logit estimations. The core finding holds that community controversies are only a significant predictor of hiring a consultant for low-reputation firms, and not for high-reputation firms.

[48] See also Lord (2000, 2003).

Table 5.1 *Negative binomial regression of the count of consultants hired by Fortune 500 firms on corporate characteristics*

Variable	All firms		Low-reputation firms		High-reputation firms	
	Coef.	S.E.	Coef.	S.E.	Coef.	S.E.
Reputation						
Fortune score, 2007	−0.038	(0.034)	–	–	–	–
Protest						
Consumer protest	0.199	(0.185)	0.578*	(0.288)	0.043	(0.225)
Labor protest	0.167	(0.231)	0.376	(0.333)	0.042	(0.293)
External controversies						
Community controversies	0.279*	(0.137)	0.709**	(0.221)	0.149	(0.162)
Environmental controversies	0.132+	(0.077)	0.304**	(0.106)	0.024	(0.104)
Internal controversies						
Diversity controversies	0.163	(0.160)	0.059	(0.237)	0.183	(0.209)
Employee controversies	−0.179+	(0.095)	−0.277+	(0.156)	−0.081	(0.114)
Stakeholder strengths						
Community strengths	0.006	(0.106)	0.058	(0.155)	−0.086	(0.130)
Environmental strengths	−0.007	(0.091)	0.055	(0.131)	0.026	(0.108)
Diversity strengths	0.228***	(0.062)	0.224*	(0.100)	0.225**	(0.074)
Employee strengths	0.033	(0.085)	0.094	(0.134)	0.011	(0.099)
Political context						
House DW-Nominate mean	0.260	(0.402)	0.252	(0.647)	0.343	(0.503)
Political activism						
Lobbying ($ millions)	0.309*	(0.150)	0.455+	(0.254)	0.265	(0.173)

	Model 1		Model 2		Model 3	
Industry						
Information	0.775*	(0.329)	0.729	(0.505)	0.863*	(0.412)
Manufacturing	−0.246	(0.245)	−0.910*	(0.398)	0.014	(0.267)
Retail	−0.294	(0.318)	−1.254*	(0.575)	0.117	(0.383)
Energy	0.393	(0.337)	0.279	(0.469)	0.353	(0.439)
Transportation	0.388	(0.386)	0.604	(0.514)	−0.208	(0.626)
Revenue						
Fortune rank	−0.002*	(0.001)	−0.002+	(0.001)	−0.002+	(0.001)
Structural characteristics						
Employees (thousands)	0.240+	(0.123)	0.522**	(0.199)	0.102	(0.153)
Cash flow ($ billions)	0.070	(0.168)	−0.463	(0.339)	0.185	(0.188)
Market-to-book ratio	−0.103	(0.133)	0.074	(0.205)	−0.213	(0.175)
Constant	−1.326*	(0.620)	−2.483**	(0.871)	−0.942	(0.695)
N	340		165		175	
Pseudo R-square	0.218		0.326		0.187	
Log likelihood	−356.0		−123.9		−214.5	

Significance levels: $^+ p \leq .10$; $^* p \leq .05$; $^{**} p \leq .01$; $^{***} p \leq .001$

as noted by management and organizations scholars.[49] Thus, the apparent bivariate effect of reputation is, in fact, an effect of revenue, in which the most resource-rich firms are among the most likely to hire a firm. The findings for *Fortune* rank confirm this, as firms with a lower rank (i.e., higher number on the ranking list) are significantly less likely to appear on grassroots lobbyists' client lists.

Comparing across the models, I find support for the expectation that organizations with external public controversies are among the most likely to mobilize grassroots participation, but that this effect is moderated by reputation. In particular, the models show that among low-reputation firms, the presence of community controversies, and poor environmental performance, and, to a lesser extent, consumer protest, are all significant and positive predictors of the count of consultants retained by the firm; none of these measures have any significant effect for high-reputation firms. Thus, comparing the leftmost model to the reputation-specific models presented in the center and right columns, it becomes clear that reputation moderates firms' responses to negative public information. In particular, additional models (not shown) illustrate that certain negative relations are among the most significant individual predictors of the volume of low-reputation firms' grassroots activities: negative economic impacts in the local communities in which a firm operates ($p < .05$), concerns about hazardous waste in the environment ($p < .05$), and evidence of environmental regulatory violations ($p < .10$). For high-reputation firms, however, none of these statistical relationships hold, as firms with a strong reputation can weather negative information without needing to engage in campaigns to mobilize stakeholders.[50] In a sense, then, reputation operates as a buffer against negative information in firms' institutional environments.[51]

A similar relation holds for protest, in that low-reputation firms that were the target of a major consumer protest were found to have significantly higher levels of corporate grassroots engagement, whereas this relationship does not hold for high-reputation firms. Thus, consistent

---

[49] E.g., Fryxell and Wang (1994).

[50] An augmented version of the "all firms" model in Table 5.1 (not shown) included a term for the interaction between reputation and community controversies. These results showed a significant ($p < .001$) negative interaction, consistent with the expectation of a moderating effect of reputation.

[51] E.g., King (2008).

with the case material described earlier, firms with poor reputations appear to engage in a strategy of fighting fire with fire: when targeted with protest, firms with relatively weak reputations do what they can to mobilize their own activism to counterbalance the claims of protest groups. Importantly, however, they do not appear to take this strategy when faced with labor protest, as only public protest by consumer groups draws this type of corporate response. Thus, although industry-leading organizations are among the most likely to face protest because they are expected to influence other firms in the field,[52] laggard firms are among the most likely to take strategic action in response to protest.

Firms that had internal controversies were generally not more likely to work with consultants, although the models show that low-reputation firms with controversies in their employee relations were slightly less likely ($p < .10$) to work with consultants; this relationship did not hold for high-reputation firms. Thus, while external controversies encourage a public response from low-reputation firms, internal controversies in a firm's relations with its employees lead these same firms to keep a lower profile.

Interestingly, I find no significant effects for three of the areas of stakeholder strength (community, environment, and, most consequentially, employee relations), and significant positive effects in one area (diversity strengths). It appears, then, that firms that have succeeded in building and maintaining diversity in their workforce and management are significantly more likely to hire grassroots consulting firms, suggesting that diversity programs are strengths on which constituency-building efforts can be launched.[53] Firms that feature such diversity programs appear to be more confident in their efforts to engage grassroots participation, even after introducing a wide variety of controls.

Moving to the control measures, I find no significant effect of the political context on firms' engagement in grassroots campaigns. For the other political measure, however, I do find a significant effect that also appears to be moderated by reputation: among low-reputation firms, higher levels of logged lobbying expenditures are associated with a significant increase in the count of consultants retained. Thus, expenditures on inside lobbying are also related to grassroots mobilization, and in a way that is also moderated by reputation.

---

[52] Rao, Morrill, and Zald (2000).   [53] See Keim (2005).

Regarding the effects of industry, I find that information and communications technology firms tend to engage in a greater volume of
grassroots mobilization, as these firms are both highly regulated and
also possess the capacity to mobilize participation using their own
technologies.[54] This sector includes a number of major media firms
that appear as clients of grassroots lobbyists (such as AT&T, Viacom,
Virgin Media, and Disney), as well as communications companies like
Verizon, Google, Yahoo!, and Sprint Nextel. This finding is consistent
with what I found in another study about the predominant role of media
and communications firms in grassroots mobilization among a broader
set, including both *Fortune* 500 companies and smaller firms.[55]
Grassroots lobbying methods rely upon the media and information
and communications technologies, and the firms that provide access
to media and ICTs appear to be its heaviest users. On the other hand,
low-reputation manufacturing and retail firms are less likely to engage
in these activities.

One of my interviews was particularly relevant for understanding the
findings of this model regarding information and communications
firms. When asked about differences across industries in their grassroots
mobilization efforts, long-standing consultant Pat Samuels explained to
me that communications firms are often at the forefront of such efforts
not only because of the regulatory issues they face, but because of their
relations with their vast consumer base:

[Companies] do unite from time to time on big issues. Usually taxes or some
sort of restrictive legislation or oversight of one kind or another. [Firms in the
telecommunications industry] deal with governments all of the time on rates.
And they do have a big footprint. They have all of these subscribers. They are
used to dealing with individuals all over the country, and they have data on all
of those individuals. There's a culture of doing grassroots within their
industry.

Lastly, coming back to the findings in Table 5.1, I found consistent
support for the argument that revenue and public prominence affect
firms' likelihood of mobilizing grassroots participation, as firms
ranked lower in the *Fortune* 500 list are significantly less likely to
hire one (let alone *many*) grassroots lobbying firms. I also find that

---

[54] For an analysis of the role of regulation in shaping trade associations' work with
consultants, see Appendix 7.
[55] Walker (2012a).

low-reputation firms use large employee bases as an asset in mobilizing participation ($p < .01$), but do not find this effect for high-reputation firms. Finally, measures of firms' cash flow and market-to-book value both have no significant effect on grassroots mobilization in any of the three models.

Conclusion

This chapter sought to examine which circumstances tend to lead large companies to engage in grassroots mobilization campaigns with the support of consultants. In particular, this chapter asked how such organizational behavior is tied to companies' relationships with their external communities, the protest they face from consumer and labor groups, and the broader political context.

I expected to find, above all else, that corporate grassroots mobilization is a strategic response to protest and poor community relations. A secondary expectation was that firms' reputations could serve as a buffer against these dual threats, such that high-reputation firms might not need to hire consultants *when faced with these challenges* (but, lacking that buffer, low-reputation firms would be forced to respond). Although both high- and low-reputation firms are likely to emphasize commitments to CSR when faced with external challenges – as both Kimberly-Clark and Wal-Mart did in the case studies described at the outset of this chapter – only firms with a weaker reputational position should respond to controversy with grassroots counter-mobilization. Accordingly, I found support for the notion that reputation moderates the relationship between the public controversies and the hiring of public affairs consultants to defend companies. High-reputation firms hire consulting firms also, but for reasons that are more closely linked to operating in a regulated industry.

Most importantly, the findings of the case studies and the statistical models presented here indicate that neo-institutionalist analysts of organizations have been correct in calling attention to the ways that corporate-targeted contention has promoted more environmentally sustainable and pro-social policies among leading companies, as well as other industry-wide voluntary programs.[56] However, it also makes clear that a firm's position relative to its peers conditions its likelihood

---

[56] Bartley (2007).

of responding in this fashion, as firms with weaker reputations may supplement their CSR efforts with stakeholder mobilization campaigns to defend the firm. Strong reputations buffer firms against contention,[57] but firms in weaker reputational positions have a freer hand in responding to negative claims.

The findings of this chapter also suggest that one of the major outcomes of societal contention directed at private businesses has been the development of corporate public affairs programs designed to mobilize the firm's primary stakeholders as a political force. As contention against firms has expanded into a more regular aspect of many firms' public existence, so too has the institutionalization of grassroots programs for *Fortune* 500 firms. Politicized industry and the expansion of citizen groups, as I argued in Chapter 3, facilitated a significant expansion in the field of consultants, and this chapter illustrates how controversies, protest, and regulation drive firms to utilize their services.

Scholars investigating the role of social movements in reshaping organizational practices and institutional dynamics, then, need to examine not only whether social movements' corporate targets are forced to concede to protest groups' demands (or engage in increased self-regulation or reporting to ward off the threat of future protest), but should also investigate how firms take strategic measures to actively challenge the threat posed by protest and controversies. It appears that although high-reputation firms are more likely to face protest, low-reputation firms are more threatened by such negative claims-making, often engaging in efforts to mobilize stakeholders when few other political options are likely to be successful.

In total, the findings of this chapter show that now that the consultant field is well established, nearly 40 percent of *Fortune* 500 firms use them to gain a political edge. Grassroots practices aren't just for advocacy organizations now that public affairs consultants can be called upon to help companies manage complex political environments.

---

[57] King (2008).

6 | Outsourcing advocacy? Consulting for associations

Introduction

Public affairs consultants are quite logical service providers for corporations. After all, corporations are built for generating profits and distributing them to their owners or shareholders, not for mobilizing public participation. Thus, when a challenge like unwelcome regulation, a community controversy, and/or a public protest comes about, corporations often find that they need to enlist public affairs consultants' services.

Advocacy organizations, by contrast, are known for their ability to connect people to politics.[1] Public interest groups pressing for social change on issues like the environment and climate change, abortion, poverty, taxation, or health policy tend to be far more likely to have strong inherent capacities for galvanizing mass political participation than corporations do.[2] Why, then, do some advocacy organizations feel the need to, in a sense, "outsource" their member mobilization efforts to public affairs consultants? And what does their doing so mean for the infrastructure of civic and political organizations in a context of expanding participatory inequality, transforming communications technologies, and professionalization in the advocacy sector?

This chapter shows that although it is relatively rare for advocacy organizations to contract with grassroots public affairs consultants – indeed, they need not search for "grassroots for hire" when they already have these capacities internally – the practice is more common among very large national advocacy organizations, especially the most well-resourced federated organizations with headquarters in the nation's capital. And, in contrast to the expectation by many that the advocacy

---

[1] Weir and Ganz (1997).   [2] Kollman (1998: 43).

sector has been transformed since the 1970s by the rise of so-called associations without members[3] – that is, advocacy groups that mobilize participants primarily as check- and letter-writers rather than as face-to-face activists – this chapter shows that such groups are not significantly more likely than member-based groups to hire a public affairs consultant.

Notably, many consulting firms and their staff are instrumental players in both the broader conservative and progressive movements in the US. For example, the Richard Norman Company (Lansdowne, VA) is deeply rooted in the community of conservative politics and can boast clients like the Tea Party Patriots, Freedom Alliance, the Conservative Caucus, and controversial voter-ID law backers True the Vote. By contrast, Democracy Partners (Washington, DC) has worked with MoveOn.org, Americans United for Change, Every Child Matters, and the American Federation of State, County, and Municipal Employees (AFSCME). The consultants at Democracy Partners, importantly, have backgrounds working as organizers in progressive advocacy groups and labor unions such as the NAACP, Emily's List, the Service Employees International Union (SEIU), AFL-CIO, and low-income community organizations affiliated with the Industrial Areas Foundation.[4] There are slightly more firms in the data that fit the profile of groups like Democracy Partners; recall from Chapter 4 that firms with a primarily advocacy clientele are somewhat more likely to be affiliated with the Democrats than with the Republicans.

There are many firms like Richard Norman Company and Democracy Partners that hold similar ideological commitments and tend to see their work as a natural extension of their respective movement, envisioning their consulting work as rooted in deeply personal hopes that their side will win. As John Crate, the founder and president of the California-based Emmitt Strategies,[5] which has a clientele comprised exclusively of progressive advocacy organizations, explained to me,

I've been doing this [organizing work] since I was in high school ... I never stopped protesting. I mean, so aside from my training, which includes training

---

[3] Skocpol (2003); cf. Walker, McCarthy, and Baumgartner (2011).
[4] Democracy Partners (2012).
[5] Both "John Crate" and "Emmitt Strategies" are pseudonyms.

from the [United] Farm Workers – which sort of was like the Harvard of organizing with their people – [I've learned that] it's really an interactive process. I'm really analyzing … "Where do you wanna go, what resources do you have to get there, and what's most important to you, and what paths would you not wanna take?" And then, I apply my own expertise, and, obviously, you know, consult other experts on data, and use data consultants and vendors for what's necessary. But, you know, I go through real analysis of how I can help them get where they think they want to go, which may not end up where we actually end up going together.[6]

John continues,

We're motivated by our interests, which are clearly progressive. That's my passion and that's what I want to spend my work time doing. So we're pretty flexible. Like if we find an organization that wants to work with us and we wanna work with them, we'll do whatever the hell they need. We've done fundraising, we've done grassroots organizing, media relations, advertising. "Hey, what do you need?"

I begin the chapter with two brief descriptions of consultants' work for advocacy groups, followed by a discussion of how their work dovetails with trends in the field of US advocacy organizations including professionalization, use of new media and communications technologies, and the changing meaning of "membership." I also describe, using the survey data, the services that consultants tend to provide to advocacy organizations. Then, using data from the client lists and from a systematic data source on national advocacy organizations, I examine which types of advocacy groups are most likely to hire public affairs consultants. I conclude by considering the implications of these findings for how best to understand the place of associations in contemporary American politics and society.

---

[6] I regularly heard from consultants that they often subcontract to other consultants when they require specific data services (e.g., targeted lists of particular demographic groups that the consultant did not already own) or if they required local knowledge of a particular community or region where the firm had not previously worked. Indeed, in the 2009 scandal over fraudulent letters sent to Virginia Rep. Tom Perriello on behalf of the American Coalition for Clean Coal Electricity, it was revealed that the responsible party for the fraudulent letters was in fact a subcontractor to the Alexandria, Virginia-based Hawthorn Group (Snyder, 2009).

Cases of public affairs work for associations

Crossroads Campaign Solutions

Crossroads Campaign Solutions (CCS) is a Washington, DC public affairs consulting firm founded in 2007, which as of this writing has a staff of sixteen consultants and a roster of fifty-five clients. Not to be mistaken for Karl Rove's nonprofit Republican-affiliated American Crossroads, CCS has a clientele comprised almost entirely of progressive advocacy organizations and Democratic candidates.[7] Consultants working for the firm have backgrounds in nonprofit fundraising, community organizing, think-tank work, staffing for policymakers, and field organizing for Democratic Get-Out-The-Vote (GOTV) efforts. The firm also has formal partnerships with Clifton Consulting (which handles training of association leaders on such skills as communications, leadership development, and media savvy) and also with Empowered Media Strategies (a one-person cause marketing firm known for its work with the viral LGBT youth project called "It Gets Better," run by a former consultant from Blue State Digital). The firm provides quite a broad range of services to advocacy organizations, ranging from activist targeting to communications training. CCS also helps advocacy groups locate and hire short-term employees to make sure a campaign has the staff it needs to be successful. As the firm describes itself on its website,

Crossroads can help organizations develop plans and gather the resources necessary to contact legislators and mobilize communities to take action on education, direct service, and advocacy campaigns. We have put together innovative strategies utilizing a variety of available tools for distributing campaign messages through traditional and non-traditional communications.

We can help your organization set up legislative meetings, create briefing material, and engage constituents through letter writing, phone call and email campaigns. Crossroads can also create person-to-person contact programs including but not limited to large-scale canvasses, forums and events, voter registration, and Get-Out-the-Vote (GOTV) efforts.

Looking at particular campaigns for associations, CCS has provided a variety of services. Working with National Council of La Raza (NCLR), CCS helped the organization to manage coalitions with over forty partner

---

[7] Crossroads Campaign Solutions (2012).

associations to "assist with field know-how, organizing tools, best practices advice, and developing print materials"; more recently, CCS has helped NCLR's organizational partners to become more professionalized through helping manage their grants, and to improve "internal processes and reporting mechanisms." For Reform Immigration for America, CCS helped the organization to develop targeting plans and to coordinate organizers and individual participants; as they describe it, they applied a "metrics-driving approach" to evaluate the effectiveness of various grassroots mobilization strategies. And, working with the Partnership for Working Families (PWF), CCS developed plans to increase organizational capacity and further build the civic engagement of participants.

Importantly, CCS makes considerable efforts beyond its work for PWF to build the capacities of the associations that hire it for assistance in their campaigns. This fits with a common theme that arose during my conversations with consultants who specialize in working with advocacy clients: they are happy to help these clients to meet their strategic goals, but also do not want to create long-term dependence on consultants. While this may seem counter-intuitive – after all, it might make more sense for a consultant to seek out retainer contracts with their advocacy clients – the consultants I talked with, like Crossroads, believe that there is a limit to what consultants should do for advocacy organizations. This is, of course, a stark contrast from consultants who work with a corporate clientele and often work their hardest to be kept on retainer (as described in Chapter 4). As Crossroads describes it, they

help campaigns and nonprofits become more effective in establishing and accomplishing their internal and public goals. We work hard to develop a strategy that aligns organizational capability with short- and long-term goals. Not content to apply a one-size-fits-all action-plan, we spend the necessary time to review and understand your organization's strengths and identify potential areas of improvement. The Crossroads team will assess current staffing, management, and capacity of your organization by participating in internal meetings, conference calls, and other activities as needed. Crossroads will then make recommendations and work with organizational staff and leadership to write plans and budgets that drive goal-oriented work.

This is quite similar to what Bill Hoover, the co-founder and president of Field Engagement, Inc.,[8] a well-connected Midwestern public affairs

---

[8] Both names are pseudonyms.

shop with a primarily advocacy clientele, told me when I interviewed him. As he made clear, consulting firms working in advocacy are often quite committed to the causes they promote for their clients, and put these values above their interest in lucrative contracts. This is not to say that such pecuniary concerns are disregarded completely, but the firm's reputation depends upon a balance:

I would say we are a grassroots consulting firm that intersects with the public affairs space, and so we're also a *value space firm*. And so as a firm of folks who all started off as grassroots organizers, our conception of the world is about building capacity ... So, our business model really is [that] if we help our clients [build capacity] and they learn how to do it well, two things are gonna happen. One, they're gonna tell others about it, and that's been the case [for our firm for] over thirteen years, and at three, or four, or five years they're gonna want to elevate to the next level of effectiveness and they're gonna come back to hire us again.[9]

Shirley & Banister Public Affairs

Shirley & Banister Public Affairs (SBPA) is a long-standing, Republican-affiliated consulting shop located in Alexandria, VA, with a mixed clientele comprised mainly of advocacy organizations, Republican candidates, and some corporations and industry groups. As a more generalist firm, SBPA provides services beyond facilitating activism, as the firm's principals also assist a number of pundits and conservative leaders in their relations with multiple media including television, radio, print, and internet-based outlets. Founded in 1987 as Keene, Shirley, & Associates, the firm today has five consultants and provides services such as grassroots coalition-building, traditional lobbying ("government relations"), and facilitating publicity events. They also carry out PR and advertising services like placing advertisements, helping clients develop a message and get it published in op-eds, and general media relations. Since 2001, the firm has been known as Shirley & Banister, after Craig Shirley offered Diana Banister – a lead consultant in organizing the GOTV efforts for the presidential runs of Bob Dole and Pat Buchanan – a partnership.

The firm's founder and CEO, Craig Shirley, is quite well known in his own right not only as a conservative intellectual and trusted consultant

---

[9] Emphases are mine.

but also as a *New York Times* best-selling author for his book about the days surrounding the attack on Pearl Harbor, *December 1941*. He had previously written two books about Ronald Reagan: one about his failed 1976 campaign that, Shirley argues, helped to revive the Republican Party, and another about Reagan's landslide victory in 1980. Shirley was not merely an outside observer to these events, as one of his first political posts was at the Fund for a Conservative Majority's "$750,000 independent expenditure campaign" in support of Ronald Reagan's 1980 campaign, followed by a 1982 stint as a communications advisor to the RNC and another as director of communications for the National Conservative Political Action Committee during the 1984 campaign.[10] His involvement with the conservative movement has continued in the years since Reagan's presidency, not only through his consulting work but also through the Political Action Committee (PAC) affiliated with George H.W. Bush's 1988 presidential campaign, Bob Dole's 1992 run, and George W. Bush's election (and the Florida recount) in 2000.

SBPA's work on behalf of associations is extensive, and includes consulting for the Tea Party Patriots, Christian Coalition, Heritage Foundation, NRA, National Taxpayers Union, and Citizens United (the plaintiff and namesake in the landmark 2010 Supreme Court decision, *Citizens United v. Federal Election Commission*, which removed restrictions on independent political expenditures by corporations and unions). And part of that work is the development of coalitions on behalf of the client, which the firm describes in the following manner:

Often, when developing a client's campaign, a key element can be the development of a coalition under which many voices can speak out in support of the client's efforts or concerns. We have developed many such coalitions dealing with a myriad of issues and have excellent relations with both Washington and state-based think tanks from the Heritage Foundation, AEI, Cato, Progress & Freedom Foundation, and Competitive Enterprise Institute to the Hudson Institute, the Manhattan Institute and many others. They can often be the difference between the success and failure of a public affairs campaign.

---

[10] Gill Report (2012).

The firm's work for particular advocacy clients has included helping to promote the Defund the Stimulus coalition, backed by advocacy groups including Let Freedom Ring, Americans for Tax Reform, and the Restore the Dream Foundation.[11] This follows earlier work in which SBPA helped Let Freedom Ring with their media relations and the grassroots presence for its WeNeedAFence.com campaign surrounding immigration reform.[12] SBPA also helped the Club for Growth with its message promoting tax reform, Social Security privatization, and "fiscal responsibility," and former CFG president Stephen Moore (now on the editorial board of the *Wall Street Journal*) suggested in promotional materials that the firm helped his organization to move from relative obscurity into being a household name during the 2004 elections.[13] SBPA also managed the Tea Party Patriots' "No Tax Compromise" petition drive in December 2010,[14] when Tea Party activists were furious over the agreement between President Obama and Congressional Republicans to extend the Bush-era tax cuts for two years while also maintaining benefits to the unemployed and temporarily cutting payroll taxes.[15]

What the work of firms like Crossroads Campaign Solutions and Shirley & Banister Public Affairs tells us is that public affairs consulting firms have become quite rooted in the advocacy communities in which they operate. They are trusted sources of guidance, providers of data, PR counselors, and advocacy experts. Consultants help to provide strategic guidance to associations' campaigns, while also extending their reach into otherwise untapped pools of support. Despite these benefits, these cases also make clear that consultants help to further professionalize associations and require that significant resources be paid to consulting firms rather than being devoted to other priorities.

As I explain in the next section, associational professionalism and contracting with consultants are tendencies that appear to go hand in hand.

Understanding contemporary advocacy

The field of American advocacy organizations has undergone some major changes over the past half-century. As shown in Chapter 3 (see

---

[11] SBPA (2011a).   [12] SBPA (2011b).   [13] SBPA (2011c).   [14] SBPA (2010).
[15] Herszenhorn and Calmes (2010).

Figure 3.2), the density of the advocacy sector has increased dramatically since the 1960s, in what political scientist Jeffrey Berry once called the "advocacy explosion."[16] Following the "long sixties" protest wave in the US and the major expansion of federal regulatory powers during that same period, organized advocates saw vast new opportunities to have their say through legislatures, agencies, and courts, which were all making attempts to become more transparent.[17] An increasingly educated populace with disposable resources to donate to advocacy causes provided further wind in the sails of civic and political associations. For Congress in particular, the 1970s-era "sunshine laws," which, of course, take their name from Justice Louis Brandeis's famous statement that sunlight is "the best of disinfectants," decentralized power in Congress and broadened the range of opportunities for advocacy groups to have a voice in legislative decision-making; one study showed that even for long-standing interest groups like the National Audubon Society and unions like the United Automobile Workers, their invitations to deliver testimony before the House of Representatives increased dramatically in the period following these reforms.[18]

The post-sixties explosion of advocacy organizations was indeed staggering. While there were only 627 national associations active on general matters of public affairs in 1972, that figure had climbed to 2,249 associations by 1990, seeing some decline but largely remaining steady throughout the 1990s.[19] Even after adjusting for population growth, the field of national advocacy groups per capita nearly doubled between 1972 and 2003.

Along with this came the professionalization of many organizations, as groups that emerged out of the sixties-era social movements of the left came to play the role of well-established interest groups with professional staff, more stable flows of resources (often from foundation

---

[16] Berry (1997); see also Walker (1991).

[17] On advocacy responses to the widening regulatory scope of the state, see Skocpol (2007); on disclosure policies, see, e.g., Fung, Graham, and Weil (2007).

[18] Heitshusen (2000: 153).

[19] Author tabulation using data from the *Encyclopedia of Associations'* "public affairs" subject heading. For a detailed description of this data source and justification for using it in research on advocacy, see Walker, McCarthy, and Baumgartner (2011: 1325–1329) and also Appendix 6.

grants), and relatively routinized means of engaging in politics. Not long thereafter, groups on the right gained traction, linked to Christian conservative organizations, right-wing entrepreneurs in the legal profession, anti-tax groups, and those pressing back against new regulations on business.[20] On both sides, groups learned how to pair the ground game of mass public participation with more professional tactics like advertising, direct lobbying, and campaign contributions.[21] Between the late 1960s and early years of the new century, there was also a large numeric (but not proportional) increase in "associations without members," including policy institutes, think tanks, centers, and research funds that advocate on public issues while not enrolling individuals as members (or, importantly, building social ties between those who engage on their behalf).[22] Membership organizations, for their part, were professionalizing their fundraising, using supply-side recruitment strategies, and packaging their activities in a desirable way for funding by foundations and other would-be patrons.[23]

Professionalization, in part, made advocacy groups more amenable to hiring public affairs consultants to help them to reach beyond their existing constituencies, especially when a pressing policy matter arose for an organization. It did so in at least three ways: by (1) Helping to redefine "grassroots" away from its traditional meaning as participation that is unique, unprompted, local, and spontaneous and shifting its meaning toward a more encompassing definition that focuses instead on mass participation in general, regardless of whether participation is prompted by an organization or professional; (2) The professionals working in public affairs firms often have backgrounds in campaign consulting and/or advocacy politics (as I described in Chapter 3), and employ many of the same tactics as advocacy groups in order to advance their client's cause; (3) The in-house staff of advocacy organizations often find that their time is quite scarce, and know that the hard work of grassroots advocacy through canvassing, signature gathering, micro-targeted communications, and phone banking can often be done

[20] Skocpol (2007); Teles (2010).
[21] See Walker, McCarthy, and Baumgartner (2011).
[22] Skocpol (2003); Walker, McCarthy, and Baumgartner (2011). See also Minkoff, Aisenbrey, and Agnone (2008).
[23] Jordan and Maloney (1997); Bosso (2005); Shaiko (1999); Jenkins (2006).

in a more cost-effective fashion by consulting shops and vendors. Some commentators worry that such "outsourcing" may be detracting from the vibrancy of civil society, while also removing the paid organizing staff of such campaigns from more meaningful political engagement.[24]

The link between the professionalization of advocacy organizations and their interest in hiring a consultant was described to me in rather succinct fashion by Bill Hoover of Field Engagement, Inc., introduced earlier in this chapter. As he argued in our conversation,

> I would say the line of demarcation [between which groups hire us versus those who don't] is one of resources. Organizations that are more well resourced tend to turn to consultants more quickly.

He continued, arguing that such associations commonly have a professional staff who

> understand ... or will have familiarity working with, other sorts of consultants, and it's just more in their culture [...] There are groups ... including some where I have good friends working, [that] think the idea of a for-profit grassroots consulting firm is anathema to their ideals, and my response to that is part of what we're able to do as consultants is stay on top of the very latest trends and developments, and we're also able to borrow and move things across worlds. So we take things from the political world to the advocacy world all the time; from faith organizing back into political organizing all the time. And when you're an organization – even if you're a really, really good grassroots organization – you're often operating in one world, and we're not.
> I think we are supported by a growing recognition that traditional [grassroots] strategies are not getting you far enough.

However, while this provides some initial indication of the factors behind advocacy groups' work with consultants, it's unclear whether resources and professionalism are the only driving forces behind such collaborations between advocacy groups and consultants. In the following section, I describe the results of a systematic analysis of the hiring of consulting firms by national-level advocacy organizations. After presenting the results of that investigation, I return to the question of how best to understand the contemporary advocacy sector and the place of consultants within it.

---

[24] Fisher (2006).

Hiring of consultants by national advocacy organizations

The evidence presented in Chapter 3 provided some indication that public affairs consultants tend to have a complementary (rather than competitive or substitute) relationship with advocacy organizations. The "advocacy explosion" since the early 1970s helped to support the founding of new grassroots public affairs consultancies. But exactly which features of advocacy groups are most complementary to the work of consultants? I now consider a number of features that, based upon previous studies of civic and political associations, should be systematically linked with such participatory "outsourcing" by advocacy groups.

Professionalization and resources

Based upon Bill Hoover's commentary above, one might expect resources and professionalization to be central to consultants' associational work. An association can be said to be professionalized when certain individuals spend full-time hours doing advocacy work, when a set of normative constraints exist on staff (such as a code of ethics), when a professional organization exists to coordinate the efforts of staff, and when members of the profession possess specialized knowledge that they employ in their service to clients. Sarah Sobieraj argues that one consequence of these transformations has been to limit the development of participants' civic skills.[25]

Professional groups often use direct mail recruitment and mobilization of members, and, more recently, appeals through mass email and blogs. Many of these campaigns target primarily those with higher levels of education and income, both because of their increased likelihood to take action as well as to provide financial support.[26]

Associations with a heavy professional staff presence, although they are only a minority of the broader associational field, are likely to differ from the more common grassroots, member-driven organizational form in a variety of ways.[27] Primarily, groups with larger staffs should be likely to call on members to lobby their representatives, because

[25] Sobieraj (2006).   [26] Brady, Schlozman, and Verba (1999).
[27] On the prevalence of grassroots associations without any paid staff, see Smith (1997).

powerful interest groups can activate their constituents both as group members and as individual voters in legislative districts. And organizations with larger staffs have a greater organizational capacity to mobilize members, and can carry out a variety of activities to get members active on pertinent issues.

In addition, organizations may not wish to tie up their staffs with the somewhat mundane functions that a consultant could provide: mass mailings, phone banks, and the like, alongside media and PR strategies to support the organization's image; because those larger staffs could perhaps be put to better use, it is also possible that professionalized organizations will be more likely to hire a firm.

With respect to resources, Chapter 4 illustrated that the services of a consultant are expensive. Although a number of consultants I interviewed reported billing associational clients at a lower rate than they require of their business clients, nonetheless consultants often require a substantial outlay of funds on the part of an advocacy organization.

Overall, then, *I expect that groups having a larger staff size and a larger budget will be more likely to contract with a public affairs consultant.*

Federated structure

While the field of advocacy organizations has changed in many ways in recent years, the trend of federation – that is, of having regional, state, and/or local chapters – appears to have remained relatively stable.[28] Although federations come with the advantage of widespread coordination across geographic regions and levels of government, there are potential costs involved in maintaining such a structure, such as divided loyalties between branch groups and the national office, the potential for conflict over resources and members between chapters, and the risk that chapters will become autonomous.[29] Regardless of these challenges, federated organizations require extensive communication and harmonization between the various organizational levels. In addition, because the existence of a federated structure suggests that such groups are politically active at multiple levels of government,[30] these groups have an interest in promoting the grassroots activation of

[28] McCarthy (2005b: 204–205).   [29] Ibid.
[30] Skocpol, Ganz, and Munson (2000).

their members while employing mechanisms for coordinating those efforts. The services of a consultant, then, *should be more common among groups with regional, state, and/or local branches.*

Membership size and structure

Alongside the widespread growth of the field of associations throughout the 1970s and 1980s, particularly at the national level,[31] both large-scale membership organizations as well as non-membership groups (foundations, centers, think tanks, and other policy-planning organizations) came to play a more prominent role in American political life.

Although having a mass membership base does not *require* that an organization utilize mass marketing and public relations techniques in order to activate members, it certainly does appear to provide incentives for such action. In large associations, even though members may express strong commitment to the group and many volunteer for the organization, such groups often use telemarketing services to send messages to members and deploy targeted direct mail. It follows that *organizations with a larger membership base will be more likely to hire a grassroots lobbying firm not just because their large member base represents a political asset, but also because with scale comes an increased need for outside, specialized technical assistance.*

It is also reasonable to expect that so-called "associations without members," or "non-membership advocacy organizations," will be quite likely to work with consultants. These are advocacy groups with a paid staff but no individuals or organizations enrolled as members.[32] Such groups depend upon interested individuals who participate in the organization only as financial benefactors or as outside advocates that can be activated in grassroots lobbying campaigns. Therefore, it seems *especially likely that non-membership organizations will hire a grass-roots lobbying firm.* Because these advocacy groups use targeted donor and advocate lists in order to recruit individuals into political participation (primarily into the act of contacting representatives), they may use firms to help create a constituency.

---

[31] Berry (1999).
[32] On such groups, see Walker, McCarthy, and Baumgartner (2011).

Founding cohort

As I described in Chapter 3, not long after the explosion of new advocacy organizations, a variety of organized interests began to focus on mobilizing public activism in lobbying efforts. The activism of the Public Interest Movement – one professionalized from the start, with a heavy focus on employing educated staff in order to shape the content of legislation – helped to make known the power of the media and negative publicity in shaping the action of political institutions.[33] I therefore *expect that organizations founded after 1975 will be most likely to hire a consultant*, because the founding of these advocacy group cohorts were contemporaneous with the rise of grassroots lobbying and the increasing professionalization of this organizational population. As Arthur Stinchcombe once argued, the formative experiences of an organization are likely to have substantial "imprinting" effects on its future actions.[34]

Capital location

Finally, the political emphasis of an association should be a strong predictor not only of an organization's likelihood to engage in inside lobbying, testimony before legislative committees, and campaign contributions, but also the mobilization of rank-and-file members. One of the central means by which an organization attempts to influence political outcomes is by having an office in the nation's capital. Therefore, *I expect that groups with a DC headquarters will be significantly more likely to hire a grassroots consultant*, regardless of the issue area in which a group is active.

Issue focus

Finally, groups interested in mobilizing their members in political action are likely to be those that engage in issues on which public input would be influential in swaying legislative decisions without requiring high levels of specialization or expertise. In addition, organizations active in lobbying are less likely to be those that engage in merely social activity – for example, a local cultural association – and more likely to engage in

---

[33] Vogel (1989).   [34] Stinchcombe (1965).

issues with broader political implications, such as those regarding public affairs, social welfare, health, and environmental quality. It was in
these issue areas that many of the new, professionalized interest organizations became active, amplifying the voices of a variety of Americans
formerly excluded from group representation.[35] It follows that I *expect
groups involved in the issue areas of public affairs, health, social welfare, and the environment will be more likely to hire a consulting firm
than groups working in other issue areas.*

Findings

Table 6.1 presents the results of a logistic regression model predicting
the likelihood that an advocacy organization will contract with at least
one grassroots public affairs consultant in 2010.[36] I use data from the
Encyclopedia of Associations to identify the population of national
advocacy associations in the US, and all data on the factors that shape
their likelihood of contracting with a consultant are derived from that
data source. Additional details about these models and the measurement of variables are available in Appendix 6.

I use a rare events logistic regression estimator because the outcome is
binary (contracted with a consultant or did not), and because only a
small fraction – 3 percent – of the thousands of national advocacy
organizations in the US hire a consultant. Although this is a small
number, one should not underestimate the importance of this subset
of the US advocacy community. Because of their immense membership
sizes and budgets – grouping this small number of associations together,
they have a combined membership of nearly 150 million[37] and an
aggregate budget of $7.86 billion – their work with consultants is
nonetheless a substantial force in American politics.

The results in Model 1 (left) of Table 6.1 provide modest support for
most of the expectations outlined above. The most statistically significant effects in the model include three factors in particular: resources
(budget), professionalization (staff size), and whether the organization

---

[35] Berry (1997); see also Walker (1991).
[36] A logit estimator was employed because the dependent variable was collapsed
into a binary; it was relatively rare for an association to appear on more than one
firm's client list.
[37] Of course, many individuals are members of multiple organizations, so this figure
is not directly applicable as a proportion of the US population.

Table 6.1 *Rare event logistic regression of hiring a consultant by an advocacy organization*

Variable	Model 1		Model 2	
	Coef.	Robust S.E.	Coef.	Robust S.E.
Resources and professionalization				
Budget (logged)	0.437**	(0.136)	0.518***	(0.092)
Staff (logged)	0.501**	(0.147)	0.291**	(0.107)
Federated structure				
Regional chapters (dummy)	0.259	(0.320)	0.185	(0.277)
State chapters (dummy)	0.762**	(0.283)	1.060***	(0.240)
Local chapters (dummy)	−0.492+	(0.280)	−0.151	(0.282)
Membership size/structure				
Members (logged)	0.171**	(0.061)	–	–
Non-membership org. (dummy)	–	–	−0.316	(0.339)
Founding cohort				
Founded 1976–1985 (dummy)	0.014	(0.378)	0.139	(0.297)
Founded 1986–1995 (dummy)	0.109	(0.793)	−0.034	(0.639)
Capitol location				
Washington, DC headquarters (dummy)	1.038**	(0.300)	1.133***	(0.245)
Issue area				
Educational	0.415	(1.134)	0.944	(1.085)
Environmental	1.945*	(0.975)	1.984+	(1.036)
Governmental	1.817+	(0.985)	1.800+	(1.049)
Health/medical	1.997*	(0.913)	1.934+	(0.991)
Public affairs	2.646**	(0.952)	2.599**	(1.000)
Religious	0.453	(1.262)	0.174	(1.395)
Social welfare	1.938*	(0.963)	1.458	(1.027)
Constant	−14.999***	(1.926)	−14.203***	(1.455)
N	2738		3628	

Significance levels: $^+ p \leq .10$; $^* p \leq .05$; $^{**} p \leq .01$; $^{***} p \leq .001$

has a Washington, DC headquarters. More specifically, these effects translate to notably higher rates of contracting for organizations with each of these characteristics: each additional 20 percent increase in budget leads to an 8 percent increase in contracting, each 20 percent increase in staff size is associated with a 10 percent increase, and organizations with a DC headquarters are nearly three times as likely as those outside the District to hire a consultant. Contracting advocacy groups have median budgets approximately fourteen times the median budget of non-contracting groups, and staff sizes around eight times larger. Above all else, then, contracting with consultants is most common among advocacy groups that are professionalized, exceptionally well resourced, and Washingtonbased, thus lending further support to the suggestion by Bill Hoover at the start of this chapter about the importance of funding and professionalism.

Other factors also have a significant effect on contracting with consultants. In particular, an organization's membership size matters quite considerably. The logistic regression estimates in Model 1 of Table 6.1 show that each additional 20 percent increase in membership size is associated with a statistically significant 3 percent increase in contracting. This finding suggests that contracting is concentrated among organizations with exceptionally large membership sizes, and is further confirmed by the fact that although non-contracting advocacy organizations have median memberships of 775, the comparable figure for contracting organizations is nearly thirty times larger, at 23,000.

Model 2, however, shows that non-membership organizations – policy-planning organizations, institutes, think tanks, and similar organizations that are dominated by paid staff and lack any membership in the usual sense – are no more or less likely to contract with consultants. Although a variety of non-membership advocacy organizations do contract with consultants – ranging from conservative groups like the American Family Foundation, Heritage Foundation, and the National Right to Work Legal Defense Foundation to progressive groups like Children's Defense Fund, NAACP Legal Defense and Education Fund, and Families USA Foundation – being a non-membership group is not systematically related to hiring a consultant. This reinforces a finding of my earlier study with John McCarthy and Frank Baumgartner: that there is a well-established division of labor in the broader advocacy community between non-membership groups and more traditional member-based associations.[38] Non-membership groups leave the mass mobilization activities to membership groups, although they often support the latters' efforts to build public participation. Part of that repertoire of member mobilization by large advocacy groups now includes work with consultants to help win in policy battles.

Returning to the summary findings in Model 1, the results illustrate that groups that are federated and have state (or, to a lesser extent, local) chapters are significantly more likely to hire a firm. Groups with state chapters are, in fact, over twice as likely to hire a consultant, although those with local or regional chapters are no more or less likely to hire a consultant than those without such chapters. Importantly, then, it appears that engagement in *state* politics in particular drives national advocacy groups to hire consultants for assistance in those subnational policy environments. Consultants help advocacy groups with gathering signatures to support or oppose state ballot measures, to lobby state legislatures on issues of interest, and to influence state-level regulatory agencies, in addition to the services they provide to organizations on the federal level.

These models also make clear that advocacy groups active in certain issue areas are much more likely to work with a consultant. Associations active in the areas of public affairs, environment, health and medical issues, and general social welfare are much more likely to be involved than the reference category (cultural organizations), and I find a weak effect for groups that represent governmental interests. Educational, religious, and governmental organizations are not significantly more likely than cultural organizations to engage the services of a consultant.

Lastly, the results in Model 1 illustrate that an organization's founding cohort is not systematically related to its likelihood of working with a consultant. Organizations founded during the peak period of the "advocacy explosion" are not any more or less likely to work with a consultant, and this finding is robust to alternative model specifications.[39] Thus, although Chapter 3 illustrated that public affairs

---

[38] Walker, McCarthy, and Baumgartner (2011).
[39] The model was also estimated using dummy variables for additional cohorts, and was alternatively estimated using a continuous measure of organizational age. None of these variables were significant in either specification.

consulting expanded considerably in the years following the vast expansion of advocacy organizations in the 1970s and 1980s, associations founded during this period are not significantly more likely to work with consultants than groups founded before this period. The factors that seem to matter more involve resources, professionalization, membership size, and a focus on federal and/or state-level policy within particular issue domains.

Conclusion

This chapter started by suggesting that although corporations are not typically structured for grassroots advocacy and require the boundary-spanning services offered by public affairs consultants, advocacy organizations have less need for consultants because they can utilize their own in-house structures. However, as shown in Chapter 4, advocacy groups still represent nearly one out of every five clients for the average consulting firm, and also represent a roughly proportional share of consultants' revenue. Thus, although most advocacy groups will not need to work with consultants, certain (typically very large and well resourced) advocacy organizations do. And, as illustrated at the start of this chapter, in the cases of Crossroads Campaign Soultions and Shirley & Banister Public Affairs, some consulting firms are playing an important and active role in the progressive and conservative movements in the contemporary United States.

Taking a systematic look at which national advocacy associations appear on their client lists, the evidence in this chapter revealed that consultants seem to complement the member mobilization strategies of advocacy groups. Although only a fraction of groups hire consultants, they represent many of the very largest advocacy organizations in the United States. Consultants are significantly more likely to be hired by advocacy groups that are more professionalized, well resourced, and have a sizable body of members. In addition, groups that have state chapters, are Washington based, and those that are active on the issues of social welfare, public affairs, health, and environment are all significantly more likely to hire a consultant. Advocacy groups with only a professional staff and no members – so-called "associations without members" – are no more or less likely to hire a consultant than traditional membership groups.

The findings of this chapter, then, indicate that consultants complement the work of advocacy organizations rather than replacing their member-mobilization capacities. My investigations of the client lists of consultants as well as my interviews with them indicate that consultants are often called upon when groups need to reach beyond their existing membership base, often either to target specific demographic groups and/or to manage coalitions and partnerships with other organizations. They often do so using strategies and data provided by the staff and members of advocacy groups themselves. In many ways, then, their work represents the next step in the professionalization of social movements and grassroots organizing.

PART III

Outcomes

7 | *Participatory and policy impacts*

Introduction

The preceding chapters have developed an account of how civic and political change made possible the development of the field of public mobilization consultants. But while the evidence assembled thus far shows rather clearly that a market has indeed developed for these services and that these consultants are used widely by diverse organizations, the account has thus far left aside the question of the *effectiveness* of these campaigns in both mobilizing the public and also in generating policy change. Although the prevalence of these practices provides some indication that these grassroots campaigns are *seen* as effective, it remains possible that, like many other well-established organizational practices,[1] usage is decoupled from efficacy. That is, organizations often adopt practices believed to be effective even when they may be fruitless or even counterproductive.

Studies by scholars of social movements and organized advocacy draw attention to a variety of factors that tend to be influential in the mobilization and policy outcomes of grassroots campaigns: the resources that groups can bring to bear, their skill in making alliances with policy elites, and their ability to carefully craft and frame their message. Although these factors tend to be applied to informal citizen advocacy groups and those who lack routine access through existing channels of policy influence, I argue in this chapter that many of the same explanations can be applied to "grassroots for hire" campaigns in which elite political consultants target key public audiences for mobilization on behalf of their paying clients.[2]

---

[1] Meyer and Rowan (1977); Tolbert and Zucker (1983).
[2] Jeffrey Haydu (1999) makes a similar argument about elite counter-mobilization in his study of employers' strategic responses to unions in the late nineteenth century. See also Useem and Zald (1982).

However, there is one key difference in the effectiveness of consultant-driven campaigns as opposed to those organized by citizen groups on their own: the ability to mobilize displays of support from apparently *independent constituencies*. Thus, when a major big-box retailer seeks to open a new grocery and retail outlet in a low-income area despite strong community opposition, no one is surprised when the company's executives make forceful arguments that the new store should be permitted. Mobilization by suppliers and distributors also isn't likely to register much attention. But when public health advocates join the campaign and note that the proposed location is otherwise a "food desert"[3] where local residents lack access to quality food, policy-makers may be more likely to notice. Similarly, displays of support for the company among low-income local residents and small business owners would also seem to suggest a certain breadth of the company's coalition, indicating that those who are not obvious corporate benefi-ciaries are also on board with the company's plans. Such has, in fact, been Wal-Mart's strategy in its effort to open a new store in New York City (as described in Chapter 5).[4] Such strategies are consistent with the expectations of the resource mobilization approach to the study of advocacy, rooted in the classic work of John McCarthy and Mayer Zald.[5] As they suggested, advocacy causes whose primary base is among resource-providing outsiders must often mobilize those in the beneficiary group for strategic legitimating purposes, as the AFL-CIO did when it organized new senior citizen constituencies in favor of Medicare legislation in the 1960s.[6]

As the big-box retailer example above suggests, these seemingly *independent constituencies* are often the disadvantaged, especially in campaigns that are initiated by an elite corporate client. But we know, of course, from bodies of research in sociology and political science that the disadvantaged are uniquely difficult for political organizers to activate.[7] The less educated often lack access to the information

---

[3] See, for example, Cummins and Macintyre (2002).   [4] Olivo (2004).
[5] McCarthy and Zald (1977).   [6] Ibid.: 1215, 1235.
[7] E.g., Schattschneider (1960); Schlozman, Verba, and Brady (2012); Verba, Schlozman, and Brady (1995); Brady, Schlozman, and Verba (1999); Verba (2003).

necessary for participation,[8] those with low incomes are forced to prioritize meeting basic needs over finding the time to become politically active,[9] and racial inequalities also distort civic and political engagement.[10] Knowing this, recruiters for political causes tend to pay disproportionate attention to soliciting the activity of those who are most likely to say "yes" to their requests, and these tend to be those educated and well-resourced individuals already over-represented in the political system.[11] This is the process of supply-side recruitment described in Chapter 2.

Putting these considerations together raises a key question of whether consultant-driven campaigns either prioritize activating independent constituencies (often the disadvantaged), or, by contrast, follow a rational actor strategy and focus on those who are easiest to mobilize (often the advantaged). The consequences of these investigations have implications for whether consultants are promoting further inequality in political representation across the US, or are instead raising up the voice of the disadvantaged. What this chapter shows is that public affairs consultants attempt to optimize by employing *both strategies*. They seek out the likely voters among those who can be framed as independent of their client's interests. They disproportionately target the highly educated, but also seek to expand their client's coalition and make it more diverse. And recall the finding from Chapter 5 that regardless of a company's reputation, firms with more internal diversity are much more likely to take a grassroots approach.

I begin this chapter by using data from the SPAPCO survey to provide some general information on how consultants tend to rate their own effectiveness, in terms of winning campaigns for their clients and mobilizing public participation. These data reveal that above all else, consultants focus on meeting both of the above goals at once: focusing on pre-existing civic activists who represent *independent constituencies* on this particular campaign. They therefore promote civic inequality in some ways but work against it in others.

---

[8] As Verba and colleagues (1995: 433) put it, education is the "prime factor in most analyses of political activity . . . it affects the acquisition of [civic] skills; it channels opportunities for high levels of income and occupation; it places individuals in institutional settings where they can be recruited to political activity; and it fosters psychological and cognitive engagement with politics."
[9] Imig (1996).   [10] E.g., Burns, Schlozman, and Verba (2001: 274–306).
[11] Brady, Schlozman, and Verba (1999); Schlozman, Verba, and Brady (2012).

I continue by describing two campaigns initiated by corporate clients, one of which failed (Working Families for Wal-Mart) and one of which was successful (rail company Canadian National's campaign to acquire another rail line despite fierce resistance). Both of these campaigns sought both policy change and to mobilize popular participation on behalf of the client. Both also developed strategic frames that resonated with key audiences, had some elite allies, brought substantial resources to bear on the problem, and faced organized opposition. However, the Canadian National campaign was successful because the company, with the help of consultants I interviewed, was able to mobilize *independent constituencies* who had an authentic grievance that aligned with the campaign's corporate sponsor. The Wal-Mart campaign failed because it was unable to generate independent participation despite substantial efforts to develop displays of political support among working-class residents, suppliers, and customers. Consistent with what other sociologists have suggested, effective campaigns sponsored by elites often "look very much like the [bottom-up] efforts that they are intended to replicate."[12]

The major implication of these cases is that although elites can generate policy change through social movement-like channels, their ability to do so is constrained, in part, by the independent force of organized civil society. Thus, a major conclusion of this book is that influence mediated by civil society cannot simply be purchased by corporations or others who hire public affairs consultants to win on policy issues.

Ingredients for success in (commercial) grassroots campaigns

Theory and research on social movements and advocacy has drawn attention to a variety of social forces that shape collective actors' capacities both for mounting a campaign and also for winning their goals. It would not, in fact, be a stretch to argue that the evaluation of movement effectiveness has become the dominant strain of sociological research on collective action.[13] And political scientists have long sought answers to the question of how we can know whether interest groups of various types are successful both in setting elite policy

---

[12] McNutt and Boland (2007: 167).   [13] Amenta et al. (2010); Walder (2009).

agendas and in generating policy change.[14] Although not typically applied to paid lobbying, some commentators have begun to pay greater attention to the role of consulting firms, political professionals, and policy elites in helping grassroots advocates to make their case to the public and to policymakers.[15]

Undoubtedly, resources and organization are a major factor in determining the policy influence of any collective actor, from a low-income community organization to a major corporate effort to have a merger approved by regulators. In sociology, resource mobilization theory offers the suggestion that collective action is most likely to be mounted not just on the basis of shared public grievances about an issue, but more in response to the availability of new resources and organization that can be brought to bear on the issue.[16] Thus, funding of issue entrepreneurship is key for giving voice to popular grievances. Those who study interest groups make quite similar arguments about the importance of elite patronage for the vitality of the interest group sector.[17] Patrons tend to have less uncertainty about supporting more professionalized organizations, which may indirectly lead to under-representation for socially disadvantaged groups that are more informal and struggle to win patronage.[18] On the other hand, a detailed recent study of advocacy effectiveness by Frank Baumgartner and colleagues showed that resources are only weakly correlated with policy success.[19]

Organizers also need the policy environment to be poised to give their issue a full hearing.[20] Collective action, even when well funded and thoroughly organized, is likely to be unsuccessful when a movement lacks sympathetic leaders in established positions of power, such as in the leadership of legislatures, regulatory agencies, or the courts.[21] Edwin Amenta and colleagues refer to this as the "political mediation" model of collective action, in which grassroots social movements are dependent upon political insiders to carry their message forward and

---

[14] Baumgartner et al. (2009); Kingdon (1984); Baumgartner and Jones (1993).
[15] Fisher (2006); Skocpol and Williamson (2010); Howard (2006); Kreiss (2012).
[16] McCarthy and Zald (1973, 1977); Jenkins and Eckert (1986); Soule and King (2008); Walker and McCarthy (2010).
[17] Walker (1991); Berry (1997). [18] Ibid.
[19] Baumgartner et al. (2009: 221–232).
[20] Meyer (2004); Amenta et al. (2010). [21] Ibid.

generate policy change.[22] Such opportunities may change depending on shifting configurations of power among political elites, whether the grassroots campaign has elite allies, how strong the opposition is (and whether the opposition can effectively shut off the claims-making of the campaign), and whether grassroots organizers are aware of such opportunities when they exist.[23]

Messaging is also crucial, especially in that advocacy campaigns need to develop a strategic frame that helps to diagnose the problem, offer a solution to that problem, and offer potential activists a compelling account to motivate participation on the issue.[24] Although effective messaging is likely to require resources, organization, and connections to elite political allies,[25] it is clear to many analysts that an advocacy campaign's broader message must resonate with audiences by seeming both credible and salient to activists.[26]

Campaigns organized by consultants need all of these factors to come together. Despite their greater level of professionalization, access to detailed data about likely activists, and backing of a paying sponsor (not to mention the sponsor's local knowledge about the issue and context), consultants nonetheless face many of the concerns of grassroots organizers of all stripes.

However, there is one factor that appears to matter even more when a paying (often elite) sponsor seeks to generate grassroots activism: *the breadth of the coalition that can be activated as a part of the campaign, especially by facilitating the support of audiences who do not appear to have an obviously self-interested motivation for engagement.* That is, in elite-sponsored advocacy campaigns, it becomes especially crucial to signal to the public and to policymakers that the campaign has support among a broad set of constituencies. Although scholars have recognized that the globalization of advocacy and changing character of civil society has encouraged a greater focus on coalition-building among collective actors,[27] the coalitions that elite actors build when seeking to mobilize participation are less well known.[28] Sometimes these coalitions are referred to as coalitions of "Baptists and bootleggers," as in

---

[22] Amenta, Carruthers, and Zylan (1992).
[23] Snow and Soule (2010: 64–86); Meyer and Staggenborg (1996).
[24] Snow et al. (1986); Benford and Snow (2000a).
[25] Ryan and Gamson (2006).   [26] Snow and Benford (1998).
[27] E.g., Van Dyke and McCammon (2010).
[28] But see McCarthy (2005a); Goldstein (1999: 106–124); Kollman (1998: 78–100).

Bruce Yandle's well-known parable; both are interested in restricting alcohol sales on Sunday, but for entirely different reasons. Still, the Baptists provide tacit moral cover for the more profane pecuniary interests of the bootleggers.[29]

The consideration of coalition breadth or *independent constituencies* offers a powerful line of defense for consultants when they are pressed by critical publics about their role in orchestrating a citizen response for a paying client. As discussed in Chapter 4, public affairs consultants are naturally quite sensitive to the concern that their campaigns might be dismissed as mere "astroturf" or ersatz grassroots mobilization. Consultants worry about this accusation and the appearance that their campaigns are subverting representative democracy. As a consultant with one of the most influential firms in the field told me,

People by definition think if you hire a Washington, DC firm, it's astroturf. You know, we're paid shills or whatever the term is. And I don't think that's entirely fair because we're here in Washington, and they're in, say, Michigan. [But] when we make a Michigan coalition, there is a Michigan chairperson, real businesses, [and] real citizens that are the members of that coalition. I think coalition-building is very important.

Given this consideration, and that their clients are often very powerful corporations, trade associations, and advocacy groups, consultants need to have a relatively light touch and build as broad a coalition as possible.

Participatory outcomes: who gets targeted

In order to focus directly on the question of participatory inequality, the SPAPCO survey asked a variety of questions about the types of demographic groups that consultant-driven campaigns target when working on behalf of their paying client. As mentioned earlier, campaigns need to balance the sometimes (but not always) competing concerns of being successful in their requests (quantity) versus establishing a broad coalition of genuine supporters (quality).

---

[29] Yandle (1983); Walker (2012c).

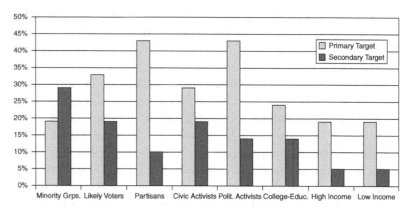

Figure 7.1 Demographic groups targeted in consultants' primary campaign (survey data)

To that end, the survey asked consultants to identify the demographic groups that they focused on mobilizing in their "primary campaign." This is defined as the campaign to which the consultant devoted the greatest amount of effort and resources (on behalf of a client) in the past six years.[30] Consultants were then asked, regarding this leading campaign, which demographic groups they targeted for activism. Respondents were given the option to identify groups as a "primary target," a "secondary target," "not a target," or "don't know." Figure 7.1 shows the percentage of respondents, respectively, who identified each demographic group as either a primary or secondary target.

Coming back to the discussion of supply-side recruitment from Chapter 2, what Figure 7.1 shows most clearly is that consultants, like other types of political recruiters, tend to prioritize those who are most likely to say yes to their requests.[31] Above all else, these citizens are pre-existing political activists and those who are strongly partisan. This partisanship may be on either side of the political spectrum, as Chapter 4 showed that the partisan consultants in the study tend to be distributed approximately evenly between the Democrats and the GOP. Consultants tend to focus on recruiting those who are most likely to say

---

[30] An overview of what distinguishes these primary campaigns was offered in Chapter 4.

[31] Brady, Schlozman, and Verba (1999).

"yes" to their appeals, and having a history of political activism and strong partisan commitments increases the chances that one is likely to acquiesce when a campaign reaches out.[32] This finding also squares nicely with the evidence presented in Chapter 3, which showed that an increasingly partisan public in the US has supported the founding of new public affairs consulting firms.

Figure 7.1 also indicates that public affairs consultants make serious efforts to reach out primarily to likely voters, civic activists, and the college educated, all of which are groups who are already over-represented in the political system. On the other hand, they do not seem to go out of their way to target particular income groups, whether those at the top or at the bottom of the income distribution. Combined, these findings make clear that consulting firms are playing a role in increasing participatory inequality in the US. This is especially signifi-cant, given that the leading campaign by the firms in the sample claims to have reached out to a median estimated 4,000 citizens and mobilized nearly 1,000 of those contacts.

While the bulk of evidence in Figure 7.1 provides support for the participatory inequality thesis, it also shows that campaigns seek a broad coalition. Importantly, nearly half of consultants said that their leading campaign involved either a primary or a secondary effort to target minority groups for participation. And nearly a quarter of con-sultants' main campaigns targeted low-income groups for participation.

As further evidence of the participatory outcomes of campaigns organized by public affairs consultants, Figure 7.2 shows how consul-tants prioritize groups of corporate stakeholders when the client is a company or industry group. Consultants were asked, again about their

---

[32] Brady and colleagues (1999: 157) find, however, that partisanship does not have an effect on requests for participation after controlling for other factors including political efficacy, information, interest, civic skills, education, and income. However, their study focuses on *any* requests received by their survey respondents, and the large majority of requests for participation come from friends, family, neighbors, coworkers, or fellow participants in civic associations (Verba, Schlozman, and Brady, 1995: 144–145). Those recruiters who are less likely to have a pre-existing personal connection to potential activists, such as public affairs consultants, need to rely on other cues that signal an individual's motivation to become active on an issue, such as whether the individual is strongly partisan. My interviews with public affairs consultants provided additional confirmation on this point, as a number of consultants noted that they focus on locating strong partisans on issues like taxation, regulation, or the environment.

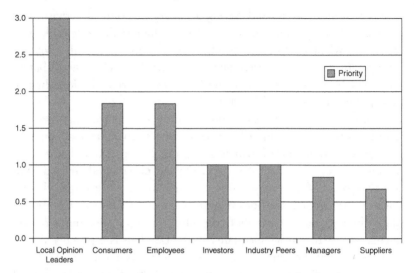

Figure 7.2 Stakeholder groups targeted for participation in corporate-sponsored campaigns (survey data)

most intensive campaign over the past six years, whether each of the following groups was a "top priority" (score of 3), a "medium priority" (2), a "low priority" (1), or "not a priority" (score of 0). The mean scores, by stakeholder type, are presented in Figure 7.2.

Figure 7.2, then, provides additional evidence that both logics of organizing – rational prospecting and broad coalitions – are at work. Consulting firms are called upon by their corporate clients mainly to reach out to the broader public and to generate displays of support by local opinion leaders (described by the industry, as mentioned earlier, as the "grasstops"). In so doing, they try to reach those who are likely to influence others in their communities to support corporate projects, especially those outside the corporation's natural constituency.

Figure 7.2 also shows that consumers and employees are an important target for corporate-backed mobilization. The average consulting firm reported that while local opinion leaders are always a "top" priority, consumers and employees tend to be a "medium" priority for activation. Employees are a particularly important constituency, as management scholar Gerald Keim argues that a firm's workers are a crucial source of grassroots support in defense of a firm or industry.[33]

---

[33] Keim (2005).

They are not quite as significant in displaying the breadth of the coalition as local opinion leaders are, but they appear be placed a rung higher than other corporate constituencies like suppliers, managers, or investors. It is also worth noting, as argued in Chapter 4, that corporate clients often *turn to consultants for that very reason*: that consultants can help companies to reach audiences that might not be accessible through a firm's internal public affairs office.

Policy outcomes: helping the client to win

How often do consultants win for their clients?

The survey asked consultants about three of their most prominent campaigns over the past six years, listed in rank order based on the amount of effort and resources devoted to each campaign. Consultants were asked to rank campaigns on a scale of one to five, in which "1" represents not successful, "3" represents partial success, and "5" represents complete success. However, because these self-reports are subject to social desirability biases and consultants may be less willing to acknowledge devoting substantial resources to a failed campaign, I move beyond these data in the case studies that follow. Despite this concern, the anonymity of each consulting firm in the aggregate data, as well as the fact that the survey did not request that the specific client(s) be identified, should mitigate this limitation somewhat.

Overall, averaging across the three campaigns reported by each consultant, firms reported a mean success score of approximately 3.8. However, consultants varied in their success rate according to where they ranked each of the three campaigns in terms of their own effort and resources. Thus, 76 percent of consultants suggested that their primary campaign was more than a partial success (> 3), 67 percent said the same about their second campaign, and only 40 percent could claim a similar victory in their third campaign.

Campaigns also reported varying levels of success depending on the policy goal of their organizational client. Figure 7.3 breaks down the distribution of consultants' assessments of their success in meeting their client's goal according to the policy target of the campaign. For each of their three leading campaigns, consultants were asked if their client's primary goal was to "influence the outcome of a piece of legislation," "influence the policy of a government agency," "influence citizens'

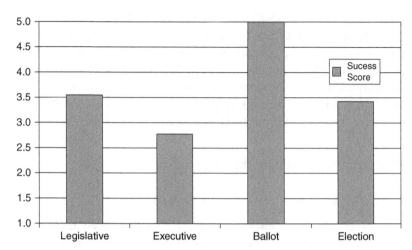

Figure 7.3 Self-reported success of campaigns, by policy goal of client (survey data)

preferences about a ballot measure, initiative, or referendum," or "influence citizens' preferences as voters about a specific candidate for office."[34] Figure 7.3 matches each success score with the client's primary goal for each campaign, and then averages those goal-specific scores across the three campaigns.

What Figure 7.3 shows most clearly is that consultants tend to report the greatest degree of success when working on shaping citizen views of ballot measures. All consultants who worked on ballot measures in one of their three leading campaigns found that they were completely successful in influencing citizen preferences about that ballot measure. Ballot measures are issue-specific and local or statewide, and voter fatigue and informational limitations plague direct democracy;[35] these factors appear to allow consultants to have a substantial influence.[36]

---

[34] Although consultants also work on campaigns that seek to influence citizen sentiments about a particular company (i.e., corporate reputation work) or the decisions of other organizations (e.g., to gain the support of a community organization, or to get another corporation to negotiate more fairly in a contract dispute), Figure 7.3 focuses on the broader public *policy outcomes* of public affairs campaigns (thus using a more restricted set of targets than those found in Figure 4.2).

[35] Bowler, Donovan, and Happ (1992).

[36] Bowler, Donovan, and Fernandez (1996).

Many consultants, in fact, specialize in getting ballot measures *qualified* rather than approved. They rate themselves much more modestly when it comes to shaping citizen opinions about a candidate for office through their grassroots mobilization services. As a consultant with Grassroots Amplifier, Inc.[37] who specializes in ballot measures told me,

[Our company has] such a simple operation ... all of our strategy has to do with just telling [our paid circulators] to keep it short and simple and understand you're not campaigning. You're just telling people, "Hey, your signature just gets you the chance to get this on the ballot." So ... when people say, "I don't know if I'm for that," well, that's OK. All that's gonna happen is that this is on the ballot. As you get more of a chance to get informed and if you're against it later, vote no.

It is also apparent that consultants have only modest success in shaping legislative decisions, and less success in influencing agency decisions. Grassroots organizing around agency decisions, as the Canadian National case below makes clear, can be more difficult. Agency-targeted campaigns are often somewhat restricted in scope due to the relatively narrow time frames of public comment periods,[38] and also because agencies themselves are constrained by the party in control of the White House and/or governorships.[39] It is also worth noting that consultants' campaigns on legislative issues were much more likely to be at the federal level (52 percent) than state (42 percent) or local (6 percent), whereas consultants were more active with agencies at the state level (50 percent) than the federal (21 percent) or local (29 percent) levels.

Lastly, Figure 7.3 illustrates that, despite the fact that a plurality of grassroots consultants got their start in electoral consulting (see Chapter 3), they report only modest success in influencing voters; consultants report slightly less success in this realm than in shaping the outcomes of legislative votes.

Tactical effectiveness

Consultants also vary in the tactics they deploy on behalf of their clients. Consistent with the findings of proprietary reports about the field of public affairs consultants[40] and other studies that have looked at how

---

[37] A pseudonym.   [38] Carpenter et al. (2012).   [39] E.g., Shipan (2004).
[40] Public Affairs Council (2008).

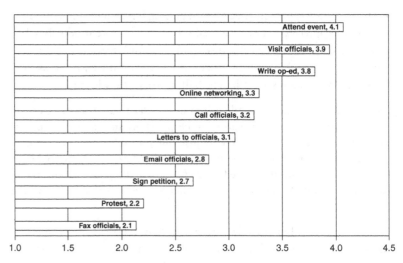

Figure 7.4 Perceived effectiveness of tactics for mobilizing public participation (survey data)

civic and political organizations mobilize public participation,[41] consultants often reported in interviews that they face a trade-off between mobilizing large volumes of participation using low-cost tactics versus smaller volumes of participation using higher-cost tactics. Although it would be appealing if every constituent from a Congressperson's district were willing to fly out for a meeting with their representative, very few are usually willing to bear that high cost.

In order to consider the effectiveness of the various forms of public participation that consultants request of those they target on behalf of their clients, Figure 7.4 displays consultants' evaluations of the effectiveness of each tactic for winning their client's goals, sorted in order of reported effectiveness.

Indeed, the effectiveness scores associated with each tactic do, by and large, fit with the expectation that high-cost tactics are most effective, while low-cost tactics that can be generated at higher volume are less effective. While this would not be surprising to political analysts,[42] it is nonetheless important to recognize that there are certain relatively low-cost tactics that consultants find effective (organizing through Facebook, Twitter, blogs, and other online networks, writing op-eds

[41] Kollman (1998); Lord (2003).   [42] See Kollmann (1998: Ch. 3).

in newspapers) and also that some higher-cost tactics are seen as less effective, at least when facilitated by consultants (such as protest). Tried-and-true high-cost methods of in-person participation – such as meeting with public officials or attending public events – are among the most effective, and low-cost mediated forms that can be generated at high volume (emailing, faxing, petitioning) are the least. The volume of such mediated communications to policymakers has ballooned in the past decade,[43] forcing leaders to turn to computer scientists to help them to aggregate the data from such messages and also raising new questions about the authenticity of communications.[44] As the consultants with Williamson Strategists described in Chapter 4, policymakers also find electronic mass communication less trustworthy.

Understanding campaign effectiveness

Introduction

In order to further unpack these findings and to provide practical examples of what makes for a successful public affairs campaign, the remainder of this chapter examines in depth two cases of grassroots mobilization on behalf of a paying corporate client. Both cases involved a client facing strong organized resistance, and in each case the client also had powerful elite allies and substantial resources to expend. The difference between success and failure, as I explain, had to do with the breadth of the campaign's coalition, especially among audiences seen as independent of the paying client.

Ineffective without a broad coalition: Working Families for Wal-Mart

2005 was a particularly difficult year for Wal-Mart, despite being able to open over 150 new retail outlets in the US.[45] The company's stock price was in serious decline, such that Wal-Mart's market value

---

[43] See the following reports issued by the staff of the Congressional Management Foundation: Fitch and Goldschmidt (2005); Goldschmidt and Ochreiter (2008).
[44] Shulman (2006, 2009). [45] Wal-Mart (2005, 2006).

dropped 17.3 percent between fiscal years 2003 and 2005.[46] A former executive at the firm was ousted from the board of directors after an internal investigation uncovered that he had misused nearly a half-million dollars of corporate funds.[47] The company's attempt to enter the online DVD rental market was declared a failure and abandoned.[48] And negative attention to the firm was mounting. For example, reports were surfacing that 46 percent of the children of Wal-Mart's employees were either uninsured or on Medicaid.[49] On top of all of this, in October 2005 an internal memo to the firm's board by Wal-Mart's Executive Vice President for Benefits was leaked, suggesting that the company was actively searching for innovative ways to hold down spending on employee healthcare, such as by discouraging unhealthy job applicants by requiring physical activity for most positions (including for cashiers).[50] As *New Yorker* columnist Jeffrey Goldberg summarized it when looking back at that period,

The company has had its bright moments, most notably in the immediate aftermath of Hurricane Katrina, when Wal-Mart mobilized its truck fleet to deliver goods to the storm zone. But that was a rare instance of good public relations. Owing in part to its status as a retail behemoth, Wal-Mart has met with resistance in numerous communities (including New York City) when it has tried to open stores. And its recent business performance has been less than stellar; sales have slowed, and the stock price is stagnant. Problems like these have concentrated the minds of Lee Scott, Wal-Mart's C.E.O., and his top executives. "We used to be the David and now we're seen as the Goliath," John Fleming, the company's chief merchandising officer, told me.[51]

It was also the year in which the United Food and Commercial Workers (UFCW) International Union launched its Wake Up Wal-Mart campaign, hoping to move beyond attempting to unionize employees and focusing instead on developing a broad-based corporate campaign against the firm. Such "name and shame" strategies against firms are common among contemporary US labor organizers, reacting to the relatively hostile environment for organized labor today.[52] The idea

---

[46] Data were derived from my calculations using S&P's COMPUSTAT data file. Wal-Mart's market value was $232.15 billion in FY2003, compared to $192.05 billion in FY2005.
[47] Barbaro (2005).   [48] Hansell (2005).
[49] Greenhouse and Barbaro (2005d).   [50] Ibid.   [51] Goldberg (2007).
[52] Manheim (2000); Martin (2008).

behind the campaign was to enlist not only the support of labor advocates and frustrated employees, but environmentalists, small business owners, and local community stakeholders worried about big-box retailers.[53] Further fuel was thrown on the fire for UFCW's organizing with the allegation by a former executive that the firm was paying individuals to "keep tabs on organizing activity in Wal-Mart stores,"[54] and the company closed a Quebec store after its employees unionized.

UFCW's efforts were complemented by a parallel effort organized with the backing of the Service Employees International Union (SEIU), which called itself Wal-Mart Watch. Wal-Mart Watch was established with the SEIU president Andrew Stern and a Sierra Club director as key members of its board of directors, operating effectively as a project of the SEIU.[55] Stern and labor leader Anna Burger had only months earlier helped to lead the SEIU's effort, along with six other unions, to break away from the AFL-CIO by forming the Change to Win Coalition. Consistent with the focus of Change to Win on developing broad-based campaigns to challenge corporate reputations, Wal-Mart Watch brought together diverse organizational partners including Sojourners, American Independent Business Association, National Council of Women's Organizations, Sierra Club, Teamsters, and, at times, also the UFCW.[56] Still, Wal-Mart Watch operated independently of SEIU, with its own thirty-six employees, fourteen of whom were active in field organizing as of 2005.[57] Wal-Mart Watch was the campaign that secured the leaked memo about the company pushing out unhealthy workers.[58]

Comparing the two, the UFCW campaign (Wake Up Wal-Mart) was widely seen as the more aggressive, as it was involved not just in organizing constituencies but also running television ads, holding a national protest bus tour in 2006, and gaining endorsements by latter-day Democratic presidential candidates Barack Obama and John Edwards.[59] Although these two campaigns would eventually join together in 2009, for the most part each was independent of the other during the peak years of contention against Wal-Mart starting in 2004.[60] In fact, these separate campaigns often ran into disagreements with one another over tactics and whether to applaud particular Wal-Mart decisions, such as the company's 2006 expansion of healthcare benefits to new groups of employees.

[53] Spence (2005).   [54] Barbaro (2005).   [55] Higgins (2005).
[56] Armour (2005).   [57] Ibid.   [58] Mui (2007).
[59] AFX International Focus (2007a).   [60] PR Newswire (2009).

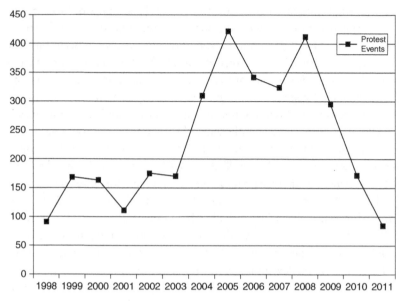

Figure 7.5 Protests against Wal-Mart, 1998–2011

Beyond the UFCW and SEIU campaigns, protests by diverse community stakeholders against Wal-Mart were also picking up steam at the same time. Figure 7.5, which uses data from the advocacy group Sprawl-Busters (which tracks protests against Wal-Mart and has been used in studies in the leading journals in sociology),[61] shows the trend in protests against Wal-Mart from 1998 to 2011. Using this data source, it is clear that protests against Wal-Mart increased 81 percent between 2003 and 2004, and an additional 36 percent between 2004 and 2005. The year 2005, in fact, represented the peak period of anti-Wal-Mart protests over the past fourteen years.[62]

Wal-Mart's response

What was the company to do under these circumstances? Consistent with earlier arguments (especially in Chapter 5), Wal-Mart found that reputational challenges, protest, and corporate controversies put them in a position to engage in grassroots mobilization that showed that they

---

[61] Ingram, Yue, and Rao (2010); Rao, Yue, and Ingram (2011).
[62] Zimmerman (2006).

have a broad coalition of support and can mobilize stakeholders in force to defend the company. But, also like other campaigns, they found that they couldn't do this on their own, especially when trying to reach beyond the company's natural allies. They needed the support of community opinion leaders, and especially those seen as concerned about local small businesses and the interests of working Americans.

At Wal-Mart's 2005 annual meeting, CEO Lee Scott sought to frame the company as embattled and facing a resourceful opposition. He said that Wal-Mart "is the focus of one of the most well-organized and well-financed corporate campaigns in history ... A coalition of unions and others are spending over $25 million this year alone to try to do damage to this company."[63] Shortly thereafter, the company's executives heard pitches from three public affairs consulting firms: Edelman, APCO Worldwide, and DCI Group.[64] Edelman's winning pitch suggested that the effort would be a

campaign with all the trappings of a US presidential bid. A war room of publicists would respond quickly to attacks or adverse news. Operatives would be assigned to drum up popular support for Wal-Mart via internet blogs and grass-roots initiatives. Skeptical outside groups, such as environmentalists, would be recruited to team up with Wal-Mart. Edelman won and quickly put its plan into practice, with three dozen staffers working on the account in Washington, DC, and Bentonville.[65]

Thus was born, six months later, Working Families for Wal-Mart (WFW), with the support of the massive public affairs and PR consulting firm Edelman (although Edelman's role in WFW was not initially disclosed). In fact, the effort was meant to appear, in part, independent of Wal-Mart. The first reports about Working Families for Wal-Mart started to emerge in December 2005, when it was announced that

With backing from Wal-Mart Stores Inc., a group of community leaders – from clergy to Latino activists to businesswomen – announced the formation Tuesday of a national group to speak up for the world's largest retailer and launch counterattacks when they sense criticism is unfair. The steering committee of 16 people, *partially funded by Wal-Mart*, organized Working Families for Wal-Mart, whose job will be to talk about what they see as Wal-Mart's positive contributions [...] Wal-Mart is the largest financial backer of the group, company spokeswoman Sarah Clark said. Neither the

[63] Hudson (2006).   [64] Ibid.   [65] Ibid.

company nor group leaders would disclose how much Bentonville, Arkansas-based Wal-Mart is contributing to the effort.[66]

The Working Families for Wal-Mart campaign's key spokesperson and central steering committee member was Bishop Ira Combs Jr., an outspoken Republican activist and African-American leader of the Greater Bible Way Temple of the Apostolic Faith in Jackson, Michigan.[67] Combs claimed that neither Wal-Mart nor WFW were compensating him for his work on behalf of the organization.[68] However, half of the steering committee members had at least some financial ties, whether direct or indirect, to the firm.[69]

Other steering committee members included singer Pat Boone, conservative economist Charles Baird, Rep. Jennifer Carroll (R-FL), and Ron Galloway, director of a pro-Wal-Mart documentary film, as well as other diverse leaders.[70] These leaders often played the role of front-line defenders of the firm, especially for its contributions in low-income and minority communities. As Rep. Carroll – who also claimed that she wasn't being paid by WFW – put it, "Wal-Mart is ... proactive in hiring African-Americans," and she noted that the company was named one of the Top 25 companies by *Black Professionals Magazine* in 2005.[71]

The campaign also kept former White House spokesman Taylor Gross on staff, who was known for his efforts to coordinate media coverage for the Republican Party during the 2000 presidential election dispute in Florida and who is himself a consultant with the public affairs firm The Herald Group.[72] In February 2006, WFW announced that its campaign would be directed by former Civil Rights Movement leader, UN ambassador, and Atlanta mayor Andrew Young, who became the group's key spokesman.[73] Although Young also claimed that he was not being compensated, he acknowledged that his nonprofit organization Goodworks International, which pairs corporations and governments to work on global issues, was the recipient of a Wal-Mart contract for an undisclosed amount.[74] Young claimed, "I like to fight poverty ... For almost ten years, I've been using in my sermons the

---

[66] Kabel (2005), emphasis added.   [67] Associated Press (2005).   [68] Ibid.
[69] Barbaro (2006a).
[70] An archived version of the Working Families for Wal-Mart website, which includes full biographies for all steering committee members, is available here: http://web.archive.org/web/20060110112339/http://www.forwalmart.com/about_steering.php.
[71] Karkaria (2005).   [72] Associated Press (2005).   [73] Kabel (2006a).   [74] Ibid.

message that fighting poverty is good business, and I've used Wal-Mart as an example. The question is how do you fight poverty – with high wages or low prices? The answer is both."[75] Young's new position alienated many of his friends and supporters.[76]

Those on the left of the political spectrum, like Young, were core players at the top of WFW's organizing and PR efforts. Although the large majority of Wal-Mart's campaign contributions prior to 2007 went to Republicans, Democratic campaign strategists were at the heart of Wal-Mart's efforts to defend itself in 2005 and 2006.[77] Wal-Mart's Executive Vice President for Corporate Affairs and Government Relations, Leslie Dach, was a top staffer for both the Edward Kennedy and Michael Dukakis presidential campaigns, respectively, in 1980 and 1988,[78] as well as one of former President Clinton's advisors during the impeachment process.[79] Edelman executive Fred Baldassaro, a former lead aide to Howard Dean, served as a Wal-Mart strategist during this time.[80] Going out on a limb, Wal-Mart chief spokesperson Mona Williams claimed that the company "is taking care of the people the Democratic Party says it represents – the poor, the middle class. The Democrats are not taking care of them. We're like Lyndon Johnson's Great Society."[81]

WFW took a broad-based approach to fighting back against those the firm saw as a threat to its operations by marshaling research, organizing online at ForWalMart.com, canvassing in communities, and attacking both the ideas and the characters of those involved in anti-Wal-Mart activism. In January 2006, the group began releasing results of a poll, done by a nonpartisan polling firm, showing that 71 percent of US adults had favorable sentiments toward the company (a figure roughly matched by a contemporaneous Pew poll), and that even 63 percent of union households felt similarly.[82] In the state of Maryland, where Wal-Mart was threatened by the 2005 Fair Share Health Care Act – a piece of legislation also known informally as the "Wal-Mart Bill" because it would have required firms with more than 10,000 workers in the state to spend at least 8 percent of their payroll on employee health benefits – WFW issued press releases charging hypocrisy on the part of union activists who made substantial campaign contributions to legislative

---

[75] Saporta (2006).   [76] Geewax (2006a).   [77] Goldberg (2007).
[78] Ibid.; Kabel (2006b).   [79] Barbaro (2006b).   [80] Goldberg (2007).
[81] Ibid.   [82] Connolly (2006).

supporters of the act.[83] WFW started a state-level chapter in Colorado in March 2006,[84] followed shortly thereafter by Michigan, California, Ohio, and Indiana.[85] In April 2006, with the support of Republican-affiliated public affairs consulting firm Crosslink Strategy Group, WFW began canvassing Atlanta and Denver-area Wal-Mart shoppers asking for their contact information for WFW's outreach databases.[86] Shoppers who were interviewed suggested that they were not informed that the company was, in large part, funding the WFW operation.[87]

The core of WFW's campaign was to mobilize not only Wal-Mart's shoppers as members of the campaign – by May 2006 the campaign claimed to have 100,000 members across the US – but also the company's suppliers.[88] WFW sent a letter to suppliers stating that "Wal-Mart is under attack, and Wal-Mart and Sam's Club suppliers have the power to do something about it and help protect their businesses."[89] Responding to the concern that WFW's effort to mobilize suppliers amounted to unfair pressure – they might justifiably fear that the company could refuse to sell their product if they didn't join the campaign – the company responded that participation was strictly voluntary.[90]

By the summer and early fall of 2006, the rhetoric became sharper on both sides. Wal-Mart began to encourage its employees to vote against candidates who spoke out at anti-Wal-Mart rallies in the upcoming election.[91] Also, after Wal-Mart Watch took out a full-page ad in the *New York Times* in May 2006, WFW issued a statement saying, "Americans have to question why the same union leaders who are failing to address diversity, transparency, accountability and sustainability in their own organizations are spending millions of dollars in union dues attacking a company that is committed to these principles and creates tens of thousands of jobs per year."[92]

Matters became even more heated as WFW started a website, PaidCritics.com, dedicated to making personal attacks on anti-Wal-Mart activists.[93] Typical web entries on the PaidCritics.com blog suggested that these activists were interested in denying jobs to local communities, insinuating that specific organizers were enjoying lavish

---

[83] PR Newswire (2006a).   [84] Arellano (2006).
[85] PR Newswire (2006b, 2006c, 2006d, 2006e).   [86] Geewax (2006b).
[87] Ibid.   [88] Barbaro (2006a).   [89] Ibid.   [90] Ibid.
[91] PR Newswire (2006f).   [92] Geewax (2006c).
[93] AFX International Focus (2006a).

lifestyles, and predicting that the campaign is likely to backfire given that the company is so popular.[94] But even Ron Galloway, a leading member of the WFW steering committee and maker of a pro-Wal-Mart documentary, suggested that this was a step too far.[95]

Things began to take a turn against WFW toward the end of 2006 with a wave of resignations. First, Andrew Young was forced to resign his leadership position in WFW after making racially insensitive remarks.[96] Then, the same week, steering committee member Herman Cain suggested that Democratic critics of Wal-Mart were operating in a fashion akin to Hezbollah in their attempts to improve access to affordable healthcare for employees.[97] WFW was forced to back away from its defense of Cain, arguing that the comments were strictly his own.[98] In October, Ron Galloway quit WFW in protest.[99] Only days later, Republican consultant and WFW leader Terry Nelson was forced to resign after his firm aired ads against Tennessee Senate candidate Harold Ford, which were widely seen as racially offensive.[100]

The negative turn of events continued with a new WFW-sponsored effort, the Wal-Marting Across America RV tour,[101] which was later exposed as not only funded by Wal-Mart but hosted by individuals with personal connections to the firm and to Edelman.[102] The idea behind the tour was that two WFW supporters named Jim and Laura would drive an RV from Nevada to Georgia, parking at Wal-Mart stores along the way and signing up new volunteers for WFW.[103] As Laura put it, "Many RVers choose to make Wal-Mart an essential part of their travels ... Throughout the tour we will highlight the stories of these RVers and everyday working families that depend on Wal-Mart."[104] Jim and Laura's blog entries were unfailingly positive about employee experiences at the company.

Only a few weeks later, Jim's identity was revealed to be Jim Thresher, a *Washington Post* photographer who was not authorized to conduct freelance work and was told to remove his entries from WalMartingAcrossAmerica.com.[105] Laura was determined to be

---

[94] The PaidCritics.com blog is archived at http://web.archive.org/web/20060819175415/http://paidcritics.com/.
[95] AFX International Focus (2006a).   [96] PR Newswire (2006g).
[97] PR Newswire (2006h).   [98] Poole (2006).
[99] AFX International Focus (2006b).   [100] Geewax (2006d).
[101] PR Newswire (2006i).   [102] Gogoi (2006).   [103] PR Newswire (2006i).
[104] Ibid.   [105] Miller (2006).

Laura St. Claire, a freelance writer with a position in the federal government who came up with the RV tour idea, then approached her brother, an Edelman employee, about WFW sponsorship.[106] Widely discredited, the RV tour has since become a well-known cautionary tale for those who engage in less than transparent uses of social media in advocacy campaigns.[107]

The outcome

The outing of the RV campaign as a Wal-Mart-sponsored PR effort led to fallout for both the firm and also for Edelman, which was revealed as the mastermind behind the WFW campaign in the first place.[108] By the end of 2006, journalist Marilyn Geewax, who had followed the campaign from its outset, argued, "again and again, WFWM's public relations efforts backfired."[109] This happened in part because of union activists' efforts to monitor the company's every move, but even more so because of the company's efforts to avoid disclosure of its role and the campaign's inability to develop an independent constituency.

By March 2007, WFW suspended its controversial PaidCritics.com blog.[110] Later that year, Wal-Mart announced that it was suspending WFW and folding it into the company's in-house PR operation.[111] The company then announced sweeping changes to its employee health plans, and the most severe criticism and protest of the firm died down.[112] Wal-Mart apparently stopped fighting and started listening to its critics.[113] At the same time that the firm's financial performance improved, it wound down its internal "war room" as well.[114] The company began to focus less on politics and more on voluntary Corporate Social Responsibility (CSR) initiatives.[115]

The Working Families for Wal-Mart campaign makes clear that "grassroots for hire" campaigns are ineffective without a broad coalition of genuine support in civil society. Although quite well resourced and with powerful elite allies from business, elected office, and the voluntary sector, the campaign was largely ineffective in generating favorable political support for Wal-Mart.

---

[106] Kurtz (2006).   [107] Goh (2007).   [108] Rubin (2006).
[109] Geewax (2006e).   [110] AFX International Focus (2007b).
[111] Kabel (2007).   [112] Barbaro (2008).   [113] Foley (2008a).
[114] Foley (2008b).   [115] Foley (2008a).

Successful with a broad coalition: Canadian National and suburban activists

The Working Families for Wal-Mart campaign, which was waged in response to community and labor contention, was unsuccessful because the firm was not able to generate the authentic and independent support of a broad coalition. They relied too heavily on suppliers, who felt unduly pressured by the retail behemoth. They had the resources, elite support, and had built some limited organizational infrastructure needed in order to mount their campaign, but they were limited by the independent force of civil society.

But what happens when a firm faces a major controversy about its practices but is more effective in mobilizing the authentic support of *independent constituencies*? The following case shows how consultant-driven grassroots campaigns can be successful in shaping participatory and policy outcomes. The key to victory is to build a broad base of support among those stakeholders who have an interest in the campaign independent of the client's financial and/or political interests; also needed is transparency by the consulting firm about their client's identity, as well as a multi-pronged approach that creatively applies a diverse set of tactics for mobilizing public support.

The case

Railroad company Canadian National (CN), a firm previously under the control of the Canadian government but which was privatized and restructured as a publicly traded firm in 1995,[116] has made major moves to expand its US holdings in the nearly two decades since. Buoyed by the increase in US–Canadian trade following the 1994 enactment of the North American Free Trade Agreement (NAFTA) as well as the increasing appeal of rail for transporting imports from Asia, the firm acquired, in rapid succession, a variety of US rail lines.[117] Although these acquisitions faced some resistance, the company's US expansion continued to press forward without very many substantial hiccups along the way.[118]

---

[116] Hallman (1995).   [117] Market News Publishing (2005).

[118] However, there were exceptions, such as when the city of Chicago sought to block CN's purchase of the Illinois Central Railroad because CN refused to stop using a controversial lakefront track in the city (Tita, 2007).

The same could not be said of the challenges faced by the firm in its next planned acquisition. In October 2007, CN announced its intent to purchase the Elgin, Joliet, and Eastern Railway (EJ&E) from US Steel's Transtar subsidiary,[119] at a cost of approximately $300 million.[120] The US government estimates that around one-third of all freight in the US passes through Chicago's rail lines,[121] and CN's existing Chicagoland holdings forced the company to route its trains primarily through grid-locked central Chicago rail lines. The idea behind the purchase was to re-route many of these trains around the city center on EJ&E's tracks that ring the city and run through suburban areas.[122] Overall, CN projected in early 2008 that thirty-four Chicago-area towns would see increased rail traffic, whereas eighty other localities would see a decline.[123] The approval of the purchase would also offer a partial solution to the city's fraught debate about whether taxpayer funds should be used to build additional tracks to relieve the congestion.[124]

Despite these benefits to many Chicago areas and to the company, and to the company's surprise, the announcement galvanized an almost immediate response of livid community protest. While the approximately 200 miles of EJ&E rail line holdings were used only lightly prior to 2007, their acquisition by CN could mean a substantial increase in the number of freight trains passing through the backyards of many suburban communities.[125] Recognizing the potential for a significant increase, suburban activists began organizing against the purchase soon after the announcement.[126] As a geographer described the dispute, CN's "opponents framed their protest in terms of a *foreign* railroad disrupting *American* communities, suggesting deeper underlying concerns about the transnational nature of the transaction."[127]

CN announced that it planned to increase the number of daily freight trains using the EJ&E stretch from five to about twenty; community activists worried that this could pick up to a volume far higher. Suburban activists, then, with the support of municipal government leaders, formed a coalition in November known as Barrington Communities against CN Rail Congestion, named after the village in Illinois where aggrieved citizens were most organized.[128] The EJ&E line

---

[119] Brooks (2007a); Associated Press (2007).   [120] *Globe & Mail* (2007).
[121] Surface Transportation Board (2008).   [122] Deveau (2007).
[123] Pyke (2008a).   [124] Tita (2007).   [125] Associated Press (2007).
[126] Deveau (2007).   [127] Cidell (2012); emphases in original.
[128] Deveau (2007); Pyke (2008a).

runs directly through Barrington and crosses through eight roads in the village,[129] three of which are within one mile of one another.[130] In Barrington's official regulatory filing against the deal, the city said that it felt forced to oppose the deal in order to protect the city's "beauty, character, and protected open spaces."[131] The acquisition also faced another immediate roadblock when the federal Surface Transportation Board (STB) announced that it would need to complete a thorough environmental review of the proposal, which could delay the deal by more than eighteen months.[132]

Federal regulators began to hold a series of public hearings on the EJ&E purchase during the early months of 2008, many of which became quite heated.[133] At a meeting on January 10, over 1,000 local residents packed the meeting space of the Makray Memorial Golf Club. Members of the federal Surface Transportation Board heard comments suggesting that the deal's approval would "cripple an entire community," that road closures due to train crossings could be the difference between life and death for those serviced by local fire departments, and similar concerns were voiced about ambulance delays.[134] Community activists noted that many of these long freight trains clog surface crossings for up to six minutes each, putting first responders in a dire situation.[135] Residents also worried about noise. Such imminent threats, sociological research suggests,[136] are quite significant in mobilizing Not-In-My-Backyard (NIMBY) opposition to local environmental "bads," and the citizens in Barrington and surrounding communities decided it was time to take action. And so-called "site fights" like these have, for good reason, drawn increasing attention from sociologists and political scientists.[137]

Forums held in other communities beyond Barrington were also venues for expressing popular frustrations about the impending deal. In a West Chicago hearing, a resident told regulators, "I love living in Bartlett [Illinois], but the train is already a sore spot ... I just want to find out all I can to help stop this project from happening."[138] The mayor of Lake Zurich, IL, argued that if the deal did go through, Canadian National should be forced to pay financial compensation to

[129] Brooks (2007b).   [130] Deveau (2007).   [131] Jang (2007).
[132] Deveau (2007).   [133] Pyke (2008a).   [134] Brooks (2008a).
[135] Deveau (2007).   [136] Benford, Moore, and Williams (1993).
[137] Aldrich (2010); McAdam and Boudet (2012).   [138] Komperda (2008).

impacted communities.[139] Concerns like these were also voiced among a number of Indiana communities in similarly contentious town-hall meetings.[140] In total, over 2,500 local citizens attended public hearings in Illinois and Indiana throughout January 2008.[141]

As the battle raged on, federal legislators started to get into the mix. Sen. Richard Durbin (D-IL) issued a public statement acknowledging that the deal would help maintain Chicago's status as the nation's leading rail hub and promote the flow of commerce, but his much larger concerns were the same as suburban community opponents.[142] Durbin called for an expanded scope of environmental review and more public hearings.[143] Reps. Judy Biggert, Melissa Bean, and Peter Roskam raised similar concerns about traffic, pollution, safety, and noise.[144]

Still, despite all of this resistance, the company remained optimistic about the deal. Despite a year characterized by high diesel prices, increasing economic instability, and threats to many US markets, in 2008 CN CEO Hunter Harris was resolute that the company would nonetheless "fight the good fight" against regulators and local community groups standing in the way of the EJ&E deal.[145] Harris also saw the vociferous community opposition to the deal as "exaggerated,"[146] and he called the demands of community groups "unreasonable." As he saw it, CN might not be "in a position to accept the burden" of these mitigation demands.[147]

Perhaps Harris felt confident because of the company's strong allies. CN knew that it had the support of Chicago mayor Richard M. Daley, who favored less congestion through inner-city routes.[148] The railway also began to find that the deal had some powerful backers among peer firms in the industry, including both the Union Pacific Railroad and Norfolk Southern Railway; both companies worried that the STB's rejection of the deal could set a dangerous precedent as railways across the nation coped with increasing demand.[149] The whole industry was watching.

Community groups, fearful that their moment to challenge the company might be passing, took an even more aggressive approach as the

---

[139] Krishnamurthy (2008).   [140] Associated Press (2008a).
[141] Brooks (2008b).   [142] States News Service (2008a).   [143] Ibid.
[144] States News Service (2008b); Associated Press State & Local Wire (2008a); States News Service (2008c).
[145] Jang (2008a).   [146] Deveau (2008a).   [147] Boyd (2008).
[148] Selvam (2008).   [149] Jang (2008b).

campaign wore on. A second community organization formed to oppose the deal, known as The Regional Answer to Canadian National (TRAC). Outside an April 2008 shareholders' meeting, leaders of both community groups held a rally, and some activists even had to be removed from the building.[150]

By the late spring, CN started to show signs that they might walk away from the deal if regulators dragged out the process for an extended period. Noting that EJ&E's owner, US Steel, had only agreed to wait until December 31, CN filed a request with the STB that the environmental impact statement be completed by November 3.[151] Sen. Durbin and Rep. Bean wrote to the STB urging the board to reject this "fast-track" of the review.[152] Shortly thereafter, then presidential hopeful Sen. Barack Obama chimed in to voice his opposition to the deal.[153] It wasn't just the company that was becoming impatient with regulators, as the US Department of Transportation began to pressure the STB to move before US Steel's offer would expire at the close of the year.[154]

Toward the end of the summer, the STB released its draft environmental impact statement and formally refused CN's request to fast-track the review,[155] although it also announced that the review would be concluded by no later than January 2009.[156] Still, CN worried that US Steel would walk away from the deal after the end of 2008, which forced CN to take legal action to try to pressure the STB to move earlier (this legal maneuver was ineffective).[157] The announcement of the draft statement initiated a new public comment period in early fall 2008, with even larger numbers of suburban citizens voicing their concerns. For example, although organizers only expected a turnout of 3,000 for a hearing in late August in Barrington, over 5,100 residents came out to have their say.[158]

Rallies against the deal continued throughout the summer and during the public comment period of the STB's Draft Environmental Impact Statement. Figure 7.6 below maps the locations of these public meetings.

Describing one such gathering, a local high school in Aurora, IL was converted for an evening into an impromptu recruiting station for local

---

[150] Brooks (2008c).   [151] Deveau (2008b).   [152] States News Service (2008d).
[153] Deveau (2008c).   [154] Pyke (2008b).   [155] States News Service (2008e).
[156] *Globe & Mail* (2008).   [157] Brooks (2008d); Associated Press (2008b).
[158] States News Service (2008f).

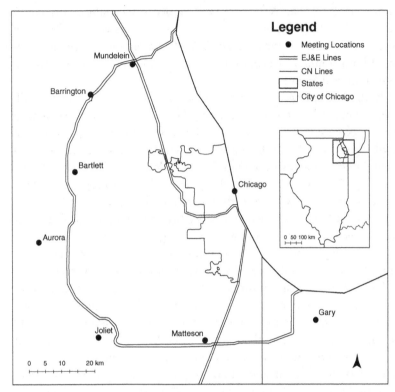

Figure 7.6 Location of the CN and EJ&E lines, and locations of public meetings concerning the STB's draft environmental impact statement between August and September 2008
Source: Cidell (2012). Reproduced by permission

protestors, with more than 600 volunteers inside the building and a line out the door.[159] Aurora mayor Tom Weisner spoke at one such rally, arguing that local citizens are "fighting a very powerful industry, a very powerful lobby. We are fighting a history of the STB almost perfunctorily approving these kinds of deals ... but with the unified voice and effort here I think we have a good shot."[160]

The summer also saw the introduction by Rep. Biggert of a bill in the US House, the Taking Responsible Action for Community Safety (TRACS) Act, which would have amended the laws governing STB

---

[159] Kmitch (2008).   [160] Ibid.

reviews of railway mergers, especially by requiring stricter mitigation conditions.[161] Although the bill failed a vote in the House, Biggert continued to press the STB to reject the deal.[162]

CN's response

Compared to the Wal-Mart case described above, CN's strategy was much more effective in generating authentic, broad-based community support for the company's interests. Importantly, they were much more successful in generating a broad coalition to back the company against its opponents. Whereas Wal-Mart took a heavy hand in pressuring suppliers and customers to participate, and did not as effectively mobilize support among community interests independent of the company, they were accordingly more open to the charge that their campaign was "astroturf" and lacked real support among the public. Canadian National, by contrast, was able to demonstrate a genuine community interest in having their deal approved by the Surface Transportation Board.

They did so by working with a public affairs consulting firm I refer to as Grassroots Advocates Company (GAC),[163] senior consultants of which I interviewed in December 2009. During the public comment periods described above, it was clear that suburban community activists were being heard loud and clear by regulators, legislators, and local government officials. What could the company do to counterbalance all of this negative attention to the purchase of the EJ&E line, especially when it was rooted in such deep local concerns as public safety, property values, noise, and traffic?

CN's answer, in the campaign that GAC helped to orchestrate, sought to mobilize a coalition of community members who resided along the corridor of CN's existing holdings, and who would stand to see a substantial *decrease* in train traffic if the deal were to go through. After all, the primary goal of the EJ&E purchase was to re-route rail traffic away from central and South Side Chicago areas that were grid-locked. Those communities would stand to benefit considerably if the purchase were to be approved, and these community members had a genuine interest in having their voice heard before the Surface Transportation Board. This was true despite the fact that the Surface

[161] States News Service (2008f).   [162] Ibid.
[163] A pseudonym; for additional details on the use of this case, see Appendix 4.2.

Transportation Board held only one of its thirty-nine hearings about the deal in the city of Chicago; as Ethan Bueno de Mesquita of the University of Chicago put it, the lesson seemed to be that "Wealthy, white suburbs have clout. Poor, minority neighborhoods do not."[164]

In response, then, residents of central Chicago communities, already facing the hazards of rail gridlock, began to send numerous letters and emails to their local, state, and federal representatives, as well as to the federal agency charged with approving the purchase. Why, they asked, should only certain communities be forced to pay the price of rail commerce through the region? Why should certain wealthy communities not share the costs? As one local official said, "all parts of the metropolitan area profit from the economic benefits [of rail transportation] . . . as such, all parts should work together to bear the burden."[165]

How did GAC mobilize the deal's local beneficiaries to have their say with the STB? GAC didn't simply call local citizens and ask that they repeat a set of talking points in the emails, phone calls, and hard-copy letters they hoped citizens would send to public officials. Instead, their staff directly called people identified as likely voters in those communities and informed them of the pertinent details of the regulatory review and how it could affect their community, a fact of which few in the community were, they say, otherwise aware. When they called, after informing the target residents of the most basic aspects of the proposed rail purchase, *openly disclosing their client's identity*, and without much additional prompting, GAC staff asked residents what their thoughts on the issue were. Unsurprisingly, many on the other end of the phone line expressed serious concerns about the existing level of rail traffic, and said they would be happy to see it decline. And, as political scientist Hahrie Han has shown in her research, disclosing their client's identity was a wise strategy, as those campaigns that do so are likely to be more effective in gaining support and raising funds.[166]

Listening closely to these residents, GAC staff recorded their concerns during phone conversations, and, at the conclusion of each call, asked if the individual would be willing to express their comments to the relevant public officials. A significant number of residents said "yes," and GAC produced a unique letter from each call, using direct quotes from the earlier phone conversations. GAC staff then sent this fully prepared letter back to the resident, asking that they sign and send it to the listed

[164] Bueno de Mesquita (2008).   [165] Silvestri (2008).   [166] Han (2009).

officials. Importantly, staff at the firm asked all those who submitted letters to send a carbon copy to the firm, which would allow them to track how many contacts were being made (and what was communicated therein). A senior representative at GAC said that they received copies of approximately 60 percent of the letters they produced, which, based on past experience, led them to very crudely estimate that a majority of their prepared letters were actually sent.

One of GAC's lead consultants, who I will refer to as Lily Abraham, described to me how this campaign was similar to others in the field of public affairs:

Say we are targeting drilling on the Arctic shelf. We might try to get people involved who are worried about high gas prices. We might work with trucking companies, Chambers of Commerce, and others who understand the impacts. We start making some calls, and we, of course, disclose who the client is that is sponsoring the call. We ask them to write a letter. But it's not standardized. In fact, what we do is get personal anecdotes. We describe the issue in general terms to them, and then ask them why they care about the issue. Then, taking those anecdotes, we craft their letter, aiding them in the process. We understand that unique letters matter more. These "cut and paste" campaigns – that's what we see as astroturf, and it's not that effective. Unique letters matter more.

Using this strategy, GAC was able to generate over eight hundred unique communications to the STB from community members who would stand to benefit from the approval of the rail deal. This included over six hundred personal letters of support, nearly one hundred patch-through calls to the STB department charged with conducting the environmental review, and multiple op-ed submissions (one of which was published in a leading local newspaper). Also, consistent with the idea that consultants seek to target their requests both at those most likely to say "yes" but also those likely to broaden the coalition, this campaign was effective in meeting both of those goals by activating likely voters who had an interest in the case independent of the consultant's corporate client.

The outcome
When the final environmental impact report was issued in early December 2008, it was seen largely as a victory for CN.[167] Although

---

[167] Pyke (2008c).

the mitigation measures it required were quite extensive – including contributions to communities to pay for rail crossings, video cameras installed so that train blockages of emergency vehicles could be monitored, and myriad noise and environmental mitigation efforts – nonetheless it pointed the way toward a closed deal for CN.[168] A wave of agreements with localities and housing developments in Illinois and Indiana followed in the weeks after, suggesting that many saw the deal as increasingly inevitable. Indeed, on December 24, 2008 the STB formally approved the deal, to the great chagrin of suburban activists and their representatives at the local, state, and federal levels.[169]

When the decision was handed down, it highlighted themes that were shared both by the firm and by the local residents mobilized by the campaign: that the rail congestion along CN's existing holdings was a major social problem that called out for relief, and that large-scale transportation decisions should be guided by concerns about what is best for an entire region rather than just certain communities. The STB's final approval statement reflected these precise concerns rather clearly in a few passages:

Many of those expressing support talked generally of project benefits, such as reduced noise or congestion along CN rail lines that would experience a decreased volume of freight rail traffic or improved regional rail traffic efficiency.[170]

Although some communities on the EJ&E line will experience adverse environmental effects, the Board finds that these effects are outweighed by the many transportation and environmental impact benefits that approval of this transaction would bring about.[171]

Many communities along CN's existing lines will experience environmental benefits from the reduction in rail traffic as CN reroutes traffic around Chicago over the EJ&E line. The Board does not believe that it is appropriate for these communities to continue to bear the full adverse environmental impacts of rail congestion in Chicago in order to protect the communities along the EJ&E line from traffic increases.[172]

What made the rail campaign so effective was not that it generated a large volume of contacts with public officials in support of regulatory approval for the rail line purchase (although, to be sure, it did that).

---

[168] Ibid.   [169] States News Service (2008g).
[170] Surface Transportation Board (2008: 35).   [171] Ibid.: 37.   [172] Ibid.: 38.

Instead, what made it so effective was the uniqueness and genuineness of the contacts that regulators and legislators were receiving. And, above all else, the campaign had a strong coalition of genuine community supporters who had a strong interest in the issue independent of the campaign's sponsor or the consulting firm who helped them to get their message out.

As Lily, a senior staff member at GAC put it, "We don't do astroturf [that is, campaigns with artificial grassroots support]. Besides, it isn't effective anyway. People on the receiving end can see right through it."

Conclusion

Building on the discussion in previous chapters on how public affairs consultants organize their campaigns on behalf of their paying clients, this chapter examined the effectiveness of "grassroots for hire" strategies in mobilizing participation and generating policy change.

Considering the effects these consultant-driven campaigns have on participation, I found that public affairs campaigns *both* reinforce participatory inequalities *and* seek to develop broad coalitions. Grassroots lobbying consultants seek, above all else, to recruit citizen activists who are most likely to say "yes" to their requests, and these are disproportionately those with a history of political activism, propensity to vote, and those known to be strongly partisan. They also prioritize civic activists and the college educated. However, consultants also hope to construct a broad and diverse coalition. Therefore, the most common "secondary targets" for consultants are minority groups. The fact that such groups are seen as a "secondary" priority by the consultants in this study suggests that a certain degree of apparent political tokenism may be at work, rather than a broad-based effort to increase the political representation of minority groups.

This chapter also showed that, even when considering evidence based upon the self-reports of consultants on how effective they are at meeting their clients' goals, consultants tend to be only moderately successful in achieving those ends. Nearly 25 percent of the campaigns that a consultant devoted the most effort to were no better than a partial success, and this failure rate increases to 33 percent for the second-highest priority campaign and 60 percent for the third. And, of course, it is worth noting again that "meeting a client's goal" is not the same thing as achieving success in generating policy change, as clients' objectives are often more modest than generating large-scale political change.

Using data from my survey of public affairs consultants, this chapter also showed that consultants tend to have a moderate degree of success when working on campaigns targeted at legislatures, government agencies, or the voting public, but have greater success in shaping the public's views on ballot measures. They also reported greater effectiveness in campaigns that were able to motivate in-person forms of public participation, such as attending events and visiting officials, with lesser success using mass contacting methods. These findings are consistent with research that suggests that political organizers often face a trade-off between quality and quantity. This trade-off helps to explain, in part, the popularity of "grasstops" or "key contact" approaches as described in Chapter 4.

Comparing the case studies of a failed grassroots campaign (Working Families for Wal-Mart) with a successful one (Canadian National's grassroots campaign in Chicago) helps to add substance to these broader findings and to further clarify the mechanisms at work. In both cases, companies faced off against contentious citizen challengers and social movement groups. Similarly, both cases involved substantial corporate resources put to work by public affairs consultants to try to develop and mobilize pro-corporate activism. Both campaigns had strong elite supporters in positions of power. But what separated the two cases was that Canadian National was transparent and able to locate and amplify an authentic and *independent constituency* who had an interest in the case for its own purposes. Although it is clear that Canadian National's consultant, Grassroots Advocates Co., helped that constituency to become aware of the issue and offered those citizens a venue to express their concerns, they were neither putting words in those citizens' mouths nor misrepresenting their ideas. GAC's consultants also made clear that they were calling on behalf of Canadian National. By contrast, Working Families for Wal-Mart was not able to broaden its coalition beyond the company's suppliers, certain consumers, and those with a financial stake in the company. They were also not transparent about the fact that WFW was funded entirely by Wal-Mart and was constructed by its consulting firm. Thus, they were not able to develop or partner with an independent constituency aligned with the company's interests.

A major conclusion of this chapter, which I elaborate further in the final chapter that follows, is that although "grassroots for hire" campaigns can (and do) have effects both on citizen participation and on policy outcomes, their force is limited by the independent power of organized civil society. They may be commercializing public participation and spending vast resources in doing so, but influence cannot simply be bought.

8 | Conclusion

Summary

The previous chapters have shown how grassroots political action, typically understood as the exclusive purview of citizen organizers, has been adapted as a commercial practice deployed by consultants on behalf of corporations, trade associations, the wealthiest and most professionalized advocacy organizations, and electoral campaigns in their Get-Out-The-Vote efforts. Although the practice of political consulting has been around for centuries and professional consulting firms have been around at least since Whitaker and Baxter opened up their firm Campaigns, Inc. in the 1930s, it wasn't until a variety of forces came together in the 1970s and 1980s that the field of grassroots public affairs consultants gained traction. These forces included the "interest group explosion" in which scores of new advocacy groups were founded, the rise of business political mobilization, and the widening gap between political partisans. This has now become a lucrative industry that is reshaping policymaking and Americans' civic and political participation.

Businesses, finding themselves on the receiving end of negative public attention through public interest advocacy, social movement pressure, and the new regulatory agencies established in the 1960s and 1970s, began to find that they needed a grassroots force to respond. A more politically partisan public was, in turn, more receptive to messages about the role of government on partisan issues such as regulation, taxation, health, and environmental policy. Once the field of consultants was established, advocacy organizations and labor unions began to find that they, too, could benefit by outsourcing a certain amount of their member mobilization efforts to the grassroots consultants who borrowed their own methods of generating mass political support. Still, only the most large and wealthy associations could afford to do so.

Consultants are having an effect both on public participation and on how policy is made. Their effects on public participation are such that, consistent with the "rational prospecting" model described by Henry Brady and colleagues,[1] consultants tend to focus their efforts on those most likely to acquiesce to their recruitment requests. But, as strangers to those they recruit, not all factors are equally important. Above all else, consultants recruit those who have a history of political or civic activism, are strongly partisan, are likely voters, or are college educated. When working for corporate clients in particular, they search out those identified as "opinion leaders" in their local community. Consultants also seek to mobilize minority groups, but this goal is only secondary, raising concerns of political tokenism. On balance, then, the work of grassroots public affairs consultants does encourage greater amounts of public participation: recall that the leading campaign by an average consulting firm targets over 750,000 Americans for participation, and that targeted requests for action are one of the most direct routes into political engagement.[2] But in doing so, these political strategists help to exacerbate participatory inequalities in the United States by amplifying the voice of those who are already over-represented in the system.

Given the major findings of this book, how best should we understand its broader significance?

Implications for the study of advocacy, organizations, and social movements

The importance of these findings for scholars of social movements and contentious politics more broadly are that both the institutionalization of grassroots organizing tactics and the creation of modular repertoires have allowed the spread of tactics well beyond other social movement actors through social contagion among fundamentally similar actors. As tactics become institutionalized (or, in Tarrow's words, repertoires become modular and adaptable to new circumstances), then, they may spread exogenously through the work of professionals such as consultants. The field of grassroots public affairs consultants represents both a mechanism for the diffusion of contentious tactics to new actors – recall Bill Hoover's remark in Chapter 6 that consultants like him "borrow and move things across worlds" – and also a means of converting such strategies into lucrative commercial services. Indeed, their practices

---

[1] Brady, Schlozman, and Verba (1999). [2] Walker (2008).

reflect the blurring of sectoral boundaries in a complex modern environment.

Although much of this organizational learning involved corporations and industry groups borrowing strategies of mass mobilization developed by increasingly media-savvy advocacy groups such as the Public Interest Movement of the 1960s and 1970s, today the well-established consultant field is facilitating advocacy groups' engagement in practices of political marketing that were originally developed for commercial applications. Similarly, today social movements regularly target corporations to encourage them to change their practices; although this may be pressuring firms to become more socially responsible, it may also be encouraging firms under certain conditions to adopt social movement-like strategies for their own purposes. As Chapter 5 showed, taking the high road of exclusive Corporate Social Responsibility (CSR) engagement represents a position of relative privilege, and firms facing major controversies or protest while also having a poor reputation are more likely to organize their stakeholders to fight back. Firms in regulated industries also do significantly more work with consultants.

Counter-campaigns organized by companies to resist social movement pressures might be seen as a form of soft repression against anti-corporate activists. The targets of social movement mobilization have a range of response options available to them beyond the expected decision of whether to partner/co-opt the movement, pre-empt its claims, concede to it, or ignore it.[3] Importantly, although scholars of social movements have paid a considerable amount of attention to repression by the state, we still know relatively little about how non-state organizations engage in forms of activist repression ranging from soft forms such as PR and grassroots campaigning all the way to more extreme measures such as the filing of so-called Strategic Lawsuits against Public Participation (SLAPPs) against social movement groups.[4] The findings of this study encourage further exploration into the dynamics of repression and co-option of activist groups by non-state organizations like corporations, educational institutions, and trade, professional, and other associations. Although these organizations lack the monopoly on the legitimate use of force possessed by the state, organizations

[3] Gamson (1990: Ch. 3).
[4] But see Meyer and Staggenborg (1996). On SLAPPs, see Pring and Canan (1996).

outside the state have considerable capacities for repressing popular activism.

This study also illustrates, consistent with the expectations of the resource mobilization theory of social movements, the important role of external patrons in funding popular mobilization.[5] However, the evidence presented here suggests that this expectation should be modified somewhat. This theory assumes that elite patrons will generally play the role of "conscience constituents": that is, those who contribute resources to a cause but will not benefit directly if movement actors win their cause. But the elite patrons who fund public advocacy through the conduit of consultants' campaigns are better understood in resource mobilization terms as *beneficiary* constituents, because they fund popular activism that benefits their own interests directly. This point is important, because it reminds us that although social movement-like tactics are *favored* by disadvantaged groups who lack resources, they are not the *exclusive purview* of those groups. Recent research, for example, on movements of the wealthy suggests similar conclusions.[6] Instead, and more consistent with the work of Schattschneider and his students, the findings of this study suggest that well-resourced elites support mass political engagement when they expect that they would otherwise end up on the losing side of a policy battle.

Accordingly, it is also worth exploring further the role of elites in contentious fields, following prominent calls for such research by Mayer Zald, Michael Lounsbury, Stephen Barley, Royston Greenwood, and others.[7] Consultants are an important type of elite in the "asteroid belt" of associations contending for power in the contemporary state, and are, in one sense, where the rubber meets the road in terms of how powerful organizations reshape civil society and policymaking domains. As experts, they attempt to distill knowledge about civic organization, the political process, and how best to market advocacy causes to distant publics. Organizational theorists, going back at least to classic work by Paul DiMaggio and Walter W. Powell, have recognized that consultants are important institutional agents, in that consultants serve as "Johnny Appleseeds" in spreading practices in

---

[5] McCarthy and Zald (1973, 1977).   [6] Martin (2013).
[7] Zald and Lounsbury (2010); Barley (2007, 2010); Greenwood (2008); Reed (2012).

mimetic fashion across organizational fields.[8] Despite the important role of elite consultants and other professional service firms in shaping the practices and politics of the leading global corporations and associations, sociological research on such intermediary organizations (and their boundary-spanning functions) is still relatively underdeveloped.[9] Thus, much more research is needed on the place of professional service firms in politics and advocacy, and particularly how such elites are reshaping both lobbying and contentious politics.

Lastly, the findings of this study help to recognize an under-appreciated point in the wide-ranging debates over the past two decades regarding the seeming paradox of declines in broad-based public participation alongside the explosion of growth in advocacy organizations. Prominent research by both Robert Putnam and Theda Skocpol suggests that we are witnessing an expansion of advocacy without a widening population of advocates, in part because many associations today lobby on their constituents' behalf without providing those citizens with meaningful, face-to-face socialization into politics. While most of the blame in these discussions was focused on the transforming structures of advocacy organizations and the changing ways that Americans spend their leisure time, existing research has largely overlooked how professional firms are generating advocacy without offering real political socialization to citizens. This is not a trivial omission, given that the aggregate campaigns of these consulting firms mobilize millions of selectively targeted citizens in what are often short-term and transactional advocacy campaigns. Campaigns like those organized by grassroots consultants allow for advocacy without the cultivation of social capital, enabled by communications technologies and media advertisements.

However, this is not to say that consultants are exclusively focused on the atomistic targeting of individuals who fit the demographic profiles desired by their client, as (a) these professionals tend to seek out those who are seen as opinion leaders in their community, as revealed in Chapter 7, and (b) they often hope that their campaign will independently take root among stakeholders, especially by using social networking technologies like Facebook and Twitter. As Owen Taylor described to me, consultants' highest hope is that local advocates will adopt the

---

[8] DiMaggio and Powell (1983: 152).
[9] Greenwood, Suddaby, and McDougald (2006).

campaign's cause as their own. In one campaign his firm organized, a local convenience store chain was seeking to open a new retail store in a suburb of a large mid-Atlantic city. This convenience store had recently begun to add gas pumps to their locations, thus threatening the interests of local gas stations, who began to lobby against the chain. Taylor described a set of fortuitous circumstances:

Everybody loves [this chain in our area], except for gas station owners who charge a lot for gas, as well as stores who sell [deli sandwiches]. So, you know, we're sort of like in a little bit of fight in [this suburb], and we've done not only traditional canvassing, but we've done a lot with Facebook advertising and things like that, and it's actually been very effective. It's so effective. One of the most hilarious things is that on the Facebook site there's a bunch of guys [from this suburb] who took up the cause. I guess they have a band, and they wrote a song and did a video, basically saying that they want [this chain to open a store in our town], and they posted it on Facebook and it circulated around. I mean, it's hilarious. And, again, that was organic. We didn't do that. But we provided the environment, you know, from a social media standpoint for these guys to do that.

Without putting too fine a point on it, examples like this show that even when such campaigns do go beyond atomistic targeting and make possible the endogenous diffusion of participation among civic and social groups, such strategies obviously do very little to encourage broad-based and meaningful public participation in which citizens generate social capital through their participation. The structures of civil society are being borrowed to help a paying client win a campaign.

Displacing the traditional grassroots?

A foremost conclusion of this book is that transformations in organized civil society in the US – particularly the political mobilization of business, the expansion of organized public advocacy, and growing political partisanship – helped make possible a market for grassroots advocacy services and promote the shift toward a subsidized public. Still, the expansion of this field need not mean that consultant-driven campaigns are necessarily *replacing* traditional grassroots advocacy by volunteers and staff of advocacy associations. In fact, the evidence presented in this book suggests that although grassroots participation consultants are, in fact, "behind the curtain" of much popular advocacy today; it also indicates that consultants have to play by many of the same rules as other kinds of organized advocates. They need to consider the decision-making processes of policymakers, study their opposition, frame their message in a resonant fashion, and effectively mobilize constituencies. While they may have more resources and better data than other kinds of organized advocates, nonetheless they face many of the same challenges. And when working with advocacy groups, consultants hope to further build associations' mobilization capacities and extend their organizational reach, without necessarily harming organizations or generating long-term dependence on outside experts. In fact, consulting firms like Crossroads Campaign Solutions and Democracy Partners, both described in Chapter 6, are integrated into the progressive movement and are committed to helping their advocacy clients win and to become even stronger associations. While only the wealthiest associations can typically afford such services, there is relatively little evidence that consultants detract from their capacity as associations.

What's more, the ad hoc nature of most of the campaigns organized by public affairs consultants makes them a far cry from the thick forms of civic and political activism for which the term "grassroots" is more commonly known: action rooted in rich networks of local community-based organizations, religious congregations, ethnic associations, and other informal building blocks of civil society. Consultant-backed campaigns are generally efforts to build upon these structures to gain political support for their client's interests, and they are more often short-term efforts that do not build long-term organizing structures. Chapter 7, for example, showed that consultants tend to target, above all else, would-be activists who have histories of political activism, thus perhaps shifting these activists over to the client's issue but focusing less on generating *new* activists. Perhaps even more importantly, I also illustrated how consultant-backed campaigns are particularly in need of sources of support that are *independent* of the paying client, such that these activists cannot easily be dismissed as those who have a personal or financial stake in the issue by being directly tied to the client. Consultants need to locate and amplify the voices of those who have a genuine interest in the issue, regardless of the incentives involved. But such voices are often difficult to locate, and when facing major crises or controversies, some consulting firms or associations may cut corners.

It also remains true that campaigns that are less than fully transparent about their sponsorship may decrease public trust in advocacy groups and lead to searches for ever-more exhaustive information on the patronage behind advocacy. But there is little reason to expect that "grassroots for hire" strategies should lead to less member participation, fundraising, or organizing by those engaged in thicker forms of civic and/or political activism. If anything, it seems more reasonable to expect that their campaigns lead to even more political activism (even if highly partisan), given that advocacy groups often need to counter the influence of consultants' campaigns. Such has been the case, for instance, in environmental groups' campaigns to counter the industry-backed mobilization in favor of the controversial natural gas extraction method of hydraulic fracturing.[10]

In sum, then, although grassroots public affairs consultants are amplifying certain voices of the privileged and politically active, they are nonetheless limited by the independent force of organized civil society. They can generate displays of mass support on behalf of elite interests, but the effectiveness of their doing so is constrained by their ability to connect those interests with those shared by constituencies who care about such issues for their own purposes. And, as I explain in more detail below, they must work particularly hard to get past the growing public perception – which firms like these have, in part, helped to create – that much advocacy today is untrustworthy, inauthentic, and covertly funded by elite interests.

Debate over disclosure

As described in Chapter 2 and in examples throughout the book, a regular concern is that consultants often fail to disclose the identity of their client to the would-be citizen activists they recruit. Consultants generally prefer to keep their own role (and their client's) in the background, such that the activism they generate appears as an independent expression of genuine public opinion rather than a top-down, elite-driven effort lacking in legitimacy. Or, at the very least, they hope that their role doesn't overshadow what may at times be a very genuine expression of popular support aligned with the interests of their client. A common refrain in my interviews was the argument that if the campaign doesn't involve fraud or a misrepresentation of citizens' authentic views, then it shouldn't matter who helped those individuals or groups find their voice.

[10] See, for example, Parks (2012).

The broader political context in the wake of the Supreme Court's landmark 2010 decision in *Citizens United v Federal Election Commission* also bears on this topic. This decision held that the US government is not permitted under the First Amendment to restrict independent political expenditures by corporations and labor unions.[11] In effect, the ruling opened up the floodgates for corporations and unions to independently – that is, without officially coordinating with a candidate campaign – express opposition or support for a political candidate through communications such as television or radio advertisements. A key additional consequence that followed from the *Citizens United* ruling was the provision that groups incorporated under code 501(c)4 of the United States Internal Revenue Code – typically described as "Social Welfare" organizations – as well as trade associations and unions, would now be allowed to make expenditures that expressly support candidates for office (although they still may not, under the law, engage in electoral advocacy as their primary purpose).[12] And, most importantly, these nonprofit organizations are required only to disclose their expenditures, not the identities of their donors, including major corporations and industry groups. Thus, a broad national debate is taking place about how these anonymous donations by corporations, the very wealthy, and other advocacy groups are reshaping elections and American democracy.[13] It is indeed quite difficult for the public to interpret these communications when their sponsors are not disclosed; even if citizens agree with the message, they might not necessarily feel the same way if they knew who was asking.

While this vast influx of dollars into third-party groups is new since the 2010 *Citizens United* decision, the strategy of funding third-party advocacy without disclosure is age-old, and raises a similar set of questions for policymakers. While the federal Lobbying Disclosure Act (LDA) of 1995 requires registration and disclosure of political activity in which a lobbyist (either in-house or for a client) seeks to influence, through their own direct efforts, the decisions of specific legislative or executive branch officials, lobbying that involves mobilizing mass public participation continues to be unregulated at the federal level. Amendments to lobbyist disclosure laws in 1998 and 2007 clarified the definition of lobbying and elaborated on which types of activities are covered by it, but nonetheless kept grassroots activities out of

[11] Winik (2010).   [12] Ibid.   [13] E.g., Lessig (2011).

that definition. Indeed, grassroots lobbying is not even considered "lobbying" under federal lobbyist disclosure laws, any more than the activity of making a rousing political speech in public is.[14] Some states require disclosure of grassroots lobbying activity, but these regulations are incredibly heterogeneous across states and difficult to enforce.[15]

First Amendment concerns, of course, are at the forefront of why grassroots lobbying is generally exempted from lobbying disclosure laws. The failure of the grassroots lobbying provisions in the Honest Leadership and Open Government Act (HLOGA) of 2007 are telling in this respect. Taken up in the months following the Jack Abramoff scandal – in which Abramoff was paid by Native American tribes in part for grassroots lobbying work – the HLOGA legislation was intended to curb lobbyist influence by integrating legislation on lobbying disclosure, gifts to members of Congress, and federal election law.[16] When introduced in the Senate, the lobbying ethics bill included a rather encompassing provision to regulate grassroots lobbying, which would have included efforts by all advocacy groups, consultants, and a range of others who encourage members of the public to engage in indirect lobbying.[17] Although supported by government transparency advocates like Common Cause, Democracy 21, and OMB Watch, it was met with vociferous opposition mainly from other advocacy groups, and the regulations on grassroots lobbying were stripped from the Senate's bill before being passed. Groups ranging from the ACLU to the Traditional Values Coalition spoke up, worried that the proposed regulations would stifle their grassroots advocacy. A provision regulating grassroots activity was reintroduced when the bill was taken up in the House, although many concerns remained. Considering how the House should address the matter, a Republican former Federal Election Commission director put it succinctly, arguing that the problem is "not that citizens are contacting Washington too much ... The purpose of disclosure is to inform the citizens of what government is doing – it's not to inform the government of what citizens are doing."[18] Although the House bill's relevant provisions were essentially restricted to the firms described in this book – "lobbying firms hired by a client to do grassroots work, and only to the firm's paid communications that urge

---

[14] Vladeck (2009: 416).   [15] Milyo (2010).
[16] Luneburg, Susman, and Gordon (2009: iii).   [17] Caruso (2007).
[18] Newmyer (2007).

grassroots action"[19] – these regulations were also eventually removed before the HLOGA's passage.

The debate over the grassroots lobbying provision in the HLOGA is important because it helps to set an agenda for federal policymakers as they consider whether to regulate grassroots lobbying activity. On the one hand, the campaigns of the consultants in this study do, at times, exploit public trust in advocacy causes and fail to be transparent. Their doing so distorts the democratic process and offers a new source of political power and influence to already-privileged elites, not to mention that the activists they target are already politically over-represented.

On the other hand, policymakers have in the past faced, and will continue to face, significant difficulties in drawing boundaries around which types of grassroots activities should require disclosure. If they require disclosure of all payments above a certain threshold to grassroots public affairs consultants, this could ensnare not only corporate- and industry-backed campaigns, but also efforts by large advocacy organizations, labor unions, and other groups. Also, since some of the work consultants do for organizations involves internal communications with their own members, employees, or shareholders, such regulations could raise concerns about whether associations have the right to expect a degree of privacy in their communications with members (or corporations with their shareholders). In sum, critics of mandated disclosure of otherwise anonymous grassroots lobbying argue that such laws could be harmful by being overly broad, restricting free speech, and violating constitutionally recognized principles supporting the use of pseudonyms or other anonymity-granting devices in making public claims (which have a long tradition in US politics dating back to the nation's founding).[20]

Nonetheless, a few sensible measures regarding corporate grassroots expenditures are advisable. Most importantly, laws protecting anonymous speech have generally covered what might best be called "anonymous speech in the public sphere" or "on the street," rather more than explicit requests for citizens to petition government bodies.[21] The courts have found compelling reasons to support disclosure of the funding sources for other forms of lobbying as well as electoral contributions through Political Action Committees (PACs), such as those required, respectively, by the 1995 LDA and the 1974

---

[19] Caruso (2007).   [20] Zellner (2010: 375).   [21] Ibid.: 382.

Federal Campaign Election Act. Given that this book has documented a lucrative industry of firms active in mobilizing grassroots support in a fashion intended to influence legislatures, agencies, and electoral decision-making, basic disclosure of funding sources would seem to be justified on similar grounds.

More specifically, it would be justified to put in place regulations that would resurrect sections of the 2007 HLOGA that were initially in the bill in its earlier form as the Lobbying Transparency and Accountability Act. In addition to expanding the definition of lobbying to include grassroots efforts, the law would have required the identification of sponsors of campaigns – involving a consultant or not – that spend over $25,000 in a quarter on paid grassroots mobilization efforts.[22] The law would have exempted internal communications within an organization.[23] Importantly for the firms in my study, it would also have required public affairs firms that receive more than $25,000 per quarter for mobilizing the public *to register as lobbyists and disclose the sources of their funding.*[24] Given the very high threshold that would need to be crossed in order to trigger such disclosure, there is relatively little reason to expect that such regulations would harm the work of advocacy groups working at even a modest-to-high scale. The vast majority of groups in civil society, after all, are small-scale and local associations.[25] Disclosure of these very large-scale campaigns, although not a perfect solution, would likely enhance trust in both government and associations. It would also impose no new limits on how much can be spent in such efforts – ensuring only that they be disclosed.

Outside of state regulation, industry self-regulation and voluntary compliance on their own are not very promising avenues, although some steps have been made in that direction. The George Washington University's Graduate School of Political Management, for example, has drafted a code of ethics for the public participation professionals, suggesting that consultants should abide by the principles that they only promote legitimate and authentic communications, that they not send irrelevant messages to policymakers, be transparent about the client's identity, and be civil and honest.[26] Similarly, the Public Relations Society of America suggests that it is unethical to create front groups

---

[22] "Grassroots lobbying" was defined as an effort to influence more than 500 members of the public to contact a federal official on a particular issue.
[23] Zellner (2010: 392). [24] Ibid.: 393. [25] Smith (1997). [26] GSPM (2012).

or to have people pose as grassroots volunteers for a cause.[27] But efforts such as these have not been welcomed by most consultants. In fact, many of the consultants I spoke with had either never heard of this proposed code of ethics or, unsurprisingly, thought it would be unnecessary. As long-standing grassroots consultant Amy Showalter put it in a co-authored essay, the industry features many friendly and personable individuals, but will never be "a profession that will naturally enjoy respect and admiration." She continues, "the public knows that we get paid to persuade. A grass-roots code of ethics that stifles free speech won't change that."[28]

Grassroots campaigns facilitated by consultants appear to be here to stay. Given the policy challenges inherent in mandating disclosure, as well as the relatively weak power of institutional pressures for normative change, two additional factors seem also to be promising in curbing some of the industry's more egregious practices: (1) strengthening advocacy associations' powers to monitor and uncover the sponsors behind campaigns that do not disclose the identity of their client, and (2) growing recognition by the industry that although a lack of transparency may be appealing when a client faces conditions of crisis or controversy, the costs are often even greater – and likely to lead to a failed campaign – when a client's covert support is revealed. Regarding the latter, grassroots consultants would be well served in recognizing that their most effective practices are those that look like traditional grassroots politics, but with a particular sensitivity to being transparent, genuine, and honest in their dealings with both citizens and policymakers.

Civil society and politics in a context of "grassroots for hire"

Elite-sponsored grassroots campaigns have become a prominent feature of American civic society and political engagement by the opening years of the twenty-first century. In a context of heightened inequality and a lack of disclosure about the funding sources of campaigns organized both by consultants and also those by other kinds of advocacy and nonprofit groups, advocacy claims are (perhaps rightfully) met with a healthy dose of skepticism. The widespread engagement of elites in mass politics has only fueled these feelings of mistrust. For example, elite

[27] Fitzpatrick and Palenchar (2006: 220).   [28] Showalter and Rhoads (2010).

advocates have become incredibly active in seeking to reshape public opinion and advocacy surrounding climate change, with some initial evidence that they have been effective in doing so.[29] The sugar-sweetened beverage industry has been mobilized in full force to press back – with varying degrees of success – against new taxes and regulations on soda sales in a variety of localities. The natural gas industry is fighting battles on multiple fronts against citizens who raise critical health and environmental questions about the safety of the new gas extraction method of hydraulic fracturing. And contention has been sustained around elite sponsorship in domains like charter schools, real estate development, gambling, food and agriculture policy, and internet regulation.

Even if consultants' campaigns may not be displacing other forms of grassroots participation, their efforts are often effective in shifting public debates and channeling participation in directions favored by elite consultants and their clients. As I have argued, their campaigns encourage participation without necessarily improving citizens' social capital or civic skills, any more than one learns how to craft a political argument or network with other activists through attaching one's name to a ready-made form letter.[30] Philip Howard has argued, along the same lines, that campaigns like the ones described in this book encourage "thin citizenship" in which democracy is reduced to short-term, transactional, and individualistic exchanges between citizens and leaders.[31] Similar to worries that some have expressed about "plug-in volunteering" in civic associations,[32] the plug-in political participation requested by grassroots consultants is facilitating the decoupling of participation from the cultivation of democratic citizenship. The toolkit of mass mobilization may have been borrowed from grassroots associations, but something significant has been lost along the way.

The hope for a revitalization of the modern public sphere, expressed by Jürgen Habermas and deliberative democratic theorists today, imagines potential futures in which the interests of capitalist markets and state administrative practices are not so powerful as to close off the independent space of a democratic public sphere rooted in civil society.[33] Theorists expect that these powerful interests will make efforts to

---

[29] Brulle, Carmichael, and Jenkins (2012). [30] Walker (2009: 84).
[31] Howard (2006: 184–191). [32] Lichterman (2006).
[33] Habermas (1987, 1989); Fishkin (1992).

"colonize" those spaces for their own purposes through advertising, public relations, and other interventions in public life.[34] However, despite these influences, there are reasons to remain optimistic that the force of organized civil society is likely to limit these colonization efforts, mainly in that the public is attentive to these strategies and often effective at discrediting them. As Habermas argued,

> Public opinions that can acquire visibility only because of an undeclared infusion of money or organizational power lose their credibility as soon as these sources of social power are made public. Public opinion can be manipulated but neither publicly bought or publicly blackmailed . . . a public sphere cannot be "manufactured" as one pleases.[35]

Accordingly, the evidence presented in this book suggests both challenges for a healthy democracy and potentials to limit what damage might be imposed by some (although not all) consultants' campaigns. The challenges are clear: the work of these consultants makes for a more unequal democracy in which narrow-casted recruitment appeals facilitate transactional participation aligned with the interests of well-resourced business groups, industry associations, elite leaders, and advocacy causes. But the limits to their influence are equally clear, in that campaigns that engage in "astroturf" strategies – heavy use of incentives, fraudulent misrepresentation of citizens' views, and/or the failure to disclose the predominant sponsorship of elite patrons – are often revealed and contested effectively by critical observers and advocacy organizations. Thus, even in a context in which mass participation is reshaped by elites, the power of critical publics to challenge those elite campaigns becomes even more important.

[34] Ibid.   [35] Habermas (1996: 364).

Appendix 1
Identifying consulting firms (baseline data)

The population of consulting firms active in providing grassroots mobilization services to organizational clients is one that has not previously been studied in systematic fashion. A number of studies nod toward the presence of such consulting firms and the role that they play in interest group or corporate politics, but these consultants have otherwise successfully remained "behind the curtain" and have been largely overlooked in such studies.[1] Thus, a crucial initial task in this work was to identify the relevant population of consulting firms. Luckily, even for a field that remains somewhat secretive, their efforts to win the business of new clients can be successfully exploited for research purposes.

Following a long tradition in analyses of organizational populations, I searched widely for a directory source that would provide a comprehensive census of organizations active in providing grassroots mobilization services. The accuracy of such a directory is crucial to minimizing systematic bias in an analyst's depiction of an organizational field.[2] When this project was still in its infancy, I was fortunate enough to locate precisely such a comprehensive directory: the listings of political consulting firms published annually by *Campaigns & Elections* (*C&E*) magazine. Perhaps even more importantly, this directory enjoys something of a monopoly on providing listings of political consultants. The directory is, as the *C&E* editors argue, the "only comprehensive directory of political consultants, political products and services, public affairs professionals, and lobbyists [in the United States]."

Indeed, the *C&E* directories are a better fit for this study than alternative sources such as the *Washington Representatives* directory, which focuses mainly on traditional lobbyists who do not include mobilizing the public in their service portfolio (for those firms that do, they

---

[1] E.g., Kollman (1998: 46, 74–80); Goldstein (1999: 2, 64); Lyon and Maxwell (2004: 563).
[2] Walker, McCarthy, and Baumgartner (2011: 1325–1331).

generally appear in the *C&E* listings anyway).[3] *C&E* is also more comprehensive than the listings provided through professional or trade groups like the American Association of Political Consultants, Public Relations Society of America, or the Public Affairs Council; a substantial subset of organizations, of course, are not members of these associations and would otherwise be ignored by an analyst who relied exclusively on such lists (even when aggregated). Further, in the interviews I conducted for this study – consistent with the field's weak professionalization – many consultants suggested that they derive relatively few benefits from joining such associations, in that this is not a field known for sharing best practices across firms. In addition, given that *C&E*'s directory is more or less the "only game in town" as a centralized source for those shopping for the services of a political professional, it would be quite unwise for a consulting firm to remain unlisted in the directory.[4]

With a team of research assistants, I collected all directory listings of firms in two *C&E* sources: (1) fifteen editions of the *C&E* "Political Pages" (CEPP) directory published annually from 1990 to 2004, and (2) a series of pullout "Grassroots Lobbying Buyers' Guides" (GLBGs) published in five special issues in 1995, 1996, 1999, 2001, and 2003. For the GLBG listings, we collected every firm listed in this pullout guide. For the CEPP listings, we collected all entries that appeared under any of the subheadings relevant for grassroots participation, taking an inclusive but not over-broad approach. Thus, the CEPP subheadings included were: "Grass-roots Lobbying," "Public Affairs – Grass-roots Strategy/Mobilization," "Petitions & Signature Gathering," and "Field Operations & Organizing."[5]

---

[3] Still, in an earlier analysis (Walker, 2009: S1) I found that less than 3 percent of the firms in the baseline data from *C&E* are focused mainly on "government affairs" (that is, inside lobbying that does not involve mobilizing the public).

[4] These listings are, as of this writing, also available online at www.campaignsand elections.com/resources/political-pages/.

[5] Other relevant subheadings were considered but then excluded. These are the following topics: "Public Affairs," "Direct Mail," "Telephone Contact Services," "Media Buying & Placement," "Database/file Management," and "Crisis Management." Since many firms in any given directory year are cross-listed under a number of categories, those which did not claim to be directly involved in grassroots lobbying, field organizing, or petitioning activity *for any year of the directory listings* were assumed to be only peripherally engaged in grassroots mobilization activity. Recall also that many of the firms in the data provide services

Our research team then reduced these grouped firm-year listings into a set of unique firms, using a set of coding rules we agreed to at the outset.[6] Thus, the baseline data include all unique firms that *appeared at least once* in either of these two *C&E* sources at some point between 1990 and 2004. The CEPP listings for every year between 1990 and 2004 offered, on average, 115 listings per year, although many of these listings overlap both within and across years. Such overlap occurred within years because consulting shops may choose to be listed under more than one of the selected headings in each year, should they wish to stand out for providing those more specialized services. As for the GLBG, an average guide provided 89 listings of individual firms, for a raw total of 445 listings across its five editions.

To merge these two sources, CEPP cases were added into a database that already included the GLBG listings as described above. Comparisons of the GLBG and CEPP entries suggest that combining both sources was necessary in order to complement one another, in that each source introduced a significant number of exclusive cases. Once all repeating firms were reduced to unique cases, the CEPP and GLBG case data produced a listing of $N=712$ unique firms to constitute the baseline data file.

For each of these $N=712$ firms, our research team also searched a number of directories, as well as firms' websites, for evidence of firms' client bases, primary service focus, partisanship, founding year, and a number of other measures. Directories searched include *O'Dwyer's Directory of Public Relations Firms, Washington Representatives,* and the Thomson-Gale *Goliath* directory of public and private firms. For each of the directory sources, we searched the firm over a three-year window surrounding the year of the firm's most recent appearance in one of the *C&E* directories. These data are used in Table A.1 below.

such as direct mail mobilization or phone calling as part of their broader portfolio of grassroots engagement practices (see Chapter 4).

[6] In the merging process, firms that have the same name but listed different cities were treated as separate cases, unless one of the addresses was in Washington, DC (which generally suggests that the firm has a branch in the capital). Firms that added an additional partner in later years were considered the same firm, whereas those cases in which the partners split up and founded a new firm were considered two cases.

Appendix 2

2.1 Identifying firms to survey

While the baseline data proved useful in developing an account of the founding patterns of consulting firms, this study, of course, required a much more in-depth account of the current field of consultants: not just about their clients, service portfolio, staffing, and revenue, but more detailed information about particular campaigns, demographic groups targeted, the outcomes of campaigns, and more. To do so would require reaching out directly to consultants through a survey. But a prior task before fielding the survey was to determine which of the 712 firms in the baseline data – again, these were firms active at any point between 1990 and 2004 – continued to be active in providing services to their clients. This is especially important to do in a relatively high-mortality organizational population such as in a field of lobbying firms dependent on variable campaign revenue.

In the planning phase of the survey in 2008, my research team made initial efforts to ascertain which organizations had survived to the present day. This was done with the understanding that this provisional list would need to be culled further once the survey would go into the field, as additional organizations would experience mortality by that point. Thus, in summer 2008, with a team of research assistants, we made efforts to contact all 712 organizations in the baseline data in order to determine whether they continued to be active. Team members first searched firm websites (where applicable) for the most up-to-date contact information for firms, cross-checking these data against the *C&E* entries from the baseline data and updating information where necessary. Then, using these updated contacts, my research assistants and I placed calls to all firms, simply requesting to confirm organizations' email and mailing addresses. We were able to directly confirm survival for 194 of these organizations through phone contacts, and we also counted as surviving an additional 39 firms for which we did not speak to an individual but

Mother Is Gold, Father Is Glass

Gender and Colonialism in a Yoruba Town

Lorelle D. Semley

Indiana University Press
Bloomington & Indianapolis

This book is a publication of

Indiana University Press
601 North Morton Street
Bloomington, Indiana 47404-3797 USA

iupress.indiana.edu

Telephone orders 800-842-6796
Fax orders 812-855-7931
Orders by e-mail iuporder@indiana.edu

Manufactured in the United States of America

Library of Congress Cataloging-in-Publication
Data

Semley, Lorelle D., [date]–
    Mother is gold, father is glass : gender and
colonialism in a Yoruba town / Lorelle D. Semley.
       p. cm.
    Includes bibliographical references and index.
    ISBN 978-0-253-35545-4 (cloth : alk.
paper) — ISBN 978-0-253-22253-4 (pbk. : alk.
paper) 1. Women—Benin—Kétou—History. 2.
Women, Yoruba—Political activity—History.
3. Mothers—Political activity—Africa, West—
History. 4. Sex role—Africa, West—History.
5. Kétou (Benin)—Social life and customs.
6. Kétou (Benin)—History. 7. Africa, West—
History—1884–1960. I. Title.
    HQ1811.Z9K487 2010
    305.420966—dc22

                                2010020121

1 2 3 4 5   16 15 14 13 12 11

For my grandmother,
Olga Wanda Semley
(1909–2005),
as promised

Contents

Preface

"You Must Be From Here"—
An Intellectual and Personal Journey

Félix Iroko, a history professor at the University of Bénin, who is originally from Kétu, liked to introduce me to his colleagues and friends in Bénin by asking where they thought I was from. Hearing my accented French and looking me over, they would guess that I was "definitely" from the north, or from the central part of the country, or maybe from Cameroon. Iroko would laugh heartily at their mounting uncertainty and say triumphantly, "She is an American." There would be momentary surprise and then recognition, none of us thinking about the implications of my "universal" appearance as Béninois, Cameroonian, or American.

Though I was born in New York City, being mistaken for Nigerian, Senegalese, or Liberian had become normal to me and almost a source of comfort since my first trip to Ile-Ifẹ, Nigeria, for a Yoruba language course in the summer of 1994. During one of our outings, to a blacksmith's workshop, an elderly man was shocked and seemingly upset when he realized that I was not Yoruba after all. I became proud of my ability to blend in, and I made use of it; once I claimed to be Nigerian, rather than American, in Senegal, and Béninois, instead of American, in Brazil. Though I sometimes spoke French in France, rejecting my relationship with loud American tourists, I adamantly displayed my American passport upon arrival in Amsterdam on a flight from Lagos, Nigeria, to avoid harassment by the authorities. Drawing on Iroko's guessing game, I sometimes asked people where they thought I was from, if they hesitantly asked whether I was from "around here." My favorite was a French man in Aix-en-Provence, who was certain I was from the Indian Ocean island of Réunion. Early in my research in Kétu, Bénin, Akande Olofindji, head of a cultural institute and a Kétu royal minister, pronounced that I *must* be from Kétu. I politely demurred, but he insisted, "Otherwise, why would you have come home?"

Had I chosen to do research in Kétu because of some deep or undefined feeling of familiarity or longing? I certainly thought I had wandered into African studies in college at Georgetown University, and later into Yoruba studies in graduate school at Yale. After taking some French-speaking African courses because I found French literature uninspiring, I completed an African Studies Certificate program in college after someone in my dorm casually suggested it. Imagining that I would become an "international lawyer," I took a job as a paralegal at the Department of Justice in Washington, D.C., but eventually decided that law school was not for me. One day, during a lunch break, I visited the Smithsonian Museum of African Art for inspiration and, there, I decided to get a Ph.D. in African history. Following the advice of my college African history professor David Johnson, I studied for a Master's in African Studies at Yale for proper training in historiography. At Yale, the only West African language offered was Yoruba and, though I wanted to study West African history, I was not sure I wanted Nigeria to be my focus. Yet when I began to learn Yoruba, I experienced moments of longing and familiarity. I became enamored with a language in which my chosen Yoruba name, Ìfétáyò̀, means "love is joy." I felt connected to a language and culture where the literal translation for the word "happy," *inú mi dùn,* is "my stomach is sweet." Hearing Yoruba and watching people converse in it tugged at my heart. I caught glimpses of gestures and facial expressions that reminded me of my grandmother, of an uncle, of a cousin. I experienced a new depth, never of pain, only of delight.

As for Kétu in Bénin, frankly I stumbled onto it when, at Northwestern University, I decided to continue my study of Yoruba history in that former French colony. A reference to a "queen" of Kétu who had commanded the town during the French colonial period piqued my interest. The story of that "queen," Alaba Ida, took me down a complicated road. She remains a central figure in this history of the changing relationship between "public motherhood" (a concept I have borrowed from literary scholar Chikwenye Ogunyemi), kingship, and marriage in precolonial and colonial West Africa.

In this book, I talk of mothers, wives, fathers, and husbands, noting the power dynamic between these identities, as symbolic as they are "real." Most often, I examine symbolic mother figures who held titled positions in West African kingdoms. I discovered that subordinate men could be viewed as "wives" and some women who were royal ministers were addressed as "Father." West African kings, on the other hand, are an ultimate "father figure," exercising a "public fatherhood" not unlike the image of "public motherhood" that is at the center of this book. These different social positions exist in relationship to one another. During my fieldwork in West Africa, I myself was cast in social roles in relation to others I met. Thus, when people called me *ìyàwó* (bride) in Kétu and even in Nigeria, they meant my youth and, potentially, junior status in a household. Often it was older women who called or greeted me in this way. On one occasion, at the house of a friend of my research assistant Alhaja Safouratou Mama, I was called upon to join other women in serving food to some visiting men. I wanted to protest, but I quickly realized that as a young woman I was expected to serve, and I complied. I regarded elderly titled women with much deference, fearing them on some level, because I was supposed to respect their power. In contrast, Alákétu Adétútù, the king of Kétu, acted like a benevolent father, one day giving me some coins and saying, "Buy something for yourself at the market." For a split second, I was going to refuse, but he was the king and he was treating me as his "child." Yet I was warned several times, with some humor, by people at the king's palace to watch my step as I approached the king's veranda. If I passed through a certain space in the courtyard, I would automatically become the king's wife; it would be as though he had "put his foot on me," so people said. The king had the power to choose any woman as his wife. It was only meant to tease me, but it had an effect; I understood the image of the king-as-husband as one of dominance rather than benevolence. These relationships into which I was drawn are not the usual data of a historian, but history overlaps the present. I came to view gender in a kaleidoscopic way, not in terms of binary opposition, as gender relationships are often expressed.

After a short summer visit in 1997, I lived in Kétu for ten months in 1998 and 1999, and for shorter stints in 2000 and 2006. Alhaja Safouratou Mama, my research assistant, helped me conduct interviews throughout the sixteen historically recognized quarters of the formerly walled center of Kétu. Each quarter, or *ita* (a square that was supposed to serve as the center of each neighborhood), had numerous lineages or extended families. The two of us would search out an elderly woman or elderly man to talk to about their lineage, the town's history, and the relationship between Muslims and Christians. Later, I added questions about marriage practices, though asking people personal questions does not come easily to me. People were generous with their personal stories. I am reluctant to expose their lives to the world, and this tension plays out in the book. When I asked one retired man about marriage practices in Kétu, a look of utter anguish flashed across his face. He was a widower whose wife had died several years before, but in that moment he was reliving his grief. People's voices are present in my text, if often submerged. It would be trite to suggest that I saw people in Kétu as my family, but I did see their stories, to some extent, as personal "family business."

Jeannette Hopkins, who worked with me on the manuscript before I submitted it to the press, insisted that I look up my genealogy because of my unusual name. Initially, I was nonchalant, perhaps protecting myself, knowing that as a black American there is often a point beyond which one cannot go. Imagine my surprise when I found out that my grandfather's grandfather had migrated to the town of Middletown, Connecticut, where I am now living and teaching at Wesleyan University. I knew that years earlier, when I had told my grandmother I was moving to New Haven, Connecticut, to go to Yale, she had mentioned that my grandfather was from New Haven. Furthermore, I now learned that in the late nineteenth century, my grandfather's grandfather came to Connecticut from the metropolitan Washington, D.C., area, where I had lived for several years after college at Georgetown and after graduate school at Yale and at Northwestern. Living in northern Virginia after college, I had once seen another Semley in the phonebook—a rare occurrence—and once tried to call, but I did not reach anyone. Though I was a budding historian, I had not thought to trace my own history in either place.

Yet now I realize that for years after my birth in Brooklyn, New York, I had been following my ancestors up and down the eastern coast of the United States without ever knowing it. Such coincidences are enough to make me think that maybe I *am* from Kétu, even though I never forgot or was allowed to forget that I was a stranger. An astute observer of Yoruba religion might tell me that the òrìṣà (deity) who rules my head has been leading me to these places. A number of years ago, when it was suggested that I had "come home" to Kétu, I was amused. Now I am more inclined to believe in larger forces ruling my head and my heart.

Acknowledgments

I did not know that this was the book I would write when I began my research several years ago. Countless people influenced the direction of my research and writing in major and subtle ways, whether through discussion in graduate courses, chance meetings at archives, or casual conversation in coffee shops. Here I will try to do justice to the insight and encouragement so many people have given me over the years.

My professors and fellow graduate students in the Master's Program in African Studies at Yale University and the history department at Northwestern University reinforced the importance of a wide-angle view of the African continent, demonstrating to me how politics, art, history, literature, environmental, and agrarian studies all intersected in the study of African history. My scholarship continues to be shaped by the work of Robert Harms, Christopher Miller, and Robert Farris Thompson at Yale and Jonathon Glassman, Adam Green, and John Hunwick at Northwestern. Though time and distance have separated me from many members of my cohort, I still would like to thank Christopher Hayden, Christopher Manning, Gregory Mann, Jeremy Prestholdt, and, especially, Sarah Fenton.

Over the years, many institutions and programs funded the research at the core of this book, including a Foreign Languages and Area Studies Fellowship, a Fulbright-Hays Group Project Abroad Fellowship, a Fulbright-Hays Dissertation Research Fellowship, and a National Security Education Program Dissertation Fellowship. Once I began teaching at Wesleyan University, funding from Wesleyan University Academic Affairs and the Colonel Return Jonathan Meigs First (1740–1823) Fund supported follow-up research trips in 2006 to Bénin, France, and Brazil.

It is not enough to arrive at an archive or library; the knowledge and assistance of the staff are crucial. First and foremost, the women and men at the Archives Nationales du Bénin always speedily obtained documents and photocopies, and even when years had passed warmly greeted with me the French version of a common Yoruba phrase, "It has been three days." In the Bibliothèque Nationale and former Institut de Recherche Appliqué du Dahomey (IRAD), librarians readily helped me locate some rare documents. At the Archives Nationales and Institut Fondamental de l'Afrique Noire (IFAN) in Senegal, I learned of the rich selection of rare manuscripts and journals in addition to colonial documents. I am also grateful for assistance I received at the Centre des Archives Outre-Mer (CAOM) [now the Archives Nationales Outre-Mer (ANOM)] in Aix-en-Provence, France; at the Archives de la Société de la Propagation de la Foi in Lyon, France; at the Church Missionary Society Archives (CMS) in Birmingham, Great Britain; at the Southern Baptist Historical Library and Archive in Nashville, Tennessee; and at the Schomburg Center for Research in Black Culture in New York. It was also a pleasure to relive my graduate school days while conducting research with the help of librarians at the Yale University Divinity Library and at the Northwestern University Library Archives and Melville J. Herskovits Library of African Studies. Finally, in Salvador, Brazil, I deeply appreciated the guidance of Angela Lühning and Alex Baradel at the Fundação Pierre Verger. They graciously gave me access to Verger's copious correspondence and hundreds of his stunning photographs of Kétu.

Reading groups, conferences, and courses I have taught at Wesleyan have been crucial during the transition from the dissertation to the book. Sara Berry, a long-time mentor and friend, kindly read many drafts of my work (some of them quite rough!) and, together with Pier Larson, invited me to participate in reading and writing workshops with other graduate students at Johns Hopkins University. As I began rewriting the book, a conference at the Université de Laval in Quebec, Canada, organized by Ana Lucia Araujo, helped me develop my concept of "Atlantic Africa." A semester at the Wesleyan Center for the Humanities in spring 2006 allowed me to draft the book's seventh chapter on Brazil. It had been spirited discussions with students in my Women's and Gender History in Africa course in the fall of 2005 that inspired the overall theme of "public motherhood" at the core of the book. In many ways, those initial conversations around motherhood culminated with a Women's Caucus–sponsored panel I organized for the African Studies Association meeting in 2008 on "New Perspectives on Motherhood, Gender, and Power in African History." I also have been inspired by the work and guidance of many specialists in my field of West Africa, including Edna Bay, Toyin Falola, Robin

Law, Paul Lovejoy, John Peel, Mariza Soares, and especially Randy Matory, for his groundbreaking work on West Africa and Brazil. I have appreciated friendship and intellectual exchange with Rachel Jean-Baptiste, Hilary Jones, Emily Osborne, and Michele Reid Vazquez. At Wesleyan, I have been grateful for the encouragement of my colleagues in the history department, especially Rick Elphick, Tricia Hill, Vijay Pinch, Claire Potter, Magda Teter, and Ann Wightman.

Friends and colleagues in Bénin and many people in Kétu have been central to this project over the years. I am grateful for guidance from Béninois historians Sylvain Agninikin, Félix Iroko, and Elisée Soumonni. Through my summer internship at the U.S. embassy in Cotonou, I met Djosse Atchade and his family, who generously provided me refuge in Cotonou, Bénin, as did Sylvie Faboumy and her family. One of my first contacts from Kétu was Akande Olofindji, who kindly introduced me to key figures in the town and offered insight into Kétu practices and history. The late Aláketu Adétútù facilitated my dissertation and his successor Aláketu Aladé Ìfẹ́ assisted me during my final visit to Kétu in 2006. Ìyálóde Basilia Abero kindly housed me during my predissertation trip in the summer of 1997, and the Fadairo family helped provide accommodation during my longer stay. I especially appreciated the lengthy interviews that the late Ìyá Libara Cathérine Oyewole Adebiyi granted me during my dissertation research. During the many months that I lived in Kétu, countless people also greeted me, encouraged me, answered my questions, asked about my work, and cajoled me. Many teased me about finishing my book someday, or at least getting married. The interviews, relationships, and research would not have been possible, however, without the help of Alhaja Safouratou Mama. More than a research assistant who took seriously the interview process, Alhaja generously welcomed me into her family, shared meals with me, told me stories, took me to family ceremonies, and helped me negotiate daily life in Kétu. She was a diligent and thoughtful research assistant and I consider her a dear friend.

Several people have been especially important in these final stages of the writing process. Reader's reports from Misty Bastian and Edna Bay were generous and constructive and shaped the final revisions of the book. I appreciate the work of many people at Indiana University Press who have guided my book through the production process and I am grateful for Scott Taylor's diligent work on the maps that appear in this book. Most of all, Dee Mortensen of Indiana University Press has been an understanding and supportive editor, encouraging my sense of myself as an author. Finally, working with Jeannette

Hopkins helped me transform multiple strands of inquiry in the dissertation into a coherent text. Her probing questions, straightforward critiques, and thorough editing helped reveal to me the book that was there all along. I am solely responsible for any errors that occur in the pages that follow.

My deepest gratitude is for my friends and family. Kimberly Dixon, whom I met at Northwestern, has remained a friend despite the comments I make just to bother her. For many years, time spent with Kathleen Noonan and Jonathan Lipson has always meant sharing great food and even better conversation. I am grateful to the Robinson family for welcoming me as a daughter/niece/sister/friend. Finally, I have known Deidre Hinds for decades; we finish one another's sentences and remember things the other has completely forgotten. She is always in the background acting as one of my biggest cheerleaders, even when I don't realize it.

My mother, Ethel Semley, never asked too many questions about my work, but she listened. In her own way, she has always encouraged me and, in imperceptible ways, has shaped who I am. My father, Arnold Semley, still surprises me with an avid interest in history that I am only just discovering. The book is dedicated to my grandmother, Olga Wanda Semley. Her strong personality, humor, and style are still the subject of many stories shared among her grandchildren and great-grandchildren, and I cannot help but picture her in my mind's eye as one of the "public mothers" that I write about in this book. It was because of her will and presence that I imagine her in this way.

Brian Robinson, my husband, has known this project from its humble beginnings. He has patiently watched it transform over time, tolerating me when I wanted to talk about it too much or too little. I love him more than he knows. Finally, our son, Elijah James Ayọ̀délé arrived very late in the process of my writing to teach me about the everyday forms of motherhood that are not discussed in great detail in the pages that follow. Through him, I also have learned of emotion for which I have no words.

Note on Orthography and Language

I have written this book as a scholarly study accessible to students and readers who are not specialists in African history. The names of peoples and places in West Africa may have multiple spellings, sometimes influenced by a French or British presence. In most cases, I have opted for the most common usage, even if that usage comes from the French language. For example, for the port city of Ouidah I have adopted the French spelling rather than the English one, Whydah. However, for the town of Kétu, I have used the Yoruba rather than the French spelling, Kétou, except in quoted material.

Yoruba is a tonal language with high, middle, and low tones that change the meanings of words. The proper tonal markings for the word "Yoruba" itself would be Yorùbá. For Yoruba words appearing in the text, I have tried to indicate the proper Yoruba accent marks and have used letters with diacritical marks that do not appear in English, including ọ, pronounced "aw," ẹ, pronounced "eh," and ṣ, pronounced "sh." While I have generally included these letters in proper nouns such as place names, I have omitted the tones. For consistency, I have not included letters with diacritical marks or tones in names of individuals, except when the usage and preference was known.

Mother Is Gold,
Father Is Glass

Prologue: "Mother is gold, father is glass"

Power and Vulnerability in Atlantic Africa

During my third extended research trip in Kétu, Bénin, in the fall of 2006, when I asked people to explain the Yoruba proverb "mother is gold, father is glass" (*ìyá ni wúrà, bàbá ni dígí*), they invariably told me a story.[1] An elderly woman explained that a mother would never let her child go hungry. "A mother's love is different from a father's love," she said. "A mirror—that breaks. The father is for everyone. The mother is your mother and she doesn't want to change you."[2] I was specifically interested in the history of women's influence in politics and society, but people told me about women, and men, in families, usually highlighting women's sacrifices in bearing and raising children, in contrast to the limited parenting by men. My research assistant became bored with people's repetitive responses and complained, "It's always the same thing," but the similar style and content underscored how central stories are to Yoruba history. While the common translation for the Yoruba word *ìtàn* is history or story, Yoruba literary scholar Olabiyi Babalọla Yai argues that *ìtàn* encompasses far more: "the verb *tàn* (from which the noun *ìtàn* is derived) means to irradiate, to illuminate, to spread, to relate, to investigate. The concept of *itàn* therefore encompasses history, geography, sociology, philosophy, and aesthetics."[3]

Similar to the "multidirectional and multidisciplinary" ethos at the heart of Yai's definition of *itàn* are several layers of meaning for the word *iyá* (mother). Any woman who has given birth to a child will become known thereafter as "mother of [child's name]" and any woman of a certain age, whether or not she has had children, is addressed respectfully as *iyá* by those who are younger. But *iyá* often serves also as part of the official title of women priests and royal ministers, and it figures in the names of both "witches" and divine or sacred women, described to me as "women whom you can't see."[4] Though the phrase "mother is gold" conjured up the image of childbearing woman in the home, the flexibility of the term *iyá* allowed me to see references to "gold" and "glass" as part of a broader and complex metaphor about gender and history.

"Mother is gold, father is glass" is a popular Yoruba saying that cannot be dated with any certainty, gold and glass having long histories in West Africa. Gold, however, is not often associated directly with Yoruba towns and kingdoms. Most of the gold in mines in modern-day Senegal, Mali, and Ghana, as early as the seventh century, was destined for the trans-Saharan trade to North Africa, Europe, and Asia.[5] With the expansion of the Atlantic slave trade in West Africa dating from the fifteenth century, some of the West African gold trade became re-oriented to the coast, away from desert caravans and toward European ships. Once slaves became the primary export sought from West Africa, Brazilian merchants smuggled gold from Brazilian mines to trade for West African slaves during the early eighteenth century.[6] By the eighteenth and nineteenth centuries, European merchants and travelers in West Africa would occasionally describe gold jewelry worn by kings, their women, and other people of wealth, the provenance of the gold unclear.[7]

While the trans-Saharan trade had extracted gold from West Africa, it brought glass in from Europe and the Islamic world, recycled as early as the ninth century into glass beads that held great economic and spiritual importance. The Yoruba town of Ile-Ife came to earn its distinction as the "cradle" of the Yoruba, partly because it was a center of production of glass beads used in trade and the arts, especially in beaded regalia. Centuries later, trade via the Atlantic coast brought greater prosperity to Ile-Ife, convincing some scholars that an association between bead production, wealth, and the female deity Olokun (Owner of the Sea) had a later origin related to the expansion of that coastal trade dating to the fifteenth century. Oral traditions claim that bead making began with Olokun, a childless, wealthy wife of the Yoruba progenitor and first king, Oduduwa, thus tracing the origins of glass bead making, in Ile-Ifẹ at least, to a childless woman who nonetheless became a "mother figure" by virtue of her affluence and transformation into a deity.[8] Thus, the *ìtàn*, or history, of gold and glass in West Africa "illuminates" a complex story of kingship, trade, religion, and ideology in the sense that scholar Olabiyi Yai uses the term.

Alákétu (king; "owner of Kétu") Aladé Ìfẹ́ interpreted the proverb "mother is gold, father is glass" to emphasize the role of fathers, saying, "Dígí (mirror) is also precious. Gold—it can become lost, you can buy another. But when the mirror breaks, it is finished. If the mother is not there, the child misses something; if the father is not there, it is worse." When I asked him how an absent father was worse, he spoke about the money fathers must spend on their children, concluding that "paternal authority in Africa is vital."[9] Thus, the saying "Mother is gold, father is glass" embodies the contradiction of gender relations in Yoruba history and culture. "Mother is gold" implies that mothers are more important in a society in which women often are dominated by fathers, husbands, uncles, and older brothers. "Father is glass" is elusive and ambivalent, portraying the relationship with fathers as fragile or even as a reflection of oneself, with the word for glass (*dígí*) also translated as mirror. But no one speaking to me used the words "fragile" or "weak" to describe fathers or a child's relationship to them, simply repeating that glass or mirrors "break." Taken at its most cynical, the phrase suggests that a father's presence is illusory or transitory even though Yoruba society itself generally subordinates women to men, especially in family relationships. Paradoxically, the proverb praises the value of women and challenges the image of patriarchal power in the household, the very setting where women potentially face the most control by men.[10]

There is tension between the power and vulnerability of mothers, fathers, wives, and husbands in politics, history, and in private relationships that plays out in Kétu, neighboring West African kingdoms, and in the Bahia region of Brazil, linked to Kétu through the Atlantic slave trade, religion, and travel. The *image* of women's power in all these places has sometimes prevailed over examples of specific women with titles or political power, especially in the past. The current study traces relationships between actual and symbolic mothers and fathers during three transformative processes: the Atlantic slave trade, French colonialism, and transatlantic travel, specifically between West Africa and Brazil.

Brazilian diplomat and author Antônio Olinto uses "mother is gold, father is glass" as an epigraph for his novel, *The King of Kétu*, about a market woman

named Abionan who wants to give birth to the next king of Kétu. Symbolizing the maternal love and sacrifice of the phrase "mother is gold," Abionan be-
friends other strong-willed women, with the honorable but transitory men in
her life evoking the image of "father is glass." But her aspirations go beyond
motherhood; she muses about the power she would have when her unborn son
became king: "transforming Kétu into a once more decisive place in the region,
and as mother of the king of Kétu she would also be able to rule and change
things."[11] Abionan's dreams of ruling the kingdom alongside her son reflected
more Olinto's own romantic notions about the origins of leading women of African descent in Brazil than the realities of women's political power in West Africa. Still, the novel, the second in a trilogy, traces the struggles and triumphs
of generations of mothers and daughters who moved between Brazil, West Africa, and Europe, recalling a history of the Atlantic slave trade and European
colonialism in Africa shaped by gender relations.

By the last decades of the twentieth century, when the character of Abionan
fantasized about restoring Kétu to a "decisive place in the region," Kétu and its
neighbors had survived three centuries of the Atlantic slave trade and seventy
years of European colonial rule, which ended in the early 1960s. Between 1620
and 1860, more than one million people from the Bight of Benin—a shallow bay
along the coasts of modern-day Bénin and western Nigeria—were forced onto
slave ships bound for the Americas.[12] As was the case in most of Africa, West
African men and boys were more likely to be shipped to the Americas, especially by the nineteenth century; the ratio of men and boys to women and girls
was 3:2.[13] Yet, as thousands of men and women captured in wars and raids were
stripped of their livelihoods, names, and families and sold on the coast, West
African kings, royal ministers, and military leaders gained wealth and power,
which they displayed by surrounding themselves with enslaved women and
wives. The Atlantic slave trade did not create West African kingdoms or cultural
concepts of gender, but the trade relationship between Africa, Europe, and the
Americas allowed some West African kingdoms to expand, reorienting their
political and economic relationships away from caravan trade routes crossing
the Sahara Desert to European ships dotting the Atlantic coast.

The Kétu kingdom stood between two formidable states that expanded
during the intensification of the Atlantic slave trade: the Yoruba-speaking Ọyọ
empire to the east and the Gbe-speaking kingdom of Dahomey to the west. The
Ọyọ empire had flourished between 1650 and 1800, imploding after it extended
its reach to participate directly in slave trading on the Atlantic coast in the
middle of the eighteenth century. In contrast, the Dahomey kingdom began a

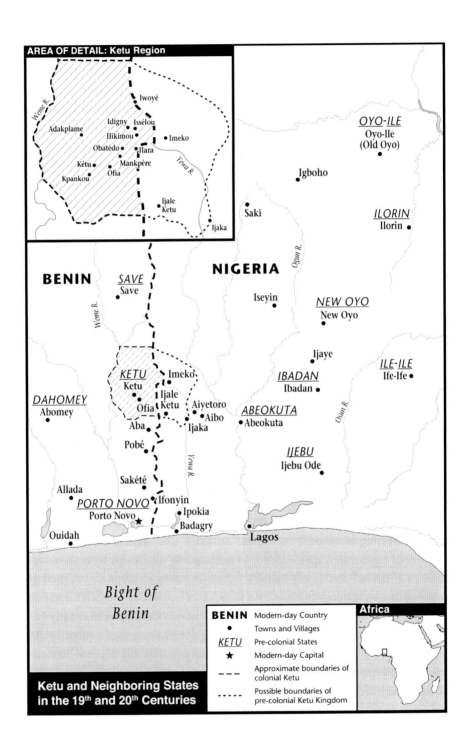

AREA OF DETAIL: Ketu Region

Weme R.

Iwoyé

Adakplame
Idigny   Issélou
Ilikimou   Imeko
Obatédo   Ilara
Kétu   Mankpère
Kpankou   Ofia

Yewa R.

Ijale
Ketu

Ijaka

BENIN   *SAVE*
Save

NIGERIA

OYO-ILE
Oyo-Ile
(Old Oyo)

Igboho

ILORIN
Ilorin

Saki

Iseyin

Weme R.

Ogun R.

NEW OYO
New Oyo

Ijaye

ILE-ILE
Ife-Ife

KETU
Ketu
Imeko

Ijale
Ketu

Ofia

Aiyetoro
Aibo

IBADAN
Ibadan

DAHOMEY
Abomey

Aba

Ijaka

ABEOKUTA
Abeokuta

Osun R.

Pobé

Yewa R.

IJEBU
Ijebu Ode

Sakété

Allada

PORTO NOVO   Ifonyin
Porto Novo   Ipokia

Ouidah

Badagry

Lagos

*Bight of
Benin*

BENIN	Modern-day Country
•	Towns and Villages
KETU	Pre-colonial States
★	Modern-day Capital
– – –	Approximate boundaries of colonial Ketu
·····	Possible boundaries of pre-colonial Ketu Kingdom

Africa

**Ketu and Neighboring States
in the 19th and 20th Centuries**

Kétu saw their stature rise and fall, from that of provincial leader to that of a mere "village chief" by the final decade of colonial rule in the 1950s.

The French were concerned with more than the women they briefly named as "queens" of Kétu and the kings they did not always fully recognize. From the beginning of the colonial era, for example, the French declared an interest in "liberating" women from forced marriages, even though local histories and colonial documents tell of more complex marriage practices in which wives of ordinary men sometimes lived apart from their husbands or left their husbands for other men. Still, the French feared West African women who were too "free," and that fear undercut colonial policies whose intent was to reform African marriage practices and bolster the status of African women within their own households. The French were more apprehensive about wives and childbearing women than about the power represented by elder "mothers."

European colonial rule, in general, reoriented West African politics and economies toward Europe, impeding the travel and communication between West Africa and the Americas that dated to the era of the Atlantic slave trade, though scholars interested in the African roots of American cultures have continued to build upon these earlier links. The term "Black Atlantic," coined by historian of African art Robert Farris Thompson, analyzed cultural borrowings from West Africa in the Americas, but Paul Gilroy's well-known book of that title relegated Africa to a place of origin long left behind as a mythical homeland. Even Africanist scholars who seek to take Africa seriously as a part of a modern Atlantic world tend to examine the nineteenth century and diverse African coastal communities but not the relationship between Africa, Europe, and the Americas in the twentieth century, during Africa's colonial period.[18]

To speak of Atlantic Africa is, however, to recognize a geographical and intellectual space covering West Africa, the Americas, and Europe and extending beyond the era of the Atlantic slave trade. The terms "Atlantic Africa" and "African Atlantic," as employed by recent scholars, place differing emphases on African history or on the history of the Americas. Anthropologist Jane Guyer has used the term "Atlantic Africa" to describe the complex monetary culture in West Africa in a wholly Africa-centered geographical space between a largely Muslim North Africa and the West African coast during the precolonial, colonial, and postcolonial eras. Historians, on the other hand, have written of an "African Atlantic" in which shared religious rituals, in particular, linked West Central Africa with the American South or colonial Brazil.[19] Kétu itself, the

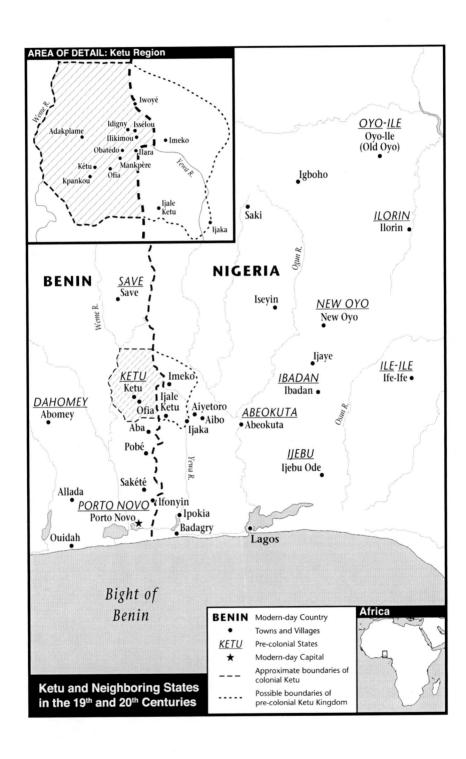

AREA OF DETAIL: Ketu Region

Iwoyé
Idigny · Issélou
Adakplame · Ilikimou · · Imeko
Obatédo · Ilara
Kétu · Mankpère
Kpankou · Ofia
Ijale
Ketu
Ijaka

Wémé R.
Yewa R.

OYO-ILE
Oyo-Ile
(Old Oyo)

Igboho ·

ILORIN
Ilorin

Saki ·

BENIN SAVE
Save

NIGERIA

Iseyin ·

NEW OYO
New Oyo

Wémé R.
Ogun R.

Ijaye ·

KETU Imeko
Ketu · Ijale
Ofia · Ketu Aiyetoro
Aba · Aibo
Ijaka

IBADAN
Ibadan ·

ILE-ILE
Ife-Ife ·

DAHOMEY
Abomey
·

ABEOKUTA
· Abeokuta

Pobé ·

Yewa R.
Ogun R.

IJEBU
Ijebu Ode ·

Allada
· Sakété
PORTO NOVO Ifonyin
Porto Novo ★ · Ipokia
Ouidah · Badagry ·
Lagos ·

*Bight of
Benin*

BENIN	Modern-day Country
·	Towns and Villages
KETU	Pre-colonial States
★	Modern-day Capital
– – –	Approximate boundaries of colonial Ketu
· · · · ·	Possible boundaries of pre-colonial Ketu Kingdom

Africa

**Ketu and Neighboring States
in the 19th and 20th Centuries**

long period of expansion in the 1720s, conquering two major Atlantic slave trading ports and falling only in 1894 when defeated by imperialist French forces. The Atlantic slave trade had reinforced existing patterns of trade, migration, and war that had spread ideas and practices between Yoruba towns, like Kétu and Ọyọ, and between Yoruba peoples and others, including Gbe-speaking states like Dahomey. Yoruba communities and Dahomey came to share religious deities, political titles, and ceremonies, especially after the fall of Ọyọ by the nineteenth century, when Dahomey raided vulnerable Yoruba towns and brought countless women to the Dahomey capital and palace where, even as slaves, they influenced kings, princes, and other leading men and women.

The nefarious Atlantic slave trade also played an unlikely role in expanding the reach of Yoruba culture to the Americas, especially to Brazil, Haiti, and Cuba, where people today claim direct religious and cultural ties to the Yoruba region, though scholars disagree over the correlation between estimated numbers of ostensibly Yoruba-speaking enslaved Africans and the impact of Yoruba culture in the Americas.[14] Kétu itself is recognized as the birthplace of the women who founded Candomblé, an Afro-Brazilian religion that employs spirit possession, sacrifice, and divination to heal and protect its followers. This image of singular and powerful women priests of Candomblé was an inspiration for Olinto's series of novels that feature leading women characters who are defined not only by motherhood but also by power and influence.

The distinction between the image and reality of women's power is an important one in West Africa, where women and men occupy a range of gendered positions. Some elder women are still referred to as "husbands" and some men as "wives."[15] The term "wife" has been as much an expression of subordination to a superior as an expression of gender. Some men who are dependents, especially to a political or religious leader, have acted out their "wifely" role by actually dressing as women. The terms "husband" and "father" have defined a position of superiority, applied both to men and to women. A woman recognized as a "father" could defy cultural norms, refusing to kneel before men or donning men's clothing.[16]

Still, the symbolic power of husbands and fathers has not been exactly the same: thus the image of the husband denoting domination over a subordinate "wife," the image of the father sometimes incorporating the ideal of benevolence, and the practice of paternalism rather than simple patriarchy. The dominant position of husbands and fathers was not absolute; nor were all mothers and wives disempowered. West African kings, the ultimate "father figures," had long faced political challenges. Yoruba kings were sometimes forced to commit suicide by discontented royal ministers and subjects. One Dahomey king was overthrown in a coup and officially erased from the historical record. Still, just as older women respectfully are referred to as *ìyá*, so older men generally are referred to as *bàbá* (father). Some terms and titles incorporate the word for father; the word for diviner, *babaláwo*, translates literally as "father owns the secrets." Whereas the contrast between the social status of biological mothers and wives and that of elderly titled mothers can be profound, men who are fathers in the literal sense and those who acquire titles later in life both exercise authority, whether in the household or over the wider community. Fatherhood is an important concept, yet it does not conjure up the same mystical allure or symbolic weight that motherhood does.

At the height of the Atlantic slave trade in the eighteenth century, kings of Ọyọ were said to have several women royal ministers, many with the word *ìyá* as part of their official title. During the era of the Atlantic slave trade, some favored royal wives were close confidants of kings. The personal power of royal wives and some women royal ministers was so defined by their relationship with the king that they committed suicide upon the king's death, which raises questions about the true nature of their authority. By the middle of the nineteenth century, many of these titled women seem to have faded from prominence as kings performed their symbolic roles as "fathers" and "husbands" by increasing the numbers of dependents or "wives," whether women or men. Numerous and visible, these dependents of the king appeared to displace women royal ministers and other "mother figures" involved in politics. Sources for this period, often imbued with the perspective of European traders and missionaries (some of them Western-educated Africans whose ideals were shaped by Western culture and Christianity), emphasized the image of women primarily as subordinate wives or mothers in the more literal sense. Yet in the early twentieth century, the French colonial administration appointed a Kétu royal wife and a woman priest as colonial agents, ostensibly a tribute to women's power in the community, though the influence of both women in the community rapidly declined. Women's power in West African societies was precarious and European colonial policies intensified the complex power dynamic between women and men.

With the advent of European colonial administrations in West Africa, kings too saw their fortunes change many times, with some kings deposed and others elevated to new levels.[17] French colonial policy, particularly, was inconsistent, weakening many West African kingdoms prior to World War I, only to try to re-establish traditional hierarchies during the interwar period. Kings of

Kétu saw their stature rise and fall, from that of provincial leader to that of a mere "village chief" by the final decade of colonial rule in the 1950s.

The French were concerned with more than the women they briefly named as "queens" of Kétu and the kings they did not always fully recognize. From the beginning of the colonial era, for example, the French declared an interest in "liberating" women from forced marriages, even though local histories and colonial documents tell of more complex marriage practices in which wives of ordinary men sometimes lived apart from their husbands or left their husbands for other men. Still, the French feared West African women who were too "free," and that fear undercut colonial policies whose intent was to reform African marriage practices and bolster the status of African women within their own households. The French were more apprehensive about wives and childbearing women than about the power represented by elder "mothers."

European colonial rule, in general, reoriented West African politics and economies toward Europe, impeding the travel and communication between West Africa and the Americas that dated to the era of the Atlantic slave trade, though scholars interested in the African roots of American cultures have continued to build upon these earlier links. The term "Black Atlantic," coined by historian of African art Robert Farris Thompson, analyzed cultural borrowings from West Africa in the Americas, but Paul Gilroy's well-known book of that title relegated Africa to a place of origin long left behind as a mythical homeland. Even Africanist scholars who seek to take Africa seriously as a part of a modern Atlantic world tend to examine the nineteenth century and diverse African coastal communities but not the relationship between Africa, Europe, and the Americas in the twentieth century, during Africa's colonial period.[18]

To speak of Atlantic Africa is, however, to recognize a geographical and intellectual space covering West Africa, the Americas, and Europe and extending beyond the era of the Atlantic slave trade. The terms "Atlantic Africa" and "African Atlantic," as employed by recent scholars, place differing emphases on African history or on the history of the Americas. Anthropologist Jane Guyer has used the term "Atlantic Africa" to describe the complex monetary culture in West Africa in a wholly Africa-centered geographical space between a largely Muslim North Africa and the West African coast during the precolonial, colonial, and postcolonial eras. Historians, on the other hand, have written of an "African Atlantic" in which shared religious rituals, in particular, linked West Central Africa with the American South or colonial Brazil.[19] Kétu itself, the

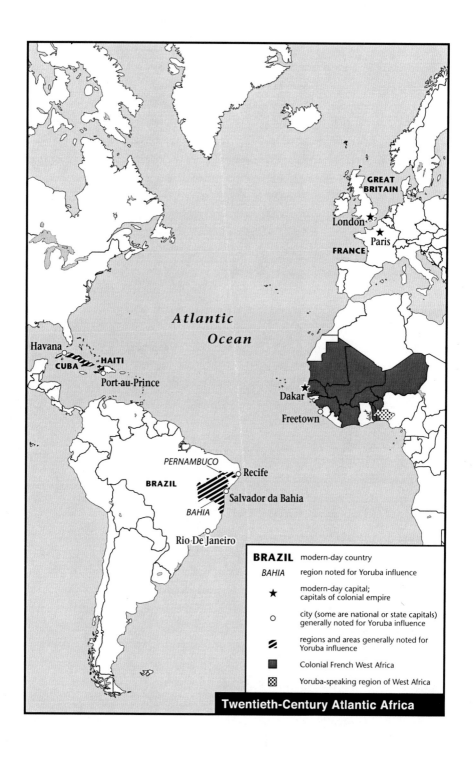

GREAT
BRITAIN

London ★

★ Paris

FRANCE

Atlantic
Ocean

Havana

CUBA   HAITI

Port-au-Prince

Dakar ★

Freetown

PERNAMBUCO

BRAZIL   Recife

Salvador da Bahia

BAHIA

Rio De Janeiro

BRAZIL   modern-day country

BAHIA   region noted for Yoruba influence

★   modern-day capital;
     capitals of colonial empire

○   city (some are national or state capitals)
     generally noted for Yoruba influence

⟋   regions and areas generally noted for
     Yoruba influence

■   Colonial French West Africa

▨   Yoruba-speaking region of West Africa

Twentieth-Century Atlantic Africa

center of this book, was physically and conceptually connected to neighboring West African kingdoms, was subject to French politics and economy, and, symbolically, was seen as part of the history and culture of Brazil. Women and men in multiple regions touching the Atlantic Ocean re-imagined their connections to one another through religious practice, politics, trade, and travel, but the attention paid to the scholars and other travelers who fostered these relationships often overshadows how mass populations in Africa and the Americas participated in these linkages between African, European, and American societies and nations.

Studies of the Atlantic world also have tended to underanalyze the multiple layers of gender relationships. Atlantic world travel has been viewed as the domain of men, young and single, as traders, sailors, and adventurers, even though wives, daughters, women traders, and women priests, too, traveled back and forth between Brazil and West Africa in the nineteenth century as the Atlantic slave trade began to wane. Indeed, two iconic images of travel between Kétu in West Africa and Bahia in Brazil are of both "mother" and "father" figures. Three almost mythical, elderly *iyá* (mothers), enslaved from Kétu, are said to have initiated the Candomblé religion in northeast Brazil in the nineteenth century, and the late king of Kétu, Alaketu Adetutu, traveled twice to Brazil in the 1990s as an honored guest.

Nigerian sociologist Oyèrónkẹ́ Oyěwùmi, author of *The Invention of Women* and frequent critic of what she calls "biologism," the equation of sex with gender, charges that a principal analytical weakness in Western feminism is that "the woman at the heart of feminism is a wife." Oyěwùmi contends that women in African cultures think differently: "In all African family arrangements, the most important ties within the family flow from the mother. . . . These ties link the mother to the child and connect all children of the same mother in bonds that are conceived as natural and unbreakable. . . . the most important and enduring identity and name that African women claim for themselves is 'mother.'" She adds, "However, motherhood is not constructed in tandem with fatherhood. The idea that mothers are powerful is very much a defining characteristic of the institution and its place in society."[20] Oyěwùmi tends to generalize across all African societies, contributing to the "natural" appearance of motherhood rather than highlighting historical processes by which motherhood takes on cultural meanings. She does not clarify the ways in which fatherhood is defined socially; nevertheless, she captures the association between the reality and representation of motherhood. If the act of childbirth makes many women mothers in the most physical sense, the powerful imagery associated with childbirth—an event at once awesome and mundane—is at the heart of the symbolism of the title "mother" bestowed on elderly women.

I draw on the concept of "public motherhood," coined by Nigerian literary scholar Chikwenye Ogunyẹmi, to explain women's political power. Illustrating the connection between the social experience of motherhood and what she calls the "politicoeconomic role of the mother without," Ogunyẹmi uses as a point of departure the Yoruba title of the Ìyálóde (Mother Owns the Outside World), who is charged with managing conflict in the town and overseeing market trade. She contrasts the social and political power of older women with the subordination of younger wives, describing powerful women as those "who have ceased to function visibly as wives and are now utterly devoted to their sons, their daughters having left home for their husband's houses. . . . While the younger woman writhes in the servility attached to wifehood, the older woman relishes the newfound power over her son's household and the community."[21] But the easy jump from "household" to "community" in Ogunyẹmi's description illustrates that women's titles may obscure the nature of women's power as much as they define it. Indeed, for Ogunyẹmi, the power women exercise flows from their role as biological mothers; she ultimately sees women as "caretakers," even in the public domain.[22]

Western feminists theorizing about motherhood have explored how it sustains patriarchy or male domination or how it functions as a lived experience to be celebrated. African American scholars, frequently challenging an idealized vision of a white, middle-class, nuclear, heterosexual household, have written about the role of "othermothers"—grandmothers, aunts, friends, lovers—in children's upbringing and in women's self-realization. But even black and white scholars who have incorporated race, class, sexuality, and also the implications of reproduction technologies in their analyses often have focused on the personal joys and traumas of motherhood, giving personal experience priority over historical and cultural settings that define motherhood.[23] Reliance on the literal experience of motherhood would make the presence of titled mothers in West Africa a function of women's bodies and sexuality rather than a part of historical definitions of power and identity. The present study is not focused on the experience of biological motherhood and avoids both Oyěwùmi's emphasis on the (perceived) "naturalness" of African motherhood and Ogunyẹmi's focus on the nurturing work of "public mothers." It seeks rather to emphasize the historical and changing symbolic power of motherhood that recognizes but also challenges men's power in West African society.

One way to rethink gender and rewrite history is to analyze constructively manhood and masculinity in terms of authority, power, and vulnerability. In a 2003 volume, *Men and Masculinities in Modern Africa,* editors and contributors differentiate between local understandings of manhood, men's adulthood, and more abstract notions of masculinity.[24] Similar to the concept of "public motherhood," a term like "public fatherhood" can be used to analyze the real and symbolic nature of men's power. "Public fathers," such as kings and other leading men in society, assume a paternal and patriarchal role over extended family members and the broader community. Dispensing money and advice, the father in the household and in the public arena may appear detached and even benevolent, but either way, as a paternal figure he wields power over subordinate women, men, and children. Perhaps because the father can adopt a position of authority, commanding larger numbers of people in ways women and younger men cannot, and because he may abuse that power, paternal affection is perceived as fragile, as a possible façade, as breakable as "glass." Matching Oyěwùmi's concept of "wife" as a problematic persona in feminist analysis, the "husband," too, represents a dichotomous authority, with power limited to control over wives, not necessarily reaching to all other family members and/or to the broader community.[25] Analyzing gender in West Africa in terms of historical and cultural understandings of real and symbolic relationships between mothers and fathers as well as between wives and husbands, for example, is to avoid some of the limitations of feminist interpretation by Western and Africanist scholars.[26]

Thus, the history of gender and power plays out in a variety of multifaceted relationships in the pages that follow: between women royal ministers, kings, and enslaved women; between Kétu's colonial "queens," French colonial administrators, and Kétu residents; between wives, husbands, and their extended families; and between researchers, Brazilian women priests of Candomblé, and men who were their partners and protégés.

1

Founding Fathers and Metaphorical Mothers

History, Myth, and the Making of a Kingdom

It is said that a "witch" named Yá Mepere (literally Mother Mepere) gave her blessing to a group of migrants—among them a would-be king and a brave hunter—who founded the settlement that became Kétu. While trailblazing men—kings, hunters, and blacksmiths—are accepted as common protagonists in West African oral histories, women leaders, feminine divine beings, and "witches" who appear beside them are viewed as relics of a long-lost matriarchal order. Such interpretations make men part of the historical past and relegate women to a mythical one.[1]

The Yoruba word for history, *ìtàn*, defines many types of storytelling, but when understood as oral traditions, it claims to provide an accurate account of the origins of kingdoms, using common elements of African oral traditions such as migration, "witches," and ritual sacrifice. Africanist historians who have long grappled with the tension between history and myth acknowledge that these oral traditions or histories, presumably passed down for generations, have been manipulated along the way. But rather than focusing on the unreliability and contradiction within oral sources, historians can embrace the very mingling of fact and fiction in oral sources as a genuine reflection of Kétu's multicultural society, its links with neighboring communities, and its cultural ideologies about gender.[2] "Mothers" may serve as a metaphor in Kétu origin myths, and that captures how storytellers, their audience, and scholars who transcribe and analyze these stories have understood the actual relationships between women and men in the historical past and in the present.

"Witches" and "Children Born To Die": Gendered Histories

When people in Kétu told me fragments of the oral traditions of the town's origins, they emphasized that Kétu's founders came from somewhere else and on their arrival in Kétu encountered two elderly "mothers" with supernatural powers and resources for survival.[3] As with many other Yoruba towns, Kétu's origins are traced back to Ile-Ifẹ, considered to be the "cradle" of the Yoruba. The migration from Ile-Ifẹ was long and complicated, with a long sojourn in at least two other towns. The turning point came when would-be king Ede and his leading hunter Alalumon decided to establish a new settlement in Kétu. Yá Mepere, the first elderly "mother," entered the story when she struck dead a young male scout who surprised her while she was half-clothed. Alalumon then greeted her properly and she granted the migrants permission to pass and access to water; she also gave Alalumon a charm for his protection. A second elderly woman, from the nearby town of Panku, known as Yá Panku (Mother Panku), recognized Alalumon from his earlier hunting expeditions in the region, and she gave the migrants the gift of fire.[4] Women and young girls in the group used the water and fire to cook, establishing the camp that would become the town. Later, to celebrate the founding of the new settlement, sacrifices were made to the òrìṣà (deities). One such sacrifice was a hunchbacked weaver. The death of this humble man reputedly gave the town its name, Kétu, when the people exclaimed, "Kétu n ke?" "Who can straighten the hunchback's hump?" The customary rejoinder to "Kétu n ke?" was "Who can destroy the town?" The town was supposed to be as indestructible as the hump on the weaver's back. Though Kétu was founded centuries ago, these mythical episodes and the sites of these events are revisited by the people whenever a new king comes to power. The rituals remind people of the role of kings, hunters, and "mothers" in the origins of the town and of the connection between Kétu and a wider Yoruba world; one of the first acts of a newly enthroned king was to send a messenger to the kings of Ile-Ifẹ and Ọyọ, who were expected to congratulate the king with a gift of luxurious fabric.[5]

Many Yoruba towns trace their origins to the legendary kingdom at Ile-Ifẹ to justify claims of kingship. Kétu, however, enjoys a degree of distinction, generally recognized among dozens of Yoruba towns, as one of the original kingdoms descended from Ile-Ifẹ. It is said that Oduduwa, the "progenitor" of the Yoruba people, descended to earth on a chain only to find it covered with water. After tossing a handful of dirt on the water, Oduduwa set down a rooster who spread the dirt, creating land that became the site of Ile-Ifẹ. This myth explains the origins of the Yoruba, if not of all humanity, and describes how Oduduwa represented an extraordinary shift in political and social organization of Yoruba states, an "experiment" in kingship. During the Oduduwa "period," kingship came to be represented by the ownership of a crown with strings of beads covering the face. It is said that six, seven, or sixteen kingdoms emerged from the sons of Oduduwa, but in the standard version, it was one of Oduduwa's daughters who bore a son who became the king of Kétu. Indeed, Aláketu Adewori, who was king of Kétu from 1937 to 1967, told British scholar E. G. Parrinder that Oduduwa was actually a woman and wife to the prince who would lead the first wave of migrants to Kétu out of Ile-Ifẹ.[6] While the image of the eminent Oduduwa as the ultimate "public mother" is an enticing one, as a myth it is symbolic, not definitive. Other stories supplant Ile-Ifẹ's predominance as a place of origin, especially stories from the once great empire at Ọyọ. In fact, the most cited work of Yoruba oral traditions was collected in Ọyọ by Christian Yoruba historian Samuel Johnson for his magisterial book *History of the Yorubas*. Ọyọ oral traditions portray Oduduwa as a migrant and claim that the Ifẹ kingship was transferred to Ọyọ with descendants of a mere slave left to serve as king of Ile-Ifẹ.[7] Other Yoruba towns assert direct ties to Ile-Ifẹ or other nearby villages, rejecting Ọyọ oral traditions that declare that other towns descended from Ọyọ's leadership or were conquered by Ọyọ.[8]

Men are the primary protagonists in most of these stories, but some women are powerful mythical figures with implications for religion and for politics, two areas closely linked in precolonial kingdoms. Given their outsider status, the founders of the Kétu kingdom, remembered as princes and hunters, had to negotiate with indigenous populations who were, in turn, represented by elderly "mothers" with supernatural powers or access to crucial resources. Partnering the "mother" with a hunter evokes the idea of African "complementarity," whereby women and men have recognized, separate, gender-specific, yet interdependent, roles in society. The concept of "complementarity," foundational to much Africanist feminist scholarship on gender in Africa (as well as in the African diaspora), has been described by Sierra Leonean–born scholar Filomina

Chioma Steady as "a total, rather than a dichotomous and exclusive, perspective. For women, the male is not 'the other' but part of the human same. Each gender constitutes the critical half that makes the human whole. Neither sex is totally complete. . . . Each has and needs a complement, despite the possession of unique features of its own."[9] Scholar Kamene Okonjo has theorized "complementarity" further into what she calls a dual-sex system in some Igbo communities in southeastern Nigeria. For Okonjo, the *omu* (mother) acts as an equal counterpart of *obi* (king), and women's power and interests are represented at all levels of society, with the *omu* "acknowledged mother of the whole community but . . . charged with concern for the female section." Theories of complementarity sometimes emphasize harmony between the feminine and the masculine, reinforcing the idea of "natural" sexual differences in what could be a range of gendered roles and social behaviors.[10] Indeed, the symbolic relationship between the "mother" and the hunter featured in the Kétu origin story is more evocative than the more common one posited between the king and the "mother." The idea that "mother figures" associated with West African kings were equal counterparts or that the women acted as "co-rulers" ignores the hierarchy and domination that characterize centralized kingdoms.

The relationship between the hunter and the "mother" in the Kétu oral tradition, in part, need not be as much about "complementarity" as about comparable forms of power. Both the "mother" and the hunter have specialized skills that can help and protect others. Together the migrant hunter and the indigenous "mother" clear the space for settlement by providing safety and the possibility of prosperity. The hunter's power derives from his familiarity with the dangerous forest, his knowledge of medicine, and his role in policing and defending the community.[11] In the Yoruba case, to see elder women's authority only in relation to biological motherhood obscures the important role of "occult power" that shrouds postmenopausal women in particular, which evokes fear as much as respect.[12] Indeed, along with the imagery of birth and nurturing embedded in the metaphor of "public motherhood" are the specters of infertility, death, and destruction. The Yoruba term *àjẹ́* often translates as "witch," though many dare not utter it, instead referring to elderly women with secret knowledge of the supernatural as *àwọn ìyá wa* (our mothers). "Our mothers" are not purely a destructive force; they are believed to bring balance, to work wonders, and to maintain social order and morality in society. Henry and Margaret Drewal, in their study of Gẹ̀lẹ̀dẹ́, the Yoruba masquerade said to honor the power of mothers, remark that the link between women's bodies and elderly women's power is, literally, not only about women's fertility and some women's supposed supernatural power to take life away but also about the perception that women can live to be old and thereby possess knowledge of the "secret of life itself." Still, the social stigma associated with being deemed a "witch" in Yoruba and other African communities may lead to persecution and exile.[13] Elderly "mothers" are often portrayed as "witches," but their power comes not from indiscriminate performance of evil deeds but from their perceived ability to control the most important life function in the community: women's fertility.[14] Thus, the fact that West African society simultaneously reveres and fears elderly women and may ostracize otherwise empowered "mothers" undercuts the authority and influence of these same women. "Public mothers" do not simply "nurture" the broader society but also embody the complexities of power, its contradictions, and its limits.

Within myths of origin, existing communities and practices are frequently incorporated into a new social order through the creation of titles and offices, recognizing the power of the ancestors and deities that inhabit the land and demand respect. Thus, Yá Mepere offers the hunter Alalumon access to water and protective medicine or a charm and Yá Panku provides fire for cooking, representing their "secret" knowledge of the local land. Though the name of the hunchbacked weaver sacrificed to the deities to celebrate the founding of Kétu is not recorded, the name of the man he lived with, Akiniko, became a royal title, evoking the weaver's story.[15] Men linked to the founding of the kingdom (including the hunter Alalumon) are honored by titles established in their name. The two elderly "mothers," Yá Mepere and Yá Panku, are remembered almost as mythical figures, yet that does not invalidate women's symbolic power, and it captures well the common image of sometimes elusive elder "mother figures" working with leading men in West African kingdoms. Most of the other wives and daughters remain nameless and in the background in Kétu's origin story, but the relationships between women, men, children, "mothers," and "fathers," formed the foundation of a lasting community, especially as the town expanded and became part of larger social and economic networks.

Nigerian historian Biodun Adediran distinguishes between "pre-Oduduwa" and "Oduduwa elements" as communities shifted from smaller, lineage-based settlements to more diverse city-states. While Adediran assumes a progression from simple, monolithic communities to complex, "hybrid" ones, he reveals a long history of ethnic diversity in Kétu and other western Yoruba towns. He

understands the early history of the kingdom as a time of great political upheaval, physical migration, and political change.[16] The initial meeting between
the would-be king Ede, Alalumon, his hunter, and the two elderly "mothers"
represents conflict and submission, and the famous walls constructed around
the town that protected Kétu from surrounding Gbe-speaking communities
are attributed to mythical kings Sa and Epo. Yet if Kétu had always been diverse in its makeup, cooperation and cultural exchange would also have been
central to the town's history from its beginnings.

Political divisions of the more recent past between Kétu and Dahomey cannot, however, be traced readily to Kétu's mythical and distant past. Scholars do
consider the conflict between Kétu and the expanding Dahomey kingdom by
the latter eighteenth century to be historical, rather than a projection of the
present into the past. Alákétu Ande, who ruled approximately between 1760
and 1780, avoided an ambush by Dahomey during the ritual bath that was part
of his enthronement ceremonies; Kétu oral traditions tell that the river ran
red with the blood of Dahomey soldiers.[17] Dahomey mounted another attack
against Alákétu Ande's successor Akibiowu in 1789; contemporary Europeans
and local oral traditions recorded its outcome differently, Kétu and Dahomey
sources associating the battle with a solar eclipse, a dead elephant, and, so it is
said, a kidnapped princess who founded a sect in the Afro-Brazilian religion of
Candomblé. Dahomey probably did not succeed in attacking or defeating Kétu
itself, but an outlying village.[18] While these eighteenth-century battles recount
the historical beginnings of modern conflict between Kétu and Dahomey, the
dispute reflects the normal competition between states rather than an example
of deep-seated ethnic hatred.

By the nineteenth century, the center of the Kétu kingdom was encased
in a mud-brick wall more than twelve feet high, with ditches eight or nine feet
deep and up to twenty feet wide; the enclosed center would have covered about
two miles and encompassed about two hundred acres.[19] A single entryway,
known as the Akaba Idena, famed for its own magical powers, marked the spot
of the hunchbacked weaver's sacrifice. Several distinct neighborhoods grew
around communal squares within the walled enceinte; by the nineteenth century, there were sixteen squares, including two Muslim quarters.[20] But, as other
anthropological and historical studies of specific Yoruba towns show, Kétu
was not a timeless Yoruba town occupied by neatly defined extended families with singular identities. A closer look at Kétu reveals a settlement of waves
of diverse migrants who arrived not only from Ile-Ifẹ but from other Yoruba
towns and from other ethnic groups.[21] Using *oríkì*, complex and poetic praise

The Akaba Idena is the famed doorway to Kétu's central town, restored and shown with some of the surrounding ramparts. The entrance was not a sign of the town's isolation but its integration in regional networks, serving as the site of the main four-day market in the nineteenth century. Photograph by author.

songs (sometimes little understood by people today who are only able to recite fragments of them), people recount with pride their origins in other West African communities such as the Baatonu (Bariba) or Tapa to the north, Weme to the south, or Gbe speakers to the west.[22] Like other Yoruba kingdoms, Kétu had amorphous boundaries spreading beyond the walled center of the town into nearby Gbe villages and other settlements more than twenty miles away in what is now Nigeria. Though some villages took on a more autonomous outlook, challenging the control of the town and the king, the links between the town and peripheral villages were strong, with most families maintaining farmland in villages and living there for months at a time during the rainy season.[23] Scholars fascinated by the density and complexity of Yoruba towns have debated whether there was a precolonial form of Yoruba "urbanism" based on agricultural production rather than industry and composed of lineages or extended families.[24] To think of agriculturally based Yoruba towns as "urban" because of their population density does challenge assumptions about the definition of cities, but the concept of a process of "urbanization" does not necessarily capture how towns actually formed, how local residents identified themselves, or how those processes of expansion reflected gender roles.

Despite the predominant theme of the independent prince or the trailblazing hunter as the iconic founder of Yoruba towns, Kétu's oral traditions subtly incorporate the image of families with wives and children as migrants and settlers. Because a bride was expected to relocate to the household of her husband with in-laws, her husband's brothers, and their families and younger siblings, women were the mobile members of the community, moving between households, villages, and towns. Like the oral traditions of the town, which emphasized migrating prince and hunter, the oral histories of individual Kétu families told of the migration, sometimes conspicuously from Ile-Ifẹ, more often from other prominent or nearby Yoruba towns, of a grandfather, a great-grandfather or a more distant, almost mythical ancestor.[25] In these family stories, individual men, portrayed as lone settlers with little reference to wives, children, and families, founded communities. To see the understated role of women in expansion as one of reproduction, sexuality, and fertility is too simplistic. Indeed, a recurrent theme in the oral histories of individual families was men's fertility and their quest for fatherhood.

Echoing the oral tradition of the town, one man told me his ancestor arrived from Ile-Ifẹ trying to escape from *àbíkú*, literally "children born to die." The ancestor, a hunter, had arrived from Ile-Ifẹ with his wife and had rested his bag on a tree where his first healthy child was born and where the compound now stood.[26] The reference to Ile-Ifẹ lends prestige and authenticity to the family's heritage, together with the familiar image of the hunter and the items associated with his work, a bag of supplies and the ability to track and scout landmarks like trees. The specter of *àbíkú* (children born to die), found too in modern Nigerian literature, appears in family histories that people tell about life-altering moments of hardship, such as displacement or religious conversion.[27] "Children born to die" may be seen not simply as a metaphor for personal anguish or modern-day angst but as defying the normal patterns of reproduction and expansion of the household by denying families children and a future. In contrast to the eighteenth century, when the Ọyọ empire, at its peak, added more royal wives and other palace dependents and politicized the symbols of procreation and marriage associated with the household, the image of the "child born to die" is linked to the itinerant club or band of men, as in the Yoruba towns that rose in the nineteenth century on the strength of their soldiers and slave raiding.[28] The story of the hunter from Ile-Ifẹ who overcame the death of his children to establish a home in Kétu is a broader metaphor for the triumph of procreation, household, and kingdom over death, mobility, and militarized states. Wives, mothers, and women's fertility may be the ultimate symbols of the household, while men suffering from "children born to die," as depicted in oral histories, link the household to men and fatherhood.

Women, wives, and even child-bearing mothers are often only secondary in family histories as in histories about the town. Though few guardians of family histories today tend to remember women as part of the founding story of a compound, there is a recurrent theme of "motherhood" in these histories, a theme less about child bearing than about age, power, and influence. Most women remembered in family histories came from more recent decades, powerful "mothers" who were most senior in the compound or women who had acquired a broader title in the community. Before I had learned of the title "Ìyá Ọba" (Mother of the King) in Kétu, a man who hinted at the prestige of his family said that one of his female ancestors, Ṣanibi, had been Ìyá Ọba during the 1920s or 1930s.[29] In one extraordinary case, an elderly Muslim man claimed that a woman blacksmith had established his family compound, extraordinary because women are seldom associated with smithing; still, blacksmiths, like elderly women, are perceived to have specialized knowledge and supernatural power.[30] Taken together, powerful mother figures and vulnerable fathers in oral traditions and family histories nonetheless do not completely subvert the gender relations in Yoruba society in which most men dominate most women.

In her study of Yoruba storytelling, Deirdre La Pin affirms that many oral forms of expression became formulaic, with stock characters, familiar hardships, and neat resolutions.[31] That oral forms can be manipulated and open to debate does not make them useless but *useful* for people who hear and tell them, who write them down or read them. Access to the oral source is seldom possible or translatable and the relationship between those who tell stories and those who write them down is lost. Whether recorded by a Christian Yoruba convert in 1853, by a local Kétu historian in the 1920s, a French administrator in the 1940s, or by me, an African American researcher, town and family histories take on diverse symbolic and historical meanings. People in Kétu may express their understanding of the past in their oral histories, may control some of the material available to researchers, and may influence the outcome, yet the writer's perspective shapes how stories about power, politics, and gender are written for a wider audience.

The Politics of Making History out of Myth

A missionary of the British-based Church Missionary Society (CMS), Samuel Crowther, himself a Yoruba man, first wrote of Kétu's origins as he learned of them during a visit in 1853: "The king of Kétu is said to be the eldest of 3 brothers viz. the Alákétu, King of Kétu, Alake, King of the Egba nation, and the youngest King of Yorùbá. . . . The king of Ife is said to be the keeper of the house of Ife. The Alákétu is the rightful proprietor of Ife at the demise of their father."[32] About forty years later, in 1894, the French had defeated Dahomey, a neighboring kingdom that in 1886 had decimated Kétu, capturing and enslaving many survivors. A French navy lieutenant and amateur topographer named Aubé, who was escorting Kétu refugees from Dahomey back to Kétu, was told, "The town of Kétu was founded by Ede, an inhabitant of Ogoudo, a village between Save and Kétu."[33] Each account addressed a radically different perspective on political legitimacy, focusing on two figures in Kétu's oral traditions. The "older brother" of the king of Ọyọ refers to Ṣoipasan, sometimes portrayed as the "husband" of Oduduwa; the villager was Ede, the man who founded Kétu, with the help of the hunter Alalumon and the blessing of "Mother" Mepere. Crowther had heard that the founders of Kétu originated in the Yoruba "homeland," and the French navy lieutenant had heard that an ordinary person established the kingdom. Neither mentioned the presence of women.

When Samuel Crowther visited Kétu in 1853, he was not a stranger. For seven years, he had been exchanging messages with the king of Kétu, Alákétu Adebia, having first met the king's messengers when the king was organizing the rescue of some of his people captured during a slave raid on another town. Crowther later helped resolve a dispute between some Kétu traders and some soldiers from Abẹokuta, where Crowther was stationed.[34] Crowther came to respect the king of Kétu early on, praising him via his messengers: "God has made him [the Alákétu] a father to his people, it was his duty to keep and protect them . . . and as long as he acts the part of a father to his people God would bless him."[35] The king himself came to see Crowther as an *awo* (intimate friend though known only from a distance), and Crowther was sheltered during much of his stay in Kétu, spending most of his time with a man named Asai, who he believed was the "prime minister" of Kétu. Asai, an apparent supporter of missionary activities in Kétu, was probably a lesser dignitary responsible for guiding visitors and probably provided the version of the oral history of the town origins that Crowther wrote down.[36]

Crowther had been rescued from a slave ship as a young boy and educated in Sierra Leone and London by the Church Missionary Society. Like other Yoruba intellectuals, including descendants of Yoruba slaves who returned from Brazil, he wished to portray a Yoruba "nation" connected by language and culture across diverse West African towns and reaching as far as resettlement communities in Sierra Leone. But Crowther had not shaped Kétu's past to his own ends; he was recording its history from the perspective of the Alákétu (king of Kétu) and other leading men. By the nineteenth century, when the Qyọ empire had been destroyed and several Yoruba towns vied to be a successor, Kétu's leadership was making a statement about the town's power and importance as the "rightful proprietor of Ife."

How different the situation was in 1894 at the dawn of French colonialism. After a nominal presence along the African coast over two centuries, European nations, spurred on by economic competition and technological advances in weaponry in the 1890s, began to undertake military expeditions to seize interior African lands. The all-European Berlin Conference of 1884–1885 had guaranteed European traders and missionaries access to the continent, often based on dubious treaties between African leaders and European representatives. While soldiers in the service of France launched a military campaign against Dahomey in 1892, Great Britain used its base in the coastal port of Lagos to complete treaties and military strikes against Yoruba towns. Kétu, recognized as a kingdom by the French, initially enjoyed "protected" status with some rights and autonomy, though in 1908 it had lost its protectorate standing along with most other kingdoms in the Dahomey. In a few decades, Africans' centuries-long relationship with Europe and the Americas shifted from one based on trade in goods and slaves to one in which French and British officials tried to shape African political and social life more closely.

When French lieutenant Aubé took down the story of Kétu's origins, he had less knowledge and less personal investment in the history of the region than Crowther had had.[37] That the refugees described Kétu's founder as neither a "prince" nor the "older brother" of another powerful king did not mean that the recent war had dampened political motivations of fifty years earlier, when Crowther collected his version of events. Aubé had been helped by a "little escort"; during the trek from Dahomey territory to Kétu's overgrown capital, abandoned for eight years, his informant likely associated with one of Kétu's five royal families that name a king to the throne on a rotating basis.[38] A man named Odu, who would take the name Onyegen as the next Alákétu, or king of Kétu, was among the refugees, as was a former wife of the previous king who would become Onyegen's senior wife, or Ida. Known as Alaba Ida, she would become a notorious figure in her local community and to the French colonial administration over the next two decades. Fehetona, another refugee, speaking to a Catholic priest who visited at his settlement near the historical site of Kétu's walled center, had claimed to be the king of Kétu in 1891.[39] Anyone with the French commander's ear would have had an interest in highlighting Kétu's independent origins.

Odu (later Alákétu Onyegen), his future senior wife Alaba, or others may have omitted parts of oral histories when they recited them. So too the writer who transcribed an oral source participated in its retelling. Oral narrative that becomes public is subject to approval or critique by any audience and vulnerable to the whims of the narrator, who may reinterpret it for political or dramatic effect. A writer, in writing down an oral history, establishes a record that may become canonical, but the actual "oral historian" who spoke to Crowther or Aubé, whether a titleholder responsible for maintaining town histories or an informant granting an interview or engaging in casual conversation, remains unknown, as does the actual and entire content of the oral history. Decades later, when Father Thomas Moulero, a Catholic priest and local historian from Kétu, and Edouard Dunglas, a French colonial administrator, took down more detailed versions of Kétu's oral history, they obscured their sources and the settings where they had collected them. Moulero and Dunglas each became "oral historians" in their own right, engaging the style and method of storytelling to convey Kétu's oral histories in writing.[40]

In 1926 and 1927, Moulero wrote a twelve-part series on his hometown's history for the religious and scholarly journal *La Reconnaissance Africaine* (African Discovery). He had been taken into the Catholic mission in Kétu as a young boy, rose quickly in the teaching ranks to become, in 1928, the first ordained African Catholic priest in the French colony of Dahomey.[41] Serving his own religious and intellectual passions, he wrote a study of the Savé kingdom's history after teaching there from 1933 to 1958, and he began a long career as a consultant and guide to innumerable foreign researchers that lasted until his death in 1974. Brazilian diplomat and author Antônio Olinto was so inspired by Moulero that he incorporated him as a character in one of his books about Brazilians who migrated back to West Africa.[42]

The French colonial administrator Edouard Dunglas was living in Dahomey when Moulero was writing his series on Kétu history. Stationed in Kétu between 1939 and 1942, Dunglas hoped to complete a study of Kétu history, but, uncovering little source material on Kétu, he turned instead to a regional

Statue of Father Thomas Moulero, local Kétu historian and ordained priest, who greatly shaped the writing of Kétu history, publishing oral traditions in the 1920s and consulting with outside researchers until his death in 1974. Photograph by author.

study of "Central Dahomey." His essay, "Contribution à l'histoire du Moyen Dahomey: Royaume de Kétou, d'Abomey, et de Ouidah" [Towards a History of Central Dahomey], appeared posthumously in 1957 and 1958. Several educated Kétu men were eager to show me hand-copied versions or excerpts of Dunglas's original undated manuscript, "Legends and History of the Kétu Kingdom," currently housed in the former Dahomey Institute for Applied Research (IRAD). The circulation (albeit limited) of the written-down oral histories within Kétu itself demonstrates how written history comes to bear on oral sources in the present.[43]

Moulero began his first article on Kétu's history as a teller of popular tales: "Here are the stories that hunters tell about the origins of Kétou during the long nights as they watch and wait for a passing herd of elephants."[44] Whether or not Moulero ever heard oral histories in such a setting, he did interview people such as an elderly woman captured in the 1886 attack by Dahomey, and some of his Savé oral histories were said to be collected from a teenage boy.[45] Many of the oral histories Moulero transcribed about Kétu were about kings, top ministers, and other wealthy male residents. Dunglas, too, sought information mainly from the Alákétu (king of Kétu), his ministers, the imam (Muslim religious leader), the French Catholic mission priest, and agents of the French administration.[46]

Moulero and Dunglas did not pretend to use only verified evidence. They both sprinkled supernatural events, songs, and aphorisms throughout their texts, in contrast to more typical modern Western historical accounts based in written evidence. Christian, Western-educated Yoruba historian Samuel Johnson also included similar magical events in his own famous *History of the Yorubas*. Literary scholar Ato Quayson explains that Johnson and his colleagues, writing in the era of rising Yoruba cultural nationalism in the face of European colonialism of the late nineteenth and early twentieth centuries, tried to represent Yoruba history in a Western mode while at the same time retaining the oral character of Yoruba culture. Moulero stated matter-of-factly that "witches" capable of powers over life and death, similar to those reputed of Yá Mepere, still existed in Kétu, and he told of a man of superhuman strength, a giant, who by himself erected the fortifications surrounding the town. He described how one side in a violent conflict in the nineteenth century protected themselves from bullets by wearing talismans. Indeed, recording a supernatural event as a historical event was not unusual for African elites writing at that time.[47] Though some of the elements Moulero and Johnson related would be dismissed by a Western reader, Moulero and Johnson attempted to transcend the contrasts by combining Western and Yoruba cultural forms.[48] They joined storyteller to writer, and spoken to written word.

Dunglas himself mocked the famous story Moulero told of the giant who dug the trench around Kétu, noting that it was the men who repaired the mud walls who recreated the large thumbprints attributed to the giant.[49] Yet Dunglas ended a chapter on the king's ministers with the story of two "witches," not unlike Yá Mepere of the standard Kétu origin story. Yá Mefu (Mother Mefu), associated with the Mefu royal family, is celebrated for bringing rain, in the past the town's sole source of water. The other "witch" was an elderly woman known as Yá Bokolo or Na Bokolo ("Na" meaning "aunt"), who like Yá Mefu was noted for disappearing into the earth instead of dying, thus able to return from time to time.[50] Dunglas tried to rationalize the lore surrounding Na Bokolo with comments that stories of the disappearance of important and powerful people into the earth were not uncommon in Yoruba towns. Dunglas reprinted and translated sayings and several songs in Yoruba and Gbe languages that marked historical events in the town, including, as had Moulero, local stories that Western standards of evidence could not explain.

Moulero's status in the Kétu kingdom and in the French colonial state affected his stake as an author of Kétu's history as much as his racial and ethnic identity did. He had familial ties to the Magbo royal family and his Western education and Catholic beliefs tied him to the colonial apparatus and to the many Westerners who visited his country after independence. Thus Moulero was an insider with the potential to observe as an outsider. Citing the work of an eminent nineteenth-century French historian of the religion of ancient Greece and Rome, he defended oral sources as superior to others.[51] Dunglas, by contrast, consulted sources based on observation or hearsay, such as traveler accounts, missionary reports, and other historical texts. In keeping with his role as a French colonial administrator, he noted colonial structures such as the administrator's residence or the dispensary and referred to notorious Kétu personalities from the early colonial period, such as the two Kétu women who had served as French colonial agents from 1911 to 1917. Reiterating that Kétu was but a provincial capital and no longer formally recognized as a kingdom (even though kingship was not abolished as in other places), Dunglas commented how the Alákétu—no longer an awe-inspiring king but the mere head of a colonial province—was able to leave the palace dressed as a "regular person."[52]

As a French colonial administrator, Dunglas could not identify with Kétu and Yoruba culture in the same way Moulero or Johnson could, even though Dunglas's portrayal of "witches," songs, and local sayings resembled that of

Yoruba cultural nationalists. Dunglas belonged to a class of French colonial administrators who conducted research and wrote studies of African history and culture.[53] In quite different ways, Moulero and Dunglas used their privilege as elite men in the West African colonial setting to obtain sources for their histories from leading men, important women, and those associated with the French colonial regime. Dunglas, as a white European man associated with the power of the French colonial state, would have been considered a man of privilege when he asked questions of those persons he interviewed. It would be surprising if Dunglas had not consulted Moulero about his work, though he did not acknowledge doing so.[54]

With access to official histories that emphasize the deeds of kings, hunters, and religious leaders, both Moulero and Dunglas incorporated mythical women like Yá Mepere. Dunglas incorporated other women with unusual power, like Yá Mefu and Na Bokolo, and also mentioned historical female figures like Alaba Ida. Yá Mepere and others, who represented myth-like figures (as did all the characters in the origin and earliest history), were depicted as elderly women with powers of their own who supported and aided leading men. Such women were potentially dangerous and commanded respect. In acknowledging and conveying this position of "mothers" in Kétu history, Moulero exposed his insider outlook despite his European and missionary education. Dunglas, in some ways, did the opposite by dispassionately including "witches" in his account, revealing his outsider status despite his deep engagement with Yoruba history and culture.

Moulero and Dunglas straddled the style of a tragic Western epic and Yoruba itàn (histories or stories), which often feature a predicament at the center of a story, leading from crisis to resolution. Deirdre La Pin writes that the role of the storyteller is "not to show the listener what is familiar in human experience, but what is uncommon and irregular."[55] During the period when Moulero and Dunglas collected Kétu oral histories about the nineteenth century, the freshest events in people's minds were steeped in war with Dahomey, in other regional conflicts, and in European colonial conquest. Much of the history Moulero and Dunglas collected rationalized the conflict with Dahomey, tracing the conflict between the two states to Kétu's original occupation of the land. Members of the Kétu community themselves even betrayed the town and helped Dahomey attack neighboring kingdoms, which led eventually to Dahomey's assault of Kétu itself.[56] To the extent these stories reflect some version of actual events or simply were created to explain the debilitating war with Dahomey, they explain the human foibles and profound crises in the style of the Yoruba *ìtàn* (history or story), while suiting Western literary modes.

Although a generation of Africanist scholars from the 1970s, drawing upon the theories of Africanist historian Jan Vansina, sought to "strip away" fabrications to get at the nugget of "truth," Vansina himself expressed doubts about this approach:

> Since a testimony is never an unbiased description of what actually happened, one must always try to check on a many sources of error . . . while at the same time avoiding a hypercritical attitude. . . . This is an attitude which could be adopted towards any kind of document— including written documents. . . . It is based on the hypothesis that it is possible to discover 'the truth' about history and the exact sequence of past events. But that is impossible. *One can only arrive at an approximation of the truth. . . . Every distortion is in itself a piece of documentary evidence, either about the past, or about present-day society,* and should be treated as such. (Emphasis added)[57]

Thus Africanist historians were challenged by three tasks: "reading" oral sources the way they read written documents, analyzing the meanings of symbolic imagery, and recognizing the role of performance.[58] Some have expressed less concern about recreating past events, or even about interpreting them, and have focused instead on process, on how oral sources are produced and preserved.[59] Although oral histories *comment* on actual events and contemporary problems, they rarely yield comprehensive or definitive answers about "what really happened" or "what it all means." Interpreting the content *and* the context of oral sources probably provides the most likely "approximation of the truth."

In their introduction to their edited volume on African oral history, historians Luise White, Stephen Meischer, and David William Cohen examine oral histories as part of the nationalist projects of the early 1960s, when many African nations were becoming independent from Europe. Writing between the 1920s and the 1940s, at the height of European colonialism in Africa, Moulero and Dunglas published their work after an even earlier period of Yoruba cultural nationalism of the 1890s, but still from a point of pride in African history and culture. Concerned about the present state of Kétu, which had not yet recovered from the war with Dahomey in 1886, Moulero hoped that a proposed railroad would revitalize the "dead town" and make it an economic center for agricultural produce.[60] Dunglas complained that the indifference of many youths to the stories of their elders made the collection and transcription of oral histories important.[61] Moulero, Dunglas, and African writers like Johnson before them had discovered the power and defended the use of oral sources decades before Vansina and his students in the 1960s.[62] The desire to "discover" and "preserve" the past often is at the heart of research on oral sources, exposing the writer's interests and bias.

The contradictions and engagement with the present in Moulero's and Dunglas's work do not detract from the historical or cultural importance of their texts, but make them more valuable sources. In a study of praise songs (*oríkì*) in a Nigerian town, Karin Barber argues that the varied and sometimes contradictory information in oral sources express the town's "inner diversity and its coherence."[63] Much of the writing on Yoruba history, especially by Nigerian intellectuals, has sought to illustrate the "purity" of Yoruba culture, but many of the oral histories scholars find reflect borrowing, exchange, and intermarriage among Yoruba towns, with other ethnic groups, across religions, and even with returned descendants of slaves from Brazil. Oral histories have been a vital source for explaining a vibrant and increasingly diverse community.

To be a resident of a Yoruba town is to be an *ọmọ*, or child of that town. To use the relationship between parent and child to refer to citizenship need not imply a limited and small, family-oriented sense of the world, but it does express power and hierarchy. In such a metaphor, the most powerful women and men are "mothers" and "fathers"; others are elder or junior sisters, brothers, aunts, and uncles, all subject to the king or a higher power as "children." Deirdre La Pin views *itàn* (histories and stories) not as mere anecdotes but as "repositories of cultural thought," as potential explanations for how and why people came to be *ọmọ Kétu* (Kétu people; children of Kétu) rather than a chronicle of a series of real or imagined events.[64] Histories and stories that reinforce ideas about mobility, diversity, and gender illustrate how people in Kétu have come to see themselves. Oral histories and founding myths remain relevant precisely because timeless themes like "mother" and "father" figures are malleable symbols of power, potential danger, cooperation, and social order, whether during the mythical past or the postcolonial present.

Oral historical narratives, whether written down later or recorded orally, are crucial and multilayered sources in African history because they purport to tell the "real" story. Oral narratives can incorporate counter-discourses, challenging, for example, expected gender ideals and notions of identity. Thus, women were not ignored as part of Kétu's oral history, and Kétu's own stories defy the idea of a "pure" Kétu Yoruba identity. European travel accounts, another vital if problematic source of African history, can similarly be read against the grain. Travel accounts from the eighteenth and nineteenth centuries in West Africa and other collected oral histories did focus on local elites, but generally within the context of a broader Atlantic slave trade, West African wars, or European competition. Though these histories, like written and published ones, show a bias in favor of elite men, they reveal that power and influence resided not only with kings, male ministers, and wealthy male traders, but also with the women—"mothers," wives, slaves, priests, and soldiers—who surrounded them.

2

How Kings Lost Their Mothers

Politics of the Atlantic Slave Trade

In his account of the past glorious days of the Ọyọ empire, Yoruba historian Samuel Johnson wrote about a group of women close to the king whom he referred to as the "ladies of the palace." There is scant historical information about these women, yet they had numerous counterparts in precolonial states across West Africa and in other parts of the continent.[1] Such women lived in and around the royal compound and performed critical duties, many bearing titles with the word "Ìyá" (mother). Women like the "mothers" of Ọyọ represented multiple relationships between gender and power. Two titled women in Ọyọ dressed as men and were greeted as Bàbá (father). At the death of the king they had served, the most important among them were sentenced to die and be buried at his side. As close confidants of the king with ceremonial and ritual duties, the "mothers" in Ọyọ stood apart from the display of the king's power that was embodied in the crowds of wives, slaves, and other dependents described in accounts of European traders and travelers.

As Ọyọ declined in the late eighteenth and early nineteenth centuries, the culturally and linguistically different Dahomey kingdom rose to prominence with a unique set of powerful women in its royal household. Most notable among them was the "Mother of the Leopard," said to reign alongside the Dahomey king. Other women carried titles as "mothers," but wives of the Dada (king) of Dahomey, with special duties and a formidable army of women soldiers, called "Amazons" by nineteenth-century European visitors, are emphasized in the historical record. Indeed, men as well as women dependents of the king who supported the functioning of the state were seen as "wives" of the king of Dahomey. Women, whether designated as "mothers" or displayed as wives, were contradictory figures, serving as valuable followers yet exposing the king's vulnerabilities.

This growing presence of "wives" and women slaves in Dahomey and in Ọyọ occurred in tandem with several forces: cultural contact between the two states; expansion in the Atlantic and local slave trades; and the peak and decline of both states. Women were not simply a possession or commodity, desired simply for their capacity to reproduce. Some women from within kingdoms and from other towns and ethnic groups could unite networks of families and states. Others brought profound religious and cultural knowledge useful to kings still considered religious and political leaders of their people. These connections across territories and cultures, facilitated by slave trading, could empower the state but weaken the king's monopoly of power. Both Ọyọ and Dahomey began to decline internally before they were defeated by external military threats: Ọyọ by a West African Muslim jihadist state and Dahomey by the French colonial army.

Though much smaller and located between these more powerful states, Kétu would have witnessed the wealth and danger brought by the slave trade, the perils of state expansion, and the threat of internal political decline. Kétu shared in the language and culture of Ọyọ but had long-standing links to the Gbe-speaking Dahomey kingdom. Gender models prominent in Ọyọ and Dahomey were relevant to Kétu not only as a neighboring kingdom, but also as a territory threatened with slave raids and war from these more formidable states. Because Kétu was connected to Ọyọ and Dahomey through trade, marriage, diplomacy, and slavery, ideas about gender and power that made "mothers" and "wives" so important to the kings at Ọyọ and Dahomey were at work in Kétu, too, shaping its development and survival as an independent kingdom.

"Ladies of the Palace": Religion and Power in the Ọyọ Empire

Using local oral histories, secondhand information, and rumor, scholars have reconstructed the history of Ọyọ's improbable rise during the late seventeenth and eighteenth centuries after conquest by a Nupe kingdom to the north.[2] The period of external conquest has been considered to explain important cultural innovations in Ọyọ associated with men's activities, including a masquerade to honor ancestors and the use of mounted horses in warfare. Ironically, according to Ọyọ oral traditions, divination, a practice largely associated with men and since linked to the later expansion of Islam, is said to have been introduced during this early period by a woman from the south. Initially ignored by the king, divination was adopted after the invasion of the north, the defeat seen as a punishment for his rejection of the practice. This oral tradition representing a foreign woman bringing powerful knowledge and skills suggests more about how people saw the spread of information through women rendered mobile by marriage practices and local slave trading than it does about the actual origins of divination.³ Thus, beginning in the early seventeenth century, not only warfare, but religion and culture contributed to Ọyọ's successful expansion and empire building in neighboring Yoruba towns. By the late part of the century, Europeans on the coast heard rumors of a "terrifying" and "warlike" kingdom in the interior. By the eighteenth century, Ọyọ's successful military campaigns had reduced Dahomey to tributary status and Europeans were learning of Ọyọ ambassadors being sent to Dahomey. Direct contact between Europeans and Ọyọ traders probably did not occur until the turn of the nineteenth century, when the once formidable state of Ọyọ was slowly beginning to come apart.⁴

Oral histories collected at the end of the nineteenth century by Samuel Johnson provide the most detail on Ọyọ's political organization, although by the 1830s the empire had completely fallen, its capital later relocated some eighty miles to the south. Johnson's discussion of the king and leading ministers in his *History of the Yorubas* mirrors the power structure of the empire, beginning with the king and palace at the center and fanning out from there to provinces and governors. Crucial to the king and his power were several layers of servants, priests, and slaves, who helped manage the state as guards, messengers, diviners, and entertainers. Among the individuals closest to the king were women who, apart from wives and slaves, held key positions as officials and priests.

Samuel Johnson's "ladies of the palace" were the eight top women ministers, eight priests, and other women of high rank, many of whom served as guardians or "mothers" over people or over religious practices, overseeing certain sections of the palace and capital. The Ìyá Ọba (Mother of the King) was said to be closest to the king, though she was a representative from among the women in the palace and not his actual biological mother. The king was not allowed to have a biological mother since the king was not to lower himself before anyone, and all children kneel before their mother. If the king's own mother was alive when he ascended to power, she was expected to commit suicide. It was an unspoken assumption that the king's biological father would have been deceased if his son had risen to the throne. On at least two occasions, biological mothers of the king were said to have ruled Ọyọ as regents for underaged sons. As the representative of the king's mother, the Mother of the King received great deference, accompanying the king during special times of worship and serving as the leader of the top noble families.[5]

It was the Ìyá Kéré (Little Mother), rather than the Mother of the King, however, who held the greater power. She was charged with guarding all the king's regalia and even with placing the crown on his head; she could register her displeasure with the king by withholding his royal trappings. She was the leader of all the king's guards and messengers, slaves known as *ilàrí*, a reference to their half-shaved heads. The Little Mother kept a statue in the likeness of each of the king's guards and messengers, with the small statues representing the king's messengers and guards' responsibility for the king's life; hence her ritual power over the king was great. As further proof of her power within the palace, the Little Mother controlled the Olosi, a top-ranking eunuch, and oversaw several governors in provinces near the heartland of \yọ.[6]

If the Mother of the King and Little Mother represented the highest forms of symbolic and political power held by senior women, the remaining female officials cultivated the king's religious and ceremonial authority. The third, fourth, and fifth key women in the palace supervised the worship of the deity Ṣango—the mythologized fourth king of Ọyọ who is associated with lightning. Led by the Ìyá Naso—a name that appears also in the origin stories of Afro-Brazilian religious practices known as Candomblé—these three women performed practical and symbolic duties of Ṣango worship. The Ìyá Naso maintained the king's personal Ṣango shrine, and her first lieutenant was responsible for the execution of any Ṣango worshipper who had been condemned to death. The second woman represented the child that the king, who, as a devotee of Ṣango, was required to dedicate to the worship of the deity. The sixth and seventh women Johnson described were linked to the king's eldest son and heir apparent as the son's mother or symbolic mother responsible for controlling a part of the capital city. The eighth woman served as the king's personal attendant. Like the other seven top women ministers, the king's personal attendant, though seemingly akin to a slave, headed a small compound of dependents on the palace grounds.[7] In 1826, Scottish traveler Hugh Clapperton, author of the first eyewitness account of (Old) Ọyọ, may have actually met this eighth woman. He told of seeing, during his visit there, two women who never left the king's side, one carrying his kola nuts and a spittoon.[8]

Johnson listed eight women priests as the next level of women in the palace, but he described few in detail, noting simply of the rest that they had titles that indicated the òrìṣà (deity) they tended to, such as Yemaja or Oṣun, both important female deities associated with rivers. The first priest, Ìyá le Ori (Mother of the House of Ori), was responsible for the king's worship of the Ori, the deity of fate, worshipped generally by both women and men. The second priest, Ìyá le Mole (Mother of the House of *Ifá*), dealt with *ifá* divination, a practice associated primarily with men, *ifá* priests known as *babaláwo* (father owns the secrets). The Mother of the House of *Ifá* participated in *ifá* ceremonies and was the leader of the *ifá* priests, though she did not carry herself as a man. Among the remaining titled women, two women lower in rank than the priests did, however, "become" men in dress and stature.

One of these eight women priests was the Ẹni Ọjà (Owner of the Market) and leader of the devotees of Eṣu, whom Yoruba Christians like Johnson referred to as the "devil." Often portrayed as a "trickster" embodying all contradictions, Eṣu is the òrìṣà (deity) of the crossroads, his shrine placed at intersections and at public places like markets. Whenever the king prayed to Eṣu at the market, he was said to lean on the arms of the "Owner of the Market," who was dressed in a man's robes.[9] The "Owner of the Market" specifically oversaw the king's market, often situated in a square before the palace; she managed two male palace officials associated with the market, one of whom was the powerful eunuch, the Olosi. It was striking that a woman dressed as a man would supervise the market, since the market was often associated with women traders and, at night, with "witches."[10]

Next, the Ìyámode led all the Ṣango worshippers, most of them women who lived around the royal burial ground. The Ìyámode—whose name includes the words "mother" and "outside"—lived in a house on the royal grounds, though her responsibilities were not directly related to the palace. All the devotees living near the royal cemetery addressed her as Bàbá (father), including the king, who knelt before her. Indeed, when the Ìyámode responded in kind to the king, she did not fully recline as a woman would before a superior. Because the king had no father and no biological mother, he prostrated before no one but the Ìyámode and devotees of Ṣango, addressing them as father, thus illustrating the supreme place of Ṣango in Ọyọ kingship.[11]

Anthropologist Randy Matory, in his study of religion and gender in Ọyọ, argues that the predominant place of Ṣango in Ọyọ specifically reinforced the image of "wifeliness." Beyond the hundreds of palace wives and female slaves, titled women, and certain priests, male slaves, known as *ilàrí*, cross-dressed and proclaimed themselves "wives of the king."[12] Because Ṣango possesses or "mounts" his devotees and because most followers of Ṣango and other deities that "mount" worshippers are women, Matory analyzes this religious practice of possession and female submission—central to Ọyọ politics even after British colonialism—as a metaphor for political power. Matory groups titled women and priests with wives and slaves, noting, for example, that the Ìyá Ọba (Mother of the King) was in fact a wife in the royal family.[13] However, Johnson emphasized that the top titled women and priests were not simply wives and were distinct from slaves. Top titled women and priests used their appearance to distinguish themselves from lower-ranked palace residents by shaving their heads and braiding or adorning their hair with feathers, not unlike the way men styled themselves as women in Matory's study.[14]

That the "mothers" in the Ọyọ palace were more than wives or slaves makes the two women who masqueraded as men more challenging to understand, though they are not the only examples of women "becoming" men in Yoruba oral histories. In addition to the Kétu oral histories that depict the first Yoruba ruler Oduduwa as a woman, some of the most powerful *òrìṣà* (deities), such as Obatala, are seen as androgynous.[15] In some oral traditions about Ọyọ's earliest history, the king who reputedly introduced warfare on horses was a woman named Orompoto. Matory recorded two versions of a story explaining how Orompoto—whose name connoted "something soft"—physically changed herself into a man, appearing naked to prove it.[16] Among the "ladies of the palace," neither of the "male mothers"—the Ìyámode as leader of the Ṣango worshippers at the royal cemetery or the Ẹni Ọjà responsible for the king's market—was one of the more important female religious or political figures who were close to the king. Their positions did not require them to work with many men as did the Ìyá le Mole, who met frequently with divination priests, or the Obagunte, a woman who represented the king in the male secret society known as Ogboni. Ironically and paradoxically, both the Ìyá le Mole and the Obagunte, who worked with powerful men outside the palace, were closer to slave status than were other female officials and priests.[17] The two "men" among the "mothers" in the palace reinforced the understanding that femininity and masculinity were part of the religious and political power structure at all levels of the state. Some "masculinized" mothers intervened in women's spaces, as in the worship of Ṣango, or in the market, while other women ministers and priests participated in rituals dominated by men, such as *ifá* divination or male secret societies.

Proximity to the king came at a cost for some women and men in the palace. Seven women and six men with the most access to the king were required to commit suicide upon the king's death, apparently to discourage assassination attempts on the king by people closest to him.[18] The doomed women fell into three overlapping categories: political, religious, and personal. The Ìyá Ọba (Mother of the King) and the two titled women associated with the heir apparent occupied the most political positions in the palace. Great deference was paid to these women by the king, by palace residents, and by leading families of the town; they had great potential to advise the king and heir apparent on policies and decisions. Similarly, because the king's political power was so closely tied to his control over religious worship, the three priests of Ṣango arguably enjoyed influence beyond their stated role in the king's worship of Ṣango. Finally, the king's personal servant had the most access to the king's person, making her extremely loyal but dangerous to the king if she turned against him. However, the forced suicide of some of these "mothers" made women's political power in Ọyọ ambivalent. In addition, most of these women were limited to the palace, its grounds, and their ties to the king. While some of the men in the royal family who held titled positions as "fathers" explicitly advised the king, and the male heads of noble families acted as "kingmakers," not even the most powerful woman in the palace was officially described as a direct counselor to the king.

Distant provinces controlled by the king but far removed from the palace were placed in the hands of governors and provincial appointees, which means less is known about women's political roles in other regions and towns from Johnson's account, written from the perspective of the capital of the Ọyọ empire. As Clapperton made his way through the Ọyọ provinces nearest the coast inland to Ọyọ in 1825, he noticed, seated on the veranda of the appointed Ọyọ official, "an ancient gray-headed set of men and women—the latter were of the greater number and appeared to be the principal officers of the household and nearest the great personage."[19] Thus the patterns of political officers and titles may have been replicated in the outlying provinces, giving women ceremonial and advisory roles. Johnson wrote that the Ìyálóde (Mother Owns the Outside World), whose title Johnson liberally translated as "queen of the ladies," was a title in the provinces of Ọyọ. Described as capable of leading warriors and as having a voice in the council of local ministers, famous Ìyálóde in Yoruba history rose to power in other Yoruba towns such as Ibadan and Abẹokuta. While most of the women in the palace at Ọyọ were concerned with the king's office and religious worship, the Mother Owns the Outside World served as a representative to whom ordinary women could express their views. But because this position became prominent during the mid-nineteenth-century wars between Yoruba towns as communities jockeyed for position in the absence of the dominant presence of Ọyọ, scholars have viewed the wealth and political power of the Ìyálóde as anomalous and "untraditional." Thus the powerful nineteenth-century Ìyálóde have been "masculinized" in the academic literature rather than considered as they are here—as part of an innovation to the idea of "mothers" of Ọyọ and other forms of Ọyọ government.[20]

The significant place of women in Ọyọ's palace and the potential influence of those patterns on neighboring towns did not lead to women being highlighted in the conventional history of Ọyọ's impressive rise and ignominious slow decline over several decades. Instead, contemporary accounts emphasized power struggles between the king and the male advisory council known as the Ọyọ Mesi. The overthrow of the king in 1796 was followed by a series of weak monarchs and Afonja, a rebellious provincial leader, helped deliver the final blow to the floundering state in 1817 when he enlisted the help of Muslim jihadist fighters from the north of Ọyọ. Soon the situation spiraled out of Afonja's control and his province became part of the expanding Muslim caliphate of Sokoto, leading to the destruction of the capital of Ọyọ by 1836. Though the king of Ọyọ managed to relocate the capital, other Yoruba towns, many of them home to waves of Ọyọ refugees, grew larger and more powerful than New Ọyọ. But the fall of Old Ọyọ and the rise of other Yoruba towns had important implications for gender relationships. Never able to replicate the grandeur of the Ọyọ empire from the previous century, new Yoruba towns emphasized military organization and personal wealth (of women and men) in contrast to the royal pomp and "wifeliness" of Old Ọyọ.[21]

But if "wifeliness" was an attribute of Old Ọyọ, so too was an ideology of "public motherhood." Other scholars who equate women's political activities primarily with "mothering" and caretaking present such skills as "natural," thus obscuring women's leadership and decision making in the ritual, religious, political, and economic well-being of the community. With different "mothers" in Ọyọ overseeing the king's paraphernalia, household, markets, and men's societies, they were not coddling and comforting society as though it was a child.[22] Yet the "public" aspect of the duties of the "mothers" was also very "private," involving religion, the king's person, divination, and secret societies. The situation was also delicate because while some women were purposefully masculinized, others, especially certain nineteenth-century Ìyálode, were criticized for "becoming like men." It is unclear how often some of these women's titles were even publicly acknowledged, especially given the fear of the supernatural power of "mothers."

By contrast, in the rival kingdom of Dahomey, the highest-ranking woman was recorded in the local oral traditions, her memory honored by a representative of her office generations later. There was not the same coterie of explicit "mother" figures in Dahomey; the consummate "mother figure" in Dahomey was surrounded instead by wives, women soldiers, and slave women who exerted power and influence, if in quite different ways.

Mothers of the Leopard and the Rise of the Dahomey Kingdom

In Edna Bay's work about the precolonial period, *Wives of the Leopard: Gender, Politics, and Culture in the Kingdom of Dahomey,* powerful princesses, often sisters of the king, served as the model for the rise of the "mother figure." A woman named Aligbonon, whose name could be translated to mean "mother of the long road," was said to have been impregnated by a leopard, their descendant later founding Dahomey.[23] Bay writes that early in the kingdom's history, princess Na Hangbe ruled Dahomey as a regent for her young nephew after her twin brother, the king, suddenly died. Na Hangbe was later defeated by her other brother, Agaja, whose wars of expansion extended Dahomey to the West African coast and into direct contact with European traders of the early eighteenth century.[24] It is said that in 1727 one of his daughters, princess Na Geze, used sabotage to help her father win control over the coastal kingdom of Ouidah.[25] Mythical and historical figures like Aligbonon, Na Hangbe, and Na Geze had no recorded titles, though "Na" itself is an honorific term for princess. Unlike "mother figures," these early mythical women were portrayed not as postmenopausal women with supernatural powers, but as young adult women associated with biological motherhood and warfare. During the early history of the kingdom, young royal women close to the Dahomey king not only cultivated a commanding role for princesses in the royal household but also paved the way for empowered, elderly, commoner women in the palace.

Historian Edna Bay asserts that the title of *kpojito* (loosely translated as "Mother of the King" but literally "one who whelps the leopard," translated as "Mother of the Leopard" hereafter) was probably created during the reign of King Agaja, from about 1716 to 1740. Adonon, the first to hold this title, was born in a village closely associated with Aligbonon, the mother of the "leopard-son" who established Dahomey. Because the founders of Dahomey had probably been strangers to the area, they drew on the region's imagery of the leopard to reinforce their own political legitimacy. Using that symbolism, Aligbonon, the mythical royal princess, and her "leopard-son," who founded the royal dynasty, embodied several overlapping relationships between mother and son, royalty and commoner, outsider/stranger and indigenous person. Beginning with Adonon, a commoner woman taken as a wife by an earlier king but acting as a "mother" to Agaja in the office of the Mother of the Leopard, these connections were re-enacted in multiple ways. Adonon, born in a territory that had been incorporated into the kingdom, represented the indigenous community drawn into a state that had been founded by outsiders.[26] Her power, influence, and historical existence has been attested to by dozens who claim to be her descendants. Into the present day, a woman is assigned to hold that title.[27] The Mother of the Leopard in Dahomey, like the Mother of the King in Ọyọ, was not a biological mother, but rather a religious and political figure embodied by an elderly woman with an ostensibly advisory role to the king but with her own wealth and followers.

After King Agaja conquered Ouidah in 1727, European traders who began to offer eyewitness accounts of his "court" noted the presence of wives and women slaves. William Snelgrave, a British slave trader, arrived in Ouidah some weeks after King Agaja attacked Ouidah and went to meet the king in the inland capital:

> His majesty was in a large court palisadoed round, sitting (contrary to the custom of the country) on a fine gilt chair, which he had taken from the king of Whidaw [Ouidah]. *There were held over his head, by women, three large umbrellas, to shade him from the sun: And four other women stood behind the chair of state, with fusils [guns] on their shoulders. I observed, the women were finely dress'd* from the middle downward, (the Custom of the country being not to cover the body upward, of either sex) *moreover they had on their arms, many large manelloes, or rings of gold of great value, and round their necks and in their hair,* abundance of their country jewels, which are a sort of beads of divers colours, brought from a far inland country, where they are dug out of the earth, and in the same esteem with the Negroes, as diamonds amongst the Europeans. The King had a gown on, flowered with gold, which reached as low as his ankles; and European embroidered hat on his head; with sandals on his feet.[28] (Emphasis added)

King Agaja's display of wealth in gold, imported fabrics, European goods, guns, and well-dressed women may have foretold Dahomey's later use of women soldiers. Snelgrave mentioned too an elderly woman who was relaying messages between the king and the "principal men of the court"; the men, who sat within twenty feet of the king's chair, "whispered into the ear of an old woman, who went to the King; and having received his answer, she returned with it to them." Known as the *daklo*, this elderly woman, whose official duty was to convey messages to the king, had close proximity to the king and royal ministers, reflecting a political role different from the display of young, dependent women and riches.[29]

Other elderly women close to King Agaja included one who fell so out of favor that the king tried to sell her into the Atlantic slave trade. Women and men absorbed into the king's household were seldom subjected to such enslavement. Nevertheless, sale to European slave traders was always a potential punishment. Snelgrave himself refused to buy the old woman presented to him, only to learn that she was to be "sacrificed to the sea." Men from Snelgrave's ship, anchored offshore, miraculously rescued her from the shark-infested waters, and despite his own wholehearted support of the slave trade, Snelgrave kept the woman secretly on board. He never learned how she had offended the king, though a Dahomey official told him she had "assist[ed] some of the King's women in their amours." The old woman surprised Snelgrave during the slave ship's transatlantic voyage; "by her talking to and advising [the Negroes on board], [she] made them easy in their minds." She calmed especially the enslaved women, who were "kept in such order and decorum by this woman, that [Snelgrave] had never the like in any voyage before." To "repay" her, Snelgrave found her a "generous" master in Barbados.[30] Among the captives on the ship from Ouidah or elsewhere who probably did not know her, she commanded respect as an elder and perhaps conveyed to them her past position of influence in King Agaja's palace.

Scholars have debated King Agaja's motives in conquering the slave-trading coastal kingdoms of Allada and Ouidah in the period between 1724 and 1727. It is Nigerian historian I. A. Akinjogbin's opinion that King Agaja actually sought to suppress the slave trade, but most have interpreted the same sources to argue that the king sought to gain control of the slave trade for himself.[31] Whatever King Agaja's plans, he faced numerous challenges from the former Ouidah king, who was trying to reclaim his throne, and from regular attacks by Ọyọ, which sought to extend its power and influence in the region.[32] Many have ignored the gendered terms in which King Agaja discussed his views of the slave trade. When Snelgrave asked for assurances about the slave trade, King Agaja said he would favor Snelgrave over other traders by treating him as "a young wife or bride, who must be denied nothing at first." The king was amused when Snelgrave bristled at the language that compared the British trader to a young woman, but the king apparently considered European traders dependents and subordinates to whom he extended favors and from whom he expected loyalty.[33] In the end, beset by attacks by Qyq and insubordination by Ouidah refugees, the king was unable to maintain his European "wives," and slave traders complained bitterly about the reduced supply of slaves.[34]

The coexistence of powerful "public mothers" and the proliferation of wives and women slaves reached a new height during the reign that followed, of Tegbesu and his *kpojito* (Mother of the Leopard), Hwanjile. As part of the new palace's bureaucracy and opulence, the new king accumulated more wives, more women guards, and more women slaves. He apparently rearranged the palace based on what he had observed in Qyq, where he had been a prisoner in his youth. During Tegbesu's long reign from 1740 to 1774, eunuchs, royal messengers, styled as *ìlàrí* with half-shaved heads, and other titled officers associated with Qyq were observed in Dahomey.[35] He initiated religious change that has been associated with his *kpojito*, Hwanjile, portrayed in oral histories as a mature, foreign woman who had married Tegbesu's father Agaja and served as a mentor to Tegbesu himself, teaching him of deities and the uses of medicines. After she was named *kpojito*, Hwanjile created two new supreme deities and a new category of deities linked to individual kings, and she encouraged the use of *fa* divination (derived from the Yoruba form of *ifá*). By tying religious worship more closely to kingship, tensions were reputedly lessened between local religious priests and the royal family.[36] Hwanjile had cultivated such power in the eighteenth century that in the 1970s, the woman designated to represent her name and title in a ceremonial position seems to have wielded enormous influence.[37]

As Hwanjile deftly used religion to cement royal control throughout the heartland of the kingdom, so Tegbesu continued to incorporate families into the palace through male officials, using the image of "wifeliness" broadly, beyond biological sex. Any dependent of the king, whether woman or man, was *ahosi* ("wife" of the king), including male titleholders, some of whom settled with their families near a palace, gaining control over land and revenue. Men who became eunuchs acted out the role as *ahosi* more actively by dressing as women. Antoine Pruneau de Pommegorge, a French trading company employee in Ouidah in the 1750s, wrote that eunuchs who dressed as women "incarnated the reverence of women." King Tegbesu bestowed wives upon the eunuchs at twenty years of age, providing for each the beginnings of a household.[38] Richard Norris, a British slave trader who visited Dahomey in the 1770s, wrote of a powerful eunuch at Ouidah named "Tanga," with numerous wives who enjoyed his riches and their freedom to take lovers and husbands from among his own slave men. In fact, "Tanga" was Norris's misspelling of the title "Tegan," which was a precursor to the position of Yovogan, "Minister of the Whites," responsible for relations with European traders at Ouidah. According to Norris, after the Tegan failed in a disastrous 1745 bid to establish himself as king of Ouidah, his many wives committed suicide rather than face punishment for supporting his campaign.[39]

The relatively short reigns of the two kings immediately succeeding Tegbesu could not compare with Tegbesu's; their "Mothers of the Leopard" also lacked Hwanjile's long-term impact. The first king, Kpengla, served for only fifteen years; his Mother of the Leopard, Chai, is remembered for bringing the wars with the neighboring Mahi to an end because she was from the Mahi region.[40] Chai is portrayed as a passive figure, representing the ties to neighboring Mahi or symbolizing Dahomey's vulnerability by dying in a battle in which the entire Dahomey community engaged. Archibald Dalzel, a British slave trader who in 1793 compiled the history of Dahomey in a pro-slave-trade tract, recorded that Kpengla's "big mother" died during a community-wide retaliation against a recalcitrant enemy and that Kpengla visited "his mother's" grave, pledging to defeat another enemy and prove himself worthy.[41]

In the even shorter reign of Kpengla's successor Agonglo, who served for eight years as king of Dahomey until assassinated in 1797, Senume, the Mother of the Leopard, played a role even more ambivalent than Chai's. Senume is remembered for her association with Christianity, then considered in Dahomey a new and possibly threatening "cult." Vicente Pires, a Portuguese priest, visited Dahomey in 1797 in an attempt to convert King Agonglo to Catholicism. He was present during the succession struggle after Agonglo's death and wrote that the most important woman in the palace was the *naie dada*, literally, "woman king." This "woman king," presumably Senume, the Mother of the Leopard, was associated with one of two women practicing Catholicism in the king's palace, their presence perhaps contributing to rumors that the king himself would convert and hence hastening the plot that led to his murder. Pires reported that several groups of high-ranking women were linked with male counterparts in the palace.[42] It is difficult to know whether the other titled women Pires observed held ministerial positions like that of the Mother of the Leopard or whether they were closer in status to palace wives and other dependents with responsibilities in the palace. During the two reigns of Kpengla and Agonglo, an increasing number of women began to take center stage in the palace and capital at Dahomey. King Tegbesu's successors continued the practice he had instituted, with hundreds, perhaps thousands, of royal wives participating in annual ceremonies to honor the royal ancestors.

Disruptions of the slave trade from Ouidah, provoked by recurring problems with Ọyọ and Ouidah refugees, were compounded in the 1780s. King Kpengla set out to attack competing ports, which encouraged African and European traders to concentrate their efforts at Porto-Novo, a port farther east, ostensibly under Ọyọ control. During the American Revolutionary War and the French Revolution, which briefly blocked French participation in the slave trade, European demand declined, and slave rebellion in Saint Domingue, which led to the founding of Haiti, shut off one of the largest markets for slaves transported out of Ouidah and the Bight of Benin region. Indirectly, these periodic declines in the Atlantic slave trade may have brought into the king's palace even more women who could not then be absorbed into overseas slave markets. The ostentatious presence of so many women compensated for the incipient socioeconomic decline of the kingdom.

When a protracted struggle between factions of women in the palace brought King Adandozan to power in 1797, he dealt a prompt blow to those who worked against him, so it is said, ordering princesses slain and sending hundreds who had opposed his ascent, many women among them, into slavery. Adandozan became known for his cruelty; so hostile was public opinion against him that once he was overthrown in a coup in 1818, he was effectively erased from Dahomey history, though Edna Bay writes that he lived for several more decades. Today, little is apparently known of his Mother of the Leopard, Kentobasin, though her name has been preserved.

In a profound reversal of fortune, Agontime, one of the many women forced into slavery in the Americas by Adandozan, was honored as the Mother of the Leopard by the next king, though it is doubtful that the actual Agontime was ever found.[43] Agontime's enslavement and attempted rescue echoed the story of the old woman expelled from King Agaja's palace who found her way onto William Snelgrave's slave ship, showing how the Atlantic slave trade continued to haunt the political landscape in Dahomey. The end of Adandozan's reign in 1818 marked the end of a century when "mother figures" were at their height of power and influence within these West African kingdoms. "Public motherhood" was integral to eighteenth-century West African kingship; so too the impact of Atlantic slave trade was vital to changing West African gender relations.

Mothers Become Wives: Silent Impact of the Atlantic Slave Trade

During the eighteenth century, while women like the Mother of the King in Ọyọ and the Mother of the Leopard in Dahomey exerted their influence in royal palaces increasingly populated by wives and slaves, hundreds of thousands of West Africans from the Bight of Benin—a bay area extending from modern Togo to western Nigeria—were forced onto slave ships. Almost 70 percent of the nearly one and a half million Africans enslaved in the Bight of Benin between 1620 and 1863 experienced the harrowing Atlantic crossing during the eighteenth century.[44] But to work with Atlantic slave trade data is to work with hypotheses, to try to give meaning to millions of anonymous lives. In a compiled database of now almost thirty-five thousand slave ship voyages, the origins of enslaved African women, men, and children, most unidentified by name, can be deduced only from piecemeal information on the circumstances of their enslavement. Neither the sex nor the age of enslaved Africans on the vast majority of these ships were recorded, and only about 10 percent of voyages noted female and male ratios during the height of the Bight of Benin trade in the eighteenth century.[45] But according to the data available, men in all periods tended to outnumber the women shipped as slaves to the Americas from the Bight of Benin. The average percentage of men hovered around 60 percent, with the slave trade itself increasing dramatically during the eighteenth century. In the first and last quarters of that century, wars of expansion ravaged the Bight of Benin region. In the early 1700s, when Dahomey was consolidating its control over Ouidah on the coast, and in the final quarter of the eighteenth century when Ọyọ was carving a path to the coast through occupied lands, the ports frequented by European slave traders shifted as Dahomey-controlled Ouidah became less popular and Ọyọ-controlled Porto-Novo more so. There is no reliable data on sex ratios of slaves sent to Brazil, where 60 percent of enslaved Africans from the Bight of Benin were shipped in the eighteenth century, but with the increased warfare and slave trading in the Bight of Benin region, more women and men could well have been captured.[46] With no evidence of a dramatic change in sex ratios of slaves sold in the Americas and given the periodic instability in the eighteenth-century Atlantic slave trade, more captured women could well have been absorbed into West African communities as slaves and wives.[47] The Americas were transformed by the influx of African slaves, but within Atlantic Africa itself potential population shifts, with increasing numbers of enslaved women held by kings and leading men, altered cultural practices and gender ideologies.

Edna Bay writes that the palace at Dahomey was a Gbe household "writ large," the king of Dahomey the supreme example of a husband and father.[48] A king's power, like that of a father in a household or extended family, depended on the presence of women not only for reproduction but for labor and prestige; the king was vulnerable if he could not maintain his wealth, followers, or dependents. Women residing in the royal palace represented the king's links to the villages and families in his kingdom and even in vanquished territories. Bay comments that while captives, especially Yoruba captives, increasingly populated the palace in the nineteenth century, the recruitment of Dahomey women also intensified from the late eighteenth century. Rather than require one daughter from every family as tribute, by the nineteenth century a Dahomey official regularly traveled the countryside to demand daughters to serve the king.[49] As part of this process, the king also redistributed women to loyal followers and commoners to illustrate his power and wealth. William Snelgrave met a woman in Dahomey in 1727 "so white, equal to our English women" with "woolly hair," who had been given as a wife to a racially mixed Portuguese "gentleman" captured by Dahomey and kept near the king's residence.[50] In the 1750s, the French slave trader turned apologist Antoine Pruneau de Pommegorge wrote of daughters given as tribute to the king; in the 1770s, British slave trader Robert Norris explained that the hoarding of women by the king and high-ranking men left commoner men with little access to women, and he described the situation as a state-sponsored form of prostitution. Attending the annual 1772 ceremony at the Dahomey capital to honor the king's ancestors, Norris reported that the king doled out women captives to commoner men in exchange for cowry shells, perhaps symbolizing the gifts exchanged between a prospective groom and the family of his future wife.[51] Thus the slave trade was a contributing factor to a changing ideology that placed more emphasis on drawing in and displaying women as wives, especially around the king.

Norris's 1772 description of the annual ceremony to honor the king's ancestors (referred to as "Customs" by Europeans) depicted groups of "ladies of pleasure," a procession of seven hundred of the king's "neatly dressed" wives and a parade of armed women. Fifteen young royal princesses marched with a retinue of women slaves. During one pageant, women who appeared to be favored wives marched at the head of armed groups of women. "She who led the van," Norris wrote, "was so universally respected, as to be too sacred to be seen; in fact that secured her effectually from my sight.... in the last troop were four umbrellas, and four favorites, very fine women, who were said to be in higher esteem with the king than any, except the lady before mentioned."[52]

It is unclear if the "sacred" woman represented the Mother of the Leopard, but these multiple processions illustrated the range of women associated with the palace, from "ladies of pleasure" to armed guards, princesses, ordinary slaves, and high-ranking wives. Many had been captives and carried various imported objects representing the military prowess and the great wealth of the king. The grand display was quite unlike the description that William Snelgrave gave of his meeting with King Agaja in 1727, when a few armed women guards and an elderly woman encircled the king's throne:

> The dresses and ornaments of the women were much more showy: the variety, and abundance of rich silks, silver bracelets, and other orna-ments, coral, and a profusion of other valuable beads, exceed my expec-tation; besides there was added another troop of forty women, with silver helmets, and there was a display of the king's furniture and trin-kets, most of the women carrying something or other of his; some of them fine swords; other silver-mounted guns; above a hundred of them held either gold, or silver-headed canes, in their hands; and that none might be unprovided, some carried a candlestick, and other a lamp, perhaps fifty at least of each, with many other articles; which were all held up for the gaping multitude to admire.[53]

Norris, who himself took some time during the ceremonies to purchase slaves and ivory, noted that interspersed with these lavish processions of women and material wealth were human sacrifices. Described in graphic detail by Euro-pean visitors, the sacrifices ordered by the kings of Dahomey were religious rituals and forms of ancestral worship.[54] At the same time, parading women were extensions of the government at the heart of the kingdom, hence crucial as symbols of its power.

There are no eyewitness accounts for Ọyọ for the same period of the eigh-teenth century, but by the early nineteenth century, the wives of the king of Ọyọ had so multiplied that they were found trading in many towns and work-ing as porters. The king mused to the traveler Clapperton that if his wives stood hand to hand, they would reach as far as Ijanna, a town nearer the coast.[55] The metaphor of his wives' outstretched arms was a powerful one, embodying the king's wealth, influence, and territory. But Ọyọ itself was in deep decline, the king's power more symbolic than real, perhaps, as was the wealth embodied in the many women surrounding him.

Troops and troupes of women also could be a liability. The king could be caught in intrigue, find his plans exposed to his enemies, or be thwarted by palace women in naming a successor to the throne. In Dahomey, King Tegbesu, angered by the praise showered on a general, planned to get rid of him. But the general's sister, living in the king's palace, learned of the plot, dispatched a secret message to her brother, and enabled him to escape.[56] During Kpengla's reign some of his wives, some known to take lovers, conspired against the king and, when discovered, falsely accused more than a hundred men, who were sent into slavery.[57] King Agonglo, who reigned for eight years, was felled by poison administered by a woman in the palace.[58] Yet hundreds of palace women were implicated in violent struggles to occupy the throne upon the death of the king. When Kpengla sought to take power in 1774, a large contingent of palace women supported him and almost three hundred were said to have died fighting. After Agonglo's demise, the battle between the female contingents of contenders led to the death of almost six hundred women.[59] To see the king's potential vulnerability simply as a manifestation of "fragility," of glass, would fail to capture the interdependent relationship between a ruler and his dependents, whether they were "mothers" or "wives."

Women, mobile and flexible symbols of religious and political power, were both vulnerable and valuable, easily sacrificed and highly praised. "Mothers" of the king, important women throughout the eighteenth century in both Ọyọ and Dahomey, for all the awe and sometimes fear they evoked, found their authority "behind the scenes" easily displaced by more amorphous crowds of wives who exercised even more ambivalent forms of power. Because the Mother of the Leopard and the cadre of "mothers" in Ọyọ were drawn from among wives and captives, increasing numbers of wives and women slaves overshadowed "mothers," some of whom had transformed their origins as slaves into positions of supreme power. The influence of "public mothers," like biological ones, subordinate at the same time to husbands and elders, could be undercut. As the "mothers" flanking the kings of Ọyọ and Dahomey seemed to decline in relationship to the sheer number of wives, the distinction between "mother" and "wife," already ambiguous, became more so. A wife of the king potentially could become an elderly "mother figure" by bearing children and/or by gaining respect and awe from those around her. Thus, by the nineteenth century, the accumulation of wives accentuated the contradictory position of "public mothers," who related to the experience of women's subordination while wielding power and authority.

Formally trained contingents of women soldiers of Dahomey organized by King Gezo in the nineteenth century occupied the gray area between "mothers" to "wives" in service of the king. The cadre of women palace guards in

Dahomey dated back to the eighteenth century, but a new women's standing army was drawn from the increasing numbers of women slaves and captives, the *ahosi* ("wives" of the king). Some *ahosi*, especially the women soldiers, enjoyed certain privileges, living in a special section of the palace and benefiting from the services of women slaves.[60] Some woman soldiers came to occupy positions similar to that of "public mothers," illustrating the slippage between the image of "wife" of the king and "mother."

A woman known as Lady Yewe, who commanded a regiment of several hundred women in the 1840s, served as the "English mother" responsible for providing British visitors with food and protection. Frederick Forbes, a British naval commander sent to Dahomey in 1850 to negotiate an end to Dahomey's role in the clandestine Atlantic slave trade, learned that Lady Yewe had personally led a battle against a town that had insulted one of her British guests.[61] Lady Yewe was part of the group of women observed by nineteenth-century European travelers who served as "mothers" to each of the ministers of Dahomey, from the highest- to the lowest-ranking. Ministerial titles for men in Dahomey had a woman counterpart carrying the suffix "-*non*" that translates as "owner of" or "mother of." Some scholars see these women either as performing the duties associated with their title within the palace or as serving as a check on the power of the male ministers who exercised their power "outside," in the kingdom itself.[62] But there seems to be a difference between this pairing of ministerial titles of women with men in Dahomey and the more singularly titled mothers in Ọyọ. Having the male counterpart underscores how doubling permeated the hierarchy in Dahomey palace organization to the point that the *kpojito* is seen as an actual reign-mate of the king.[63]

American anthropologist Melville Herskovits wrote that the "mothers" of the ministers reported to a mysterious group of women known as the *kposi* ("wives" of Kpo).[64] *Kpo* is the leopard deity associated with the royal lineage of Dahomey, making the *kposi* "wives" likely priests of the deity. While often described in nineteenth-century sources as favored by the king and superbly dressed, the role of the "leopard wives" was unclear. Edna Bay contends that as religious figures linked closely to the king and answering only to him, the *kposi* as "wives" of the leopard deity marked a profound shift from the more autonomous position of Mother of the Leopard to an emphasis on the king's personal power.[65] Though Herskovits alone asserted that in the nineteenth century the *ahosi* or "wives" who acted as "mothers" of the ministers answered to the "leopard wives," the symbolism in placing "mothers" below "wives" would be significant. Indeed, Edna Bay argues that during the same period when the power of Dahomey "mothers" was being displaced in the nineteenth century, the long-held influence of sisters of the king, princesses, was also being challenged as sisters of the king increasingly became known as wives of high-ranking officials, thus as "wives" of the king (their own brother) himself. In assuming palace titles reserved for *ahosi*, princesses, after occupying such important roles in the lore of the founding of the kingdom, became "wives."[66] Though with important duties and responsibilities in the palace, women who had in the past been more "equal" to the king as "mothers" and as "sisters" were becoming symbolically subordinate and dependent to the king by the nineteenth century.

To argue that the overlap between "public" mothers and "wives" had always been the case, even during the eighteenth-century heyday of Ìyá or "mothers" in Ọyọ, and the *kpojito* or Mother of the Leopard in Dahomey, would deny the complex and shifting meanings behind these terms. Johnson wrote that most of the titled "mothers" of Ọyọ commanded their own land and followers, indicating a degree of autonomy that belied one of the core tenets of "wifeliness": dependence on the king. The *kpojito* or Mother of the Leopard in Dahomey controlled her own people and land, partly evident from preservation of each *kpojito*'s office and scores of descendants claiming each woman's name. While it is more difficult to trace how the Ìyá in Ọyọ shifted from the eighteenth century to the nineteenth century, it is said that by the nineteenth century the *kpojito* in Dahomey was the biological mother of the king, undermining the idea of autonomy and partnership at the heart of her office.[67]

Most scholars have paid less attention to the significance of "public motherhood" in many of the same published travel accounts of the eighteenth and nineteenth centuries, in which I have found an alternate reading of gender and politics in Ọyọ and Dahomey. Both Edna Bay and Randy Matory have recognized how ritual, titles, and dress conferred a range of genders on women and men in Ọyọ and Dahomey: for example, male Ọyọ messengers who dressed as "wives" and, in Dahomey, cross-dressing eunuchs who married women. However, they both focus on the image of "wifeliness." Considering the varied women and men who acted as "mothers," "fathers," "husbands," and "wives" highlights the profound power of symbolism and culture in defining gender identities. Recognizing gender flexibility does not ignore the subordination experienced by many women wives and slaves. Even the role of "mother" in Ọyọ or Dahomey may have been a bittersweet one; to be a powerful woman in the palace may have meant first being subordinate wife, if not a slave.

By the nineteenth century, Kétu women were among the thousands of foreign women in the palace of the Dahomey kingdom. Before Kétu was defeated by Dahomey in 1886, visitors to Kétu emphasized the ubiquitous presence of royal wives surrounding the king. Indeed, the only mention of potential "public mothers" in Kétu came in passing from Charles Gollmer, a German missionary of the British-based Church Missionary Society, who traveled to Kétu in 1859. During one of Gollmer's final days in Kétu several delegations came to visit him, including a group of royal wives followed by three unassuming elderly women. After Gollmer gave a few pieces of cowry shell money to the old women for their greeting, he inquired who they were and was told that they were the "mothers of all Kétu." Gollmer, assuming this meant heads of important families, did not enquire further.[68] With his several years of residence in West Africa and in Yoruba-speaking areas in particular, Gollmer had probably witnessed before the power and influence elderly women could wield in extended families, but he did not fully acknowledge the ways the king displayed his power and good will through women.

My attempts to find out which Kétu women may have been designated by such a vague phrase as "mothers of all Kétu" have been fruitless; people would only guess who the "mothers" may have been, and it is impossible to date many of the higher-ranking titles for women in Kétu. Like the "ladies of the palace" in Ọyọ, close confidants of the king of Kétu may have had religious authority with specific duties both inside the royal household and in the town. Several titled "mother" positions in Kétu in the latter twentieth century did involve such responsibilities, including the Ìyá Libara, Ìyá Ọba and Ìyálóde. Therein lies the controversy: the Ìyálóde is a new title in Kétu and the origins of the position and meaning of Ìyá Libara—a title seemingly specific to Kétu and notably occupied by a sister of the king—are in dispute.

It would be easy to compare the displaced "mothers of all Kétu" to public mothers in Ọyọ and Dahomey, who also seemed to become overwhelmed by the presence of royal wives and other dependents of kings by the nineteenth century. But in Kétu, the story is not only of royal wives but also of *other* wives who, buried in the sources, tell another version of Kétu's history, of a time when new religious practices expanded in the town and a destructive war marked the end of an era.

3

Giving Away Kétu's Secret

Wives on the Eve of War

When Scottish traveler Hugh Clapperton met the Aláàfin (king) of the declining Ọyọ empire in 1826, the crowd of women encircling the king seemed too dense to count.[1] By the nineteenth century, the kings of Ọyọ and Dahomey had surrounded themselves with hundreds of wives, staking their power and authority on the image and work of women. At mid-century, kings of Kétu dispatched groups of wives to greet visitors to the kingdom, and one king referred to his "favorite" wives as his closest confidants. But ordinary men, not only West African kings, displayed dependence on wives. Kétu oral histories tell of a Muslim named Sofo, meaning "old man" in Hausa, who arrived in Kétu and established a home outside the town fortifications. He received visits and gifts of food from the many Kétu women he married, the women actually and metaphorically giving birth to Kétu's Muslim population.[2] Unlike the royal wives who appeared frequently in written sources, wives of Muslim men and enslaved women, some of whom became wives, were often invisible to outsiders who visited Kétu.

In addition to ubiquitous royal wives and hidden wives of Muslim men were women from Kétu captured during the devastating 1886 war with Dahomey who became part of the Dahomey king's contingents of wives and dependents. The nineteenth century was a time of profound change when wars and raids moved large numbers of women about the region as captives. The Atlantic slave trade was in decline at the time, but many women found themselves in an ambiguous position between marriage and slavery. As wives of Muslim men or as captives in foreign towns, or as women seemingly isolated in royal households, women appeared as marginal figures. And yet through their relationships and sometimes their own actions, they illuminated the dynamics of power and vulnerability during a pivotal era when gender ideologies were both reinforced and profoundly challenged by intensifying Muslim conversion, by the new presence of Christian missionaries, and by the realities of war.

Knowing Islam, Meeting Christianity: Gender and the Politics of Religion

A popular Yoruba proverb says that the Yoruba met or knew *ifá* divination and Islam *"ní ayé"* ("in the world") but that Christianity arrived at *"òsán gangan"* ("high noon").[3] More than a simple chronology, the saying is a commentary on the nature of religious encounter. In it, *ifá* divination and Islam appear comparable, both religions part of "the world."[4] Indeed, Muslim divination practices dating back centuries relate to *ifá* divination, with the reading of signs etched in sawdust on a sacred board. Yoruba language exhibits an initial Muslim influence from the more distant Mali empire to the northwest, though Muslim Hausa practices just north of Yoruba towns became a dominating influence on Yoruba Muslims.[5] The conquest of the Fulani-led jihad state of Sokoto over the Hausa states at the turn of the century had ironic effects on Yoruba religions practices: Hausa slaves in Yoruba towns spread their Muslim religion, and Yoruba who were enslaved in Sokoto raids after the 1810s were liberated in Sierra Leone and became educated Christian converts. Some, like Samuel Crowther, returned years later to the Yoruba region as missionaries— figuratively at "high noon."

Even *"ayé"* ("the world"), where the Yoruba reputedly "met" *ifá* divination and Islam, encompasses more than a physical location or time. Referring to the past, present, and future, including the ancestors, "the world" is also a metaphysical space, sometimes translated as "humankind" or "life." In fact, the first line of the proverb about the relationship between *ifá* divination, Islam, and Christianity may be translated to say that *ifá* divination and Islam are both "as old as life."[6] By comparison, portraying Christianity as arriving late on the scene suggests that Christians forged a particular relationship with Yoruba communities, especially with the advent of European colonialism. During a brief period of the nineteenth century when direct "competition" existed between Muslims and Christian missionaries in Kétu, the ensuing dialogue raised questions not only about gender relationships but also about Kétu identity itself.

Oral histories of Islam's arrival in Kétu link kinship to politics, supplementing the image of Sofo—as an almost mythical Muslim progenitor—with stories of itinerant traders and personal stories of religious conversion. A group of Muslim men known as Kanike, a name associated with the Hausa to the north, reputedly brought better Muslim practices to the town.[7] Another story claims that itinerant traders who were Ọyọ Yoruba Muslims brought Islam to Kétu.[8] Yet many indications suggest that the majority of Muslim families in Kétu today are descendants of women and men who converted before and after the war with Dahomey.[9] Like many other Yoruba towns, Kétu probably received its first Muslim visitors by the latter eighteenth century. The origins of Islam's establishment in Yoruba towns remain murky; while many nineteenth-century sources do not record the arrival of Islam, they do record established Muslim quarters in Yoruba towns. By mid-century, Muslims regularly visited and resided in Kétu. A Muslim quarter known as Masafe existed; its reputed meaning, shortened from "Masafejo," was "do not involve me (in your stories)."[10] The name of a later offshoot of the Muslim Masafe quarter known as Yawomi, meaning "come and see," appears to project a more welcoming stance.

The contrasting images of isolation and invitation well characterize the Muslim community in Kétu. Regardless of the probable descent of Kétu Muslims from Kétu converts, Kétu Muslims are sometimes cast more readily as *àlejò*, or strangers, and only begrudgingly as *ọmọ Kétu* ("children of Kétu"/ members of the community). Perhaps unsurprisingly, the Kétu Muslim community of missionary accounts is portrayed in stories of men who were advisors, military leaders, and traders, not stories of families with wives, children, and in-laws.[11]

When Thomas Bowen, a white American Southern Baptist from Georgia, reached Kétu in 1851, he lived as a virtual hostage for several weeks because some royal ministers feared that the "white man's" visit would lead to the de-

My research assistant Alhaja Safouratou Mama with two Muslim men at Jingiri Mosque in Kétu in October 2006. Said to be the site of the oldest mosque in Kétu, the original building would have dated to at least the nineteenth century. Photograph by author.

struction of the town.[12] Yet the few times when Bowen dared to venture out, he publicly insulted the Muslim men he happened upon, calling them "slave-traders" who were willing and capable of selling off townspeople into slavery.[13] Bowen had come to West Africa to search in the interior of Nigeria for a region he erroneously called "Central Africa," hoping to find "Hamites," a mythical race of "white" Africans, associated in West Africa with cattle-herding and with Islam.[14] Because Yoruba communities were familiar with Islam, a monotheistic religion based on sacred texts, Bowen considered them more "civilized" and more likely (and better) converts than people on the coast.[15] Indeed, Yoruba language and culture fascinated Bowen during his six years in West Africa; he took such an avid interest in the language that he published a Yoruba-English dictionary and later, on assignment in Rio de Janeiro, Brazil, planned to use his knowledge of the language to gain Baptist converts and recruit missionaries among the slave and free black populations.[16] But earlier, during his stay in

Kétu, he showed little understanding of the complexities of Kétu society and the place of Muslims there.

Samuel Crowther, famed Yoruba of the Church Missionary Society who traveled to Kétu in 1853, was also suspicious of the Muslim presence in Kétu. His relationship with Islam, however, was more personal and more ambiguous. Crowther himself had been enslaved as a boy by Muslim jihadists and as an adult married the daughter of a Muslim man.[17] Crowther assumed Muslims in Kétu were among the "adherents to the king of Dahomey" who had caused problems for the king, Alákétu (meaning literally "owner of Kétu") Adebia; the king's palace had burned down and Crowther was aware of threats to Bowen himself two years earlier. So when two Muslim dignitaries, along with some other royal ministers, visited Crowther, he took joy in making them uncomfortable by preaching at length from the Bible.[18] His assumption that the king of Kétu had "Muslim" difficulties ignored the complexities of Kétu society that Crowther himself had chronicled. In one long passage, Crowther described the vibrant market day that attracted traders from up to two weeks' caravan travel from to the north, from the coast and from various Yoruba towns to the east, and from Dahomey only a day and a half away.[19] Some periodic visitors to Kétu's market day, like a Muslim man named Ali, a caravan leader, became quasi-residents, and some Gbe-speaking people from Dahomey settled within the boundaries of the Kétu kingdom, itself encompassing some Gbe villages.[20] Kétu's population and relationship with the outside world was thus multifaceted, making any threat of war, as one from Dahomey, a trade partner, more complex than a dispute based on ethnicity or religion.

Whatever the Muslim presence in Kétu in the early 1850s, Crowther, like Bowen, did little active proselytizing, both men preaching on few occasions and with small groups and merely suggesting what Christianity and "the Book" had to offer. Only when Crowther sent his protégé James Barber, a West African catechist named to Kétu to follow up on his own choice of a mission site, did Kétu residents experience an earnest, albeit short-lived, attempt to spread the "Word." And because Barber was received coolly by Alákétu Adebia, who had expected the return of his friend Crowther, Barber spent most of his three-week visit preaching to, and debating religion with, the Kétu women, men, and children who attended his services sporadically. He did not meet extensively with the king nor was he greeted by dignitaries or Muslim residents.[21] Barber's quick return visit to Kétu after the king's sudden death revealed that the king had acted alone in inviting Bowen and, especially, Crowther. The royal ministers said they knew nothing of a planned Christian mission station, though they appreciated his explanation. In the light of early Christian missionaries' uneven efforts in Kétu in the 1850s, it is difficult to imagine that these sporadic visits rivaled the presence of Islam in Kétu.[22]

Charles Gollmer of the Church Missionary Society, a German by birth, traveled to Kétu in 1859, and his encounters with Muslims aroused no such suspicion or rancor. Unlike Bowen, he had no quest to find "white" Africans among Muslims in the interior and no personal history with Islam like Crowther's. Muslims offered greetings and help, and Gollmer was mostly gracious in response. A man described as the Muslim chief, "a wealthy and influential man," offered a gift of sheep and cowries and visited Gollmer several times; another Muslim man provided him and his entourage with fresh drinking water.[23] Gollmer also met Muslims in villages outside the central town; "twenty young Mahomedan men" visited him in one town on his journey home.[24] Despite his more cordial relations with Muslims in Kétu, Gollmer offered no more insight into their community and, like his predecessors, only described Muslim men as individuals or in groups, but never with wives, children, or families.

Nigerian historian Biodun Adediran speculates that an uneasy anti-Christian missionary alliance between Muslims and senior Kétu royal ministers that broke down by 1858 accounted for Gollmer's "positive" encounter with Muslims there. In 1858, a man from an outlying Kétu village accidentally killed the king of Dahomey, increasing the threat of an attack from Dahomey and even leading to the forced suicide of Alákétu Adebia's successor, Alákétu Adegbede, soon afterward. Alákétu Adegbede had been besieged and weakened by factions in the town from the beginning of his reign in 1853, and forced suicide was not uncommon in the history of Yoruba kingdoms.[25] With an increasing threat from Dahomey, many in Kétu looked to missionaries as new allies who could offer political, military, and perhaps even spiritual protection.[26]

While Adediran appropriately emphasizes the instability of the times, it is unclear whether the fundamental interests of the king, of Muslims, of senior royal ministers, women traders, or Kétu farmers would have varied greatly on matters of trade and insecurity. In 1853, the missionary, Barber, described civil unrest unleashed by the king's death as political strife between allies of the king, outlying villages, and royal ministers.[27] In extended interviews between CMS missionary Crowther and Alákétu Adebia in 1853 and CMS missionary Gollmer and Alákétu Adiro Olumaja in 1859, neither king spoke of a specific Muslim threat. Indeed, the missionary accounts, coupled with oral histories about the nineteenth century, show Muslims embedded within the Kétu community, even though the wives and children that linked individuals and families remained obscured.

Given the fateful war with Dahomey that destroyed Kétu in 1886, many oral histories of the nineteenth century, whether transcribed or not, relate to that war directly or indirectly, foreshadowing in retrospect the treachery and mistakes that led to Kétu's defeat. Muslims who appear in such stories have contradictory roles as members and as strangers of the town. For example, both Father Thomas Moulero, a Kétu historian and ordained priest, and Edouard Dunglas, a French administrator, collected stories about a wealthy Muslim man who became a favorite counselor of the king. His name, Arigba, referred to personal prosperity, and translated from Yoruba it means "he saw two hundred (bundles of cloth)." According to Moulero, in an elaborate downfall marked by intrigue, sex, and war, his enemies hatched a plot against him; Arigba fled with the wife of a top military official, then initiated an armed battle in Kétu with the help of allies from a rebellious outlying village of the kingdom. He was executed by fellow members of the Kétu Muslim community.[28] Dunglas's version did not identity Arigba explicitly as a Muslim but noted that he was head of a local *egbẹ* (club) of wealthy town residents and Muslim traders, the larger rival club composed of farmers and royal ministers, led by the top military leader. According to Dunglas, the armed conflict began after Arigba seduced the wife of a leading royal minister and after his club organized a festival where derisive songs mocked his cuckolded rival. Arigba later died at the hands of his enemies.[29] His story provides insight not only into the nineteenth-century history of Islam, but also on the role of women and marriage in that history.

Arigba straddled Yoruba and Muslim identities and practices, with ties to the Kétu king and outlying villages, as well as to the Muslim quarter in the walled town.[30] The story of the Muslim club's dance festival, one of the best examples of this intersection, showed Muslims as part of local singing and dance, ordinarily prohibited by the Muslim faith. Tales of seduction point to another important feature of the relationship between the local and Muslim communities; marriages, controversial or not, incorporated Muslim men into Yoruba families and could expand the Muslim community through conversion and the birth of children. Such stories of marriage present women in a contradictory light. Women seem passive, married off to Sofo or seduced by Arigba. But their actions could have been more provocative. The story of Sofo's many wives may be about women who were seeking out the powerful foreigner as a suitor; it was not said that Arigba kidnapped the general's or royal minister's wife, but that she ran off with him. Still, women remain ambiguous in these images of treacherous seduction versus consented marriage. This distinction mirrors an underlying theme in Kétu's history of Islam: the contrast between the celebration of Muslim loyalty and the threat of Muslim betrayal.

Such contrary imagery was especially acute during the war with Dahomey that occurred in two phases in approximately 1884 and 1886, during which some Muslims participated as soldiers on behalf of Kétu, with some, such as a general named Pakoyi, mourned as fallen heroes.[31] The story of someone like Pakoyi has been thoroughly overshadowed by the opposite image embodied by the more infamous Kétu Muslim cleric Arepa. Arepa, known for making òògùn (medicine, amulets) for Kétu's royal ministers and military leaders, is remembered as a close advisor to the king of Dahomey and for "giving away Kétu's secret." With the Dahomey army ready to abandon a blockade at the lone entrance to the walled town during its second attack on Kétu in 1886, Arepa told them that Kétu's food and water would be running out. Dahomey officers lured Kétu's top military leaders out of the protected enceinte with false promises of a truce, killed the Kétu leaders, then entered the defenseless town. Arepa performed ablutions at all the town's sacred sites after its destruction to calm the fears of the king of Dahomey that angered spirits and deities of Kétu would exact revenge.[32] Not until Dahomey and Kétu had become part of the French colony was Arepa able to return to Kétu; he was greeted with derisive songs blaming him for Kétu's destruction and died soon afterward, mysteriously, in a fire.[33]

Some portrayed Arepa's involvement in the war quite differently to me, emphasizing that Arepa had been kidnapped and forced to serve the king of Dahomey, unaware that his advice was used to mount a war against Kétu. They credit him with "saving" many captured Kétu women from slavery by taking them as "wives" when they were brought to Dahomey.[34] In a variation of that story, the great-grandmother of my research assistant reputedly rejected Arepa's offer of marriage. In retaliation, Arepa later sent the woman's daughter (perhaps with a Dahomean prince because the daughter was said to have ties to the royal family of Dahomey) to Kétu, where the girl was raised by a Muslim family and later married a Kétu Muslim.[35] This alternative vision of Arepa's role in the war highlights another, perhaps underemphasized, aspect of Kétu Muslim community: regardless of the story of Arepa and his reputed role in the war, Muslim families were part of the rebirth of the town after the war.

Indeed, Sofo, Arigba, and Arepa are remembered, to varying degrees, as "husbands," illustrating the tenuous power some men wielded over their wives. Though stereotyped as prolific "fathers" and "wife stealers," these men sought to marry local women to establish kinship links in a town where they were strangers. A Muslim man, as a stranger and as a husband, tried to establish himself as the founder of a family and compound by attracting wives and keeping control over his children. Since marriage involved entire extended families, especially elder men and women, Kétu families ideally would have had to sanction these unions. With marriage came the possibility of women's conversion and the rearing of children as Muslim, since children traced their kinship principally, though not exclusively, through their fathers.[36] The invisibility and silence of the wives of these Muslim men may suggest, however, that Muslim men did not also succeed in converting their wives or maintaining control over their children.

Rare memories of nineteenth-century marriages between Muslim men and Kétu women tell the complex history of Islam and of marriage across religious faiths in the town. Two elderly Muslim Kétu men shared with me their stories of female ancestors who married Muslim men before the war with Dahomey and who converted when they married. During the war, one woman, from a family that worshipped Ṣango, the òrìṣà (deity), escaped to Porto-Novo carrying her infant son on her back. Years later, her Muslim relatives paid visits to their in-laws to acknowledge ceremonies celebrating Ṣango.[37] Another Muslim man told me that his great-grandmother had begged her family to allow her to marry a Muslim man; she gave birth to a daughter before the war. The man was uncertain whether his great-grandmother had converted and he did not provide her Muslim name; the man himself had built a home in the compound of his Kétu relatives, who were not identified as Muslim.[38]

Even with scant evidence of interfaith marriages in nineteenth-century Kétu, the town appeared to be diverse, with resident traders from distant communities, including Yoruba migrants, Baatonu (Bariba) traders, and Gbe speakers from Dahomey and other towns. Bowen estimated that between 10,000 and 15,000 people lived in the walled town with perhaps 60,000 in outlying villages.[39] All Kétu residents, including Muslims, established multiple links across a heterogeneous community threatened by war. Fluidity and instability in Kétu and across the region made it possible for Muslim men to have local women as wives. Uncertain times reinforced local residents' suspicion of "strangers," forged alliances, and encouraged efforts to seek out assistance and information from visitors. One Muslim man told me that as a show of hospitality, a Kétu man might offer his daughter as a wife to a visitor or temporary resident, even if the stranger was a Muslim man. Such a story evoked the one told so often about Sofo.

Nevertheless, marriages across religious faiths may well be the best-kept secret in Kétu's history. Contemporary Christian missionaries and later scholars generally ignore West African women's conversion and participation in Muslim communities. Christian emissaries' notes about Muslim traders, chiefs, and clerics are detached from any reference to dependents, spouses, or kin, yet Kétu residents knew Islam in their own homes, in their celebrations, through friends, and through their children's spouses and their grandchildren. The oral histories that survive suggest that marriage and political intrigue accompanied the expansion of Islam into Kétu daily life. By contrast, the initial fleeting introduction to Christianity at mid-century has been largely forgotten. The origins of Christianity in Kétu, specifically of Catholicism, have been traced instead to the 1890s, after Dahomey's defeat by French forces and the start of the return of Kétu captives from Dahomey and refugees from other neighboring towns.[40]

Royal Wives: Secrets of the King's House

Among the survivors and returnees after the war with Dahomey were former women slaves in Dahomey who witnessed the war and aftermath and also the lives of royal wives in Dahomey at the end of the century. Assétou Ayouba, a Kétu woman taken captive during the war, gave such an account to Kétu priest and local historian Father Moulero, though she did not make clear her specific situation as an *ahosi* (dependent, "wife" of the king) in Dahomey. Instead she spoke in general terms about older women who were sent to labor on the king's farms (presumably closer to the palace) while younger women were sent to cultivate crops on farms in other villages. Other women, perhaps Ayouba among them, were kept at the palace to perform in music and dance groups.[41] Another unnamed Kétu woman, interviewed by a French scholar and by two American anthropologists in the 1950s, served as a slave to two royal wives in Dahomey; she was a slave to women who were themselves "dependents" of the king. She explained the hierarchy of wives from the most senior to the mere "wives in the yard." Some wives received permission to attend ceremonies and others accompanied the king of Dahomey onto the battlefield.[42] By the end of the century, royal wives at Dahomey were part of a complex bureaucratic system developed over the course of two centuries whereby women came to serve the king of Dahomey and the operation of the kingdom as a whole.[43]

Certainly, the scale of the royal palace in Dahomey in the 1890s contrasted with the situation described by missionaries who visited Kétu in the 1850s. All the missionaries did not personally encounter royal wives; the American, Bowen, was sequestered in his quarters and the West African catechist, Barber, was largely ignored by Alákétu Adebia. Bowen, rather than meet royal wives during his 1851 visit, encountered vulnerable West African women who were slaves or war captives, inadvertently providing insight into interrelated experiences of West African women as slaves and wives. Bowen wrote about one woman he met, originally from Kétu, who had been captured and incorporated into the Dahomey army; she was discovered wandering in Kétu territory after Dahomey's unsuccessful attack on the Yoruba town of Abẹokuta, to the east of Kétu. When she was brought to the Kétu market to be ransomed to Dahomey traders, the woman's Kétu family recognized her and tried desperately to pay her ransom, but she declared that she would "go back to her master."[44] As a soldier in the Dahomey army, she was an *ahosi* (dependent, "wife" of the king). Historian Edna Bay denies that women in the palace were either simply wives or slaves. Women who were "wives" of the king could not divorce him as women of ordinary men could, and in the palace, some slave women could attain power and rank that could "overshadow" their slave status.[45] When the captured woman soldier from Kétu declined to stay with kin in Kétu who sought to ransom her, she demonstrated the position of privilege or deep loyalty (perhaps induced by fear) generated by her role in the Dahomey army.

Bowen wrote in his missionary journal of another woman trader who had been captured at work in a market outside of Ọyọ and passed from one slave owner and market to another before finding herself in Kétu, where she appealed to Bowen to purchase her. Slaves were not sold openly in the market in Kétu, but she feared she would be sold again and forced onto one of the few slave ships that still plied the West African coast. Having had several owners and with no attachment to a household, she was particularly vulnerable.[46] Several historians, writing in the volume *Slavery in Africa: Historical and Anthropological Perspectives,* have examined slavery as an "institution of marginality," with slaves employing various forms of social mobility to alter the "degrees of marginality" and gain fuller "incorporation" in the slaveowner's society. Many who were slaves in Africa, rather than experience the utter "social death" described later in Orlando Patterson's study of slavery in the Americas, found some flexibility in their status.[47] The woman trader who asked Bowen to purchase her may have been trying to control her destiny by choosing her own patron/master/"husband."

Bowen's indirect comments on wives and gender relationships contrasted with Crowther's very direct discussion of the king of Kétu's royal wives. Crowther, unlike Bowen, was an honored guest of Alákétu Adebia, who had contacted him years earlier, and he was able to circulate freely in the town and receive numerous visitors, including the king's ministers, royal wives, and Muslim residents. His first comments were approving observations of women traders in the town doing their washing in the trenches that surrounded the town; as itinerant traders they had no access to the limited water supply, which was chiefly rain water people collected at their homes.[48] He praised the freedom with which women walked freely in the town, even at night, and he remarked on the absence of certain indigenous religious ceremonies that restricted women's movement.[49] Yet when several dozen royal wives paid Crowther a visit, he noted their impoverished dress and limited mobility, and learned that they earned money from tolls collected on market day, amused themselves by dancing (as long as they had no contact with men), and farmed a small plot near the king's palace.[50] They had limited independent income and saw virtually no one except other royal wives. His sense of them as the most "wretched" and pitiful he had seen ran counter to, perhaps, Western assumptions about women who were called "royal wives," and it contrasted with his other observations of women in the town.

In the past, women and men could take refuge at the palace, becoming a wife or servant to the king. To this day, there is a fabled spot in front of the palace of the king of Kétu that if traversed by a woman or man compels the man to become a servant of the king and the woman to become a wife. As in Dahomey, where Edna Bay argues against the idea that royal wives and other dependents of the king were slaves, Kétu royal wives were not portrayed as slaves. Indeed, Crowther said that the king of Kétu, unlike most other kings he had met, kept no slaves. He was told that royal slaves were an "annoyance" to the rest of the population, implying that even as slaves, they might use their association with the king to exert influence and make demands on the king's behalf.[51]

Royal wives lived in a household that exaggerated the practice of polygyny, men with multiple wives—a practice at the center of debates in Church Missionary Society policy. Crowther, who disapproved deeply of polygyny, accepted it as a reality, believing that through education, men and women eventually would abandon such practices. He wrote that monogamy was not a "minimum requirement for salvation" and that women in such marriages, as "involuntary victims of a social institution," should not be denied baptism. Nigerian historian Jacob Ade Ajayi points out that Christian missionaries who attacked the practice of polygyny forced converts to reject African household organization in the family compound of extended families, including multiple wives, and their children—all of them potential converts. Despite some of Crowther's other harsh statements on polygyny, he, like many other educated elite converts of his time, took a more practical and a more generous view, that "sinful" social practices did not preclude an invitation to religious salvation. In 1891, Crowther was replaced as the head of the Niger Mission for being perceived as a defender of the lax Christian practices of African members of the mission.[52]

Crowther had written of the day of his own enslavement as a "blessed" day because it led him from the "land of heathenism, superstition, and vice," despite his profound pain at separation from this mother and sisters after they too were captured. He later revealed that his own father had five wives before he was killed soon after Crowther's enslavement. But in that polygynous household and extended family, women had not been "wretched"; his grandmother claimed descent from an Ọyọ king and his mother from an important priest.[53] In a most improbable reunion in Abẹokuta in 1846, Crowther's mother and a half-brother found Crowther. His mother was living with her daughters and grandchildren in a nearby town, and the extended family had gone to great lengths to protect one another. Relatives had bribed slave traders to rescue his mother and sister from slavery, and his sister had paid a large sum to free his mother, re-enslaved three times during the twenty-five years before Crowther returned home. With Crowther's triumphant homecoming, his family spoke of his assuming his rightful place as the "father" of the family. Crowther welcomed his mother into his home and she soon converted and lived for nearly another forty more years as a Christian.[54] Crowther's personal relationship to powerful and resilient women in his life embodied the tension between his connection to, and rejection of, Yoruba culture and religion; yet, in Kétu's royal wives, he only saw "victims" and the sin of the Yoruba culture he had largely forsaken for Christianity.

When West African catechist James Barber traveled to Kétu a few months later, he met none of the royal wives formally, though one quietly attended one of his services alone, an unusual event in that she was apparently not there to represent or send greetings on behalf of the king.[55] Only when Barber returned suddenly to Kétu months later upon learning of the death of the king did he learn anything of the royal wives, their symbolic power, and their vulnerability.

Kétu was in an uproar after Aláké tu Adebia died, with some groups demanding the death of certain allies of the king. Barber learned that two royal wives had accompanied the king in death to serve him in the afterlife, one, according to later sources, the *ida* (senior wife) and the other the *ramu* (favorite wife). Barber was told that the two women—one of whom was the mother of an infant— had consumed large amounts of rum and danced around the town declaring their fearlessness before death, then had taken poison. Three men named to accompany the king in death fled, were exiled, or had their titles taken away in order to avoid submitting to the ritual death. Barber attributed the town's change of heart about the ritual death of the three men to the influence of missionary visits, but he described how the condemned royal wives embodied the king's power in death as in life.[56]

In fact, when Adebia's successor, Aláké tu Adegbede, was forced to commit suicide after his short-lived and tragic reign from 1853 to 1858, the senior wife and favorite wife were also to accompany him in death and again the favorite wife, so it is said, was the mother of an infant. Before her death, the young mother pronounced a curse on Kétu that was later taken as a foreshadowing of the town's destruction by Dahomey decades later. Her defiant action as the young royal wife challenged Crowther's portrayal of such women as "wretched" and as wholly submissive.[57]

The only other nineteenth-century missionary to have met with Kétu's royal wives was the German Charles Gollmer, who, as a well-known member of the Church Missionary Society, was invited in 1859 to come to Kétu by Aláké tu Adiro Olumaja. Gollmer had been living in Yoruba areas for more than ten years and was fluent in Yoruba language, and the sight of royal wives did not affect him in the same way that it had Crowther.[58] Gollmer remarked on Kétu royal wives before he even reached the town, having encountered them in small villages on his travels to Kétu. Once at the walled capital town of Kétu, Gollmer one morning received twenty young royal wives as visitors. When the king asked Gollmer later that day to choose one stick among twenty laid before him, Gollmer refused, perhaps suspicious at the question. He learned that the king had heard that Gollmer had "eyed" one of the twenty wives who visited him—a woman believed to be a troublemaker. The wives themselves had devised the scheme to get Gollmer to use his "supernatural power to read the heart and tell the good and evil thereof." Gollmer quoted the Bible to dismiss the idea that any human could read the heart of another and defused the situation, somewhat to the amusement of the king.[59]

Alákétu Adiro Olumaja bared his fears and desires to Gollmer, sharing his concerns about war, prosperity, and his own reign as king and pledging to open his town fully to CMS missionaries. He hoped to avoid the plague of war, fire, and "sudden death" and was adamant that Gollmer must help him attain a crown befitting a king. With increased production of cotton, the king planned to revitalize Kétu's trade networks.[60] The king recounted his special relationship with two of his royal wives, probably his senior wife and favorite wife: "They never leave me and there is no secret I keep from them or they from me and on the day of my death they follow me. . . . I show you all that is in my heart and all the secrets of my house." Gollmer instructed the king on the sins of human sacrifice, to which the king replied, "Manners and customs religious and social are like stupendous mountains, not to be removed in a day, except by the grace of God."[61] The exchange between Alákétu Adiro Olumaja and Gollmer captured the complex negotiations at hand between African communities and Christian missionaries who sought to reconcile divergent ideals and expectations about the Christian missionary enterprise in West Africa. With the king seeking assurances for the safety and prosperity of his town, and Gollmer himself more concerned with the sin and with morality according to Christian doctrine, the mutual misunderstanding of the missionary and the king was profound.

The night before his departure, Gollmer discovered that the king planned to give him a slave girl as a parting gift! He was outraged, whereupon the king gave him a large gift of cowry shell money instead.[62] The next day the king, presumably, arranged for Gollmer to meet the three elderly women described to him as the "mothers of all Kétu." Alákétu Adiro Olumaja had truly shared with Gollmer the "secrets of his house," through candid discussion and meetings with delegations of royal wives and because Gollmer was the only European traveler to Kétu to meet the official or unofficial "public mothers" of the town.[63] Thus, missionary accounts permit a glimpse of Kétu before the 1886 defeat by Dahomey, which marked a key break with the past.

Wives of War

When I interviewed people in Kétu in the late 1990s and early 2000s, "before" and "after" the war was still a salient way of demarcating eras, even if knowledge of the late nineteenth century was extremely remote. Though men's exploits ordinarily dominate histories of war, images of wives, slaves, and even "mothers" surface repeatedly in oral and written histories of the period. French accounts of the war with Dahomey and of the flight of Behanzin, king of Dahomey, in 1892 estimate that the soldiers, wives, ministers, and prisoners, including several Brazilians Behanzin took with him, numbered in the hundreds, if not thousands, before 1893, when they began to desert him or died of smallpox.[64] Kétu historian Thomas Moulero's informant, Assétou Ayouba, recounted Behanzin's strange rituals meant to forestall the advancing French army. In a speech to his entourage, Behanzin said, "I traveled to Goho with one of my wives to see the general and ask for amnesty because two great men cannot catch each other. Then I disappeared from before his eyes and returned before you. But in three days I will return with a coffin." Three days later in that coffin he placed the head of his mother, whom he had sacrificed.[65] This most desperate act was to no avail; he surrendered to the French and with the one wife he had kept at his side, he was deported with several other family members to Senegal, to Martinique, and finally to Algeria, where he died ten years later.[66]

In addition to the historical roles accorded to public mothers and royal wives, Dahomey had been known for its unique army of women soldiers, composed of "wives" of the king, such as the Kétu woman American missionary Thomas Bowen met in 1851 trying to find her way back to Dahomey. Another woman soldier of Dahomey, originally from the Ohori region to the south of Kétu, told Dahomean historian Paul Hazoumé in 1917 that she too had served the king and one of his royal wives. The king rewarded her fearless fighting in a battle by "marrying" her. She became pregnant, but pregnancy by a member of the women's army was forbidden, and when she gave birth, she kept the identity of the father a secret, though she could not hide the infant. She was beaten and forced to do hard labor as a punishment for her transgression, whereupon the king admitted his role and commissioned a series of inlaid sculptures to be placed in the wall of a newly built palace in honor of her bravery on the battlefield. He formally recognized her as a wife and bestowed upon her the honorary title of Queen Ajashe (the Yoruba name for the town of Porto-Novo).[67] Although other royal wives scorned her humble origins, she felt vindicated both by the king's lavish, if late, attention and by the successful birth of a son.

Despite the earlier enslaved status of Queen Ajashe, Assétou Ayouba, and the third unnamed Kétu woman who served at the Dahomey palace, their stories were told from each one's perspective as an elderly woman who came to command respect. In Thomas Moulero's photograph of Assétou Ayouba, she is seated, dressed in multiple layers of fabric and in sandals as a woman of some rank. The unnamed woman who had been as a slave to a royal wife of Dahomey had a son who served as an informant and interpreter to several visiting Western scholars in the 1950s. Hazoumé was so intimidated by Queen Ajashe, the former soldier, that he did not have the courage to ask her life story until he had visited her several times. Of the three women, indeed, only Queen Ajashe revealed details of her own personal experience.

It is fitting that Kétu women's accounts of the war with Dahomey should have been published; the actions of young women and mothers during and after the war are among the few stories people tell about the conflict today. Many of these stories resemble the one a Muslim man told about his grandmother who fled toward Nigeria with her infant on her back. Young women escaped, as Father Thomas Moulero's own mother did; some were married to men in other towns and many had children in the years between the time of Kétu's destruction and its rebuilding. Moulero's mother's family took care of him before he was forced into the Catholic mission; later he went of his own accord. One of the stories most repeated about the war and survivors in Kétu is that of Agiri, an important man close to the Alákétu who lived well into the colonial period. Many say he survived after being buried alive for several days by the Dahomeans, but in fact he was hidden by his own parents in a shallow hole in the earth during the Dahomean attack and later rescued.[68]

Because most Kétu women captured during the war were taken to Dahomey, many became slaves and wives of Dahomean men and mothers to their children. Some had been given as slaves to leading men in the port of Ouidah, which Dahomey conquered in the 1720s, gaining direct access to the Atlantic trade. Because a husband and the husband's family had primary rights over children, some in Kétu said that, for that reason, women were slower to return to Kétu in 1894, when the reconstruction of Kétu began.[69] As late as 1904, a French colonial administrator was alarmed to find that Kétu messengers went to Ouidah to beg the many Kétu women there, some faring well as traders, to return to help rebuild Kétu. One woman told me that one of her ancestors, fearing that her husband, a powerful Ouidah merchant, would track her down if she left with his children, changed the markings scarred on the child's face to match those of the people of Kétu.[70] Thus, not unlike the exceptional trajectory of three women who recounted their experiences in Dahomey, other Kétu women who traveled that slippery slope from slave to wife redefined themselves as traders in their new homes or attempted to shed their status of slave/wife.

Besides those captured and enslaved, there were Kétu refugees like those encountered in 1891 by a French Catholic priest named Pied, who was traveling in the general vicinity of Kétu, in search of the destroyed town. Pied came across a group of women and men led by a man named Fehetona, who had proclaimed himself Alákétu. Other Kétu residents became refugees in other Yoruba towns and villages and some were sold into slavery as far as the island of São Tomé, off the coast of West Central Africa.[71]

In 1893, those who were able to return found a town in ruins, overgrown with vegetation. A French Catholic priest who traveled to Kétu in 1897 found the community still encamped in makeshift abodes on the market square outside the town.[72] These earliest days of rebuilding coincident with French colonial rule were extremely slow yet heady with change. It was a time when women and men in Kétu first opened their hearts and minds to Christianity, though more extensive conversions would happen later over the course of the twentieth century. Many of the dependent villages that constituted the larger Kétu polity in the nineteenth century would become part of British-controlled Nigeria, raising questions about people's identity as Kétu, about their link to the king of Kétu, who was recognized by the French colonial regime, and about their relationship to wives and "public mothers" linked to the Kétu king.

Thus, in a turbulent century that culminated in Kétu's downfall, women as wives, refugees, and slaves played important roles. This same flexibility allowed certain women to exercise power as "mothers" and permitted some wives to enjoy influential positions despite the realities of their inferior "wifely" status. So, too, when Kétu emerged from ruin, royal wives, as well as "public mothers," took on new and controversial roles in both a reborn Kétu kingdom and a new French colonial administration.

4

"Where women really matter"

*The "Queens" of Kétu and the Challenge
to French Imperialism*

On April 20, 1911, after a disgruntled man in Kétu shot and killed a visiting African translator, town residents steeled themselves for a severe reprisal by the French colonial regime. Instead, a small force of police guards arrived, and a local French administrator made an unprecedented decision, naming two Kétu women as colonial intermediaries. The appointment was a startling step for several reasons. At the time, in France's federated colonies of French West Africa, not a single French colonial official or African agent was a woman. The French generally believed that African women occupied only lowly positions in African society and women were subordinate in France itself.[1]

The administrator who appointed Alaba Ida and Yá Ṣègén, the two "queens," as the French called them, explained to his superiors that "these measures should not cause alarm in the Nago [French term for Yoruba] region where women really matter."[2] Within four years, the French governor of Dahomey declared that "rule by a woman went against Nago traditions," and by 1917 both women, who had been compelled to issue unpopular demands that turned their own people against them, were deposed.[3] Elderly Kétu residents today who have heard of the two women often refer to Alaba Ida, the more infamous of the two, as an *aya ọba* (royal wife), but rarely as a "queen."[4] Alaba Ida is immortalized, but in derisive songs. The second "queen," Yá Ṣẹ̀gén, faded from colonial reports and many people's memories, though her priestly title persisted after her death. As elderly women, both Alaba Ida and Yá Ṣẹ̀gén had evoked the image of the "public mother," but they did not fulfill that role in similar ways. Local Kétu society came to emphasize Alaba Ida's subordinate status as a royal wife. On the other hand Yá Ṣẹ̀gén, as a priest, was actually a titled "mother" but of a lesser known *òrìṣà* (deity), one more popular in outlying villages than in the central town. From their unusual positions within Kétu, each was affected differently by the changing nature of the king of Kétu's role as a "father figure" under French colonial rule.

The "reigns" of both Alaba Ida and Yá Ṣẹ̀gén "were possible because in the period before the shock of World War I, the French believed that certain women could assist them in implementing colonial policies, though as the war stoked fears of anarchy and "emasculated hierarchies" in Africa, if not back home in France, both "queens" quickly fell from grace. The stories of Alaba Ida and Yá Ṣẹ̀gén illustrate the shifting roles of "mothers" and wives in early colonial Kétu while shedding light on French imperialism itself.

"Life itself is rendered completely incomprehensible": The Rise and Fall of Alaba Ida and Yá Ṣẹ̀gén

Alaba Aduké was born around 1854 in Kétu. She became an *aya ọba* (royal wife) of Alákétu Ojeku and had a daughter and a son with him.[5] When the Alákétu (king; "owner of Kétu") was slain in the war with Dahomey in 1886, Alaba Aduké, like many others, was captured and brought to the Dahomey capital, Abomey. Seven years later, France defeated Dahomey, whereupon Alaba Aduké agitated for a return to Kétu and may have been among the first group of refugees to accompany the victorious French army officers to Kétu.[6] According to a British scholar, Alaba Aduké was about forty years old at the beginning of French colonial rule and still a "fine-looking woman."[7] Some residents of Kétu said that because she was beautiful, Ojeku, the king, had "put his foot on her," demanding that she become his wife.[8] By tradition, the new king, who took the name Onyegen, inherited all the wives of his predecessor, and during Onyegen's reign Alaba assumed the influential position of *ida* (senior wife) and was known thereafter as Alaba Ida.[9]

Alaba Ida became an outspoken supporter of the French during the time of the 1906 Anglo-French Boundary Commission that drew up the borders between French-controlled Dahomey and British-controlled Nigeria, perhaps out of loyalty to the French for defeating Dahomey and supporting Kétu's reconstruction. Two years later, the king began to lose power as he became blind and more infirm and as France reorganized its West African colonies. In the restructuring of the colonies, most kings, Alákétu Onyegen among them, were demoted, first to *chef supérieur* (superior chief) and then to *chef du canton* (district head or "chief"). William Ponty, the new governor general and director of the federation of French West African colonies based in Dakar, Senegal, was convinced that local elites, particularly kings and royals, were corrupt and dictatorial, and hence promoted a policy that elevated non-elites to "district chief," assigning them the tasks of collecting taxes and recruiting labor and soldiers.[10] Because of Ponty's policy and Onyegen's illness, an additional *sous-chef* (assistant chief), Abimbọla Otupepe, was appointed. Alákétu Onyegen's physical and political weakness and Otupepe's ineffectiveness paved the way for Alaba Ida's recognition within the French colonial administration.

Though Alaba Ida took on most of the duties of the "district chief," including military and labor recruitment, taxation, and supervision of subordinate village heads, she was never formally given the title of *chef du canton*.[11] The French instead referred to her by her title "Ida," meaning senior wife, which the French translated as "queen," often rendering her name "Queen Ida" in the colonial records. From the beginning, the French were reticent about the power they had accorded to Alaba Ida, but, whether or not people in Kétu acknowledged that she held an official position in the colonial administration, today they allude to her special relationship with the French. "Alákétu Onyegen went blind," one man told me, "and did not notice when the European held out his hand [in greeting]. Alaba Ida shook hands with the European instead and became very powerful."[12]

The second "queen," whose given name was Akanké Owebeyi Aduké, lived in a village about ten miles northeast of the former walled center and heart of the Kétu kingdom.[13] As a priest, she was an *iyálorìṣà* (mother-in-deity) of the *òrìṣà* (deity) named Ondo, and in that role, apparently at around twenty-eight years of age, assumed the title "Yá Ṣègén" (probably a shortened version of Ìyá Ṣègén or "Mother Ṣègén"). The *òrìṣà* are believed to have been women or men worthy of praise and worship because of remarkable lives in earlier times. Ondo and his wife Are, for example, are celebrated as founders of Pobé, a town outside the Kétu region and the original home of Yá Ṣègén and her fellow Ọbatẹdo villagers. Òrìṣà have particular dispositions and favorite foods, and some, like Ondo, "mount" or possess priests and initiates. It is said that Yá Ṣègén took her title in Pobé in 1868. Several decades later, in 1902, when she and her followers tried to resettle in Kétu, Onyegen, the king, allowed them to stay, but on land outside the town; the name of their new village, Ọbatẹdo, meant "the king built this."[14]

Yá Ṣègén does not appear in the French colonial record until 1906, when the French colonial administrator speaks of her as "almost a divinity."[15] Her religious duties remained paramount even though she was filling a political role in working for the French. Because òrìṣà (deities) dictate certain taboos for people initiated into the group and because followers of Ondo are forbidden to ride in a hammock, Yá Ṣègén, unlike Alaba Ida, never journeyed to meet French colonial administrators. Instead, French officials came to her in Ọbatẹdo or nearby.[16] She was assigned specific responsibility for eastern villages in addition to Ọbatẹdo, several of them—Ilikimu, Issélou, and Idigne—recalcitrant and troublesome ones. Therefore, Yá Ṣègén was not simply a "village chief" but almost an "assistant district head." But, as with Alaba Ida, her formal administrative title was never stated.[17] The French at first admired Yá Ṣègén's influence as a religious leader, but in the end they were not impressed with her ability to carry out orders on their behalf.

The precipitating event that led to the appointments of both Alaba Ida and Yá Ṣègén was the murder in 1911 of a visiting African interpreter named Georges Mensah, a murder remembered in Kétu as the "one-gunshot war" because witnesses had heard only a single shot. A man named Fagbité, who was accused of the translator's murder, explained that his gun had misfired, causing him to shoot the wrong man; he had intended to kill Abimbọla Otupepe, the assistant chief appointed after Alákétu Onyegen lost his sight. His motive was to avenge a male relative who had been fined and jailed by Otupepe for insubordination.[18] He and an accomplice had planned the shooting to occur in the presence of a visiting French colonial official and a French Catholic priest to "really show the whites that we were unhappy."[19] Alaba Ida spearheaded the investigation and, years later, was considered a key witness in the case against the accomplice.[20] Fagbité was imprisoned and sentenced to death, his sentence carried out in a spectacular fashion—he was compelled to walk a distance with nails pressed into the soles of his feet and then executed on the spot where he had fired his gun.[21]

The "one-gunshot-war" contrasts with the much longer "war" between areas neighboring the Kétu region and the French, underway since the 1894 founding of Dahomey colony. Fagbité's misbegotten revenge was an incident in a broader pattern of disorder and resentment in Kétu and other villages populated by Yoruba-related subgroups, known as Ohori and Adja Ouéré. Kétu, Ohori, and Adja Ouéré villages, linguistically and ethnically related in varying degrees to the Yoruba, fell within a *cercle* (circle) based at Zagnanado, about thirty miles away. Circles, the largest French colonial administrative unit, were headed by European officers. The circle could be divided into subdivisions, provinces, cantons (districts), and villages. In the circle of Zagnanado, most of the other towns and villages were ethnically and linguistically Gbe-speaking and had been part of the former Dahomey kingdom. But with insufficient administrative personnel to cover the entire territory and with the French colonial emphasis on the region of the former Dahomey kingdom, Kétu and the Ohori and Adja Ouéré villages were out of the range of immediate oversight of the French colonial administration. As a result, additional loyal African intermediaries like Alaba Ida and Yá Ṣègén were needed.

In the first years of French colonial rule, tax evasion, illicit cross-border trade, and general insubordination were rife in Ohori and Adja Ouéré villages and in Kétu itself. Yet by 1909, the French governor of Dahomey was still reporting to his superiors that in Dahomey "peace has never been disturbed since 1893."[22] French policymakers before World War I concentrated on the use of railroads and trade to gain support and cooperation from African populations and otherwise claimed to respect African practices as long they were not offensive. But gradually, French administrators began to be troubled by a growing threat of "anarchy," and the shooting of the interpreter was seen as an ominous climax to the growing disorder. The governor of Dahomey and other French colonials higher up in the bureaucracy forbade outright force in response, and interim governor Raphaël Antonetti deployed sixty-five guards in Kétu, only to discover that people outside Kétu were saying, "The people in Kétu [had] killed a white man. They [the French] sent guards there but there is no need to be afraid of them because the guards don't have the right to burn villages or even kill the shooter."[23]

In this sprawling and hostile environment, French colonial administrators decided that the two women leaders, Alaba Ida and Yá Ṣègén, would serve as crucial allies. An undated, unsigned colonial document of the 1910s described Alaba Ida as "alert, despite her age, very authoritarian, with an intelligent and lively spirit . . . a precious resource for the administration of this unusual Nago [Yoruba] race whose distance from Zagnanado gives them a bit of independence."[24] An earlier French administrator, in contrast, had criticized the king and Kétu's senior leadership for a lack of "paternal power," and this perceived weakness in male leadership could have contributed to the conviction that "women really mattered," cited to explain the 1911 appointment of Alaba Ida and Yá Ṣègén.[25] French treatment of Kétu was consistent with its broader colonial intent to "respect" African customs and to bring "civilization" through colonialism, and by insisting that women's power was integral to Kétu culture, French administrators justified placing women in positions of power, ignoring the fact that French society itself, and colonial policy generally, had historically denied women overt political power.

Both of the two "queens" brought strengths to their new role. At first, terms like "intelligence" and "devotion" appear in French documents praising Alaba Ida, while the French valued Yá Ṣègén for her power as a priest.[26] And yet from the beginning, the rebellious setting and the power dynamic between the population and the French challenged and eventually undermined both women's exercise of power. When one village complained that a 1912 French redrawing of the boundary with British-controlled Nigeria had relocated its sacred shrine in British territory, and its residents moved over to the Nigerian side of the border, Yá Ṣègén pleaded with the community, "Consult your deity and see what he says. You are children of Kétu and you cannot abandon your ancestors."[27] French administrator Louis Duboscq gave the villagers an ultimatum: return and enjoy exemption from taxes and labor demands for three years or leave permanently and face confiscation of fields that remained within French territory. The village leaders responded defiantly but coolly that since all their farmland was actually in Nigeria, they had no reason to stay in French territory. A second village abandoned or burned its houses on the French side of the border and rebuilt on the British side. Unperturbed by the presence of the French administrator, villagers told his guide that after that year's harvest, they would no longer cultivate French soil and therefore would owe no more taxes.[28] The population of a third village, two months later, replaced the local leader the French had appointed in preparation for relocation across the border.

Duboscq, well aware that other populations were watching to see if villagers would succeed in such plans, took a strong line. On a journey with a guide and a few guards, he arrested several men and put them on public display, threatening to "make gunpowder talk" if defiance of the French continued.[29]

Local populations, despite his threats, blamed the demands for taxes and laborers on Alaba Ida and Yá Ṣẹ̀gẹ́n. Kétu villagers complained of orders from messengers of the "queens" to report to hearings or pay fines. Duboscq affirmed that those orders came from the French, yet in his tour he neither traveled with Alaba Ida or Yá Ṣẹ̀gẹ́n nor explicitly and publicly backed them (or, indeed, the Alákétu earlier) with the threat of the French military.[30] Hence, Alaba Ida and Yá Ṣẹ̀gẹ́n had to impose their demands on the population on behalf of the French colonial administration in person or through messengers, and as a consequence, both became targets of growing resentment.

A major grievance was the military recruitment drives. Even before the crisis of World War I, and soon after the appointment of the two "queens" in 1911, young men emptied Kétu and nearby villages when news of military recruitment campaigns came. Alaba Ida warned the French that continued demands for recruits would prompt flight across the border, but the French colonial administrator simply threatened her with fines. Village leaders ignored new demands for volunteers, and the French rejected, citing age or poor health, the handful of men Alaba Ida managed to press into service over the next two years. Not until the defeat of the German colony of Cameroon in 1914 did Kétu supply men to serve as porters, and even then the twenty-six provided were far fewer than Kétu's prorated share.[31] By the following year, in the midst of the war effort, the French colonial administration threatened to abduct recruits or force Kétu village representatives to appear at the colonial offices in Zagnanado. Guards transporting two village leaders back to Zagnanado were confronted by armed men from Kétu who in turn freed the village leaders and fled to Nigeria, accompanied by three entire villages. Within two weeks, Alaba Ida reported to the French that the leaders of the deserted villages were calling for her dismissal and for the return of her husband, Alákétu Onyegen, the infirm king, as head of the district.[32] Her precipitous decline as a colonial agent had begun.

In August 1915, when two to three hundred hunters gathered near Kétu under the pretense of a ceremony to honor their patron òrìṣà, the deity Ogun, Alaba Ida fled to the French colonial station in Zagnanado, declaring that her life was in imminent danger.[33] When the governor of Dahomey, Charles Noufflard, went to Kétu to investigate, Alaba Ida retracted her story. Her infirm husband, Alákétu Onyegen, and other prominent village leaders allied with the French denied the existence of a plot against her and Onyegen explained that the ceremony was simply to encourage the return of villagers who had fled to Nigeria. The governor, unconvinced, ordered dozens of rifles confiscated and destroyed, arrested forty-eight men, imposed fines and work orders, and, in a town meeting, reprimanded the population for ignoring its "debt" to the French by refusing to supply recruits. Fully revealing the limits of French support for their "queen," the French governor spoke dismissively to the community of Alaba Ida as a mere "agent" for her husband; she was not an independent leader—as he heard villagers believed—trying to "free herself of her husband's oversight."[34]

After the governor departed, both Alaba Ida and Alákétu Onyegen admitted to the local French administrator their ignorance of the reason why the hunters had gathered. Only later had Alaba Ida and Alákétu Onyegen learned that a man, who believed that the king had "lived too long," had prodded the hunters to act, promising to take Onyegen's place and remove his wife from her position of authority. Alaba Ida said she fled when the hunters demanded that the Alákétu commit suicide; she knew her own life depended on her husband's since, as the king's *ida* (senior wife), she would be expected to "disappear" upon his death and be buried with him.[35] The hunters, fearful of French reaction, had appealed to Onyegen for protection and he in turn had concocted the story of the peaceful ceremony.[36] Alaba Ida, defying her husband, now forced him to join her in admitting the truth, confirming her continuing loyalty to the French.

It was too late; Alaba Ida's loyalty no longer mattered. The French had decided that neither Alaba Ida nor Yá Șègén had made effective colonial intermediaries. By 1915, with World War I underway, the French changed leadership and shifted policy on colonial intermediaries. Local French administrators now rejected the premise of female rule, calling it "untraditional" and unacceptable for Kétu. For two years, however, no direct action was taken to remove either woman, though French authorities in Dahomey were interested in finding an "energetic" and "devoted" replacement for Onyegen after the events in 1915, showing that they still considered the king a *chef du canton*, a "chief" or "head of district."[37] The two "queens" had stayed in power for six years.

Today, people in Kétu speak less of Alaba Ida's relationship with the French colonial administration and more of her position as a royal wife. Though the wives of the Kétu king had been described as impoverished and "wretched" by Yoruba missionary Samuel Crowther some sixty years earlier, one nineteenth-century Kétu king had spoken of sharing much with his two special wives, presumably his senior (*ida*) and his favorite (*ramu*) wives.[38] Today, most in Kétu deny that wives of the king ever advised the king in any official or unofficial capacity. Those who say Alaba Ida "governed" explain that she did so in place of her husband. (The term for "govern," *jǫba*, has at its root the term *ǫba*, technically meaning "ruler" but often translated as "king.") Some in Kétu do use the term "queen," but one brusque man insisted to me that she was *not* a queen at all but an *aya ǫba* or royal wife who gave orders simply because her husband, the Alákétu, was blind.[39] An elderly woman noted that in the past, wives of the king were supposed to help govern but "they have changed everything now."[40] Some deny that Alaba Ida could ever have left the *àáfin*, the king's palace, since as a royal wife she was secluded so that men could not see her or relate to her freely.[41] A man caught looking at the wife of the Alákétu was said to be subject to corporal punishment, even death; royal wives' shaven heads and plain clothes were intended to discourage the advances of other men. Also, royal wives carried calabashes or large dried gourds in public so they could sit on them apart from others.[42] In the past, even the Alákétu themselves, like other Yoruba kings, had been shrouded in mystery and rarely seen in public.[43] Alaba Ida had disregarded this expectation of seclusion, frequently visiting the lone French officer posted to Kétu, accompanying Administrator Duboscq to visit Yá Ṣègén, and fleeing all the way to Zagnanado when she feared for her life. She may even have attempted to appropriate the hammock, shoes, and drums associated with the office of the Alákétu himself, perhaps in an effort to take on his stature by association.[44] An elderly woman insisted to me that as a small child she had seen Alaba Ida fall out of a hammock and drop her medicines at the daily market in a failed effort to adopt these symbols of the king's office.[45]

Most in Kétu who are willing to talk about Alaba Ida describe her as "severe." Some say she killed many people. In the late 1960s, some fifty years after Alaba Ida's "reign," Nigerian historian A. I. Asiwaju collected Gèlèdé songs about events of the colonial period. In Gèlèdé ceremonies, male dancers wearing elaborate sculpted masks on their heads don the shirt, skirt, and headtie of a woman, ostensibly to honor "mothers" or to placate "witches." One song Asiwaju recorded portrayed Alaba Ida's leadership as disastrous, bringing death and disease:

> Ida expelled us into the forest hideouts
> And brought smallpox epidemics on the community
> And this led to the death of several persons
> Many were kidnapped and sold into slavery all in the reign of
>   Onyegen-Asakaisha
> Life itself is rendered completely incomprehensible.[46]

More telling is people's association of Alaba Ida and Aláké̩tu Onyegen with the continued slave raiding and displacement of the nineteenth century. The threat of kidnapping, coupled with the French demands for labor, had put great pressure on a population still recovering from a destructive war and experiences of captivity.

To associate Alaba Ida with death is to portray her as a "witch," a common accusation against elderly women seen as "public mothers" with some knowledge of religious ritual and other secrets. Some today scorn Alaba Ida's origins or her femininity; she was not really from Kétu, they say, or she was barren and childless. Some even hesitate to utter her name. History is particularly harsh to Alaba Ida because of her final act as *ida* (senior wife). Upon Aláké̩tu Onyegen's death in 1918, as the senior wife, she and the *ramu* (favorite wife) were expected to be buried with him to serve him in the afterlife.[47] It is unclear whether Aláké̩tu Onyegen had named a "favorite wife," but the French colonial administration refused to permit the sacrifice of anyone and tried to send Alaba Ida to O̩bate̩do for safety. There the villagers refused to help, saying that they were unable to acknowledge Alaba Ida's existence after the Aláké̩tu's death. Alaba Ida was brought back to Kétu and installed in a building on the outskirts of town, and is said to have called out to passersby, "It is because of the French that I could not disappear." Ordered from there to Pobé, rumored as the home of her son, a former *tirailleur* (African soldier), Alaba Ida fled to a French military outpost within two months after her guards in Pobé, so she said, tried to harm her.[48] She wandered many days in the forest with nothing to eat but wild birds she had carried with her, and some said she emerged from the brush to take food from cast iron pots outside of people's homes.[49] Eating birds and roaming in the forest at night symbolize witchcraft in Yoruba culture, especially when practiced by old women. Stories of wandering and paranoia allude to senility, a state Alaba Ida is said to have exhibited late in life. She died ignominiously some twenty years later in a garbage heap, a death captured in a song a young man in Kétu sang to me.[50]

It was fear that turned the town against Alaba Ida, several people explained to me, denying that she had been rejected because she was a woman. Some said they would have accepted her as a replacement for her husband had she done "good things."[51] Still, one woman said to me of the concept of a woman Aláké̩tu: "Who ever heard of such a thing?"[52] According to Karin Barber's study of oral poetry in a Yoruba town in Nigeria, the achievements of "big men" or powerful males, even the violent and tyrannical, were celebrated in *oríkì* (praise songs), but women who achieved notable success and wealth were never so honored;

they were instead accused of "going too far."[53] An infamous example was Efunsetan Aniwura, the Ìyálóde (Mother Owns the Outside World) of the late nineteenth-century Yoruba kingdom of Ibadan, one of several Yoruba towns that vied for a supreme position in the region after the fall of the Ọyọ empire a century earlier. As Ìyálóde, Aniwura had solved disputes between women and overseen certain ritual ceremonies for the kingdom. She also was a slave trader and arms dealer, like many leading men in Ibadan, including the ruler himself. After her only daughter died while trying to give birth, Aniwura was said to have become—in a noted play on her life by Akinwumi Isola—bitter, sinister, and brutal toward her pregnant slaves. Aniwura fell out of favor with the leader of Ibadan and was assassinated.[54] Though Aniwura's *oríkì* (praise song) likened her brazen strength to that of a military leader who "owns horses she doesn't ride" and "instills fear in her equals," her story makes a play on her status as a "mother."[55] By threatening the life and fertility of her pregnant slaves, Aniwura became like a "witch" or *àjẹ́,* a woman with supernatural powers to whom people can only refer as "our mothers," *àwọn iyá wa.* While "mothers" generally were seen as elderly women who displayed wealth, influence, wisdom, character, or some combination thereof, as in the case of Alaba Ida and others such as Iyalode Efunsetan Aniwura, attaining power brought charges of witchcraft and of "going too far."

A figure comparable to Alaba Ida outside of the Yoruba-speaking and French colonial setting might be Ahebi Ugbabe of the southeastern Igbo-speaking area of Nigeria, described by historian Nwando Achebe as a woman who "became a man" and a "king." Ugbabe's rise to power and fall from grace has important similarities to and differences from the story of Alaba Ida. Ugbabe was exiled from her own town and forced to live in a foreign West African community, only returning to her homeland with British colonizers in the 1910s. Soon taking on the duties of a "warrant chief" or intermediary between the local population and the British, she displaced the council of male elders who were recognized by the people as communal leaders. In an unprecedented move, Ugbabe assumed the title of *eze* (king) for herself, though kings had never existed in her town. Playing on her position as a colonial intermediary and a "king," she settled disputes, enforced colonial policies, and cultivated an even larger image of supernatural power. She took dependents, "marrying" wives for the men in her household and claiming their children as her own descendants. Only when she attempted to create her own masked spirit—the masquerade being considered a domain solely of men—did her people reject her and the British sanction her. She stayed in power, but she was weakened; a song mocking her spoke of how in trying to bring out a mask to enter into the realm of men, she was reduced to a mere woman.[56]

Ugbabe's relationship with the British, her aura of power, and her sudden demise mirrored Alaba Ida's trajectory in some ways. Still, Ugbabe seems to have been attempting a different route to power—expressedly as a man, "husband," and "father" before her own community and before the British. Neither Alaba Ida nor Ahebi Ugbabe was rejected simply for being a woman—otherwise they would have never has gotten as far as they did. The issue for them both was how, acting as "mothers," "wives," or even "men," women could use and expand the available channels for women's power in politics, the economy, or religion.

The collective silence about Yá Ṣègén stands in contrast to the vivid stories and contemptuous songs about Alaba Ida (or even Ahebi Ugbabe). If the Alákétu and Alaba Ida had been expected to be secluded, priests like Yá Ṣègén were to move about in public, conduct rituals, and acquire followers.[57] Though Yá Ṣègén had migrated with her òrìṣà (deity) from Pobé to Ọbatẹdo, she was limited in her movement, especially as she aged, because traveling in a hammock was a taboo named by her òrìṣà. Thus, as an agent of the French colonial administration, she was unable to travel extensively and perform her expected duties. That French officials visited her instead may have enhanced her prestige.[58] And yet Yá Ṣègén has not survived well as an individual in the oral historical record. Even in her hometown, where she acted as the primary colonial official, she is referred to as an iyálorìṣà (mother-in-deity). Yá Ṣègén, the "queen," is merged with others who succeeded her and also bore the title "Yá Ṣègén." Thus, in the oral historical record, her service to the French colonial regime is not mentioned or perhaps not even remembered.[59]

The images of Alaba Ida and Yá Ṣègén—as "queen," "mother-in-deity," or "witch"—did evoke the power of their womanhood, and yet both were severely constrained by their status as colonial intermediaries. People resented the orders Alaba Ida was compelled to give on behalf of the French and disappointed by her repeated attempts to fulfill the demands the French required of her.[60] The first call for her dismissal came from hunters and villagers who had fled from military recruitment into Nigeria. In Kétu and elsewhere, colonial intermediaries who were not from ruling families, like Abimbọla Otupepe and Alaba Ida, and later in the 1930s like Bankole Okanleke, became objects of popular hostility, linked closely with their colonial contacts.[61] In contrast, Alákétu Onyegen and the kings who succeeded him managed to distance themselves from the colonial administration while still retaining their local title and the respect of the people.

Also, both Alaba Ida and Yá Ṣẹ̀gẹ́n were defined by their relationship to male figures, Alaba Ida to her husband the Alákétu, Yá Ṣẹ̀gẹ́n to her òrìṣà (deity), Ondo. Although both tried to establish an independent base of power by retaining messengers, giving commands, advising, and administering punishments, neither was able to build an autonomous base of wealth or support. One man maintained that the king's ministers and chiefs had become Alaba Ida's, but in fact as a royal wife, she had no personal wealth. Though royal wives sometimes conducted trade at the market, they could not set up the personal networks other established women traders could. Alaba Ida, without brothers, land, or livestock, had to depend wholly on government subsidies and gifts. Yá Ṣẹ̀gẹ́n, with access to some income and resources through a small piece of land cultivated by her followers, had more opportunity to generate wealth, but priests redistribute their wealth for ceremonies and dependents. Moreover, Yá Ṣẹ̀gẹ́n's òrìṣà probably was not popular throughout Kétu, linked as it was to the history and identity of the town of Pobé and its immigrant community in Ọbatẹdo.[62]

One woman minister insisted to me, in defining her own political office in Kétu, that Alaba Ida was not charged with official duties but simply served as the wife of the king.[63] Because neither Alaba Ida nor Yá Ṣẹ̀gẹ́n was an official titled minister of the kingdom, holding recognized authority over the general population, the power delegated by the French colonial administration was easily called into question by the local population. Of the two, Alaba Ida was more vulnerable to criticism because her influence derived almost solely from her association with the king and the French colonial administration, while Yá Ṣẹ̀gẹ́n commanded authority primarily from her religious role. Yá Ṣẹ̀gẹ́n's religious office drew upon the concept of *ìyá* as a "public mother," while the designation of *ida,* senior wife, emphasized Alaba Ida's ambivalent position in the palace and the community. In the end, Alaba Ida may have enjoyed important standing among the king's wives, but to Kétu residents she appeared as the epitome of subordination, a wife of the king, who was that much easier to renounce in the historical record.

Though a nineteenth-century Kétu king had spoken of his most important royal wives as close confidants, their relationship would have been hidden from public view. At best, any political influence exercised privately by royal wives was an "open" secret, perhaps known, but not acknowledged. French officials could not know all the nuances of gender and power in Kétu, and they probably did not care if they undermined Alaba Ida's influence in the palace or Yá Ṣẹ̀gẹ́n's role in religion. They had selected women as "queens" not as a tribute to their gender but as an instrument of exploitation by colonial authorities.

That both women in turn may have consciously tried to expand their position in society by working for the French tested gender norms but did not overturn local practices. What made life under Alaba Ida and Yá Ṣègén "completely incomprehensible" in the eyes of the people was not simply their challenge to gender relationships but how and in what context they defied idealized hierarchies and customs. The insult to the Kétu community was not the image of a woman giving orders but that of a royal wife publicly uttering commands.

Also, with the "reign" of Alaba Ida and Yá Ṣègén came a critical historical moment of rebuilding, when French colonial demands conjured up recent experiences of war, enslavement, and displacement. The French, recognizing that West African practices allowed power to certain women based on age and gender, had simply tried to appoint women who could serve French interests best. As the French grew more anxious about women and gender at home in France, they concluded that the image of powerful African women did not safeguard French imperial authority, but undermined it.

Emasculated Hierarchies as Threat to Empire and Republic

As elderly African women, the "queens" of Kétu deviated from concepts cultivated in France of womanhood, domesticity, and motherhood, steeped as they were in rhetoric about rights and based in policies on women's reproduction. During the Third Republic—spanning the seven decades from 1870 to 1940, much of the period of France's overseas colonial empire in Africa—kings, emperors, and parliaments had ruled France, and even during the first decade of the Third Republic, it was uncertain that democracy would prevail. By the turn of the twentieth century, France's new African empire exposed how the French Republic, both at home and in its empire, was unable to reconcile racial and gender difference with its own image as an exclusively white- and male-dominated nation. "Universal suffrage" and "brotherhood" were not intended to embrace women even in France; women did not get the vote in France until 1944 during the provisional government following the liberation of Paris and the end of World War II. Politicians and activists had sought to define womanhood and regulate motherhood according to the concept of the duty of women as mothers and procreators of the strength of the nation, dating back to the eighteenth century's revolutionary ideal of the "virtuous" mother of the republic who bore citizens for the state. Although the nineteenth century's "cult of domesticity" provided status to middle-class French women searching for a role in society, and women gained limited rights in education, legal status, and control over wages, many fundamental rights—especially women's right to control their own bodies—were suppressed in the interest of the state to stimulate population rates and thus improve the general strength of the nation.[64]

To historian Joan Scott, the history of women and Western feminism within republican democracy is a "paradox," with republican democracy centered on the rights of the individual but the individual assumed to be, and idealized as, a man. French feminists who claimed political rights as individuals had to acknowledge that male-dominated society viewed them as women and hence as inferior. Scott writes that French feminists "refused to be women in the terms their society dictated, and at the same time spoke in the name of those women," exposing the limits of republican concepts of the individual and rights while ensnaring feminism in the same trap.[65]

Further, from the inception of republican democracy, the individual has been not only male but white or European, and the French "civilizing mission" for the most part denied freedom and equality to colonized people largely on the basis of race.[66] In his book *French Encounter with Africans: White Response to Blacks, 1530–1880,* William Cohen argues that French ideas about race were remarkably static between the sixteenth and nineteenth centuries, with negative imagery toward blackness and African culture remaining constant, though the specific explanations for African inferiority changed over the centuries. Thus, writers from the sixteenth to eighteenth centuries blamed the lack of Christianity or the environment for what they saw as African inferiority; by the nineteenth century science and biology were used to demean Africans and people of African descent and to help justify the enslavement of Africans in the Americas.[67] Although the French Revolution of 1789 marked a pivotal moment in the formation of the French republic and the idealization of individual rights, the slaves of the French colony of Saint Domingue rose up in rebellion in 1791, claiming the same ideals of liberty and equality. The independent state of Haiti, established in 1804 with a population largely descended from African slaves, also exposed the contradictions between French revolutionary ideals and French imperialism and racism.

By the time Alaba Ida and Yá Ṣẹ̀gẹ́n had been chosen as French colonial agents, French ideals about imperialism, gender difference, and racial hierarchy had been adapted to the colonial situation in Africa, where fewer European settlers and no official system of slavery existed. Governor General William Ponty, head of the French West African federation from 1908 to 1915, made important political decisions that allowed Alaba Ida and Yá Ṣẹ̀gẹ́n to rise to prominence. In 1909, he distributed an important tract on the *"politique des races,"* or "racial policy," a directive promoting more "direct contact" between the French colonial administrator and African communities, thus protecting African populations from exploitation by local African leaders.[68] Still, Ponty's "racial policy" assumed the continued use of African agents, with French administrators encouraged to select African intermediaries who had no birthright to positions of authority. Instead, some literacy in French or demonstrated loyalty to the French colonial regime was prized. Alaba Ida, Yá Ṣẹ̀gén, and their contemporary, Abimbọla Otupepe, all allies of the French, fit the definition of "new men" because none of them descended from royal families and because they supported the French colonial administration and its policies. But before long these "new men" were displaced by the return of "old elites."[69]

Ponty had stressed another central element of France's "civilizing mission," that Africans be permitted to progress according to their own practices and beliefs.[70] Ponty's concern with the difference between West Africans and the French was reflected in his modification of the court system, education, and administration in the colonies, each reform revealing his prejudice. Thus, of his education policy Ponty noted, "it has not occurred to me to give anything other than simple, primary instruction. It is necessary to take into account the stage our populations are in their development."[71] When Ponty admonished French courts involved in disputes between Africans for interference with "the guarantee of justice based on their customs," his "racial policy" assumed that African communities were made up of small, isolated units, not of states, kingdoms, or empires.[72] That women, such as Alaba Ida and Yá Ṣẹ̀gén, could occupy a position as "new men" was never simply an observation that "women really mattered" in Kétu but implied the West African town's backwardness in comparison to the French republic.

Until the bitter end, however, Ponty had confidence in the eventual triumph of the "civilizing mission," despite hostility to French policies within its African colonies. In the final months before his death in 1915 came an uprising in 1913 and 1914 in the Ohori region, to the south of Kétu, provoked, so Ponty wrote to the minister of colonies, by "superstitious fear of the European rather than irrational hatred." His advice was to "leave the population with the impression of our force in order to demonstrate that firmness does not exclude good will. . . . patient penetration and a policy that is both energetic and humane have become classic in West Africa."[73]

After World War I, French confidence in the "civilizing mission" was never quite the same; the new colonial leadership doubted the value of rule by "new men." While Ponty's immediate successors as governor general confronted harsh realities of war at home and widespread revolt in West Africa, his policies were pushed aside, particularly his approach to local African agents. The first of the two successors, François Clozel, author of two books on Côte d'Ivoire and an amateur ethnographer, was convinced that African kings and elites made better colonial intermediaries than "new men," who would not have been "traditional" authority figures.[74] In his previous assignment in Upper Senegal-Niger (modern Mali), Clozel had developed a favorable relationship with France's Muslim allies, and he gave a speech to the Colonial Government Council praising their loyalty and quoting a qur'anic verse he had learned from a Senegalese Muslim leader.[75] Yet his sympathy for African culture did not keep him from taking a hard line against rebellions spreading across Dahomey; he explained "sporadic troubles" there as caused by the most "pagan, ignorant, and estranged" populations in the colonies.[76]

By July 1917, with the disastrous socioeconomic effects of the war felt deeply in France and its colonies, the new governor of Dahomey, Gaston-Léon Fourn, sent a letter of alarm to the new governor general, Van Vollenhoven, warning of "the intentional destruction of indigenous hierarchies." "We need hierarchies," he wrote, "but respected, honest ones controlled by our Administrators."[77] About a month later, Van Vollenhoven issued a circular on "indigenous chiefs," effectively repealing Ponty's "racial policy" and opening the way for the return of male elites and kings to positions of power. Echoing Dahomey governor Fourn's appeal for hierarchies, he wrote that African communities needed indigenous chiefs as a child needed parents, because of their "infantile" status. Indigenous local leaders were "indispensable" as intermediaries to the French colonial administration. However, a local leader was not a "legendary black king," but an "instrument" of the French administrator.[78] Van Vollenhoven's policy continued to disparage leaders like the Alákétu, who identified themselves and were viewed by others as kings. The shift in colonial policy was about underlying French notions of racial difference and about the practical difficulty of controlling populations in an area nine times the size of France itself.

Following Van Vollenhoven's policy paper, the governor of Dahomey explained Alaba Ida's dismissal in his next report. Alaba Ida had been able to "impose her authority over the population thanks to her energy, intelligence, and action," but her severe attitude and "venality" had caused hostility in the town. According to local custom, the king himself, her husband, could not be replaced before his death, so the governor had installed the top minister to serve as the *chef supérieur du canton* (superior district head).[79] (Yá Ṣ̀ègén, the second "queen," was not mentioned explicitly in the report and was probably replaced around the same time as Alaba Ida.)

The dismissals of the two women did not mark a simple retreat back to a French colonial policy that emphasized the role of local elites and royals, since concern about women and gender had taken on new significance during the war and was affecting French colonial policymaking in Africa. Women were at the center of larger political debates in France itself, debates about the family—especially mothers, but also about fathers and "endangered" children—debates that dated to the beginning of the Third Republic. Concern about depopulation in France had led to legislation in Paris to encourage and regulate motherhood by laws on, for example, wet nurses, the length of the workday, and maternity leaves. The war had affected women's identities—as mothers of recruits, as victims of rape by German soldiers, and as workers—encouraging a reconsideration of the recognition and protection of women, but particularly of mothers.[80] Mary Louise Roberts writes that the emergence of the "modern woman" and the "single woman" represented the traumatic change wrought by the war, but that the "mother" remained an enduring and comforting icon.[81] Underlying concerns with the health of infants, the education of school-age children, and protection against child labor were assumptions about the centrality of paternal power and fatherhood to the rebuilding of France.[82]

French colonials grafted rhetoric and anxieties about family and morality in France onto their African policy while at the same time preserving the sense of distance and difference in race and culture. In 1917, Governor General Van Vollenhoven wrote to the minister of colonies in Paris:

> *Social discipline and the family were respected everywhere,* moreover there were ruthless sanctions against those who disobeyed. We created civil justice but *native society was frightened by the rights accorded to individuals, especially rights given to women and youths, boldly defying marital and paternal authority,* traditional bases of the African family. We got rid of the large, feared and respected African forces but in doing so we deprived people of a certain degree of tyranny that provided a secure foundation. . . . *the rigorous hierarchy of the past has been replaced with a benevolent but emasculated one.*[83] (Emphasis added)

Van Vollenhoven saw the same elements of the family, rights, and paternalism in West Africa that were at issue in France, but he emphasized a different remedy. The "well-intentioned" French imperial regime had, unwittingly, weakened the family and paternal power in the colonies. Male dominance in the African household had been threatened, with women and children exercising too many rights—a power that was presumed unnatural in the traditional hierarchical and patriarchal family in Africa. Traditional authority was oppressive, perhaps, but it was an authority that discouraged dissent and disorder. African women, like French women, needed to be put "in their place," in France with the "protection" of motherhood, and in West Africa with the reinstitution of "a certain degree of tyranny."[84]

Governors General Clozel and Van Vollenhoven and Governor Fourn of Dahomey were, in effect, seeking the return of a "masculine" hierarchy headed by a male elite figure, ideally a "father" or, more precisely, a patriarch. Once the French had adopted language that bolstered masculinity, patriarchy, and the old hierarchies of their African colonies, neither Alaba Ida nor Yá Ṣègén could continue as colonial intermediaries. In France and in its colonies, politicians hoped fathers and husbands and, especially after World War I, the image of women as mothers—child-bearing mothers rather than the elderly "mothers" of leadership represented by Alaba Ida and Yá Ṣègén—would help restore order and stem the threatening tide of precipitous social change.

In response to perceived social upheaval at home and in its French empire, the French government turned to more "rational" and technical forms of government that shifted the government to the right in the late 1930s and early 1940s and culminated in the fascist Vichy regime under the German occupation of World War II. By the 1920s, French colonial policy too, under the framework of *mise en valeur* or "rational development," encouraged forced labor and emphasized "chiefly authority" to improve the "material and moral situation" of the colonies. Governor Fourn's 1925 annual report predicted the "disappearance of local customs" and "profoundly modified social practices," in contrast with earlier reports' language about respecting African culture.[85] Local customs and practices did not disappear. In response to changing gender ideals in France and it the colonies, a shift in French rhetoric was the significant change.

The reasons the French appointed Alaba Ida and Yá Ṣègén as intermediaries in the first place remain unclear. Both women seem to have given the impression that they could give orders and gain compliance from women and men throughout the community. Were the French inadvertently, and unwittingly, placing themselves as "father figures," with "mother figures" beside them, or were they displaying their own power by placing women in their service as so many kings and leading men had done before them? The French appeared to understand neither the symbolism in West Africa of having "mothers" work on their behalf nor the controversial sight of a royal wife commanding men. As the situation in Kétu deteriorated, the French fell back on what they continued to believe about women, both French and West African: that they were inferior and subordinate to men. If French administrators wanted to control women as mothers and wives, people in Kétu wanted royal wives to act properly and kings and elders to be able to rule. Too easily the desire for order, in both places, translated into calls for more control over women.

5

"Without family . . . there is no true colonization"

Perspectives on Marriage

In 1902, Monseigneur Alexandre Le Roy, an archbishop in the French Catholic order of the Holy Ghost Fathers Congregation, published a provocative essay about the importance of stable African families to French imperial policies: "without morality, there is no family; without family, there is no society; and without a productive society that works, consumes, and produces, there is no true colonization, the peaceful and fecund colonization that we would want."[1] Le Roy was probably the key figure behind a 1910 survey on marriage and the family in Africa distributed by the French Antislavery Society (of which Le Roy was a prominent member) in France's West and Central African colonies. Authors of the survey intended to reveal the immorality and social disorder caused by French colonialism and also to boost support for civil marriages between African women and men as a remedy to perceived depopulation. But two decades passed before the results of the survey were published in 1930, and by that time the French colonial administration was promoting its own strategies to quell disorder and increase productivity through legal reforms that also focused on marriage.

The French Antislavery Society survey on African marriage and families tapped into dual aspects of French colonial legal reform: the court system and research on local African customs. From very early on, as the French sought to define the parameters of courts in its West African colonies, repeated efforts to obtain ethnographic information on marriage, kinship, and property as the basis for African "civil law" courts proved inadequate. French colonial administrators at various levels were frustrated by their inability to control, influence, and understand African cultural practices that shaped legal cases, especially those on women, marriage, and families.

Le Roy's alarmist language at the turn of the century had been prescient in its focus on the "disorganization" of families, a term increasingly used to describe French and African societies after World War I. By the interwar period, related concerns arose about birth rates and economic productivity, especially the physical and social health of African families, which resembled similar debates in France. Ineffectual laws in France were encouraging French women to serve the state by having babies. In Yoruba culture, on the other hand, the idealized image of the subordinate wife had long been complicated by the role of elder women and by the changing nature of marriage itself. Yoruba marriages were open to debate and variation in ways that dismayed French officials devising and enforcing laws for the colonies.

"Mitigated by Matriarchy": Yoruba Marriage and Families

The goals and role of the French Antislavery Society itself differed significantly from earlier abolitionist movements, partly because its first chapter was not founded until 1888, after the transatlantic slave trade and slavery in the Americas had been abolished. Slavery and slave trading persisted in Africa and the Middle East as European nations began to establish new overseas empires. The eighteenth-century abolitionist movement had been linked to Protestantism; the new antislavery societies were linked to the Catholic Church. The French Antislavery Society maintained close ties to the Catholic missions and to the French colonial administration in France's new West African colonies. Governor General Ponty distributed the society's survey in 1910 via the *Journal Officiel de l'Afrique occidentale française* (Official Journal of French West Africa).[2]

Nonetheless, full emancipation of all former slaves in West Africa had no support in the French Antislavery Society. A speaker at an Antislavery Congress in 1901 frankly declared, "I am not partisan to the mass liberation of slaves. . . . That would ruin the country and cast most slaves into the ultimate misery."[3] Catholic missionaries in West Africa focused their attention instead on trying to form families among the young Africans who came to live at their mission in search of refuge or opportunity. French missionaries, writing in the journal of the French Antislavery Society, told of their efforts to attract women to the mission, framing the antislavery movement in a context of morality, women, and marriage. Le Roy, in particular, who described the plight of the African woman who "belong[s] to her husband who paid for her," proposed the untenable idea of civil marriages to resolve the "disorganization" of the African family.[4] Given the small communities of converts in some French African colonies and French colonial rhetoric that vowed to help Africans "progress" only at their own pace, widespread African civil marriages may have seemed as "untenable" as the idea of the mass emancipation of slaves within Africa.

The story of Antoinette, a Kétu woman, published in the journal of the French Antislavery Society, bridged the antislavery mission with the Catholic mission's purpose of gaining converts and forming Christian families. Antoinette had been captured during the war with Dahomey in 1886 and incorporated into the royal household. She was among the enslaved children and women whom Dahomey's king Behanzin took with him in exile into Martinique in 1892. "Overwhelmed by homesickness," Antoinette was brought back to the new French colony of Dahomey after interventions by a priest; she came to live at the Catholic mission in Porto-Novo, marrying a formerly enslaved, converted Kétu man there. Returning to Kétu, she helped convert her mother and siblings and they all came to live at the *village de liberté* (freedom village), the Catholic mission set up at Zagnanado for former slaves. Antoinette supported herself as a laundress and through small-scale commerce that allowed her to "live easily." She took in two young girls who had been seized from a slave trader and who were to be married to "Rough Tom" and "Peaceful Jacques," Christian men in the compound.[5] Thus Antoinette, once a slave, then a Christian, had expanded the Christian community by converting her family and by becoming a "mother" to young women who would be wives of converted men.

The inspiring news of Antoinette's redemption through work, religion, and family contrasted with the image of the African family projected by the Antislavery Society's survey. The seventy-three questions of the survey assumed the limitless power and rule of an autocratic male head of household. Thus question twelve asked, "Doesn't the head of household abuse his authority in order to divert the family wealth to himself and in order to acquire women whom he must later send off into prostitution?" Several of the questions focused on the age and consent of the bride, taking exploitation of wives and depravity of African marriage practices as a matter of course. Question twenty inquired, "Does the wife's family regularly seize the woman on certain occasions under various pretexts, refusing to return her to her husband unless he pays them? Is this abuse authorized by local custom?" The survey invited the respondent to muse on useful reforms to "prevent the exploitation of the husband, wife, and child and how to bring more dignity, morality, and freedom to families."[6]

Catholic missionaries themselves wrote many of the responses to the questionnaires, with the editors of the volume that appeared two decades later condensing information or combining it with other reports, including some material prepared by colonial administrators.[7] Most likely it was Father J. Vallée, a priest stationed in Kétu between 1907 and 1914, who provided the commentary on Kétu. Yet despite the leading questions, the descriptions of marriage practices in Kétu and neighboring regions do provide insight into the changing situation of young wives and elder women at the turn of the century, and they foreshadow shifts in French colonial policy in the 1930s.

Of the role of patriarchy or control by men in the household, the survey's description of Kétu acknowledged that "the most senior woman also plays an important role in relation to all the women and girls [in the family], in terms of women's labor. The senior male has nothing to do with this issue. Thus it generally is a patriarchal family organization mitigated by matriarchy.... The head male rules autocratically.... But before ordering anything from the women, when the need arises, he must consult first with the senior woman."[8] Thus, patriarchal authority was one of several, sometimes overlapping, hierarchical family relationships. If a man had more than one wife, the first wife exerted power over those who came after. Widows became the wives of younger brothers or nephews of the deceased husband. Motherhood and child care hinged on these multiple family relationships; young daughters were entrusted to a matron, ordinarily a senior woman in the paternal family, who became her "mother," responsible for arranging her marriage. A grandfather or an uncle frequently mentored young male relatives who assisted them in their work. Age, rank, and gender guided all relationships within the household.

Still, patriarchal control was not wholly unchecked; in Kétu, for example, husbands could not pawn their wives or give them away as gifts, though children, including young girls, could be given as pawns to pay back debts.[9] According to the French author of the report on Kétu, a woman could obtain a divorce without difficulty: "No woman getting married has the idea that it will last a lifetime." Indeed, two years earlier, Father Vallée had reported that within Kétu's fledgling Christian community, one young wife, encouraged by her mother, who had wanted her to marry a different man, left her husband.[10] Women left their husbands, so it was said, under various pretexts and returned to their parents' home, leaving children with the husband. Of one woman's visit to the homes of her several ex-husbands, the French writer declared acerbically, "Thus, polyandry combines with polygamy," a suggestion that women could have several husbands in one lifetime, not unlike men who married multiple women. The mother/ex-wife maintained an interest in the children she left behind, particularly her sons, and used her own savings to help pay their bridewealth, a series of gifts, money, and labor paid by the groom and his family. Negatively portrayed by the same writer as "buying [her son] a wife," the mother was actually investing in future labor and wealth for herself as the paternal grandmother, since she would have access to her son's children. Women like these elderly "divorcées" gave outside observers the impression that many wielded "matriarchal" influence and challenged the overall male dominance in the household.[11]

By the early twentieth century, local marriage practices were changing in Kétu. Young couples were both affirming and undermining men's established control over women. Although parents still arranged marriages and received gifts or bridewealth on behalf of their daughters— portrayed as "merchandise" by many European observers—the society's survey reported that some young women refused the man chosen for them and convinced family members to accept bridewealth from preferred suitors instead. Some couples were running off together, challenging male privilege and elder authority even more audaciously.[12]

The tension between patriarchy and so-called polyandry, that is, women with multiple husbands, had less to do with an actual "matriarchate," a group of ruling women, than with a drawn-out marriage process involving entire extended families. On engagement and the marriage process, so the report said, the "genesis" of marriage in Kétu began with the birth of a child, already a prospective bride or groom, and with initial negotiations for marriage, involving several consultations with a diviner, between two families. Hence the formal engagement ideally occurred when the future bride was a young girl who could hardly refuse her parents. Over the years between childhood and the appropriate age for the marriage itself, the fiancé's family provided gifts of local food and drink, labor, and resources. If the woman broke the engagement, the fiancé was entitled to the return of the money he and his parents had spent. Again, local practices were now shifting, with greater tolerance of broken engagements, though sometimes with demands for interest on the money spent during the engagement process. The actual marriage ceremony itself still established the young woman's incorporation into her new household; the new wife promptly demonstrated her subordinate status by ritually sweeping the courtyard and cooking food for her in-laws.[13]

The writer or writers of the questionnaire responses reflected his or their own affiliation with the Catholic Church, describing the plight of "our missions" and critiquing the French colonial administration for discouraging what Catholic missionaries would have defined as "social and familial reform." In attempting to change local practices, Catholic missionaries in Kétu and neighboring towns found themselves fulfilling roles of the extended family in the marriage process, finding prospective brides, paying bridewealth, and trying to reconcile estranged couples.[14] Christians in Kétu were wary of performing Christian marriage ceremonies out of fear of reprisals from others or from local deities. Thus, the civil Christian-based marriages proposed by the French Antislavery Society to remedy what French observers saw as moral decline would not have enhanced the situation for Kétu's small Christian community.[15]

Court cases like the 1915 custody battle between a Muslim Kétu man named Souleymane Adekambi and his Gbe wife Adogbonu exposed this gap between French colonial (if not also missionaries') understanding of African practices and their desire to control these relationships through legal reform.[16] The couple—notably of different ethnic and religious backgrounds—had married in the wife's hometown near Zagnanado after her father consented to the marriage because she would continue to live with him and raise her three children. When, after her father died, Adogbonu refused to move in with her husband Adekambi, he cut off financial support for their children and demanded custody of their daughter, who had begun schooling at a Catholic mission. To the dismay of the Catholic mission and to the confusion of the French colonial administration, Adekambi successfully argued for custody before a colonially appointed court of elder local men.

The French administrator, Louis Duboscq, not understanding how a married woman could live apart from her husband, assumed mistakenly that the couple was divorced.[17] Elders appointed as advisors for the local court informed Duboscq that married couples in fact did not always live together. One elder explained, "Frequently, married women live with their children outside of the conjugal home, in their father's house if he is living or at the mother's house." Husbands were to provide financial support to wives who lived separately.[18] The governor of Dahomey had suggested that marriage and child custody practices from other regions of the colony might apply to the case, suggesting that the couple had entered into *ha dido,* or "free union," as practiced only by princesses in the former Dahomey kingdom; he proposed the use of child custody practices prevalent in Savé, a Yoruba kingdom north of Kétu. But the governor's ideas of "free unions" and custody rights were misguided because Adogbonu's father had consented to her marriage; theirs was not a "free union." If it had been, the mother would have retained custody of her children.[19]

When Duboscq questioned Adekambi, he insisted that spouses in Kétu could live apart and that women could end marriages, especially if a husband did not provide material support for his wife and children. According to Nago (Yoruba) practices, men nevertheless retained custody over their children after a marital relationship ended.[20] Like the elders in his wife's hometown, Adekambi was defining marriage broadly, citing comparisons with other Yoruba towns in British-controlled Nigeria and considering local practices negotiable and full of possibilities. French authorities, taking a much more narrow view, suspected that "immoral speculation" was at the heart of the matter; they assumed that the parents sought custody of the daughter to profit from gifts and labor from a future fiancé. But the daughter could have entered into a marriage in which elaborate gifts were not exchanged, as her parents themselves seemed to have done. A Catholic priest accused the colonial administration of being "pro-Muslim" in allowing Adekambi to remove all his children from the mission school.[21] As with the documentation of many court cases in colonial Africa, the final outcome of this case was uncertain; French officials were never quite clear about the motives underlying the case or the practices shaping it.

Basing their decision on Gbe customs, which the wife shared, rather than on the husband's foreign Nago (Yoruba) practices the local elders could not be expected to know, the elders in the Adekambi case failed to honor a 1912 colonial decree that ordered African women to submit to the "customary law" of their husbands, even though the case was still decided in the husband Adekambi's favor. Not long after, in a similar dispute in which wife and husband were from different ethnic groups, the wife was forced to return to her husband's household because his cultural practices did not allow women to seek separation or divorce. French officials ignored whether the woman was acting according to the norms within her own community.[22]

A lawyer by training, Governor General Ponty would have known of a similar recent law in France that stated that women automatically adopted the nationality of their husband; the law was repealed in 1927 after more French women began to marry European men who were not French.[23] Thus, French policymakers' decision to try to monitor formally the processes of marriage and divorce in the West African colonies was not a sudden change in the 1910s or the 1930s, but part of long-standing concerns about women, marriage, and families, connecting policies in France with those of its colonies.

Nigerian scholars who published studies of Yoruba society in the same period, between the turn of the century and the 1930s, were reporting on changing marriage practices, but with interests and in styles quite different from French colonial administrators and Catholic missionaries. Reverend Samuel Johnson, A. K. Ajisafe, and N. A. Fadipe were more concerned with establishing the historical and cultural record of Yoruba society than with proposing ways to alter it by applying practices and standards of Western (Protestant) religion. They showed respect for Yoruba practices while hinting at changes underway under British colonial rule, thus portraying more broadly how the image of women as wives and mothers had evolved across Yoruba communities by the early twentieth century.

Samuel Johnson's foundational six-hundred-page tome *History of the Yorubas,* completed in 1897, was not published until 1921, twenty years after the author's death. It portrayed a grand Yoruba "nation" that originated at the town of Ile-Ifẹ and flourished in the kingdom of Ọyọ before decades of war and the onset of British colonial rule. In this comprehensive political history, only a few pages were devoted to marriage practices. Johnson discussed the role of extended families in finding spouses and the array of gifts marking the engagement process over the years before the formal marriage ceremony, the *ìgbéyàwó* (carrying of the bride), during which the new bride was escorted to her new home in her husband's family compound. On the formal day of marriage, the young bride would be directed to the "head lady" of husband's house, reminiscent of the "matriarch" in the Kétu survey. Johnson described how female members of a family chose wives for young men in the household, echoing the stories of Kétu's Catholic missionaries about the strong intervention of mothers in the marriage of sons. Johnson denied the existence of divorce except in rare cases, asserting that a divorced woman could never remarry legally. Sometimes, however, a young girl refused her parents' choice and, if recognized by her own chosen suitor's family, she might become the man's lawful wife.[24] Although other elite Yoruba Christian converts of the late nineteenth century criticized the recently arrived British, who increasingly discriminated against them, Johnson, a Protestant minister, praised the end of warfare and the spread of Christianity under the British. To him Christian conversion was a solution to certain social ills. Still, proud of Yoruba culture and history, he maintained that the Yoruba were actually reclaiming a Christian faith lost in the distant past.[25]

A. K. Ajisafe's *Law and Customs of the Yoruba,* published in 1924, originated with research in 1906 among the Egba Yoruba around Abẹokuta, Nigeria. Its spare text of just more than eighty pages reads like a legal code but with insightful descriptive passages. Overall, it has little analysis of the impact of British colonialism and Christianity. Ajisafe explained how, out of respect, the fiancée hid her face before her husband's family or friends until she was acknowledged or had given birth to their first child.[26] Pampered with cooked meals in the first days after the wedding ceremony by the senior woman of the compound, a younger wife would thereafter assume a larger share of the most onerous domestic chores.[27] Over time, she could gain access to resources or build her own wealth through inheritance from paternal or maternal relatives; even a husband could not seize land his wife inherited. Though Ajisafe denied divorce as a traditional legal practice among the Yoruba, he took care to explain the procedure that followed after a woman left her fiancé or husband for another man.[28] Some elder women could play intermediary roles in the marriage process as the *alárenà* (one who opens the way), receiving presents for their advice and their intervention on behalf of the future groom. Some might rise to importance as the Ìyálé (Mother of the House), opposite the male head of household, or might become leader of a club (*ẹgbẹ́*).[29] Johnson himself had written of several titled royal women, specifically in the Ọyọ kingdom through the nineteenth century, but Asijafe recognized only one powerful, titled woman in Yoruba society, the Ìyálóde (Mother Owns the Outside World), leader of all the town's women.[30] Still, in all, Ajisafe captured the vulnerable position of the young wife, whom he classified as "movable property" along with furniture, cattle, and slaves, and contrasted it to the more secure position of senior women.[31]

N. A. Fadipe's thousand-page dissertation was completed in 1939 and edited and published in 1970, long after his premature death in 1944, in an abbreviated form as *The Sociology of the Yoruba.* Fadipe revisited Johnson's broad and comprehensive study. A student of sociology at Columbia University and the University of London, he had conducted several fieldwork trips to Nigeria between 1932 and 1935. He considered both Islam and Christianity more fundamental than the fact of imposition of British colonial rule to the changes in Yoruba society. If Le Roy and others warned of "disintegration" in African communities, Fadipe saw Yoruba society as "integrated" and as a "compromise" between cultures.[32] In the 1930s, sociologists studied "complex" industrialized societies; only non-Western sites, deemed more simplistic, were considered the proper domain of anthropology. Fadipe, in presenting Yoruba society as "complex" and as a product of "diffusion" or cultural exchange rather than as a "primitive" society devastated by contact with the outside world, made a deeply theoretical and political point.

Fadipe considered shifts in marriage practices at the center of overall social change, the mutual consent of the woman and the man and increased divorce rates being especially important. Like Johnson and Ajisafe, he described the marriage process in terms of engagement, payment of bridewealth, and the "carrying of the bride," but he also explicitly addressed the mundane and emotional aspects of marriage over a lifetime. When a young woman left her own family to assume a low status as a wife in another household of not only her husband but also probably of his parents, brothers, aunts and uncles, and their wives and children, almost every other woman there (including the wives of brothers and uncles) was senior to her.[33] She could form alliances with other "wives of the compound," who arranged themselves according to age and status, and also would rank higher than any woman who married into the household after she did. In her latter years an elder woman, by then the actual and figurative "mother" to many, could speak more freely and exercise some authority in the compound.[34] Indeed, both the model of the subservient wife and that of the powerful mother and elder persisted in Yoruba society.

Johnson, Ajisafe, and Fadipe all took care to discuss Muslim marriage practices as well, which were important in Kétu in the early twentieth century though ignored by Catholic priests in their correspondence with the French Antislavery Society. In the Muslim marriage ceremony, *yigi,* derived from the Hausa term for marriage, *igiyar arme* (the Hausa to the north had a large influence on Yoruba Muslim practices), Muslim fathers sometimes gave daughters in marriage as *sàráà,* a sort of almsgiving, instead of exchanging the elaborate series of gifts over a long engagement.[35] But the household organization of Muslim families would have mirrored those who practiced indigenous religion and even Christianity, despite the restriction on multiple wives. Islam was both integrated with and segregated from the rest of the Kétu community through marriage practices and broader political relationships. Kétu, with its seasonal roads and a population as small as two thousand at the turn of the century, did not share the same colonial experience as Nigerian cities like Lagos, Ibadan, and Abęokuta, which were subject to intense British colonial activity through missions, railways, and schools. That Kétu exhibited the same complexity of powerful elder women, divorce, and Muslim influence as larger Yoruba towns under British colonial rule meant that the presence of Europeans or Christianity was not the sole factor bringing about change in marriage practices in Yoruba communities.[36]

Every aspect of the marriage process in Yoruba society—the art of negotiation, the involvement of extended family, and ongoing exchange in gifts— invited change and modification. Although written accounts from both French observers and Nigerian scholars were biased and politicized, sometimes an author, perhaps unwittingly, portrayed an image quite different from the model West African family of subordinate wife and young mother in recounting elopements and divorces that challenged the power of elders, especially of senior men. Young married women did not always conform to expectations and older women sometimes exercised privilege and authority. As a result, French colonial administrators, though claiming to act on behalf of oppressed West African women, engaged in confused and short-lived efforts to reform marriage practices, undertaken precisely because West African wives and mothers deviated from French expectations of womanhood based on the image and reality of French women's lives.

Custom-Made: "Manufacturing" Blackness for France's African Empire

When Monseigneur Le Roy stated, in a 1902 speech about African society, that "the indigenous family is so disorganized that it no longer exists," he was drawing on fears about depopulation in France stoked by a growing natalist or pro-birth movement at the turn of the century.[37] Le Roy's reference to the need for a more "fecund" colonization in Africa echoed concerns over the lack of *fécondité* (fertility) in France itself. Émile Zola published a novel with that title in 1899. Celebrating family and child rearing within a large extended family, Zola's novel contrasted a woman expecting her fifth child with a woman who abhorred the idea of childbirth. Zola highlighted women's responsibility for ending the French population crisis and applauded men's virility. His story takes a remarkable twist near the end with the return of a long-lost relative who had been living in West Africa with a large family of his own. The young man speaks at length of the "father" Niger River "impregnating" the soil and of the "creation of another France." The elaborate metaphor cast the perceived fertility of Africa's very soil as a solution to France's population crisis.[38]

With a social hygiene movement also spreading in France around the same time, concerns about birth rates and public health in France was translated into policies concerned with family life in West Africa. Initial measures to contain contagious disease, to improve sanitation, and to instruct in personal hygiene, based as they were on the more urban context of France, failed in West Africa.[39] After World War I, concerns over both birth rates and public health began to converge with racial ideologies. French eugenicists, believing not only in increasing the birth rate, as natalists did, but also in improving the racial "stock" of the nation, spoke of increasing the number of births in "quality and quantity" and promoted theories on *puériculture* (child rearing).[40] In 1924, the French colonial government established the National Office of Social Hygiene, the principal goals of which, borrowing from the language of social hygienists and eugenicists in France, were "the establishment in France and in the colonies of a continuous and methodical propaganda to the public . . . necessary for the maintenance of health, the fight against social diseases, and the preservation of the race."[41] In a 1926 circular to the governors of the French West African colonies, Governor General Jules Carde wrote of "develop[ing] the native races in quality and quantity" and of "educat[ing] mothers and increasing diffusion [*pénétration*] of child-rearing skills [*puériculture*] into households."[42] In a 1929 report on the medical assistance program in Dahomey, an inspector echoed Carde's policies, summarizing the goals of French initiatives: "protection of public health," "education of the native in matters of personal hygiene," "improvement and increase of indigenous races."[43]

In 1931, a top colonial administrator, Dr. Séverin Abbatucci, head of the office of social hygiene, explicitly connected perceived low birth rates in France's African colonies to the health and social situation of African women. Abbatucci restated bluntly what Le Roy had warned decades earlier about productivity and labor. African women were to "manufacture blackness [*fabriquer du noir*] . . . in the same way that we must enforce the manufacture of whiteness in the metropole."[44] French colonial authorities sought to boost their budget for health reform in the late 1930s and outlined plans to build hundreds of medical units, birthing centers (*maternités*), and other treatment facilities.[45] While French politicians were seeking in vain to control French women's bodies, French colonial policymakers, less familiar with the circumstances of diverse populations of African women, tried to redirect African women's social experience within families and households as daughters, wives, and mothers.[46]

The same year that Dr. Abbatucci wrote about African women's duty to "manufacture blackness," Governor General Jules Brévié (later to serve under the fascist Vichy regime) distributed a circular to the governors of all French West Africa colonies announcing his plan for sweeping changes to African "customary" law, which defined legal procedures based on local African practices. "Customary" law had been an integral part of French colonial policy since the beginning of the French West Africa federation in 1895. While citing France's long-standing avowed respect for local African practices, Brévié argued that a new "complete" inventory of African customs was now necessary. "Customs and legal institutions," he wrote, "especially the organization of the family and property, are directly linked to society, beliefs, and religion." Pronouncing ignorance and preconceived notions about local practices dangerous, he encouraged colonial administrators to develop new codes from a "strictly indigenous" point of view and not from a French one, suggesting that the legal codes would not be "eternal" but that they would be "flexible enough to adapt to the diverse stages of evolution of our subjects."[47] Yet when Brévié proposed his significant changes to customary law in 1931, he simply attached as a guideline a 1901 questionnaire on family and property, ironically reflecting the same lack of imagination he cautioned against in his own circular.[48]

Since the early years of French colonial rule, administrators had expressed an interest in documenting West African customs, working within the two underlying French ideologies: "assimilation" and "association." To assimilate Africans was to bring them "civilization" and get them to conform to French cultural ideals. The principle of "association" promised to "respect" local practices and permit colonial subjects to evolve within their own cultures, often under the leadership of traditional elites. For much of the colonial period, these two approaches coexisted. Africans exposed to education and training were more likely to experience, and even to welcome, assimilationist policies, but mass populations were expected to change only as the broader society changed around them. After the upheaval of World War I, French colonial policymakers touted association even more vocally over assimilation, concerned about the rising demands of some educated elite Africans for citizenship and other rights.[49]

But to "associate" with African society—manipulating and encouraging even slow change within it—French colonial administrators had to understand local practices. Some French officials had compiled distinguished monographs based on African practices in specific regions, but many efforts to gather information and to implement reforms systematically across all of French West Africa fell short.[50] Indeed, Dahomey was the only colony to complete a law book in response to Brévié's 1931 circular. Published in 1933, the *Coutumier du Dahomey* (Customary Law Book of Dahomey) reads like a legal code with more than three hundred articles and only intermittent references to specific ethnic groups. With its sparse ethnographic detail, the book apparently did not capture what Brévié had in mind, and it was six years before customary law guides for each of France's West African colonies were available.[51]

Kétu itself was not mentioned as a specific research site in the 1933 or 1939 questionnaire, yet descriptions of the broader region of southern Dahomey, where Kétu is located, echoed what French observers had written about Kétu in response to the 1910 Antislavery Society's questionnaire.[52] In the 1933 customary law book, published in response to Brévié's 1931 circular, Yoruba communities were portrayed as politically unstable, with the *chef de famille* (family head), the most senior man of an extended family, said to have more power because Yoruba communities were "disorganized." But the family head could share his power with "old women with good advice," conjuring the image of "patriarchy mitigated by matriarchy," as expressed in the Antislavery Society survey response.[53] Among the Yoruba, it was said that the approval of the family head made a marriage "regular" and therefore that the consent of the couple was only a "formality," with the future husband consulted and the bride not, except among some elites.[54] As wives, women had no legal status, each living with her husband but maintaining a role in her own family. A Yoruba woman was said to maintain a position in her natal family, inheriting from either parent and exercising influence once she became an aged women with a "reputation for wisdom."[55]

Whatever the actual content of French sources on African customary law, within all of these publications the subordinate position of African women, specifically wives, was incidental and assumed by French policymakers. French colonial administrators themselves were unwilling to take any far-reaching action that might threaten existing social hierarchies in Africa. Governor General Brévié thought the "delicate tasks," required by a 1932 decree that compelled French officials to hear any cases involving marriage, divorce, or child custody in the customary courts, should be presided over by French authorities to demonstrate intense French interest in African family life and the need for customary law guidebooks to aid officials.[56] Enacting policies first proposed by Brévié, Marcel de Coppet, governor of French West Africa during the short-lived, leftist Front Populaire regime of 1936 to 1938, announced changes to colonial policy on indigenous marriage, establishing minimum ages of fourteen for girls and sixteen for boys, requiring the consent of the couple to marry, and defending the woman's right to seek divorce. Still, he reminded his colleagues, "What we have promised our natives, is not to brutally substitute our laws to their ancient institutions, we are also not opposed to their free development because of concern with rigid conformity to outdated customs. . . . But we must not put more at risk the current structure of the native family."[57] In much of the colonial record and legislation, African wives and young mothers are the "unfortunate victims" of "native customs" for whom the French could do little, even through legal reforms. By relegating women to discussion of marriage and the family, French authorities denied the impact of women and gender in shaping their policies and West African society in general.

In the 1930s and 1940s, two unusual French women, Denise Moran Savineau and Sister Marie-André du Sacré-Cœur, published studies on West African women, offering perspectives outside those expressed by French men with their vested interest in maintaining white European colonial power in Africa and male dominance in French African colonies. Savineau, who had worked several years in Chad before an assignment as an educational consultant to the French colonial administration in Dakar, was appointed by Governor General de Coppet to lead an inquiry into African women's roles in the family, education, and work. She traveled for seven months in 1937 and 1938, visiting the French Soudan (Mali), Niger, Dahomey, and the Côte d'Ivoire, and produced reports on each colony as well as a comprehensive general summary.[58] She examined women outside of the home, as well as on farms, in courtrooms, and in prisons, considering them as part of the cultural and social "evolution" in France's West African colonies.

Savineau's final report began by dismissing the Europeans' search for "authentic native custom." "There is no 'true' custom," she wrote, "but, witnessing shifting traditions, a collection of practices constantly in the process of becoming," with French colonization an important part of this process of change and discovery.[59] She coupled her discussion of local practices with that of reform of colonial courts, outlining general aspects of marriage and family life, followed by an overview of the prison system. Bridewealth payments, forced marriage, polygamy, and childbirth were part of the civil justice system, while the operation of prisons was part of the criminal justice system. While Savineau presented many local practices in a negative light, she was ambivalent about the power of French policy to change them. On men taking more than one wife, she wrote, "It will not be a question of fighting against polygamy, neither by force nor by persuasion. . . . But if fairly recent practices of polygamy seem to prevail over monogamy, here or there, almost everywhere, the demands of fathers for bridewealth and those of women who want to free themselves of it, will end by bringing about monogamy."[60]

Though Savineau believed that African culture, with its "vast masculine authority," would modify itself, as it always had, she thought the colonial administration played an important role in the outcome. She concluded, "All native society, evolving on its own, tends to reinforce the power of men over women and fathers over children. These dominators wait for us to help them maintain or bolster their supremacy. But we are not inclined to follow them blindly, we want to preserve individual liberty, sometimes increasing it. The oppressed know it.... They run the risk of overstatement, of provoking a kind of anarchy. We have pointed out that it is in our interest to clarify our doctrine, in order to avoid a double failure."[61] Savineau's vision was far-reaching: "These new households that we are going to form, households of leaders, but also of students, we must prepare them for a new family life and society.... We are raising individuals, pushing them toward a profession, we are not preparing them to be husbands and wives." As an educational advisor, she advocated the use of schools to advance French policies, and she perhaps identified more with educated elites and with wives of functionaries in a well-maintained home with a salon, dining room, and maids. "And why not tell them that to take good care of your husband is a way of keeping him?" she asked, suggesting that good housewives could enjoy a monogamous relationship. Meanwhile, she described the masses of African women as an "obstacle to evolution," portraying them as traditional and religious.[62] She saw most African women as victims in need of guidance, but she considered them responsible for changing their own lives.

Also in 1939, Sister Marie-André du Sacré-Cœur, born Jeanne Dorge, published her book *La Femme noire en Afrique Occidentale* (The Black Woman in West Africa). Sister Marie-André had completed law and doctoral degrees before becoming a nun in Algeria in 1927 at age twenty-eight. Her subsequent work as a nurse in mission clinics in North and then West Africa exposed her to the lives of African women and encouraged her to become an advocate for women's rights. She applied her knowledge of legal institutions to examine the role of customary law in improving women's lives. She later served in international organizations and in 1959 addressed the UN Commission on the Status of Women. She always maintained the link between her legal, medical, and advocacy backgrounds and a relationship with the French colonial administration.[63]

Sister Marie-André believed that African women were being ignored even as colonialists wrote studies and reports on African culture and society. She based *La Femme noire en Afrique Occidentale* on several ethnic groups with whom she had extensive experience in French Sudan (Mali), Guinée, Côte d'Ivoire, and Gold Coast (Ghana), and she argued that there were certain similarities in their family organizations and marriage practices. Unlike Savineau, who was interested in highlighting change, Sister Marie-André emphasized continuity, noting that these communities distant from the coast had not experienced European influence until the late nineteenth century and that the women in particular had lived much as had their "very distant ancestors."[64] A supporter of French colonialism in Africa, she praised policies on public health and education, though she admitted that masses of African women did not benefit from them. She focused on the plight of the educated elite woman subject to customary law and criticized the "respect for custom" the French applied to avoid conflict with African local practices and religious beliefs.[65] Her deep disapproval of the "fearfulness" of the colonial administrator faced with familial questions stemmed from her belief that the French colonial administration was responsible for changing existing practices. "When civil law recognizes all 'matrimonial freedoms,'" she wrote, "European domination will really be for them [women], a liberation."[66]

Sister Marie-André's confidence in the potential of colonial legal reform and education was manifest in her work with the United Nations after most African nations became independent in the 1960s. In a 1962 book, *The House Stands Firm: Family Life in Africa,* she wrote of "women of the new Africa," by whom she tended to mean educated Christian activists. Like the increasing numbers of European women participating in international organizations after the interwar period, Sister Marie-André expected women, including African women, to serve in a variety of positions outside the home and, by the 1960s, to have "new responsibilities—social, civic, and political." After independence from European rule in much of Africa in the 1960s, African women continued to fight to reform marriage practices such as minimum age, consent, and bridewealth payments, which called into question whether French and other colonialists were ever truly interested in, or indeed had the power to affect, social change and thereby "liberate" women.[67]

It is worth considering the work of Savineau and Sister Marie-André within the longer trajectory of Western feminist writing because American and European feminists have examined gender relationships in their own and in other countries through the prism of Western society, politics, and family.[68] Though feminists in the United States, Great Britain, and France, for example, have generated multiple theoretical approaches to wifehood and motherhood, all three bodies of literature have encouraged some form of "sisterhood" that ignored race, class, culture, and sexuality. In the United States, black, Latina, Asian, Native American, and poor white women had critiqued the dominant middle-class, white, heterosexual narrative in the literature, especially by the twentieth century.[69] Nineteenth- and twentieth-century British feminists tended to focus on class, but their work did not extend to the experiences of African, West Indian, and Asian women living in the British colonial empire and in Great Britain itself.[70] The French feminist movement, contrary to both the North American and British movements, actively evoked the image of motherhood and sexual difference between women and men in the struggle for rights, beginning in the early twentieth century and continuing in the postwar welfare state, focused as it was on social programs. When French feminists addressed the situation of Arab, African, Asian, and West Indian women in the French empire, they too were likely to evoke solidarity that glossed over racism and power, engaging in what several authors have termed "imperial feminism" or "feminist imperialism."[71] Even with their attention to African culture and their sharp critiques of French colonial policy, Savineau and Sister Marie-André made assumptions about African society based on their Western experiences. Much like the French colonialists who hoped to manipulate cultural change in Africa to suit their own vision of empire, both women hoped that certain colonial policies would, one day, bring their vision of modern womanhood to Africa.

Legal reforms on marriage, health, and education never had the heart or the francs behind them to work. French colonialists did not want to spur dramatic change; rather, they were interested in African marriage practices and family life in order to monitor and control them through courts and customary law. Already by the 1910s, and still in the 1930s, various marriage practices in Kétu did not conform to French assumptions; some wives lived apart from husbands and a number of women gained influence in their households with old age. As Savineau had reported, African women and men themselves modified their customs with or without French intervention. This social change has been recorded and remembered differently by those with African and those with European perspectives.

When Marriage Became "Spoiled" in Kétu

The stories people told me about marriage practices in Kétu in the past corroborated information in written sources, while adding a new layer of emotional complexity. Elderly Kétu residents today are ambivalent about the past, disparaging it as a time of ignorance or *ojú dúdú* (eyes closed black), yet nostalgic for the way children used to "obey their parents." Marriage has become "spoiled" since the coming of "civilization" or *ọlàjú* (the opening of the eyes), with "civilization" generally dated from the final decades of colonial rule in the

1940s and 1950s, not to the beginning of French administration at the turn of the twentieth century. As in the written accounts of marriage in the early twentieth century, contradictions are embedded in people's stories. "In the time of my older sister," one Catholic woman explained to me, "the family of the boy would go to the family of the girl and ask for her in marriage. It is not like today where the boy goes and sits in the girl's house, chats with her, and she does whatever she wants with him."[72]

Many elderly people distinguish between the way their older siblings or parents married and the way they met their own spouses. Before the 1930s, a recurrent image was of an elder male approaching a neighbor to say, "I would like someone to draw water for my child," a reference to a wife (especially a junior wife), charged with hauling water and with other domestic duties. In contrast, those who married in the 1940s and 1950s talked of meeting their spouses at the night market and courting without any involvement of family members. They spoke to me of *owó ìfẹ́* (love money) or *owó orí* (head money) to celebrate their engagements. Changes in the form of "love money" occurred during the pivotal period when the French were trying to devise their customary law books. In the 1930s, "love money" increased substantially, from about 100 to 1,000 francs, some claim, with a new type of "secret" gift, called *ètepélóòru* (tiptoe in the night gift). Secret gift giving may always have been part of the marriage negotiation process, but often the "tiptoe in the night gift" was imported alcoholic beverages, which people ordinarily shared and consumed publicly. The presence of imported drinks indicated socioeconomic change; since Kétu did not have easy access to overseas imports, liquor was either carried over the Nigerian border illegally or obtained from the coast via Abomey.[73]

By the late 1930s and 1940s, an increase in the Kétu population brought more stability and more opportunity to marry. Competition for spouses may have spurred the introduction of new and expensive or rare gifts and clandestine gift exchanges. Repeatedly, elderly women and men in Kétu spoke of the difficulty in earning money in the past through selling produce or small-scale trading. Thus, elder men with resources controlled the marriage process, though in the decades that followed, some young men pooled their own resources to pay bridewealth themselves. The potentially higher stakes in marriage may have encouraged young women and men to assert their desires, though the French Antislavery Society survey, the Adekambi-Adogbonu case, and the customary law books all suggest that some couples had already done so. One remarkable woman said in an interview that she had chosen her own husband when she married in the late 1910s and that her daughter did the same in the 1930s.[74] But these two women were not the norm. Even in the 1930s, one woman who refused two men her parents suggested was forced to choose one of the two.[75]

The prevalence of marriages between women and men of different religious faiths—indigenous, Muslim, or Christian—also challenged the image of a past when "children obeyed parents." People in Kétu today who relate across religious faiths as friends and neighbors still bristle at the suggestion that people of different religious faiths married in the past when marriages were expected to occur only with the approval of parents and other elders. Yet marriages between Muslim men and women who practiced indigenous religion are part of the lore and oral history of the Muslim community in Kétu, including the popular story of the Muslim Hausa man, "Sofo," who married multiple Kétu women, who in turn gave birth, literally, to the Kétu Muslim community.[76] Sofo's story assumes that the children were Muslim and may even imply that the wives converted. Muslim law requires that a woman who does not practice a "religion of the book," meaning Christianity, Judaism, or Islam, become a Muslim before marriage, but some wives and mothers neither moved into their husband's household nor converted.

Sitting in the shadow of the Catholic mission in Kétu, one elderly woman spoke to me of an aunt who married a Muslim man in the 1920s or 1930s and never converted; she stayed in her natal compound and raised her Muslim children there.[77] Another Catholic woman who married a Muslim man in the 1920s and went to stay in the Muslim quarter despite her family's fierce disapproval continued to attend the Catholic church, though all of her children were raised as Muslim.[78] The religious identity of the child of such marriages was not always clear-cut. A Muslim woman whose mother was a Catholic spoke of her Muslim grandmother who had married a Muslim man but later had children with a Catholic man. Each of the woman's siblings took up different religious practices.[79] In the 1940s or 1950s, the French photographer Pierre Verger took a picture of a Kétu woman named Koyato, a powerful ìyálorìṣà (mother-in-deity) of the local òrìṣà Buku. As "Ìyá Buku," Koyato married a Muslim man, had two sons, and continued as a leading figure in indigenous religion. She converted late in life, taking the name Awaou and offering many sacrifices to her òrìṣà so that the òrìṣà would release her and allow her a proper Muslim burial.[80] Thus Koyato's story and her image captures not only the symbolism of "public motherhood" but also the complex history of marriage and religious identity in Kétu.

Described by photographer Pierre Verger simply by the term "orishas" (deities), several people in Kétu identified this woman as Koyato, the former Ìyá Buku of Kétu. Her *òrìṣà* or deity may have been similar to Nana Buku, who is said to control birth and death. As Ìyá Buku, Koyato embodies the symbolic power associated with "public mothers." Foto Pierre Verger © Fundação Pierre Verger.

Elders, with an air of resignation, told me dramatically how people handled disobedient youth who married outside the family's religion: "If you don't let them marry, they will throw themselves into a well." But there were consequences. Marriage into Islam or Christianity meant, in principle, that a child could no longer participate in the *ifá* (divination) or *òrìṣà* (deity) worship, which was central to family ceremonies and even to the identity of families of diviners or *òrìṣà* priests. Inability to take part in rituals and practices challenged the authority of elders and threatened the well-being of relatives and their relationship with ancestors. Difficult to accept as they were, such marriages and conversions nevertheless occurred, with women and men relating across the religious boundaries in everyday life. One man said that his wife's family, known for their *babaláwo* (father owns secrets) or *ifá* diviners, allowed her to convert after she married him. The man's own father, known for drumming in religious ceremonies, had been introduced to Islam by a Muslim friend and business partner. On his conversion, he had to appease family members and friends with gifts.[81]

Women often are placed at the center of so-called "syncretic" or mixed religious practices in Africa, with wives and mothers still connected to indigenous religious practices or marginalized by the general predominance of male leadership in both Islam and Christianity. John Peel posits, in his study of Christian conversion among the Yoruba, that women in the nineteenth century were reluctant to convert to Christianity out of concern for their own fertility, which they protected through worship of *òrìṣà* (deities) and consultation of *ifá* divination.[82] But, in the different setting of Lagos, Nigeria, so Kristin Mann's study of urban elite Christian couples reports, elite Christian women in particular were drawn to the monogamy of Christianity, a doctrine their educated Christian husbands disregarded when convenient.[83] Other factors, such as threats to family and health, challenged the faith of both Muslim and Christian converts. In 1908, Father Vallée wrote of a Catholic convert who, upon the death of his young child, pledged repentance for resorting to *ifá* (divination) when the child became ill. One Muslim woman explained to me how her father's repeated experience with infant deaths, *àbíkú* (children born to die), led him to seek out indigenous medicine and religious intervention, until he came to trust fully in the power of Muslim prayer.[84] Women and men of various religious backgrounds looked to religion to aid them in times of profound distress, allowing them to move between, and occasionally to marry across, religions. Ignored or misrepresented simply as lax religious practices by French officials and missionaries, cultural "diffusion," as the term is used by Nigerian sociologist N. A. Fadipe, was fitting for Yoruba communities, even in a smaller town like Kétu.

While Monseigneur Le Roy blamed social disorder on the repression of women, he would hardly have approved of the increasing "freedom" of women in the 1940s and 1950s that marked, for some, the era of "spoiled" marriages. Some women became engaged only after they were pregnant, forgoing bridewealth gifts and money. Men talked of marrying second or third wives for whom they paid no bridewealth because the women were pregnant or had been married previously. Other women and their families demanded more exorbitant amounts for bridewealth, and some women abandoned their fiancés for other men. These young wives did not gain newfound freedom or power suddenly as marriage practices began to challenge the model of power enjoyed by the most elder members in families; even women who chose their own spouses or stayed in their parents' compound continued to be subject to hierarchies based on age and rank that constricted their own choices and duties. Nor did shifts in the marriage practices emerge out of thin air. Rather, decades earlier, in the time of "eyes closed black," local processes that included the introduction of European goods and Christianity made change possible. Still, though the relationship between youth and elders on marriage choices had begun to change, husbands and fathers continued to exercise authority over wives, buttressed by half-hearted French legal reforms that were not designed to transform social norms even when they appeared to serve the interests of women.

The language of health and population growth, resembling that current at the time in France, was altered to mesh with French views of West Africa during a time when French policymakers prescribed the colonial program of "development" in the colonies that began in the 1920s. Such policies implicitly required a robust population of workers, and marriage and motherhood was thus integral to the policies. In France, women were encouraged to rescue the nation from the crisis of depopulation and degeneration by having babies, specifically French babies. The low birth rate, disease, and moral decay were viewed as symptoms of overall social and biological decline, and after the war, immigration, even of other Europeans, threatened to lower the "quality" of children born in France.[85] New laws regulated the work day and maternity leave. Medals were awarded to mothers of large families to encourage a boost in population rates. With European immigration and the presence of mixed-race children in African colonies, French lawmakers pondered laws about French citizenship, about whiteness, and about whether French "blood" was passed by mother to child.[86] In West Africa after World War I, there was newfound interest in birthing hospitals and child care, despite little funding. The minister of colonies, in Paris, expressed concern about the effect of "hygiene" and "moral decay" on the "development of the native races." Historian Alice Conklin writes that the interest in "regeneration of the races" in Africa was linked directly to rational development policies and forced labor practices in the colonies.[87] To "save" Africans from further "degeneration" meant emphasizing African women's roles as mothers who bore children—not as elderly women who ruled.

After World War II, French colonialists, while never fully abandoning their concern about women's fertility as wives and mothers, began emphasizing the roles of men in new ways, especially those called *évolués* (evolved men), that is, educated elites, by extending voting rights and changing labor laws. By the 1950s, France, like other major colonizing European nations, was trying to shed responsibility for its colonies, but without entirely losing influence over them. Men from all walks of life in Kétu—traders, husbands, Muslims, youth, fathers, and traditional elites—while distant from the centers of French colonial politics and power, at the same time were initiating their own forms of social and cultural change, ultimately redefining what it meant to be men.

6

"The Opening of the Eyes"

The Politics of Manhood on the Eve of Independence

A Muslim man named Alhaji Moussa Mama, commonly known as Moussa Laurent, is often credited with ushering in the period of *òlàjú* (the opening of the eyes) in Kétu. Working with a couple of Muslim friends, Alhaji Moussa Laurent began to travel to Lagos, Nigeria, in the 1940s to buy gunpowder and later bicycle parts to sell in Dahomey. Others who approached Alhaji Moussa Laurent and his friends to hear about their newfound success were soon trading or working as apprentices and transporters.[1] With access to such new goods and revenue, a young man could purchase a gift for his girlfriend and save money for marriage ceremonies rather than have to depend on the assistance of older male relatives and patrons to pay these expenses. Young men, as a consequence, could gain more control over how they became husbands and fathers.

But French colonial authorities considered the cross-border trade that circumvented markets in Dahomey to be smuggling, especially since these traders rarely declared their goods at customs checkpoints. To evade customs officers and their fees, transporters hired by the traders took circuitous routes at unusual hours, a practice that became known as *fàyàwọ́* (literally "pulling chest to ground"; translated here as cross-border trade). People today remember and talk about these new opportunities to make money, about diverse modes of transportation, and about changes in marriage practices as evidence of the coming of ọ̀làjú, a term often translated as "civilization."

That "civilization" or even modernity came to Kétu via men who carried bits and pieces of it on their backs contrasts with the narrative of a French "civilizing" mission under the guise of French imperialism. By the post–World War II period, when cross-border trade was increasing in Kétu, the French colonial administration had instituted major political reforms that ostensibly opened the door to modern representative politics across its African colonies. Initially, however, the idea behind the political reform was not to decolonize but to shift responsibilities onto the colonies and African representatives. Unlike the interwar period, when French colonial policy sought to deepen control over African communities through legal reforms aimed at the household and women, as colonialism began to wane, the French turned to politics and to the men to whom they expected to hand over control. Convinced that newly formed elected councils would reduce the remaining influence of any local kings or ministers, including the king of Kétu, who had retained recognition in the colony, the French played closer attention to the political climate among évolués, or "evolved Africans," often men who were educated or had been exposed to French culture.

Whereas French policymakers had thought of West African women and French women in similar ways, as wives and childbearing mothers responsible for boosting the population, African husbands and fathers were not viewed in quite the same way as their French counterparts. In postwar France, the men at the center of political debates had shifted away from an idealized vision of fathers of large families, the model patriarch, to French families and social welfare. Some African men were trying to assert their identities as workers, but French laws in the changing French empire required that African men be defined first as fathers of families in order to collect worker's benefits. Such debates, taking place among labor unions, African politicians, and French policymakers, did not necessarily resonate with men in rural areas who were involved in cross-border trade or working as apprentices and transporters in order to become husbands and fathers. Yet elder and younger men in Kétu did participate in the broader political reforms sweeping France's West African colonies in the postwar era, blurring the distinctions the French wanted to make between the "evolved" Africans who would lead and the "masses" who would follow. Thus, the vectors for "the opening of the eyes" in Kétu were multiple; Kétu traders, politicians, kings, and young men were redefining their relationships with women, wives, and mothers, while directly and indirectly engaging with a waning French colonial empire.

Self-Made Men: Cross-Border Trade and the Redefinition of Marriage, Family, and Community

In his study of the Yoruba Ijẹṣa region of Nigeria, John Peel defines ọ̀làjú as an indigenous concept of "development," considering "the opening of the eyes" as opening land for cultivation, opening minds through (mostly Christian) education, and opening outlooks through personal mobility/trade and political participation.[2] Kétu residents themselves associate ọ̀làjú with similar external markers, such as long-distance trade and Islam, emphasizing the personal experience of exposure to change and innovation. Whether "civilization" or "development," broad examples of social change in Kétu itself were defined in local terms of new trading networks, in changing marriage practices, and in the appearance of new mosques and Arabic-language learning.

But evidence of long-distance Kétu trading appears in mid-nineteenth-century sources from Christian missionaries based in Abẹokuta (now Nigeria) who regularly met and received messages from Kétu traders. Though the Kétu traders were not named or described in any detail, they did travel frequently between the towns and to the coast. By the 1890s, French colonial documents described Kétu traders as Muslims and/or foreigners; a French official complained in 1894 that "foreign" Muslim traders or *aloufa* (scholars), primarily from Lagos, constantly crisscrossed the border and refused to declare their "nationality."[3] The problem was "contraband" from Nigeria, which included imported fabrics and ammunition, and Muslim merchants threatening to entice local products away from the port of Porto-Novo in Dahomey to the Nigerian port of Lagos. At the turn of the twentieth century, at the onset of colonial rule, the French were well aware of long-standing trading patterns that spanned the arbitrary boundaries between French-controlled Dahomey and British-controlled Nigeria.[4]

As early as 1901, the governor of Dahomey mentioned that Yoruba populations (Nago in French documents) on both sides of the border were participating in illegal cross-border trade. Muslims "without a nation" from the Lagos region were infiltrating communities in Dahomey to establish links to interior markets to the north. The governor warned that Muslim Nigerians readily gained converts and allies among the Yoruba populations. Cross-border trading practices, described decades later in Kétu, had already surfaced to the south at the turn of the century:

> One must note the connection between the frequent incidents of fraud in the region and the activities of Muslim Nago who constantly cross the British border between Badagry and Kétou. Muslims know that they must hide their goods as they reach the border so they are not alone in this activity. Certainly by the Muslims' initiative British imported fabric is purchased at a low price at the moment of liquidation. *Fetishist Nago residing in the country transport the items.* In Sakété in particular, every house becomes a warehouse for contraband. Recently established *customs agents reap benefits from this illicit activity* but this does not happen without angering the inhabitants who are incited by Muslims to arm themselves and fight arrest by Customs agents. They even attack the customs posts at night with the support of groups of individuals who make up the floating population on the frontier. [5] (Emphasis added)

From the description, the key perpetrators in this earlier period of cross-border trade appear to be outsiders, but Kétu residents too engaged in regional trade. In a rare case from 1916, French authorities arrested an array of Kétu traders and Muslims from Lagos and charged them with smuggling ivory from Dahomey to Nigeria.[6] Still, the distance and cost of transport of bulky agricultural products, such as corn and cocoyams, were likely to discourage Kétu traders from venturing into Nigerian territory with such trade items. Instead, Kétu women engaged in a local regional trade to the south in the Ohori region, Sakété, and Pobé, selling lightweight agricultural products such as *gari* (manioc flour), calabashes (dried, decorated gourds), and indigo dye.[7] Kétu men had not set up the extensive networks of transporters and customs contacts that the governor of Dahomey remarked upon in towns further south.

In 1915, after hunters in Kétu threatened to overthrow the senior royal wife and French colonial agent Alaba Ida, soldiers sent to the region seized contraband and guns found at a local customs office that had only been created the year before. Kétu residents told Nigerian historian A. I. Asiwaju in the 1960s that the office was later closed because of abuses by the customs agents. It is unclear if these "abuses" involved the bribery or confrontation between agents and the population as described in 1901 further south of Kétu. A 1935 colonial decree that officially closed the customs post did not mention whether funding or popular opposition was the reason. But when I asked people myself about customs offices near Kétu before the 1940s, they denied that any existed, so strong was their belief that there had been no cross-border trade before the 1940s or 1950s. "There were no roads," several people insisted.[8]

Yet a Catholic Kétu woman said her husband's older brother paid for her wedding gifts in 1933 by purchasing white fabric in Abẹokuta and selling it to women to dye. Though her husband became a man of some means, his older brother did not appear to work with others in this business.[9] Another Catholic man said that his father traveled by foot to sell palm nuts in Nigeria (an unusual practice, considering that Kétu was too far north to produce palm oil). By purchasing palm oil products further south and selling them on the coast, he tapped into a vibrant palm oil trade.[10] With his profits, the man's father was able to do in the 1930s what few in Kétu could do for a decade or so: purchase a bicycle; with his new transport, he traded contraband over the border.[11] He even went to Lagos to obtain gifts for his *iyàwó kékeré* (junior wife).[12] By the 1940s and 1950s, trade patterns increasingly involved a hierarchy of traders, intermediaries, and transporters rather than individual men.

Thus a great deal of forgetting shapes the stories people tell about the coming of "civilization" in Kétu. People easily recall Alhaji Moussa Laurent and his Muslim friends as the leading figures in this cross-border trade, while often overlooking other men and women who were not Muslim but who also participated. Only leading figures in the Kétu trade network—not all of them Muslims—knew the pertinent contacts in Nigeria. A leading figure of *fàyàwó* (pulling chest to ground; cross-border trade) was a Catholic man named Sylvain, and some of the trade companions of Chitou, Alhaji Moussa Laurent's eldest son, were Catholic.[13] "Everyone did *fàyàwó*," one Catholic man remarked to me. "Since it was a Muslim that began it, people say that Muslims do it."[14] Though Alhaji Moussa Laurent came from a well-established Muslim family, as a young boy he had insisted on attending the Catholic mission school, hence his more common name, Moussa Laurent. Before he became involved in cross-border trade, he worked as a weaver, and, with his education and growing stature in the town, he served as an impromptu translator when French officials arrived.[15] His son Chitou and others expanded the enterprise, taking goods to various interior markets in central and western Dahomey. Others began moving goods across the border on bicycles.

Forgotten traders who preceded the celebrated pioneers of *fàyàwó* (pulling chest to ground; cross-border trade) and those who followed the example of Alhaji Moussa Laurent shared a key characteristic: they traded their goods to help with major life expenses, like marriage. Cross-border trade also gave them access to earnings of their own, in contrast with laboring on their fathers' farms or on farms of other male patrons. With this new independent source of income, these young men accumulated resources to pay *owó ìfé* (bridewealth, literally "love money") themselves. The man who exclaimed that everyone, not just Muslims, did *fàyàwó* told me he had earned 2,500 francs working as a transporter for Alhaji Moussa Laurent in 1958 and had given the money to the family of his fiancée.[16] Some who married in the 1940s and 1950s and engaged in cross-border trade did not want to farm, and others believed they could earn money faster. Sometimes men worked in cross-border trade for a few years or used it, over the long term, to supplement their work as farmers.[17]

Women, too, were caught up in the new trading networks, building on existing markets for produce and prepared foods, such as the alum and potash used in dyeing and soap making, acquired from markets in Meko, Nigeria. When these women encountered customs agents, they covered the goods on their heads and pretended to be returning from work in the fields. A Muslim woman named Sekinatou (the first Kétu woman to complete the pilgrimage to Mecca) is remembered as one of the first to engage in this new form of trade. Some Muslim and Kétu women began to sell fabric known as *bogi*, obtained from Nigeria.[18] By the 1960s, customers were buying manufactured bowls, pots, and serving trays from Lagos as wedding gifts. Women supplemented items bought in Nigeria with similar items purchased in the coastal cities of Porto-Novo and Cotonou in Dahomey, so that if customs agents caught them illegally moving Nigerian goods across the border, the women could still profit by selling the products from Dahomey.[19] They took a career path different from that of men, who might begin, as young unmarried men, as transporters to avoid labor as a farmer; young women saved or skimmed money from their work as apprentices to their mothers or other female patrons to save up enough to begin commerce of their own after their marriage.[20] Cross-border trade did not necessarily replace farming, but it altered young men's and women's perspectives about livelihoods, opportunities, and responsibilities to parents and guardians; the promise of goods and revenue from *fàyàwó* (pulling chest to ground; cross-border trade) was changing the expectations of young women and young men.

A small number of court cases from 1963 and 1964 indicate the larger sums of money and gifts that changed hands when women and men became formally engaged in the late 1950s and early 1960s. Initial gifts to the family of a bride could total more than ten thousand francs, with contributions to ceremonies, food, drink, and other miscellaneous expenses perhaps doubling or tripling that amount.[21] Testimony in the court cases also recount stories of wives who refused to live with their husbands or became pregnant by other men, thus brazenly defying custom and their own families, future spouses, and in-laws. One man requested the return of his *owó ìfẹ́* (love money; bridewealth) and other gifts after his wife had three children with another man.[22] Another man's mother brought a complaint against the family of a wife who refused to move into her husband's compound, with the woman's family responding that the husband had not presented money and gifts for the marriage in a timely manner and, as the family of the bride, they had loaned money to his family for part of the marriage ceremonies.[23] Another woman appeared in her husband's household pregnant by another man, and, although her husband accepted her as his wife, she fled to the home of the father of her child, and her family defended her actions on the grounds that her husband had offended her and refused to apologize.[24] Though men could earn their own money through cross-border trade to pay for wedding expenses—a husband in one of the cases was a trader who traveled to Lagos—extended families were still heavily involved in marriage disputes.

If new trade earnings affected marriage relationships between Kétu residents, money and travel also changed how Kétu Muslims in particular were seen as "strangers" within the town and how they related to the outside Muslim world. Muslims, as well as those who practiced indigenous religion or Catholicism, associated *ọlàjú* (the opening of the eyes) with Muslims and their religion, some believing that Muslims possessed worldliness and business acumen because they were "strangers." The same Catholic man who reminisced about working with Alhaji Moussa Laurent to earn money for bridewealth said, "He [Alhaji Moussa Laurent] was civilized since he had done Mecca by foot. He understood how to do commerce."[25] Indeed, that Alhaji Moussa Laurent was one of the first Muslims from Kétu to complete the *hajj* to Mecca, then an arduous overland route, only added to the lore surrounding him.[26] Such reactions about Muslims built upon stereotypes, still prevalent in some academic literature, that define Muslims as the quintessential long-distance merchants, thus tying exposure to trade and travel to Muslim religious conversion. Muslims in Kétu today often talk of their own lack of familiarity with Muslim religious practices, laws, and texts in the past.[27] In 1914, when a Muslim visiting from Nigeria preached reform of certain religious practices, local Muslims assured the French colonial administrator that they would continue to participate in local dances, ordinarily prohibited by Muslim faith.[28]

None of the stories people tell to explain how Islam arrived in Kétu—of Sofo, the famed progenitor of the Muslim community, or of the Kanike, who reputedly instructed existing Muslims in Kétu on Islam—suggest that the first migrants brought Arabic learning with them. During the first decades of the twentieth century, however, Kétu Muslims had increasing contact with learned Muslims in Nigeria, either through relatives or visiting Muslim clerics. Moussa Olokoto, a Muslim man from Kétu who had resettled in Abẹokuta, is said to have returned to Kétu sometime in the 1920s to serve as imam, religious leader of the Muslim community.[29] After the 1940s, Muslim visitors were invited to speak, particularly during the holy fast of Ramadan, which contributed to the idea that a new period of "reform" of Muslim religious practices had begun in Kétu.[30] New mosques were being built and more clerics were setting up qur'anic schools where young children learned to memorize the Qur'an. Until about the 1960s, two qur'anic schools dominated in Kétu; several men set up other, short-lived schools, usually headed by Kétu Muslims rather than outsiders, that used the method that simplified Arabic pronunciation and spelling rather than the more standard Arabic.[31] Alhaji Nassirou Raji, who served as imam in the 1990s, remembered learning actual Arabic language from a visiting Nigerian cleric sometime during the reign of Alákétu Adewori, which lasted from 1937 to 1963. In the 1950s, a Nigerian cleric took a group of students from Kétu to Lagos to learn Arabic.[32]

Access to more Islamic schooling and knowledge brought more opportunities to women. The Ìyá Sunna (Mother of Muslim Customs) may have been recognized from the 1920s; she is the one who is primarily responsible for preparing deceased women for burial. In the past, the Ìyá Sunna may have repeated memorized verses; in more recent decades, women, like men, study the Qur'an and learn Arabic.[33] The first woman to complete the holy pilgrimage to Mecca was known to have participated in cross-border trade, demonstrating how access to goods and revenue allowed some Muslims to deepen ties to their religious practices. Muslim women in Kétu today, in groups known as *asalatu* (from Arabic *salat*, meaning "prayer"), learn Arabic verses from the Qur'an. People in Kétu recognize women's involvement in cross-border trade, their increasing role in Muslim institutions and education, and their participation in the pilgrimage to Mecca as part of the coming of "civilization."

In other Yoruba towns, particularly in Nigeria, elite status came with knowledge of English and work within the British administration. In Kétu, residents identify the coming of "civilization" during the colonial period with Muslims, seen as the more worldly and cosmopolitan members of the community.[34] The exposure to "civilization" that came through contact with Nigeria had a special significance for Kétu Muslims seeking religious knowledge from other Yoruba who shared their language and culture. But Muslims in Kétu did not form a separate or exclusive community; residents worked, married, and socialized across religious boundaries. What it meant to be Muslim changed in Kétu as the town as a whole was transformed through new relationships, ideas, and experiences.

Today, when one hears talk of the coming of "civilization" to Kétu, one might gather that the French had little to do with it. French officials were wary of the transnational nature of cross-border trade and of the involvement of Muslims on both sides of the border. *Ọ̀làjú* (the opening of the eyes) occurred through the initiative and innovation of men like Alhaji Moussa Laurent, who helped create a complex network of traders, transporters, and apprentices. Contrary to the image common in both scholarly and popular accounts of long-distance trade as dominated by Muslims and men, Kétu men and women of varied backgrounds had been involved in such activity since before the colonial period. By participating in cross-border trade after the 1940s, men in Kétu were beginning to redefine how they became husbands and fathers, altering relationships with their own parents and wives.

The Decline of the French Father and the Rise of the African Worker in the Postwar French Empire

In France itself the image of the powerful *père de famille* (father of a family) was in decline after the aggressively masculine and pronatalist rhetoric of the fascist Vichy regime of World War II. Postwar policies in France that began to focus on the family and labor were translated in turn into colonial policies in West Africa centering on working men and their families. Anxieties over depopulation and "degeneration" in France and France's African colonies had implicated not only women, wives, and mothers, but men and fathers as well. Kristen Childers's study of the changing meanings of fatherhood in interwar France argues that the iconic image of the *père de famille* inspired political debates on citizenship, masculinity, and the family. Like women and mothers, fathers were expected to lead France out of decline by producing and being responsible for children. Politicians and activists debated a range of policies to support fathers, including a forty-hour workweek and a family vote that would give a father one vote for himself, one for his wife, and one for his children. To recognize the greater responsibilities of men of large families not only extolled fatherhood but also permitted a pointed critique of men who were single or childless. Not unlike women and mothers who were at once honored and cajoled by policies that provided subsidies and medals for having children and ostracized for having none or not enough, men and fathers were looked upon as a cause of, and a solution to, France's social woes of the 1920s and 1930s. The image of the father with three or more children and a wife at home was an ideal; there was great disdain for alternative male figures, such as the *célibataire* (single, childless man), the alcoholic and negligent father, and men who "morally endangered" children.[35]

By the 1930s, the emphasis in France was shifting to a "politics of the family," with increasing concern for the rights of children and families, addressed partly by legislation establishing family allowances for working men, beginning in 1932. Susan Pedersen mentions, in her comparative study of the origins of the welfare state in France and Britain, that family allowances, seemingly a boon to fathers, especially those who received a larger bonus for having more than three children, at first were a means for large industrial employers to control workers.[36] A longer history of family associations dating to the late nineteenth century, the Family Code of 1939, and the family politics of the fascist Vichy regime contributed to the shift in focus to the family itself and the state's role in the welfare of society in general. Family allowances came to incorporate the father into the family, if not into society, rather than setting him apart as patriarch. France's national family policy, especially the development of state control over family allowances, redistributed the cost of raising children across the entire French population.[37] With postwar political reforms, including the right to vote for French women, granted in 1944, the special position of fathers was even more compromised. Childers remarks that the end of the war brought the era of the *père de famille* to an end.

During the early postwar years, however, West Africans began pushing for their rights both as workers and as fathers of families in the new French Union of 1946. The devastating losses of the war had led France to reconsider its relationship with its colonies and to propose a new arrangement that offered political reform in the form of voting and representation within the framework of French empire.[38] The constitution adopted in 1946 was more conservative than initially proposed; it granted voting rights only to groups of Africans who met certain criteria. The limits within the new constitution prompted African nationalist leaders in the French Assembly to look to their own trade union backgrounds to push for social reform for workers. The practice of forced labor, unpaid and compulsory labor in France's African colonies, was officially declared illegal in 1946. There was an attempt to pass a worker code with separate sections for European and African workers, but the measure failed as strikes organized by African workers effectively challenged the idea of separate codes and launched a decade-long debate on a unified worker code in the French parliament. French officials were most opposed to including family allowances in the new code, refusing to apply the image of worker and family to Africans in the terms that had been applied in France.[39]

The language of "family" used by French officials was striking in contrast to the language of universalism and citizenship used by African activists and politicians themselves. In a council meeting on the unified worker code, Senegalese deputy Lamine Guèye asserted that "the Frenchman of Brest or of Lille will not be considered more French than the Frenchman of Africa." In similar language, a trade union paper from the French Soudan (Mali) drew broad similarities between the Frenchman born on the banks of the Seine and the Frenchman born near the Senegal River.[40] There were vociferous debates over family allocations, with the French expressing doubt that they could apply family allocations to African families with multiple wives and numerous children. Leopold Senghor, African deputy and future prime minister of Senegal, asserted that many African workers were single or childless; they were men and workers, not fathers of a family. His comment is intriguing and could be interpreted in various ways. On one hand, it was the symbol and the right to a family allowance that inspired Africans to act and argue for equal status as workers and as men. If, on the other hand, most men would not immediately qualify for a family allowance as married men with children, it is unclear whether some men were thinking more broadly about how the family allowance could apply to parents, siblings, and dependents other than one's biological children.

Fred Cooper's magisterial study of labor and the decolonization policies of France and Great Britain emphasizes that by the time family allowances were implemented in 1956, French policymakers had come to see them as a means of reproducing desirable, nuclear, and monogamous European-style families, verified by marriage certificates, prenatal doctor visits, and payment of school fees.[41] By focusing the debate over family allowances on a certain type of family—and policing those families—French policymakers tried to minimize the broader implications of social and political equality between African and French communities. But most African households could not replicate the European ideal of the nuclear family, especially one where only the husband worked and the wife stayed at home with the children. With most Africans unable to attain that European standard, the French came to compartmentalize Africans as "evolved," as workers, as peasants, or as uneducated masses, while claiming to have incorporated its colonies into a French Union after 1946 and thereby to have recognized all Africans' rights and privileges as citizens.

Because maintaining the boundaries between "proper" African families and other categories of Africans was important, the shifts in a place like Kétu, in terms of Muslim identity or in terms of the coming of "civilization" through cross-border trade, were problematic. For the French, Africans either went to school, worked, and developed a "modern" lifestyle or were part of rural communities that transformed at a pace amenable to indigenous beliefs and local social organization. The way educated elites, traditional leaders, farmers, and young people were participating together in a changing and already modern society was lost on a French colonial administration struggling to maintain control over African territories that, as late as the early 1950s, the French did not imagine they would lose.

Modern Men: Politicians, Kings, and Youth

In his 1954 book *Réactions Dahoméennes* (Dahomean Reactions), Réné Grivot, a former administrator in Dahomey, outlined Dahomean responses to "modern life." For him, all the trappings of modernity came from the French, the "tutoring power," whether it was education, economic opportunity, or judicial reform.[42] Africans, Grivot said, simply accepted, rejected, or misunderstood French policies, without any power to redefine social and economic changes in local terms. He contrasted the educated elite with a general population still mired in indigenous beliefs. Elites were inevitably male, and though the term "masses" was not gendered, it conjures up crowds of men, perhaps dangerous men. So important was the distinction between the *évolués* (evolved ones/men) and the masses that Grivot believed the elites formed "a weak minority that the masses are still a long away from following," which threatened the stability of the country.[43]

Grivot saw a crisis within the indigenous leadership, particularly among kings, referred to as "chiefs" by the French. Hereditary leaders had been ignored and replaced by favorites of the administration during some periods, especially before World War I, with kings rehabilitated during the interwar period, only to earn the ire of the local population because of the forced production and heavy taxation of World War II. Postwar political reforms called for the election of members of the Council of Notables, diminishing the little authority and prestige kings still enjoyed through their birthright. Grivot wrote how these "chiefs" bristled at the changes, one of them remarking, "It is useless to introduce European ways, let us name kings [chefs] according to our own ways."[44] This local ruler spoke of "traditional" ways in contrast to colonial policies, but African customs, rituals, and hierarchies had always been a part of the French colonial project, even when radical change was introduced, including the broad political reforms of the postwar period.

A few months before the liberation of Paris in June 1944, General Charles de Gaulle, leader of the Free French, convened a conference in Brazzaville, Congo, in West Central Africa, to propose landmark changes in the relationship between France and its colonies in Africa, Asia, and the Americas. Echoing an opening speech that promised to consider "the incorporation of the indigenous masses into the French world," General de Gaulle proposed that the measure of true progress was a man's ability to participate in the management of his own country.[45] The idea that France needed to guide Africans through this process explained the contradictions embedded in the conference's recommendations. While the French empire would remain intact, with local African leaders providing counsel through "traditional institutions" and assemblies, the true power to legislate and make decisions would remain with the French governor and other administrators.[46] The changes were still profound; eligible Africans would eventually elect their own "traditional" leaders at home and gain limited representation in the National Assembly in France. French colonial administrators, like Réné Grivot, continued to presume a great chasm between the masses and elites, which led the French to encourage both democratic reform and kingship, leading to modified forms of each.

All West Africans did not suddenly become citizens of France. At the constitutional conference of 1946 to found the Fourth French Republic, participants voted on whether to grant all Africans citizenship in the French Union.[47] The initial constitution was rejected, and a second, more conservative assembly adopted a constitution that reaffirmed Africans' lesser status as colonial subjects rather than as French citizens. There were two electoral colleges—one for French and naturalized citizens, a second for subjects. The voting rights of African subjects changed continuously thereafter to permit more individuals the right to vote as veterans: civil servants, people literate in French or Arabic, property owners, and pensioners. Few African women would have met these requirements. Only after 1951 could a woman vote, and only if she was the mother of two war veterans.[48] Though more than 330,000 people lived in Dahomey by 1951, only about a fifth of the adult population was eligible to vote for the representative to the French National Assembly. Kétu residents could more effectively voice their opinions in local contests for heads of *canton* (districts) and villages, affecting the real and symbolic power of the man recognized as the king of Kétu.[49]

It was in response to World War I–era uprisings and rebellions across French West Africa, including several in Dahomey, that the governor general for French West Africa reinstated "chiefs" like the king of Kétu; many kings had been divested of titles or supplanted by French colonial administrators or their appointed agents under early colonial policies.[50] This restoration of "chiefs" reinforced what the French saw as a patriarchal order threatened by women and youth. While such a policy appeared to echo concerns about fathers in France during the same period, the French were talking not as much about the heads of families as about bolstering political hierarchies to regain order. But the power of these kings would be controlled in terms of French interests. Governor General Joost Van Vollenhoven, for example, made it clear that "chiefs" served under the firm authority of French officials. By 1932, Governor General Jules Brévié envisioned that "chiefs" would "again become, in some degree, what most of them were before our arrival, namely chiefs; but chiefs animated by our ideas, imbued with our desire to assure the natives a better future." In an attempt to create these modern and loyal intermediaries, ones legitimate in the eyes of local populations, he called for re-establishment of the "Commissions of Notables" in which the opinions of these men would "carry more weight."[51]

In Dahomey itself, a year or so before Brévié's declaration on the new roles of "chiefs," the governor reorganized the indigenous administration, with the responsibilities of village leaders supervised by regional heads.[52] A few years later, an interim governor fretted over the strains placed on indigenous leaders, who also were paid by the French colonial administration but could not legally receive the types of gifts and services from the local community that would legitimize their authority.[53] The colonial administration's rhetoric spoke of "chiefs" sharing in French "ideas" and "desires" while demonstrating how much the French expected that African politics would take place under the cloak of local rituals and beliefs.

The resurrection of African "chiefs" in Dahomey angered educated elites, especially those working in the lively local press in the capital, Porto-Novo. *Évolués* resented the power these authorities wielded and the exactions they demanded, precisely in the forms of those gifts and services that the French authorities recognized as so central to indigenous power. Fearing that traditional authorities were being severely undermined by elites, Governor General Brévié met with editors of the local press to discourage propaganda campaigns against named "chiefs."[54] Thus the debate over "chiefs" in Dahomey responded specifically to years of fierce antichief rhetoric that elites wrote of in their newspapers. Once electoral reform began in 1946, the French governor of Dahomey, considering "chiefs" less relevant, shifted attention to the actions of *évolués* on the coast, those more likely to have the right to vote and voice their opinion.

Aláikétu Adewori experienced these shifts in French policy personally; he was a king not initially recognized as a *chef du canton* (district head) by the French colonial government. His two predecessors had been weakened but not deposed brusquely as other kings in French West Africa had been. The infirm and blind Aláikétu Onyegen, whose senior wife Alaba Ida had played such a controversial role as a colonial agent in the French administration, had been officially replaced by his most senior minister one year before he died. Though Onyegen's successor Aláikétu Odemufekun, who reigned from 1918 to 1936, was recognized as *chef du canton*, French officials often wrote in their correspondence of unseating him. Following the reign of Odemufekun, a returned World War I veteran, Bankole Okanleke, usurped the local leadership position as *chef du canton*, normally held by the king, and it was said that he tried to be named as Aláikétu, or at least to halt the naming of the new king. Aláikétu Adewori was named in 1937, but a territorial reorganization that made Kétu a part of the subdivision based at Zagnanado demoted his status to *chef du village* (village chief). Aláikétu Adewori, not officially recognized as a *chef du canton* for about ten years, won that distinction by popular vote in 1947, and Kétu even became its own subdivision.[55]

The French governor of Dahomey subsidized the installation ceremonies for Aláikétu Adewori two years later to ensure Adewori's prestige among fellow leaders in Nigeria.[56] Pierre Verger, a visiting French photographer and researcher of Afro-Brazilian culture, captured stately images of Aláikétu Adewori in full regalia in 1949 on a throne, parading with his entourage and greeting French colonial administrators. Aláikétu Adewori seemed to be living up to his full chosen name, "crown is now too securely placed on the head to be removed by anyone."[57] But the rehabilitation of the throne and the town declined, ironically, with the electoral reforms adopted in 1958, two years before independence. The town ceased to be a subdivision or even a *canton* (district) and was referred to as a village, with the king again becoming *chef de village* (village chief). Alákétu Adewori was formally recognized as king by the French only to see his town's status and his own prestige decline with democratic reform.[58]

While there was talk of "chiefs" and kings in Kétu, some Dahomean men were politicking on a national and international scale, seemingly contrasting the experience of modern elites with the "traditional" masses. African leaders based in Paris, Senegal, and the Côte d'Ivoire pushed for more rights, especially around labor issues. The three men who rose to prominence in Dahomey itself, however, seemed to embody a backward-looking ethnic regionalism. Yet the first political party founded in Dahomey, the Union Progressiste Dahoméenne (Progressive Union of Dahomey) (UPD), originally presented itself in 1947 as a "party of the masses that joined together all the people of Dahomey regardless of ethnicity, region, religion or class."[59] Sourou Migan Apithy, originally from Porto-Novo, a member of the Progressive Union and the first deputy to the French National Assembly from Dahomey, founded his own party in 1951. The Parti Républican du Dahomey (Republican Party of Dahomey) (PRD) came to be associated mainly with the southeastern and coastal region of the country. At the same time, members of the Progressive Union from the northern regions of the country clamored for a candidate from the north to run for a second deputy position from Dahomey. When their demands were ignored by the Progressive Union, they started a party called the Groupement Éthnique du Nord (Ethnic Groups of the North) (GEN), nominated Hubert Maga as their candidate, and won the second deputy position. Rivalries within the Progressive Union brought the brief era of the nationwide "party of the masses" to an end, leaving a dangerous north-south divide in its wake. Though a third party, the Union Démocratique du Dahomey (Democratic Union of Dahomey) (UDD), formed in 1955 to appeal to young Dahomeans with a "pan-African" vision, managed to organize throughout Dahomey and later won seats in the southwest, southeast, and north, its party leader, Justin Ahomadegbé, was associated with the central region of the former Dahomey kingdom.[60] Though for a time Ahomadegbé's party brought together laborers, farmers, government functionaries, and small business owners, the political map in Dahomey remained tripartite, with the Republican Party in the southeast, the Democratic Union in the center, and the Ethnic Groups Party in the north.

Alákétu Adewori, pictured here greeting French colonial authorities, was king of Kétu from 1937 to 1963, but only recognized by French colonial authorities in 1947. The French administration later sponsored these ceremonies for his enthronement, only to later demote his status (again) to that of "village chief." Alákétu Adewori was both vulnerable to French colonial policy and able to exist as a king outside of recognized colonial hierarchies. Foto Pierre Verger © Fundação Pierre Verger.

The French West African federation of colonies was decentralized in 1956, making self-government inevitable and increasing the stakes for the three political parties in Dahomey. Just prior to independence, Africans in France's colonies were granted universal suffrage, and by 1960, Dahomey and the other former French West African colonies celebrated the end of colonial rule. Using tactics that merged the interests of kings and politicians, Apithy and Maga increasingly depended upon regional heads to influence votes for Apithy in the south and Maga in the north. Ahomadegbé's Democratic Union Party would engage in local politics that linked politicians and kings, though these tactics could backfire. Indeed, Alákétu Adewori lost his government title in the 1960 election as a member of Ahomadegbé's party, which people associated with Gbe-speaking Dahomey and the devastating war that had destroyed Kétu in 1886. The candidate from Apithy's party won, though Alákétu Adewori remained king.[61] Rather than simply dividing the nation between "traditional" masses and urban elite, national politics created cross-cutting alliances between men the French courted as future leaders of the nation and masses of men and women who elected them into office. Elites may have controlled political parties, but the general population could still influence national and local politics.

The French had tried to manipulate who gained political power and influence as "modern" men by extending specific political reforms step by step during the 1950s and by organizing *conseils de la jeunesse* (youth councils) across French West Africa in 1952. Described by scholar Tony Chafer as a "rising generation of 'Young Turks,'" these younger (though not necessarily young) men, educated and involved in newspaper publishing in Dahomey, soon joined in the debates between pro–French Union nationalists and more radical voices, some of the latter Marxist-influenced.[62] These "young turks," many of whom were civil servants, fit the mold of the "modern" man, yet they challenged the political reform process the French sought to control. The movement for creation of youth organizations, which continued after independence, posed a threat to the new independent nation, spiraling into new directions probably not envisioned by the French.

The many regional youth organizations forming between 1960 and 1964 were to engage in more revolutionary and pan-Africanist rhetoric under the umbrella student organization, the Union Général des étudiants et des élèves du Dahomey (General Union of Students of Dahomey). Béninois historian Sylvain Anignikin writes that the group declared plans to "integrate the working masses and peasants and educate them to participate . . . in the revitalization of avant-garde organizations, essential supports for an anti-imperialist front for the liberation and true unification of Africa."[63] Because of their strike activities, the General Union of Students was banned by the government and resurrected, more than once, between 1961 and 1971. When Kétu's youth association, the Association des Jeunes de Kétou (Youth Association of Kétou), formed in 1967, Dahomey had been independent for seven years and had experienced several civilian and military regimes. For elections organized by the military regime in 1970, the Kétu youth association put forth an independent candidate who won the local election, with the results later annulled. After two years came the military dictatorship of Major Mathieu Kérékou; Kérékou tried to use the General Union of Students to legitimize his takeover until he himself in 1974 accused them of "verbalism and infantile Left-Wingism" and banned the group.[64]

In his book *Birth of a Black State,* Béninois scholar Maurice Glélé concludes that expanding trade to urban centers and the proliferation of radios emancipated rural populations from traditional authorities, who also lost influence in the face of political parties, especially after independence in 1960. Yet at the same time, Glélé cites a general lack of political consciousness and a certain passivity instilled by tradition that lasted through the first few years of Dahomey's independence.[65] In contrasting the image of "modernity"—in the form of trade, cities, and radios—to "tradition," Glélé obscures more complex relationships between rural and urban; between educated elite and farmer; between politician and king; between youth and elder. Many of these categories were gendered male in an era when French policymakers and Dahomean nationalists were envisioning the leaders of a new nation whom they could only imagine as "modern" men. Other men, younger, less educated, rural, or associated with "traditional" power, did not disappear. In a place like Kétu, it is likely that a man involved in local youth organizations perceived as a threat to the fledgling, independent state could, at the same time, have traveled dirt paths, "pulling chest to ground," to transport goods that would help buy a gift for his girlfriend or the family of his fiancée.

Post–World War II French colonial policy seemed a reversal of much that had just come before it: African women and men (technically) enjoyed political rights; "traditional" rulers were repudiated; and men, explicitly and implicitly, were at the center of French colonial ideologies and programs. But the changes were not as stark and revolutionary as they appeared. For example, there had been a time, just before World War I, when African kings were displaced by more educated intermediaries. So, too, men had always figured in French colonial concepts of the idealized head of household and patriarch in its African colonies. While there was a qualitative shift in the French rhetoric around "modern" men as African independence loomed nearer, "traditional" kings and women did not vanish as objects of colonial or postcolonial policies or as political actors in their own right. Thirty years after independence, when the king of Kétu re-emerged in local and national politics with "public mothers" at his side, another historical force played an unexpected role in the resurgence: research and travel linking this part of West Africa to the Bahia region of Brazil. Again the relationship was not a new one, but one that had been transforming societies connected by the Atlantic Ocean since the era of the Atlantic slave trade.

7

Mothers and Fathers of an Atlantic World

When French photographer Pierre Verger left Brazil for his research trip in Kétu in late 1948, he could not have known the significance of that year or of his own eventual relationship with the image of public motherhood" and kingship in the Atlantic world. While in Kétu, Verger witnessed and photographed the king of Kétu's long-delayed enthronement ceremonies, marking the beginning of an erratic rehabilitation of kingship in Kétu. In Brazil, some months earlier, journalist Edison Carneiro's publication of the book *Candomblés da Bahia* (Candomblés of Bahia), on the Brazilian African-based religion of Candomblé, declared that women or "mothers" were the predominant and preferred priests in the religion. Carneiro's text and other studies, including the 1947 ethnography *The City of Women* by American anthropologist Ruth Landes, would foster the image of matriarchy in the religion and the renown of women priests like Maria Bibiana do Espírito Santo, also known as Mãe Senhora ("Mother Madame"), a Candomblé priest who was a spiritual "mother" to Verger. Both Verger and Mãe Senhora benefited from their ongoing relationship that was not unlike the interdependent one between West African "public mothers" and the king as "father figure." Thus the historical relationship between "public mother-hood" and kingship in West Africa not only illuminates gender and power relationship on the continent but also provides a new way of understanding the links between Kétu and Brazil and the power dynamic between "mothers" and "fathers" in Brazil's Candomblé religion.

Many followers and scholars of Candomblé emphasize the Yoruba influences in the religion, accepting as true the ethnic labels associated with different Candomblé groups, especially those who identify as "Kétu" or "Nagô-Jeje" (Yoruba-Gbe).[1] In fact, Brazil's Candomblé religion blends rituals from diverse African groups as well as from Catholicism and Native American cultures. Its members engage in divination, spirit possession, veneration of saints, ancestor worship, and healing. They are led by women and men priests known as *māe-de-santo* (mother-in-saint) and *pāe-de-santo* (father-in-saint), but, partly because of the scholarship, the emphasis is on women priests.[2] Analyzing the image of women in Candomblé as part of the concept of "public motherhood"—the recognized social and political power of elder women within (African) communities—establishes what anthropologist Randy Matory calls an "Afro-Atlantic dialogue": "interacting and changing sets of participants in a conversation."[3] Often the African side of the exchange has been viewed only in terms of the transatlantic slave trade rather than in terms of other forms of trade and contact.

Verger's research and travel experience followed in the footsteps of Brazilians of African descent who regularly, over the centuries, returned to West Africa as traders, priests, and immigrants, carrying with them information and ideas. European and American scholars (both North American and Latin American) interested in the origins of black culture in the Americas have followed similar routes between West Africa and Brazil, some of them, like Verger, revitalizing these exchanges. Both West African and Brazilian communities were transformed by Atlantic world travelers, "mothers" and "fathers" who altered the nature of gender, religion, ethnicity, and nation on both sides of the Atlantic Ocean.

"We Brazilians, we come, yes": Atlantic Travelogues and Dialogues

In a conversation recorded by African American linguist Lorenzo Turner, Martiniano do Bonfim and Anna Santos recalled a song heard in the port of Lagos in modern-day Nigeria in the nineteenth century when arriving Brazilians of African descent, also known as *agudás,* caught sight of West Africa:

We come, yes. People, come, see the sailboat, yes.
We Brazilians, we come, yes. We come, yes. People, come,
See the sailboat, yes. We Brazilians, we come, yes.
We come yes. People, come, see the sailboat, yes.
We Brazilians, we come, yes.[4]

Martiniano do Bonfim, a renowned diviner born in Brazil, had spent eleven years in Lagos where, in his words, he "reached the age of understanding." Anna Santos, born in Lagos, traveled in the other direction when she was twenty years old, migrating to Salvador, Brazil, with her father and siblings in 1908. Their stories reflected centuries of forced and voluntary travel between an area of West Africa that now encompasses Bénin, Nigeria, and Togo and the northeastern Bahia region of Brazil.

Martiniano do Bonfim himself, with Candomblé priest Anna dos Santos, also known as Mãe Aninha (no relation to Anna Santos), engaged in an important collaboration during the first quarter of the twentieth century. Randy Matory writes that the two created a narrative about African purity through innovative titles and rituals within the Brazilian religion of Candomblé.[5] Bonfim assumed a role as teacher, if not "father," in their relationship. Arriving in the British colony of Lagos in 1875 at age thirteen, Bonfim learned English and *ifá* divination. His knowledge of English would bring him prestige and fame among Western researchers, and his training in Africa as a *babaláwo* (father owns the secrets) gave him power and influence in the Brazilian Candomblé religious community as well as in the Western academic world.[6] In 1938, he expressed concern about the direction of Candomblé to American anthropologist Ruth Landes, reminiscing about Mãe Aninha, who had just died the year before: "She really tried to study the ancient religion and establish it in its African purity."[7]

Bonfim's narrative of purity was as much about race as about ritual, ironically, at a time when Gilberto Freyre's influential *Masters and the Slaves* (1933) was celebrating racial mixing in Brazil and obscuring the realities of prejudice and inequality. Bonfim told Ruth Landes that before emancipation in 1888 in Brazil, slaves and freed blacks known as "old Africans" had lived in his neighborhood in "a whole village of blacks." Landes reported not only what Bonfim said but tried to convey his attitude and tone: "'Both slaves and freedmen . . . stayed in town to do special work for their masters living in the country. . . . the stevedores used to congregate on certain corners on Sundays and holidays, the free ones wearing frock coats and silk hats!' He laughed. 'But they were true Africans,' he said seriously. 'No white was mixed with them, and they knew their religion.'"[8] For Bonfim and other Atlantic world travelers like him, even though being black could mean doing "special work for masters," being black also could mean being modern, traveling, or sporting European dress. American anthropologist Donald Pierson, studying "race contact" in the region of Bahia, found black Brazilians who kept copies of Nigerian newspapers or photos of a Lagos school, and one with a biography of Pan-Africanist Marcus Garvey and a copy of *Negro World*, Garvey's publication.[9] But in early twentieth-century Brazil, "whiteness" meant higher status and "blackness" conveyed a stigma of inferiority.

In the 1890s, Martiniano do Bonfim had participated in interviews with a physician, Raimundo Nina Rodrigues, whose pioneering study of African-based religion in Brazil concluded that blacks, because of their deep connection to African culture, were not properly integrated into Brazilian society.[10] Later students of Brazilian race relations would highlight Brazilian "exceptionalism" in comparison to segregationist policies and racial tensions in the United States. A student of Nina Rodrigues, Arthur Ramos, declared that "the Negro participated fully in the social life of Brazil, and no laws restricted participating in the exercise of the legitimate function of Negro citizenship."[11] American anthropologist Donald Pierson deemed ideas of white superiority prevalent in Brazil "cultural" and not "racial," yet his own statistics showed that whites tended to be of higher economic status and blacks on the lowest rungs of society.[12] Nonetheless, in the 1930s, when Martiniano do Bonfim referred to himself in a mocking tone as a "poor black," he identified with several communities he portrayed as modern: black/African, Candomblé, and Brazilian.[13]

Many other scholars have examined male immigrants and traders who traveled between the Bight of Benin and Bahia, in particular, in the nineteenth century, but families and couples were also an important part of this travel and dialogue into the early twentieth century.[14] In an article, "Some Contacts of Brazilian Ex-Slaves with Nigeria, West Africa," Lorenzo Turner told of several women traveling from Brazil with husbands or parents. One such woman was Isadora Maria Hamus, born in Brazil in 1888, the year of emancipation there; much like Martiniano do Bonfim, she had lived in Lagos, Nigeria, for several years before returning to Bahia to become a leading figure in the Candomblé religion. Another Brazilian woman from Rio de Janeiro had traveled with her family to Lagos and met and married a Brazilian man there. Their son later returned to Bahia to trade in African agricultural products, such as kola nuts, pepper, and cowry shells used in Candomblé ceremonies. Anna Santos's father and mother, who had been born in Brazil, emigrated as teenagers with their families to Lagos. They married in Lagos and had nine children. Anna Santos's father, Marcos Cardoso, was a successful carpenter who designed several churches and schools in Nigeria and Dahomey; after his wife died, he brought seven of his nine children back to Brazil. Anna Santos's siblings had lived in Bahia and Rio de Janeiro; an elder brother stayed in West Africa in the Gold Coast (Ghana). She married a Nigerian man with a Portuguese name, though she said that he frequented "the cult of the idol worshippers."[15]

This intense travel of Brazilians between the Bight of Benin and Bahia had slowed by the time many scholars came to study Candomblé in the late 1930s, but researchers themselves now traveled between Africa and the Americas, seeking to trace the origins of the African-based religion and culture they had found in the Americas. Anthropologist Melville Herskovits, the leading figure in this field, conducted fieldwork between 1928 and 1942 in the Americas in Suriname, Haiti, Trinidad, and Brazil, and in Dahomey in West Africa.[16] Originally a proponent of the idea of assimilation and trained at Columbia University by Franz Boas, a leading figure in the study of American anthropology and race relations, Herskovits came to adopt the concept of "acculturation," that contact between cultural groups results in changes to both.[17] Herskovits's theory of contact and change could be seen as a precursor of the metaphor of "dialogue," borrowed from Matory and employed here. But Herskovits himself, like many of his students and others influenced by his work, focused instead on degrees of "acculturation," used as a near-synonym for "assimilation" for people of African descent in the Americas. His *Myth of the Negro Past*, published in 1941, saw African cultures as an unchanging "baseline" against which to examine the degree of change in the Americas; his interest, ultimately, was less in ongoing change and interaction between Africa and the Americas and more in the ideal of "retentions" or "survivals" in the Americas.[18] In such a formulation, Afro-American cultural forms change in relation to their contact with modern Euro-American society. Cultural change in Africa or in the Americas becomes a "loss" of African culture rather than part of dynamic change to Atlantic world societies, combining African, European, Native American, and Asian elements.

French photographer Pierre Verger was a scholar who affected the cultural and intellectual exchange between West Africa and Brazil; a documentary honoring his life refers to him as a "messenger between two worlds."[19] Verger was an inveterate wanderer. He visited several continents, including Africa, before arriving in Salvador, Brazil, in 1946. It became his home base for the next fifty years. He said that in Paris in the 1930s he had frequented the Bal Nègre, a fashionable night spot known for "beguine," a form of Martinican music and dance.[20] A club popular with blacks not only from the Caribbean but from West Africa and the United States, the Bal Nègre was known as a place where artists and writers went to "dance with blacks." Verger later commented that the "hot and exotic nights" there influenced his interest in West Indian, Brazilian, and African culture.[21] Becoming a prolific researcher of Afro-Brazilian Candomblé, Yoruba *ifá* divination, and trade relations between West Africa and Bahia, he went beyond the "hot and exotic" to the historical and the intellectual.

Verger navigated "between two worlds" with the help of a longtime friend, Maria Bibiana do Espírito Santo, known as Mãe Senhora ("Mother Madame"), powerful *mãe-de-santo* (mother-in-saint) in the Candomblé religion. Verger had become intrigued with Candomblé soon after his arrival in Salvador in the Bahia region of Brazil. He received a research grant to West Africa to study, as he put it, "the origins of what is going on still in Brazil and West Indies," especially in "regions 'broken' by the kings of Abomey—'Ketou' in particular."[22] Verger depended heavily on references and guidance from contacts in the Candomblé religion in Brazil. Though he met Mãe Senhora for the first time not long before he left Salvador, she, in a ceremony, consecrated his head to the òrìṣà (deity) Xango (Portuguese spelling of Ṣango) for his protection.[23] Later she bestowed an honorary title upon Verger, who referred to her as his "mother," honored to be one of her "spiritual sons."[24]

While deferring to Mãe Senhora, Verger, in shifting his attention from Kétu alone to the broader coast and interior of Atlantic Africa, began to recreate and reinvigorate the very transnational exchanges he was studying through his own research, photography, and correspondence. He wrote in a letter to American anthropologist Melville Herskovits that people in Kétu responded well to pictures of their "cousins" from the Bahia region of Brazil.[25] Upon his return from West Africa, Verger told Herskovits, "It was I believe the first time in this century that somebody came to give them information on their own people sent abroad in the past."[26] His book *Flux et reflux de la traité des nègres entre le Golfe de Bénin et Bahia de Todos os Santos, du XVIIe au XIXe siècle* (Trade Relations between the Bight of Benin and Bahia) was based on the intense nineteenth-century communication and travel across the Atlantic; the more descriptive, original French title used the terms "flow" (*flux*) and "counter-flow" (*reflux*). His own relationships recaptured the broader sense of the Atlantic world, encompassing Europe and involving exchanges within Atlantic Africa and within the Americas.

Some of Verger's closest confidants indeed were a trio of French research-ers: anthropologist Alfred Métraux, who conducted important work in Hawai'i and in Haiti with South American indigenous populations; sociologist Roger Bastide, whose research included Candomblé in Bahia, Brazil; and Gilbert Rou-get, an ethnomusicologist who accompanied Verger on several of his trips to West Africa.[27] In 1948, Métraux showed pictures Verger had sent him of Bra-zilian Candomblé to a local man he was working with in Haiti and was amazed how his informant "identifie[d] without blinking the *loas* [deities] that possess the people in the photographs" and "discover[ed] all sorts of parallels with Haiti that have escaped me."[28] In 1953, after Verger, in Kétu, was initiated into *ifá* divination as a *babaláwo* (father owns the secrets), he exclaimed in a letter to Roger Bastide that he had taken the name "Fatumbi," which he translated as "Ifá gives birth to me again." He added, "What is interesting from the point of view of Brazil is that I have discovered several stories that are found in the notebook on divination by cowry shell that our mother Senhora gave me."[29] Religious and cultural knowledge flowed in multiple directions and forms be-tween Verger, his friends, and those who supplied stories and information to them. Verger became more than a "father" of the secrets of *ifá*; he emerged as a "father figure" in the study of the "flow" and "counterflow" of scholars and information across the Atlantic.

Verger held fast to the belief that the association of Kétu with Candomblé in the Bahia region of Brazil was a literal connection that continued through priests like Mãe Senhora. He escorted Mãe Senhora's biological son Deoscóredes Maximiliano dos Santos (also known as Mestre Didi) to Kétu in 1967, while the son was on a research grant to compare sacred art in Nigeria and Bénin. Mestre Didi said he had always heard that he was descended from a royal family in Kétu, but when he met Aláké́tu Adetutu, who had come to power in 1964, he realized he could not converse too long in the Kétu dialect and instead sang a song. The king and his ministers apparently recognized some of the words in the melody. Coaxed by Verger and his wife, Mestre Didi then recited a short series of words known as an *oríkì* (praise name) he had learned from his mother, Mãe Senhora. One term, "Aṣipa," was recognized by the king; he asso-ciated it, he said, with a family in Kétu and told Mestre Didi, "Your family lives over there." The king arranged for Mestre Didi to be led to a household whose residents welcomed him. Mestre Didi recalled feeling too overwhelmed to respond. He came to view himself as a descendant of the Aṣipa-Alapini family and returned to Kétu in 1983 to receive from Alákétu Adetutu the honorary title of Baba Mogba Oga Oni Ṣango. Aṣipa is a high-ranking title associated with the hunter's association in Kétu, and Alapini, a Yoruba title associated with the Egungun masquerade, a dance of reincarnations of the ancestors. Alapini is also the name of one of the five recognized royal families in Kétu. The name Aṣipa is known in other Yoruba towns in Nigeria as well; Samuel Johnson listed it, alternately, as a military title found in Ọyọ and as a title used among the Ogboni secret society in Abẹokuta.[30] Three years after receiving the honorary title in Kétu, Mestre Didi founded a cultural center, Ilê Axipá (House of Aṣipa) in Salvador, Brazil.

Despite the alterations to African "tradition" he chronicled in his own research and despite his participation in conversations and movements that contributed to change, Verger ended his book on trade relations between the Bight of Benin and Bahia with the remarkable story of Mestre Didi's return "home." He claimed, in language reminiscent of Herskovits, that Mestre Didi's experience reflected the "fidelity with which certain African traditions were conserved in Bahia." Hopeful, he asked if Mestre Didi's discovery meant that the old ties between the Bight of Benin and Bahia could be restored.[31] Mestre Didi's revelation was a fateful moment that reinforced Verger's belief in Kétu's special place in Bahian Candomblé and deepened his own unique relationship with Kétu on both sides of the Atlantic through Candomblé and *ifá* divination. As a biological and symbolic mother, Mãe Senhora had mentored both men, bolstering the claims of each to African and Afro-Brazilian culture, while she herself was part of a larger dialogue about gender, race, and power.

Rethinking Black Atlantic Motherhood

The trilogy of novels by Brazilian diplomat turned author Antônio Olinto, set mostly in West Africa, *Casa da agua* (The Water House, 1969), *Rei do Keto* (The King of Kétu, 1980), and *Trono de vidro* (The Glass Throne, 1987), begins with the return of an African-born former Brazilian slave, her free daughter, and granddaughter to Lagos, Nigeria. His part history/part memoir, *Brasilieros na Àfrica* (Brazilians in Africa), that preceded and inspired his trilogy, had been based on a period from 1962 to 1964, when, as the cultural attaché for the Brazilian embassy in Lagos, Olinto had been drawn into the local Afro-

Brazilian community.[32] In his memoir, Olinto wrote of a returned Brazilian woman named Maria Romana de Conceição, who had arrived from Brazil in 1900, surviving an outbreak of yellow fever on a ship stalled at sea. In *The Water House*, Olinto told this story through the eyes of the character Mariana Silva, who, though widowed with young children, became a successful entrepreneur, buying up property on the West African coast; her son was elected president of the newly independent fictional West African nation of Zorei. Mariana became like a "public mother" in the young nation, known as the First Lady of Zorei to her son, also as widower before he himself was assassinated.[33] By the third novel, *The Glass Throne*, written in the 1980s, her granddaughter and namesake is seeking the presidency of Zorei.[34] Olinto drew upon what he saw in West Africa and on his experience with "mothers," the women priests of Candomblé, and Kétu's mythical role in Afro-Brazilian religion and culture.

Indeed, the Kétu Candomblé of Bahia became the most studied and renowned of the Candomblé houses. A *mãe-de-santo* (mother-in-saint) or *pãe-de-santo* (father-in-saint) heads each house or *terreiro* (literally yard), presiding over officers, sponsors, and initiates known as *filhas-* or *filhos-de-santo* (daughters- or sons-in-saint). Daughters- or sons-in-saint are also known as *iaô*, from the Yoruba *iyàwó*, meaning wife or dependent, demonstrating their subservience to their deity. Women and men join Candomblé houses because they are drawn to the *òrìṣà* (deity, saint) and take part in rituals and festivals where they offer sacrifices and gifts to *òrìṣà*, who sometimes possess or "mount" participants. Initiates hope that by serving the *òrìṣà*, the deity will provide protection and help with life's difficulties. Although Candomblé houses have long claimed links to diverse African and Native American "nations" or ethnic identities, Kétu, Angola, and Jeje (Gbe), among others, Candomblé is often associated with Yoruba religious practices. In the 1930s, journalist Edison Carneiro, who identified seventeen nations among the sixty-seven houses he had studied in Bahia, asserted that the oldest was a Kétu house founded a century earlier.[35]

Carneiro wrote that three black women from "the coast," Iyá Adêtá, Iyá Kalá, and Iyá Nassô, established this first Candomblé house, also known as Ilê Iyá Nassô (House of Iyá Nassô), after one of the women.[36] The links to West Africa and (Ọyọ) Yoruba culture are tempting; Ìyá Naso was a title in the Ọyọ kingdom for the woman priest of the Ṣango worshippers in the king's palace.[37] Forms of these names, collected in oral histories, appear in a Yoruba prayer song Melville and Jean Herskovits recorded during fieldwork in 1941 and 1942. The song's recurrent phrase, *mojuba* or *mojubare*, "I bow down before you," pays deference to "mothers" *and* "fathers" who were ancestors and founders of these early Candomblé houses, specifically referred to as Kétu Candomblé.[38]

Verger wrote that the two founding women of Engenho Velho had traveled to West Africa, one dying there and the other, Iyá Nassô, returning after spending seven years there (Verger assumes in Kétu) with her daughter and granddaughter. The granddaughter was pregnant with a third daughter on the return voyage and that third great-granddaughter, named Claudiana, was the mother of Mãe Senhora. A Yoruba man named Bamgbose was said to have accompanied the women back to Brazil, his "Africanness" lending authenticity to the women's religious practices.[39] Others spoke of a man named Babá Asika, who helped Iya Nassô found the Candomblé house; his name was recorded in the song Herskovits collected. After Iya Nassô's successor died, two women competed to be the *mãe-de-santo* of Engenho Velho; the one who was denied the post founded her own, Gantois, after the French landlord who rented them space. The successor of Gantois, Mãe Menininha, who served a long term from 1926 to 1986, was perceived as a gatekeeper of the Kétu tradition. Another dispute at Engenho Velho in 1890 led to the rise of Eugenia Anna dos Santos, known as Mãe Aninha; twenty years later, she founded her own Candomblé house, Ilê Axé Opô Afonjá, with the help of a man named Joaquim Vieira.[40] She was an outsider to Yoruba language and culture but adopted Yoruba (Nago) practices.[41] Years later, Mãe Senhora became mother-in-saint at Ilê Axé Opô Afonjá, which had by then, in some respects, transferred the Kétu lineage away from Engenho Velho.

Another Kétu Candomblé house, one known as Alaketo (title of the king of Kétu), claims a long tradition and direct ties to Kétu, its oral histories saying that its founder, Otampê Ojarô, had been kidnapped from the Kétu kingdom in the late eighteenth century and was freed by a kind stranger, the personification of an òrìṣà. Otampê Ojarô, who traveled back to Kétu as a young woman, married a man there named Babá Laji, who returned to Bahia with her to found a Candomblé house, Ilê Maroiálaji, or Alaketo. In anthropologist Vivaldo da Costa Lima's interviews with Alákétu Adewori in 1963 in Kétu, the king verified a late eighteenth-century Dahomey attack when members of the Aro royal family were kidnapped; one of the captives was a young girl named Ojarô.[42] However, tracing the founders of Candomblé to Kétu is still an extraordinary feat and one scholar associates the term "Kétu" less with an ethnic identity than with the forms of worship and ritual.[43] Whether or not Iyá Nassô or Otampê Ojarô actually came from Kétu, they embody important cultural symbols of the Bight of Benin and Brazil, as "mothers" and as travelers in the Atlantic world. The long-time priest of Alaketo, known as Olga do Alaketo, was famous for her frequent travel back and forth to West Africa during more than a half-century while she headed the house of Alaketo until her death in 2005.[44]

Scholars and the tourist industry in Bahia have played heavily on the image of "mothers" in Candomblé, obscuring the role of men. So, too, women and men in West Africa and the Americas have debated and transformed the concept of "public motherhood" in the Bahian context. Though the popular image of Bahian culture is the *māe-de-santo* or, at least, the Bahiana, a Bahian black woman in flowing skirt and headwrap, the founding of all the famed Kétu Candomblé houses involved men, Bamgbose and Babá Asika for Engenho Velho, Joaquim Vieira for Ilê Axé Opô Afonjá, and Babá Laji for Alaketo. Their names are preserved in the oral traditions of Candomblé houses as honored ancestors. Within Candomblé ritual itself, men serve as diviners, drummers, and sponsors. Indeed, by the 1930s, the white and mixed-race intellectuals who studied Candomblé and participated as *ogā* (sponsor, literally, "priest who is not possessed") provided support and helped portray Candomblé for public consumption. As Matory shows in his study of Candomblé, *Black Atlantic Religion,* there has always been a "dialogue," but it is important to recognize that these are conversations between women and men, between elites and Candomblé priests, and within a network of West Africans and black Brazilians.[45]

Candomblés da Bahia, the key 1948 publication by Brazilian journalist Edison Carneiro, was released one year after American anthropologist Ruth Landes referred to Salvador, the capital of the state of Bahia, as the "City of Women." Carneiro and Landes collaborated during Landes's fieldwork in the late 1930s. Carneiro's slim volume mentions that women priests were influential in Candomblé religion, but the central theme of Landes's entire book is the "cult matriarchate" or "ruling women" of Candomblé. Her focus on women priests was taken up by other scholars, notably women, from the impressionistic description of Candomblé by French feminist Simone de Beauvoir in the 1960s to the more recent scholarship by Kim Butler and Rachel Harding.[46] Black feminists working primarily in the United States also have been intrigued by the idea of continuity between West African women's economic independence in marriage and the image of dominant black mothers in African American families. Many scholars have eschewed "retentions" of African practices in the Americas for socioeconomic explanations, recognizing that racism and poverty contribute to the prevalence of single women as heads of households.[47]

Still, Candomblé women are viewed in isolation from men, and some scholars harbor an ideal of the West African motherhood and family life that does not incorporate cultural change in West Africa or ongoing communication between West Africa and the Americas.

Matory argues that the collaboration between Carneiro and Landes in the late 1930s completely redefined Candomblé religion. Their writings played up the power and influence of women priests at the expense of male priests, denigrated as "passive homosexuals," who let themselves be penetrated by men and "mounted" by the gods. Tracing how Carneiro's discussion of male priests changed after Landes published her writings, especially her *City of Women* in 1947, Matory blames the emphasis on "mothers" in Candomblé almost entirely on Landes's white, Western, feminist project.[48] Focusing on Carneiro and Landes's relationship denies a role to Candomblé priests and followers who were Carneiro's friends or also provided information to him. Participants in Candomblé religion and ritual asserted the authority of women Candomblé priests as religious leaders and "mothers." Donald Pierson, writing before Landes published her work, noted that "several of the more prominent and influential *candomblés* in Bahia now have women leaders." But Pierson attributed the positions of the women to their tendency to be "traditional" in contrast to black men's increasing social mobility and contact with whites.[49] Ironically, Melville Herskovits, highly critical of Landes and Carneiro's emphasis on the role of women in Candomblé, viewed the economic independence of black Bahian women as a "survival" from West Africa. Of the Afro-Brazilian household, he wrote, "The man's role is one of co-operation rather than of dominance . . . the woman knows that freedom is hers for the taking."[50] While Pierson's comments may today be considered sexist because he assumed women were "traditional" or even "backward," and Herskovits's ideas presumptive and outmoded in his search for "survivals," the strong presence of women in Candomblé and in Afro-Brazilian society was observed by others who did not share Landes's "matriarchy" thesis.

Even if male Candomblé priests dominated in the nineteenth century, not unlike "fathers" and kings in West Africa, they were surrounded by and dependent upon women as evidence of their authority; many of the followers and organizers in Candomblé have been women.[51] Rather than see women's and men's power in Candomblé as a zero-sum game, where women *or* men must dominate, Candomblé can be seen in terms of the dialogues and partnerships emphasized in the oral histories and structure of the religion itself. Partnerships between women and men and between Africans and Brazilians existed not only in the oral traditions about the founding mothers of Engenho Velho and their transatlantic voyages, but also in the examples of men like Martiniano do Bonfim and Pierre Verger.

Verger cultivated multiple partnerships, with Mãe Senhora, with West African kings, and with Western and West African scholars. Each of his relationships illustrated the "unequal exchanges," "imagined communities," and "human agency" Matory emphasizes as defining aspects of a "dialogue."[52] As a white European man, Verger could use his "whiteness" to gain access to rituals and interviews for his writings and photographs, but he depended on his Brazilian and West African contacts for information and guidance. Verger was deeply reverential towards Mãe Senhora. He helped her make contact with West African kings, such as the Aláàfin (king of Ọyọ) Adeyemi, who bestowed a profound honor on Mãe Senhora when he repeatedly referred to her as Ìyá Naso (known in Ọyọ as the priest of the Ṣango shrine) in his letters to her.[53] Maria Stella de Azevedo Santos, known as Mãe Stella, head of Ilê Axé Opô Afonjá since 1976, said in an interview in the 1998 documentary film "Pierre Verger: Messenger between Two Worlds" that Verger had come to Bahia because "Xango (Ṣango) ruled his head," that is, he was born to serve the òrìṣà (deity) Xango and was led to Mãe Senhora's Candomblé house, where Xango is a primary deity.[54]

The shifting power dynamic between black Candomblé women priests and white and mixed-race elite men is part of the racial tension that permeates Brazilian society and history even today, most acutely expressed in the image of the "Black Mother" in Brazilian lore and modern politics. Gilberto Freyre's *Masters and the Slaves* (1933), celebrating the image of racial mixing at the heart of Brazil's history, established the myth of "racial democracy." Freyre presented the romanticized image of the "Black Mother" and other gendered and sexualized images of race: "we almost all of us bear the mark of that [Negro] influence. Of the female slave or 'mammy' who rocked us to sleep. Who suckled us. Who fed us, mashing our food with her own hands. The influence of the old woman who told us our first tales of ghost and beast. Of the mulatto girl who . . . initiated us into physical love and, to the creaking of the canvas cot, gave us our first complete sensation of being a man. Of the Negro lad who was our first playmate."[55] In Freyre's ideal world, the elderly black woman served as a veritable "mammy" or submissive matron and the mixed-race woman fulfilled sexual desire, with black men passive allies in an idealized patriarchal order dominated by white men.

In the late 1920s, journalists, politicians, black political organizations, and eventually Candomblé groups took up this image of the Black Mother [Mãe Preta], calling for a commemorative day, statues, and honorees. Black activists in Sao Paulo first promoted "The Day of the Black Mother" to mark the anniversary of the 1871 Law of the Free Womb that automatically freed children born to enslaved women. The figure of the Black Mother also literally and figuratively honored the long history of black women who had served as nursemaids to white children, evoking both the dominance and intimacy embedded in the practice of slavery. The shared experience by black and white (men) of the black woman as "mother" created a bond of "brotherhood," palatable to white intellectuals and to the Brazilian nation as a whole.[56] Thus the image of the Black Mother was fraught with symbolism of "racial democracy," with black women's submission and sacrifice, and—with the repeated references to a Brazilian nation suckling at the breasts of black women—sexuality. It was in 1955 that the first statue of the "Black Mother" was erected in Sao Paulo, and a decade later Mãe Senhora was celebrated as the "Black Mother of Brazil" in Rio de Janeiro. A statue in her likeness was erected in Rio de Janeiro after her death.[57] Still, Afro-Brazilian activists and white intellectuals, by themselves, did not dictate the transition of the Black Mother's image from a slave woman and wet nurse to a Candomblé priest; black women leaders of Candomblé also contributed to the charged imagery that surrounded them.

In 1938, American anthropologist Ruth Landes interviewed Mãe Menininha and found quite a different image of her as a "mother figure":

"My deceased aunt"—she [Mãe Menininha] touched the ground again—"inherited her position from her mother, the great deceased named Julia"—she touched the ground—"and Julia founded the temple after she arrived in Brazil. First she served as a priestess in Engenho Velho—mother and daughter served together. . . . *You know how it is in Europe, my lady. We mothers are like royal houses, we pass our offices to kinsfolk only, usually women.*" She shook her head and sighed. "The candomblé is a great responsibility. Often I wonder where I can get the strength to go on with it, and whether I have the right to burden my daughters with it."

"Why is that?"

"*I have no time for myself! I am a slave of my people, two hundred of them who depend upon me absolutely! Imagine!*" She shrugged, but her look was not really troubled.

"There is a great deal I need to learn, my mother," I [Ruth Landes] said, sighing to think of the tremendous imponderables of life in Bahia. "You see, we have no candomblés in North America."

"No?" She was surprised and disapproving, "Don't your people believe in God?"

"Oh, yes, but we show it in other ways. Still, we have much to learn."

"You want to learn from us?" Her tone was cold.

"Yes," I ventured.

"But there are secrets here you may not learn."

"It is not the secrets I want, my mother. I want only to understand your beliefs. I want to learn more about God, and about men because they are my brothers."

Menininha did not answer.[58] (Emphasis added)

Mãe Menininha portrayed herself as a servant of her people, but she touted her privilege and compared herself and her ancestors to a royal family of women. That Mãe Menininha received coldly and with suspicion Landes's thinly veiled submissive posture belied the accommodation and openness implied by the image of the Black Mother associated with Candomblé priests.

Mãe Stella of Ilê Axé Opô Afonjá, one of the most popular and well-known Candomblé priests since the 1990s, projected a contradictory image of women's predominance in Candomblé in a 1995 interview with a Brazilian newspaper:

It is a matriarchy. This is due to the fact that when Candomblé came to Brazil, this practice we know today, began with three Ladies. . . . This does not mean that men have no capacity to be a Babalorixá [father-in-saint, priest], but *the woman is the maternal figure, and when people come to Candomblé, they often look for a sort of maternal comfort and kindness [aconchego]. The woman is more able to give this.* That is the only reason. Suddenly there is the fact that women follow the African tradition that, *at Xango's house or Xango's cult, he is the boss, but there is a predominance of women because they have the title of Iyá Nassô:* the woman is the main Ayaba [royal wife; queen] of Xango's house and *she is the one who gives orders. But men and women have the same capacity.* [59] (Emphasis added)

Mãe Stella evokes "maternal comfort and kindness" yet speaks of women "giving orders" and as having the "same capacity" as men. In fact, she does not deny men a role in Candomblé, noting that they can become *babalorixá*, the Portuguese version of the Yoruba (Nago) word for *pãe-de-santo* or father-in-saint. In an interview for a documentary film released in 2005 called *A Cidade das Mulheres* (City of Women), which pays explicit tribute to Ruth Landes's work, Mãe Stella and other priests and scholars make even stronger statements about the role of men in Candomblé. Mãe Stella jokes at one point, "I think a matriarchy is wonderful. But what is a temple that only has women? What a bore, right? It has to have men. The men have their own functions in Candomblé. . . . There are posts that only men can hold just as there are so many others that women hold and men can't." An ethnolinguist interviewed in the same documentary analyzed the situation further: "Candomblé is a great example of innovation of an alternative lifestyle within a patriarchal society. . . . In Candomblé women have power without being matriarchal per se in the sense of oppressing or excluding men. Women have power . . . but without negating the male (masculine) principle."[60]

In both interviews Mãe Stella implied that African traditions require that men be "the boss" in the worship of the òrìṣà (deity) Xango but that male authority is countered by the title Iyá Nassô. But by describing the Iyá Nassô as an *aya ọba* (royal wife) rather than an *iyá* (mother) in the newspaper interview, which she seems to interpret more as a "queen" with the power to command, Mãe Stella provides a contradictory image of Iyá Nassô's mythical and symbolic power. In the kingdom of Ọyọ, the Ìyá Naso was responsible for the king's Ṣango shrine, and the name Iyá Nassô is recorded in the founding of Candomblé in Salvador. Drawing on the historical image of the founding "ladies" of Candomblé and the title of Ìyá Naso, Mãe Stella asserts the image of independent women leaders. But her consistent reference to an ideal of "maternal kindness," embodied by the Black Mother, can merge easily with the submissive image of the "mammy" described by Freyre. The continued importance of the perverse Black Mother image shows that black women try to redefine racial and sexual images associated with them. But the image of the Black Mother distorts biological motherhood and obscures the concept of "public motherhood," associating the mature, postmenopausal woman with child rearing and turning "mother figures" into "queens," technically wives defined by their relationship with "kings."[61]

It is tempting to see simple parallels between the Bight of Benin and Bahia, as expressed in the work of Pierre Verger, which places images of rituals, architecture, and bodies from West Africa and Brazil side by side to stress the shared style, pose, and expression.[62] His most extensive book of juxtaposed photographs, *Òrìṣà: Les Dieux Yoruba en Afrique et au Nouveau Monde* (Orishas: Yoruba Gods in Africa and the New World), intrigued my research assistant as she waited for me at the Bénin National Archives; she said that she wanted to go to Brazil to see "all the things that we have here." Several months earlier, at the Pierre Verger Foundation in Salvador, Brazil, I had been struck by the similarity between photographs of Alákétu Adewori that Verger took in Kétu in early 1949 and others of Mãe Senhora taken sometime later. In both series, the king and priest are seated outdoors in flowing robes, their rich fabric glistening in the sunlight in almost the same way. In several shots, Mãe Senhora is even wearing her beaded crown, modeled after the headdress worn in West Africa only by Yoruba kings. The photography archivist suggested that the resemblance was not an accident, but that Verger had been inspired by the regal bearing of Alákétu Adewori and had placed Mãe Senhora in a similar pose.[63] Thus Verger linked the West African king or "father" and the Brazilian priest or "mother" figuratively and literally through a photograph. Participating in this "dialogue," Alákétu Adewori and Mãe Senhora each looked boldly at the camera. Perhaps in a way that fits too neatly with the saying "mother is gold, father is glass," Alákétu Adewori would die in 1963 after losing an election and much power but retaining his title as king, and Mãe Senhora would die in 1967 at the height of her power and popularity, having been named the "Black Mother of Brazil."

To conceptualize black womanhood or motherhood in the Americas in terms of "survival" from Africa, or as consequence of poverty and racism, is to overlook the role of migrating Brazilians, West Africans, and Western researchers. The story of black women in the Atlantic world cannot be told in isolation from men or from the Western world. The shift from West African "public mothers" to Brazilian "Black Mothers" is not a simple echo or transformation or perversion of "traditional" African ideals. In both West Africa and in the Americas, the image of the mother figure has always been fraught with paradox and contradiction. In their comparative study of black and white feminisms in the United States, American authors Gloria Joseph and Jill Lewis try to capture this ambivalent ideal of black motherhood: "The Black mother, however, is also a woman, and herein lies the great contradiction. The 'honored' mother is the same second-class citizen who is often regarded and treated as an object to be used, bruised, and abused. . . . The societal attitude toward Mother is one of both idealization and degradation. The mother's role in the family is symbolic of contradictions and contrasts."[64] While Joseph and Lewis are writing of black American women, it is difficult to talk about the "Black mother" without conjuring up an image of Africa. Their observation emphasizes that the ten-

Alákétu Adewori during his enthronement ceremonies, photographed by Pierre Verger. The similarity between his posture and that of Maria Bibiana do Espírito Santo, or Mãe Senhora of the Ilê Axé Opô Afonjá (*next page*), raises questions about how women and men visually represent their power as "public mothers" and kings and about the role of the photographer and "subject" in determining poses. Foto Pierre Verger © Fundação Pierre Verger.

sion between women's power and vulnerability lies beyond the physicality of biological motherhood. And if "mothers" are surrounded by blind reverence and mystique, they run the risk of being misunderstood, even when they are neither defamed nor forgotten.

Indeed, "mothers" and symbols of their power have persevered on both sides of the Atlantic in the form of West African "public mothers" who are allied with kings and Brazilian "mothers-in-saint" who are partnered with men.

Maria Bibiana do Espírito Santo, or Mãe Senhora, was head priest or *mãe- de-santo*
of the Ilê Axé Opô Afonjá from 1942 to 1967. She descends from one of the three
"mothers" said to have established the Candomblé religion in Salvador, Brazil.
Her son, artist Mestre Didi, claimed ancestral ties to Kétu through a praise name
that she taught him, thereby reinforcing her renown and authenticity as a "Black
Mother" in the Candomblé community and the Brazilian public.
Foto Pierre Verger © Fundação Pierre Verger

Such relationships evoke several pairings in the study of Africa and a broader
Atlantic world that are more complex than they seem: motherhood and fatherhood; power and vulnerability; gold and glass. Even during the "second" independence of Africa—the democratic renewal of the 1990s—these concepts
have shaped Kétu's evolving relationship with Brazil and the "rediscovery" of
"public mothers" and kings.

Epilogue: A Rebirth of "Public Mothers" and Kings

In 1994, Kétu celebrated the centennial of the "rebirth" of the town, recalling Kétu's destruction in a war with Dahomey in 1886 and its renewal under the aegis of the French colonial state eight years later. By the end of the twentieth century, fewer than forty years had passed since French colonial rule came to an end in 1960. But Kétu had been "reborn" in multiple ways: as a town and kingdom, as part of a newly democratic Béninois nation, and as part of an Atlantic world. Scheduled events during the week-long celebration showcased Kétu's prominent place in a broader Yoruba culture and the "multiethnic" nature of the Kétu region. In a booklet commemorating the occasion, one commentator spoke of "a demonstration of national culture and an occasion to reunite people from Kétu scattered around the world."[1]

The era of democratic renewal serves as a fitting conclusion to the present study. Kingship and "public motherhood" in Kétu had been redefined with royal women ministers and with a new woman mayor, demonstrating the town's "rebirth" and transformation in terms of gender and power.

"Rebirth" of a King

The language of "rebirth" was part of the national rhetoric of Bénin during the period of democratization, which began in 1989 and culminated in 1991 with the multiparty election of Nicéphore Soglo. Rosine Soglo, the new president's wife, even founded a new party evoking this theme of new beginnings, the Renaissance du Bénin (Rebirth of Bénin Party). At the same time, kings like Alákétu Adétútù were reclaiming power and influence lost in the two decades of dictatorial rule under Mathieu Kérékou. Kérékou, who took power after a 1972 military coup, had reduced even the symbolic power of kings by eliminating the title of "village chief," used in the colonial period for men formally recognized as kings and for local elites who competed for such positions. Titles like "delegate" and "mayor" had been substituted. Alákétu Adétútù, though still recognized as king, lost the contest for mayor to his own cousin.[2] Such "traditional" leaders faced strong antagonism, if not outright attack, from the Kérékou regime, as kings across Bénin strove to reassert their power and formed the General Council of Kings, Queens, and Traditional Chiefs of Bénin in the early 1990s. Kérékou's authority, in a stunning reversal, was for a short time "effectively emasculated," as one scholar put it.[3]

Within months of the 1990 National Conference, which appointed Nicéphore Soglo as interim prime minister, Alákétu Adétútù was on a goodwill tour to Brazil sponsored by the Béninois and Brazilian governments.[4] The voyage drew not only on a history of government-sponsored travel and closer diplomatic and economic ties between Brazil and the Bight of Bénin that began in the 1960s, but also on forced and free travel in the era of the Atlantic slave trade.[5] The king of Kétu was accompanied by the minister of foreign affairs and a friend representing the head minister of Kétu in a trip that presaged Soglo's own interest in developing tourism around the history of the slave trade in Bénin. During his presidency, two UNESCO-funded programs—the Ouidah 92 Vodun Art Festival and the Route des Esclaves (Slave Route Project)—sought to remember the transatlantic slave trade while celebrating African history and culture. The Slave Route Project, launched in Ouidah in 1994, has educational, artistic, and tourism components; a declaration was made in Accra, Ghana, vowing to "identify, restore and promote sites, buildings and places of memory linked to the slave trade and slavery in order to develop a tourist trade focused on remembrance."[6] Alákétu Adétútù's venture to Brazil pointed out that the slave routes emanating from the coast of Bénin had origins in the African interior. As emissary of the newly democratic government of Bénin, Alákétu Adétútù embodied this history and memory of the Atlantic slave trade that had connected West Africa and Brazil, but as the king of Kétu, he evoked something more. The oral and written histories linked the founding of the Afro-Brazilian Candomblé to women who traveled back and forth from West Africa and, some say, specifically back to Kétu.[7]

Alákétu Adétútù's second trip to Brazil in 1994, just before the centennial celebration, was funded by an Argentinian cultural institute that sponsored the king's visit as an honorary guest at the Second International Congress of Afro-American Culture in Salvador, Brazil.[8] Associates of the king of Kétu had taken the initiative in contacting sponsors, but it is unlikely that the king, who identified himself as Catholic, was seeking to emphasize his authority in Yoruba religion. In the late 1990s, when a Brazilian musician turned government official, Gilberto Gil, arrived in Kétu to trace French photographer Pierre Verger's research in Kétu and other parts of West Africa, Alákétu Adétútù reminisced about the Yoruba religious shrines Verger had shown *him* in Brazil.[9] Alákétu Adétútù could make use of symbolic authority as the king of Kétu without abusing his own stature.

This appeal to the past glory of kingship during this historic moment of democratization in Africa was not contradictory. To evoke "tradition" was neither simply backward-looking nor overtly patriarchal. The revitalization of the king of Kétu's stature depended on a new national and international prominence that used the *image* of tradition since the precolonial political power of kings could not be resurrected in any substantive way. Even though Alákétu Adétútù was mainly exercising the most symbolic aspects of his rule after decades of dictatorial rule, his prominence during the new era of democratization was still a true resurgence.

Alákétu Adétútù's "rebirth" occurred within the context of his own transit (by plane rather than ship), flying above the routes of slave passages across the Atlantic Ocean, which, like the paths of migration from the Americas to Africa, was strongly defined by gender as well as by race. Over the centuries of transit in both directions, the percentage of men was higher, and the common image of the slave and the Brazilian traveler often was that of a young man. Yet the mythologized history that links Kétu to Brazil actually illuminates quite diverse travelers, including young enslaved girls from Kétu and mature and elderly women priests from Brazil. That it was a king of Kétu and male ministers who traveled to Brazil need not deny the image and presence of women as slaves, priests, and travelers in an Atlantic world. The image of a jet-setting king was incorporated into the tribute to kingship in the 1994 centennial events, and

Alákétu Adétútù, king of Kétu from 1963 to 2002, was invited to participate in the Second International Congress of Afro-American Culture in Salvador, Brazil, in 1994; he is pictured here with Kétu royal minister Antonin Iko Alayé to his left. The king's visit echoed the fabled, forced migration of the Kétu "mothers" said to have established Candomblé and the more recent migrations of scholars and travelers who have voyaged back and forth between Africa and the Americas. Photograph courtesy of Ilé Àṣe Oṣun Doyo, Instituto de Investigació y la Difusió de las Culturas Negras [Institute for the Investigation and Diffusion of Black Cultures], Buenos Aires, Argentina.

Kétu residents understood the contrast between Alákétu Adétútù's extensive tours and the past seclusion of the kings of Kétu. The celebratory pamphlet also drew special attention to the role of women royal ministers associated with the king; "public mothers" were an important part of Alákétu Adétútù's reign, a period that evoked past practices but reconfigured them in the present.

"Mothers of All Kétu" Revisited

Unlike the eighteenth- and nineteenth-century accounts of mother figures associated with the kings of Ọyọ and Dahomey, only in the postcolonial period are there definite records of royal women ministers in Kétu. The nineteenth-century "mothers of all Kétu" are unnamed, and the information on official women ministers and other prominent women in Kétu, even as recently as the

early to mid-twentieth century, is disputed. Before I ever inquired about female ministers in Kétu, I heard of a woman named Ṣanibi, important during
the reign of Aláké̩tu Odemufekun, king from 1918 to 1936. Her own descendants
said she had been Ìyá O̩ba (Mother of the King), a symbolic role, but a few elderly persons remembered her as another top female minister, the Ìyá Libara.[10]
Adrien Adegnika, a retired schoolteacher and member of the Mefu royal family
from which Odemufekun and Ṣanibi hailed, referred to Ṣanibi as an Ìyá Kétu
(Mother of Kétu). He told me that Mother of Kétu was a supreme title of honor
for women who intervened on behalf of people to resolve their problems. Chosen based on age, attitude, and appeal, such a woman would have been recognized by the entire population. Adegnika denied that women were ever recognized as ministers of the king, but he reconsidered his assertion about women
as royal ministers when he began to talk about the position of the Ìyá Libara,
providing the only attempted translation of her title as "mother who rids us
from misfortune."

Many would agree that the Ìyá Libara, described in the centennial publication as a "Grande Royale," was foremost among women titleholders, a member
of the royal family who served as an advisor to the king. Adegnika asserts that
this title first appeared under Aláké̩tu Adewori, king of Kétu from 1937 to 1963.[11]
Pictured in an old photograph in the 1994 pamphlet was the Ìyá Libara during Aláké̩tu Adewori's reign, a woman named Okonou Iko Adeoti who was so
popular and effective as Ìyá Libara that she continued to serve under the next
king, Aláké̩tu Adétútù, until her own death in 1982, even though Aláké̩tu Adétútù was from a different royal family.[12] Her successor, Ìyá Libara Cathérine
Oyewole Adebiyi, also featured in the 1994 publication, told me of the importance of the Ìyá Libara title, declaring that had she been a man she could have
been king.

The Ìyálóde (Mother Owns the Outside World) Adunni, described as a
minister of women and religion, is still fondly remembered as a powerful woman,
though a successor, Ìyálóde Basilia Abero, had been named to that post when I
arrived in Kétu for the first time in 1997. A controversial figure, Ìyálóde Basilia
Abero has been a target of hostility. During an interview one man compared
her problems to those of Kétu royal wife and French colonial agent Alaba Ida.
Though the title of Ìyálóde dates back at least to the nineteenth century in Yoruba towns, it is a new title in Kétu. Aláké̩tu Adétútù, known for bestowing
honorary titles on wealthy patrons and visitors, introduced the title of Ìyálóde
in Kétu after learning that it was a historical title in major Yoruba kingdoms in
Nigeria.[13] The role of the Ìyálóde was described as a female advisor to the king

especially charged with the affairs of the market, but in Kétu, the title partly duplicated that of Ìyá Libara; the reigning Ìyá Libara and Ìyálóde whom I met each told me that she was the "leader of all the women."[14] Nor was it uncommon for people to say that Ìyálóde had existed in the past. While I was interviewing one Kétu Muslim man, he asked some elderly women sitting nearby for names of important women from the past. The women mentioned a woman, a Muslim woman even, who they said had been Ìyálóde before the time Alákétu Adétútù was said to have brought the title to Kétu.[15] They laughed and shook their heads at the suggestion that the title of Ìyálóde in Kétu was only a recent creation.

The third woman pictured in the 1994 brochure was Ìyá Afọbajẹ (Mother Who Ends the Time of Spoiling) Salamantou Egunlope Brouaima, a woman charged with naming and installing kings. Although her title was described to me as "honorific," suggesting that it was newer and not the same as the ministerial ones, Ìyá Afọbajẹ Salamantou Brouaima was, in fact, one of the most respected women in Kétu in the late 1990s.[16] Well-versed in the town's oral history, she found herself caught between her titled role in the kingdom and her identity as a Muslim woman. She told me that women in her Muslim prayer group, or *asalatu* (from *salat*, Arabic for prayer), which met to study the Qur'an, rejected her because she wore the beads indicating her role at the king's palace. (Beads are associated with indigenous religion, linking the spiritual and social worlds.)[17] That these most powerful women were still vulnerable to challenges to their authority and person captures well the contradictory nature of their position as "mother figures" in West African history.

Despite the strong and stately presence of these women ministers in Kétu in the postcolonial era, most of their predecessors have been lost to the historical record, whether women with established titles or women more informally recognized by the town. I used my one piece of evidence about the precolonial existence of publicly recognized women in Kétu—the brief note in Charles Gollmer's 1859 missionary account about the three "mothers of all Kétu"—to preface my questions about high-ranking women ministers in Kétu in the past. Inevitably, people mentioned the Ìyá Libara, Ìyá Ọba, and Afin Ọba Obìnrin, a woman charged with handling worship of *òrìṣà* (deities) for the king. No one could reliably name previous Ìyá Libara or Ìyá Ọba, much less Afin Ọba Obìnrin for the nineteenth century or even for the first half of the twentieth century, during the colonial period.[18] It would be ahistorical to project these women's titles into nineteenth-century Kétu, even with the written accounts and oral sources describing similar titled women in other Yoruba towns. The top women ministers in Kétu in the 1990s also diverged in one significant way from the titled women in Ọyọ in the eighteenth and nineteenth centuries discussed in chapter 2. The "public mothers" in precolonial Ọyọ were drawn from wives, dependents, or slaves living in the royal residence, while the Ìyá Libara, Ìyá Ọba, and Afin Ọba Obìnrin in Kétu were said to have been named from the paternal side of the king's family. The Ìyá Libara and the Ìyálóde could live and operate outside of the king's residence, unlike the Ìyá Ọba and Afin Ọba Obìnrin who were said to stay close to the king.[19] Because they were not wives who had risen in the ranks of the royal household but women translating their power within the ruling family into a role related to kingship and town government, perhaps the highest ranking women ministers in Kétu were acting as "public mothers" in a sense more similar to that of the king as the ultimate "public father."

In contrast to the invisibility of Kétu women ministers during the precolonial and early colonial period, over the border in Nigeria, a British colonial officer reporting on the history and politics of the town of Abẹokuta in Nigeria in 1937 commented, "Today, women's affairs are mostly petty matters of sanitation, they told me with disgust; in the old days they were concerned with war."[20] Women ministers and officials continued to serve in Yoruba towns in Nigeria during the colonial period; another British colonial administrator listed the top women minister for more than twenty towns in one Yoruba-speaking district. The top woman minister, whether an Ìyálóde or a similar official, named other women as her assistants.[21] In Kétu in the summer of 1997, a group of women, some of whom held various titles, accompanied Ìyálóde Basilia Abero as she greeted a group of Béninois government officials. Because I was staying in her compound at the time, I too was swept up in the ceremony as a dancing member of her entourage.[22] Considering the ongoing communication and travel between a town like Kétu in Bénin and other Yoruba towns in Nigeria, it would be surprising if there had been no similar titled positions for women in Kétu dating to the precolonial period and extending, albeit transformed, during the colonial period. Still, it is difficult to know how and when certain titles for women came into existence in Kétu during the period before 1960. Because of the elasticity of the use of the title Ìyá (Mother) for elder women, priests, and divinities, people in Kétu disagree, each remembering differently the significance of women in "public" positions.

For some, the ambiguous power of these women suggests two opposite trends: the resilience of long-lost matriarchy or the maintenance of patriarchy. But neither scenario alone is a useful way of thinking about these com-

The late Cathérine Oyewole Adebiyi, Ìyá Libara of Kétu, shown here in 1999, once told me that she could have been king had she been a man. Photograph by author.

plex relationships. Women ordinarily did not rule over the entire community through these titled positions, and the women's political relationship with the town was defined through a link to the king. It is the connection between kings as ultimate "father figures" and these symbolic "mothers" that is most significant, not simply for collaboration in decision making but for the way symbolic fathers and mothers defined one another. Often this connection is overlooked when the power of kings and other leading men is emphasized. Sometimes the influence of certain well-placed women is highlighted without reference to men. The seductive concept of "complementarity"—the idea that African women were historically equally represented in politics, society, and households by women who were counterparts to leading men—builds too easily upon certain fixed assumptions about femininity versus masculinity; private versus public; religious versus political. These simple contrasts are at the heart of the limits, hierarchies, and inequalities that shape the lives of women, youth, junior siblings, widows, and anyone with less access to resources.

The popular saying "mother is gold, father is glass," used as a point of departure, captures these multiple and changing relationships between women, men, power, and vulnerability, especially in Kétu as kingship and public motherhood have been "reborn" in the decades since independence. While neither the idea of women royal ministers nor of transatlantic ties is new for Kétu, the concepts of "public motherhood" and a "black" Atlantic world were still transformed even more when a woman become mayor of Kétu in 2005.

Meet Madam Mayor

Mayor Lucie Sessinou Tidjani, a Gbe (Mahi) woman from Kétu, began her improbable rise to her position of power through local political party work. Drawn to the development issues that continued to plague Kétu, including road construction, education, maternal health, and general poverty, she saw opportunities to address issues facing women and children. By 2003, she was the first assistant to the mayor—the top three positions in the Kétu council must be shared between the Kétu, Gbe (Mahi), and Ohori populations that make up the region.[23] The sudden death of the mayor, followed by the resignation of his successor, led to an emergency session in which the local council unanimously voted Tidjani into office as mayor on July 4, 2005.

Tidjani's appointment as the third woman mayor in Bénin—the first in Kétu—occurred during the time of the new decentralization policy put in place by then president Mathieu Kérékou, who had ruled as a dictator for almost two decades but who had refashioned himself in the years after the period of "democratic renewal," whereupon he served as president from 1996 to 2006. Since 2002, decentralization policies have mandated that individual communities in Bénin be self-supporting and self-sufficient. Tidjani was searching out development partners around the world to advise and support an ambitious set of projects in Kétu ranging from sanitation, improved facilities at the main market, and agricultural development to a cyber café, museum, and shopping mall. To realize these plans, Tidjani was eagerly seeking organizations in the United States and Europe and was traveling internationally; she attended a meeting of African mayors in Nairobi, Kenya, the week before I met with her in October 2006.[24]

Tidjani's tactics and vision suggest an image of women's power beyond that of "mothers" or "wives," even though she frequently touts her own personal experience as a woman, mother, and wife when discussing her work. In a 2006 interview that appeared on the official government website for the region, she responded to the charge that she is a "fervent militant for gender and development," saying, "The only thing that I know is that as a woman, for the past two and a half years, I have tried to demonstrate that I am capable, I worked, I tried to show men through my work that a woman is capable of many things. Besides, women address and better manage things than men. . . . It is that men don't pay attention, a woman, she observes the most minor details. When ready, she does everything to succeed."[25]

While Tidjani uses the image of "mother" and "wife" literally, she recognizes the symbolic power of the king and his women ministers in the community. Outside the mayor's office I met two women who now hold honorific titles bestowed by the current Alákétu Aladé Ìfẹ́. As much as Tidjani asserts her power as a woman who used the challenges she faced as a wife and mother to prepare for her political career, she does not ignore the profound vulnerability of wives, grandmothers, and daughters. She wants to encourage women to become political and to participate in local development, because "if women suffer, it is the whole community that suffers."[26]

On one hand, Mayor Tidjani captures how women's experience and the study of gender merge in daily life, and she reorients the relationship between Africa and the African diaspora. On the other hand, as a middle-aged woman, Tidjani does not fit the mold of the symbolic elderly "mother figure" who historically wielded power in Kétu and elsewhere in the Bight of Bénin. Instead, building on her identity as a woman, mother, wife, and activist, she potentially defines a new era of politics. Rather than seeking connections through the former slave trade routes that connected Kétu to the Bahia region of Brazil, she sees new possibilities in Europe, North America, and Africa itself. By 2009, following an apparently controversial re-election bid by Tidjani, a Kétu man assumed the position of mayor and Tidjani was back to being a regional counselor. Only time will tell how people will recall and represent this historical period in the future. [27]

My title, *Mother Is Gold, Father Is Glass,* seeks to convey the tension between the rhetoric of women's power as "public mothers," "queens," and priests in West Africa and the realities of women's subordination and vulnerability as wives, young mothers, and slaves. Shaped both by their links to "fathers" and husbands and by larger cultural ideals of power and identity, some women have been highly valued by kings, others have been abandoned by husbands, and still others objectified by French colonial policies. As part of a collection of kingdoms and towns that shared—sometimes closely and other times loosely—a religion, culture, and language, Kétu women and men did not come up with ideals about gender and power in isolation. The transatlantic slave-trade transported ideas and practices to the Americas, but never whole and always altered in form and meaning. The image of mothers and wives has been tenacious across West Africa and in the Americas, though these concepts have been flexible and adaptable, reflecting the impact of the Atlantic slave trade, French colonialism, and more recent travel between West Africa and Brazil.

The question then becomes whether societies and scholars can understand the multiple identities women (and men) have occupied historically, and sometimes simultaneously, as priests, travelers, slaves, royal ministers, traders, and government officials, while pushing the boundaries of their symbolic positions as "mothers" and "wives" (and "fathers" and "husbands"). The slippage between the realities and symbolism of motherhood is not unlike the blurring of sex and gender in academic writing and popular culture; historian Joan Scott observes that "academics are not much better than the general public at maintaining the distinction between the physical and the social (nature and culture, body and mind) that the introduction of 'gender' was meant to achieve."[28] The widespread failure to differentiate between the physical nature of sex and the social definition of gender in academic writing and popular culture is precisely the point. The social definition of gender is so powerful that it seems "natural" even as scholars have shown that the physical definition of sex itself based in appearance and in scientific testing is not a given.[29] Though in many African societies, cultural processes and ceremonies define gender together with the physical body, the connection between women's sexuality and motherhood is often assumed, thus obscuring broader cultural ideas about motherhood and power.[30]

Linked to the confusion over sex and gender is a distinction some scholars would like to make between women's history and gender history—differences that reflect ongoing debates over feminism and feminist theory. Some Africanist scholars, more likely perhaps to identify themselves as women's historians, highlight the "resilience of (colonial) patriarchies." Those Africanists who use "gender" more deliberately as an analytical tool seek to examine "social and symbolic relations" and to shed assumptions about women's subjugation, resistance, and "universal" experience.[31] Still other Africanists, some with African backgrounds, question the Western feminist ideals that have shaped the debate between women's and gender history. Several African feminists, many of them literary scholars, have developed alternative concepts for African feminism(s) that emphasize the importance of diverse African cultural practices, the African "tradition" of "complementarity" or power sharing and negotiation between African women and men, and the larger social and political problems confronting African women and men.[32]

Debates over women's and gender history reveal what may come to be a fruitful middle ground that encompasses "feminisms" between and among Western and African scholars. Zimbabwean writer and economist Paul Tiyambe Zeleza acknowledges that "gender history cannot go far without the continuous retrieval of women's history, while women's history cannot transform the fundamentally flawed paradigmatic bases of 'mainstream' history without gender history."[33] By echoing the concept of "complementarity" espoused by some Africanist feminists, scholarship on women and gender could "balance" one another not because they are so different but because both women's and gender studies endeavor to rewrite traditional history and transform society.

Thus feminist scholars and activists of Africa, Asia, and Latin America have taken up issues such as access to clean water, housing, war, human rights, and development policy, showing how society itself, not just women's place within it, may be reconfigured.[34] In these intellectual and political endeavors, diverse experiences, local practices, and ideologies of womanhood and manhood must be taken seriously. Still, the ultimate challenge lies in a thorough reconceptualization of research and activism that is no longer a reaction to Western models. Broadening the time and space of the African diaspora to include the post–Atlantic slave trade era and the period of European colonialism in Africa encompasses the more complex experiences and relationships among all Atlantic communities—African, American, and European. To think creatively about the connections between gender and power on all sides of the Atlantic Ocean is to reveal more than a "renaissance" or a transformation of society; to write such a history gives birth to something entirely new.

Essay on Sources and Methodology

Like other Africanist historians, I have been eclectic and have sought to be innovative in gathering and using evidence. Thus I have juxtaposed my reinterpretation of archival sources and analyses of ethnographies and I have examined works of fiction alongside unpublished field notes of researchers. While this diversity of research materials attests to Kétu's rich and complex history within West Africa and a broader Atlantic world, it also demonstrates the particular challenges and rewards of writing Africanist history. I have elaborated in the text on source materials where appropriate. In this essay, I discuss how I have woven sources together, reflecting the concept of "dialogue," as used in the book, to describe Kétu's ongoing relationship with the Bahia region of Brazil. By placing written and oral sources in a conversation, I have tried to capture the dynamism of African history itself.

Oral traditions—defined as town histories and genealogies passed down for generations—are one of the classic sources for precolonial African history. The conventional guides to using such sources, Jan Vansina's *Oral Tradition: A Study in Historical Methodology,* trans. H. M. Wright (Chicago: Aldine Publishing Co., 1965), David Henige's *Oral Historiography* (Oxford: Clarendon Press, 1982), and Joseph Miller's edited volume, *The African Past Speaks: Essays on Oral Tradition and History* (Folkestone, England: Dawson; Hamden, Conn.: Archon, 1980), provide scholars with tools to analyze facts embedded in oral data likely to have been manipulated and used for political purposes. Because of such problems with oral traditions, some scholars have ceased to use them to help reconstruct the past. Contributors to the volume edited by Luise White, Stephen Miescher, and David Cohen, *African Words, African Voices: Critical Practices in Oral History* (Bloomington: Indiana University Press, 2001), explore the symbolism, performance, and power relationships represented in oral traditions more than the historical content itself.

I myself decided that the methods offered by Vansina, Henige, and Miller would keep my own focus too narrow and that the approach of White, Miescher, and Cohen would distance me from the historical narrative I was trying to recreate. Borrowing from both, I took a middle road: to examine oral traditions seriously while simultaneously demonstrating their historical and symbolic power and value. So, for example, while oral traditions of Kétu's history, written down as early as the mid-nineteenth century, tell of a kingdom founded by "fathers" yet incorporate "mother figures" and wives as participants in the historical process of establishing the settlement, I do not focus on whether such stories could have been reliably handed down over the centuries. Instead, I discuss how these stories reflect contemporary ideologies about the role of "public mothers" in politics and religion, looking at oral sources more broadly and symbolically and in relation to the historical context and neighboring states. Broadening my perspective beyond Kétu meant I could draw from a larger body of texts, yielding a more forceful argument about the contradictory nature of gender relationships in West Africa and the connections to ideologies within a colonizing French nation. Viewing Kétu through a wide-angle lens also opened up links with African diaspora communities in the northeast Bahia region of Brazil.

If African oral tradition represents a valuable, lost, insider perspective, the European man's travel narrative epitomizes an outsider, and often male, bias. A close reading of texts can allow scholars to, in the words of historian Marc Bloch, "overhear what was never intended to be said."[1] European travel accounts that are often pro–slave trade or anti–slave trade do not only reveal generalities on kingship, religions, slave trading and culture, but also a historical trajectory of tension between the role of "mothers" and the role of "wives" throughout the eighteenth and nineteenth centuries. Though the European authors of these travel narratives did not realize it, these written sources chronicle the increasing presence of royal wives. They also foretell France's anxiety about the social and legal position of African wives in its West African colonies. Inspired by Robert Harms's *The Diligent: A Voyage through the Worlds of the Slave Trade* (New York: Basic Books, 2002), which weaves many of these travel accounts into a compelling narrative of eighteenth-century West Africa, I looked further for stories and conversations in European accounts. William Snelgrave's stories about the elderly woman from the Dahomey palace rescued off the shores of Ouidah, or about his own conversation with the Dahomean king, revealed a great deal about the historical context. Thus stories and conversations embedded in traveler accounts offer a window onto the attitudes and ideas of African women and men and of European men toward them in the precolonial era, whatever the interests and perspective of the author.

European missionaries, like European traders and travelers, were outsiders, but with their proselytizing efforts, their often longer stay in Africa, and their more intimate knowledge of local culture and language, European, American, and especially West African missionaries exposed more of their personal experience in their accounts. Missionaries' reports and letters home were part descriptive account and part conversation among missionaries and between missionaries and potential converts. In his *Religious Encounter and the Making of the Yoruba* (Bloomington: Indiana University Press, 2000), John Peel emphasizes the individual histories and religious imagery central to missionary writings. Though I examined the original journals of missionaries at the Church Missionary Society archives in Birmingham, Great Britain, and later reviewed them in microfilm at Yale University, it was in the collection of letters written by Southern Baptist missionary Thomas Bowen at the Southern Baptist Convention library in Nashville, Tennessee, that I recognized the stylized emotion yet deeply felt fervor of evangelical revival still prevalent in the nineteenth century. Thus, I analyzed missionaries' stories of sentiment as part of larger issues of religion, race, and gender.

For the period through World War I, before colonial documentation became increasingly bureaucratized and formulaic, the reports of French colonial administrators, especially lower-ranking ones on the ground, are also detailed and descriptive, exposing more of the relationship between colonial authorities and local African populations than perhaps colonial officials intended. Debates over the performance of Alaba Ida or Yá Ṣẹ̀gẹ́n as colonial agents or over a rare child custody court case in 1912 are part of a series of letters, opinions, and judgments that were, sometimes and sometimes not, shaped by what people in Kétu were doing in everyday life. In examining these documents, I have been influenced by the "culture and colonialism" concept explored in Frederick Cooper and Ann Laura Stoler's edited volume *Tensions of Empire: Colonial Cultures in a Bourgeois World* (Berkeley: University of California Press, 1997), which emphasizes the interplay between European and African ideas about labor, gender, sexuality, and citizenship. Often I have found the European perspective explored more fully in such studies, hence, as my historical narrative moved on multiple levels from specific West African kingdoms to the broader West African region, as well as to Europe and the Americas, I endeavored to keep Kétu central to the story.

I interviewed about a hundred individuals in Kétu (several more than once) in the summer of 1997, from September 1998 to June 1999, from April to June 2000, and in October 2006. The majority of the interviews were in Yoruba and French, conducted with the help of my research assistant Alhaja Safouratou Mama. I had prepared questions for her to use as a guide. While I could understand the general flow of the conversation and ask for clarification, she translated my questions from French and the interviewee's responses from Yoruba. Once we had completed several interviews, she was able to conduct them more like a conversation, picking up on the tangents that she knew interested me, pressing on points that she and I had discussed about the history of Kétu. Because I had talked to both women and men, I found, embedded in those discussions, a crucial theme of my book on women and gender: men, and to some extent fatherhood. Ironically, however, I initially found it difficult to portray or to use those conversations in the book, though I had read and taught several books and essays on the nature of interviews, the power dynamic between researcher and interviewee, and the performance that is part of the interview process.[2]

This book is about the concept of "public motherhood" first and kingship and marriage second; it is the image of "public motherhood" that raised the theoretical and historical questions about social change and power at the center of the book. Though I have been critical of studies of gender that exclude men and masculinity, at first I myself did not intellectually engage with the kings, missionaries, and traders who were popping up in my own book and *their* relationships with women. By beginning to incorporate the conversation between "public mothers" and kings, between spouses, and between women and men who were spiritual and intellectual partners in the Brazilian religion of Candomblé, I was able to trace more sharply the changing meanings of "public motherhood" in precolonial and colonial Kétu and in a broader Atlantic world. In the process, I have carved out a "middle way" for myself, bridging the work of scholars like Edna Bay and Randy Matory, whose different approaches to gender and culture in West Africa and Brazil ultimately focus on "wifeliness."[3]

I had not at first planned to include the Brazilian story in my book, but I concluded that it was an important part of the history. I first learned of Pierre Verger's extended stay in Kétu by chance, during an interview with a descendant of the *babaláwo* (father owns the secrets) or diviner who had initiated Verger and instructed him in *ifá* divination.[4] Although I did not conduct fieldwork on the Brazilian religion of Candomblé, I was able to examine the rich history of the religion through ethnographies, letters, and unpublished field notes. I visited the Pierre Verger Foundation in Salvador, Brazil, to examine Verger's extensive scholarship on Atlantic world exchanges and, recalling the fortuitous remark from my field interview, came to realize his particular connection to Kétu. Letters written by Verger and other scholars, taken together with their published accounts, also revealed paradoxical concepts about women, men, and power in Candomblé, conjuring up similar images of "public motherhood" and kingship that I was examining in Atlantic Africa.

I also have incorporated a broader Atlantic world into my study to demonstrate the cosmopolitan history of a place, Kétu in Bénin, long considered a backwater. When I told my research assistant, herself from Kétu, that a nineteenth-century missionary wrote of hundreds of people attending a market day in Kétu, she did not believe me. Yet in the nineteenth century, traders from distant interior towns, and missionaries who were international travelers, passed through Kétu; by the twentieth century, different forms of those travel routes from and to Kétu were opening up again. Kétu's connection to a wider world embraces not only international travel but also regional trade and identities. Kétu residents themselves were, and are, diverse and engaged with multiple local and global contexts; the border with Nigeria, a few miles away, linked Kétu to other Yoruba-speaking towns and offered Kétu access to part of the British colonial empire.

The disparate sources I have explored have forced me not only to go beyond the usual sources in my research and analysis, but also to reconceptualize African history. I have been inspired by these texts and by my own multidisciplinary way of teaching African history with primary sources, novels, ethnography, and film. Taking into consideration the range of materials with which I seek to engage my students and illustrate Africa's dynamic history, I have tried to present the same vibrant story in this book.

Notes

Prologue

1. Linguist Oyekan Owomoyela reports the saying in its entirety as "mother is gold, father is glass; the day the mother dies is the day the gold is ruined; the day the father dies is the day the glass is gone," but he does not offer any date or source. Owomoyela, *Yoruba Proverbs,* 307. Owomoyela uses the Yoruba word *jígí* for glass.

2. Egunlete Elegbede, interview with the author, September 22, 2006. There is also a popular song originally released in the 1950s by Dele Ojo and His Star Brothers Band called "Iya Ni Wura," which celebrates women's sacrifices in motherhood. *Iya Ni Wura,* Deje Ojo and His Star Brothers Band, http://www.youtube.com/watch?v=PBTHDuhMcU8 (accessed July 14, 2009). People in Kétu often referred to a more recent song called "Iya Ni Wura" during my interviews in 2006, but I could not verify the singer or lyrics.

3. Yai, "Review of *Yoruba: Nine Centuries of African Art and Thought,* 24.

4. Alaketu Aladé Ìfé, interview with the author, September 19, 2006.

5. Garrard, "Myth and Metrology: The Early Trans-Saharan Trade," 460. Garrard even suggests that there was the potential for gold production in the region of Ile-Ifè.

6. Pierre Verger, *Flux et Reflux,* 129.

7. For examples, see Snelgrave, *A New Account of Some Parts of Guinea and the Slave Trade,* 34; Clapperton, *Hugh Clapperton into the Interior of Africa,* 96, 184.

8. Drewal and Mason, *Beads, Body, and Soul,* 39.

9. Alákétu Aladé Ìfé, interview with the author, September 19, 2006.

10. For a general short discussion on the ambivalent image of women and gender in Yoruba proverbs, see Yusuf, "Contradictory Yoruba Proverbs about Women, 206–15.

11. Olinto, *The King of Ketu,* 5.

12. "Voyages: The Trans-Atlantic Slave Trade Database," http://www.slavevoyages.org.

13. Eltis and Engerman, "Fluctuations in Sex and Age Ratios in the Transatlantic Slave Trade," 310. For a more complex explanation of the changes in the ethnicity and gender of people enslaved in the Bight of Benin, see Lovejoy, "The Yoruba Factor in the Trans-Atlantic Slave Trade," 40–55.

14. Eltis, "The Diaspora of Yoruba Speakers: Dimensions and Implications," 17–39.

15. Amadiume, *Male Daughters, Female Husbands*; Niara Sudarkasa, *The Strength of Our Mothers,* 171–72; Oyèwùmi, "Introduction: Feminism, Sisterhood, and other Foreign Relations," 15–16.

16. Rev. Samuel Johnson, *History of the Yorubas from the Earliest Time,* 65–66.

17. Asiwaju, "The Alaketu of Ketu and the Onimeko of Meko," 134–60.

18. Thompson, *Flash of the Spirit*, xiii–xviii; Gilroy, *The Black Atlantic*. For an overview of African diaspora studies, see Mann and Bay, "Shifting Paradigms in the Study of the African Diaspora," 3–21.

19. Guyer, *Marginal Gains*, 4; Young, *Rituals of Resistance*; Sweet, *Recreating Africa*. For some, "African Atlantic" is another way of writing about the African diaspora, especially for a period prior to the nineteenth century. Other scholars use the term "Atlantic world" to examine earlier European colonial empire in the Americas. For example, see Bailyn, "The Idea of Atlantic History," 19–41. For an overview of Atlantic world scholarship, see Games, "Atlantic History."

20. Oyěwùmi, "Family Bonds/Conceptual Binds," 1094, 1097. Several African feminists have emphasized a mother-centered ideology in African society. For example, see Acholonu, *Motherism: The Afrocentric Alternative to Feminism*.

21. Chikwenye Okonjo Ogunyẹmi, *Africa Wo/Man Palava*, 10, 46.

22. Some scholars examining how women have translated "private" roles as mothers into political organizing in African, Western, and Latin American contexts have defined such action as "maternalist" politics. Maternalist politics is defined narrowly in terms of a specific (often confrontational) relationship that self-defined mothers establish with the state. Examples of maternalist politics vary and include southeastern Nigerian women's "war" against the threat of taxation during the colonial period, black South African women's protest of pass laws restricting movement in urban areas, Argentine women's ongoing demonstrations for those who "disappeared" during the military dictatorship between 1976 and 1983, and Western women's demand for welfare rights in the twentieth century. While many scholars debate whether such maternalist activism is "feminist" or not, others focus on the symbolism behind maternalist politics. For a general overview of maternalist politics internationally, see Jetter, Orleck, and Taylor, *The Politics of Motherhood*; Wells, "Maternal Politics in Organizing Black South African Women," 253; Walker, "Conceptualising Motherhood in Twentieth Century South Africa," 417–37; Wolfe and Tucker, "Feminism Lives," 448; Koven and Michel, "Introduction: 'Mother Worlds,'" 2. In terms of case studies, research on the Igbo Women's War in 1929 in southeastern Nigeria has recognized, in different ways, how economic change and colonial taxation were perceived as threats to womanhood, whether in terms of social roles or fertility. Van Allen, "'Aba Riots' or 'Women's War,'" 59–85; Ifeka-Moller, "Female Militancy and Colonial Revolt," 127–57; Bastian, "'Vultures of the Marketplace,'" 260–81. Diana Taylor, in her creative interpretation of gender and the state in Argentina, argues that the activities of the Grandmothers of the Plaza de Mayo operate as a "bad script," replicating the victimization of women and the feminization of the general population under the masculinized military regime. Taylor, *Disappearing Acts*.

23. For overviews of feminist literature on motherhood, see Snitow, "Feminism and Motherhood," 33–51; and Arendell, "Conceiving and Investigating Motherhood," 1192–1207. For African American critiques, see Collins, *Black Feminist Thought*; James, "Mothering: A Possible Black Feminist Link to Social Transformation?" 45–56.

24. Lindsay and Miescher, "Introduction: Men and Masculinities in Modern African History," 5.

25. In 1999, a special volume on fatherhood in the *Journal of Family History* acknowledged that race was not addressed constructively in any of the contributions, none of which addressed Africa. Griswold, "Introduction to the Special Issue on Fatherhood," 251–54.

26. Relationships between siblings and other extended family members, such as aunts or elder mentors, could also be explored in more depth. On sisters, see Sacks, *Sisters and Wives*.

1. Founding Fathers and Metaphorical Mothers

1. Specific to Kétu and neighboring kingdoms, see Adediran, *The Frontier States of Western Yorùbáland*, 42, 68; Barnes, "The Many Faces of Ogun," 4–7. More generally on the theory of a matriarchal African past, see Diop, *Cultural Unity of Black Africa*; Amadiume, *Re-Inventing Africa: Matriarchy, Religion, and Culture*. For a general discussion of the matriarchal myth, see Eller, *The Myth of Matriarchal Prehistory*.

2. For an examination of how history, symbolism, and gender operate in oral histories in Dahomey, see Blier, "The Path of the Leopard," 394.

3. Iya Afobaje Salamantou Egunlope Brouaima, interview with the author, November 2, 1998.

4. Dunglas, "Contribution à l'histoire du Moyen-Dahomey," vol. I, 29. In Moulero's version, the person who assists them in Panku is another man, a hunter. Moulero, "Essai historique sur la ville de Kétou (suite)," 6.

5. Moulero, "Les rois de Kétou: Ordre de succession et éducation du candidat au trône," 11; Dunglas, "Contribution à l'histoire du Moyen-Dahomey," vol. I, 49–55; Parrinder, *The Story of Ketu*, 73.

6. Parrinder, *The Story of Ketu*, 11; Adediran, *Frontier States of Western Yorùbáland*, 68.

7. Johnson, *History of the Yorubas from the Earliest Times*, 3–12; Law, *The Oyo Empire, c.1600–c.1836*, 27–29.

8. Barber, *I Could Speak until Tomorrow*, 310n16; Apter, *Black Critics and Kings*, 31–34; Law, "Local Amateur Scholarship and the Construction of Yoruba Ethnicity," 55–90.

9. Steady, "African Feminism: A Worldwide Perspective," 8; Also see Steady, "The Black Woman Cross-Culturally: An Overview," 1–41. For an overview of literature tracing the concept of "complementarity" or "parallelism" in Latin American and Pacific societies, see Stoeltje, "Asante Queen Mothers: A Study in Female Authority," 44–45.

10. Okonjo denies that the "mother" and the king ever "clashed." Another scholar does find evidence of nineteenth-century conflict between a specific *omu* (mother) and king and refutes the claim that "mother" and king were literal counterparts, with equal or "parallel" power. Okonjo, "The Dual-Sex Political System in Operation," 47; Henderson, "Onitsha Woman: The Traditional Context for Political Power," 225, 238.

11. Barnes, "The Many Faces of Ogun," 2, 8.

12. Ogunyẹmi, *Africa Wo/Man Palava*, 46.

13. Comaroff and Comaroff, eds., *Modernity and its Malcontents*; Geschiere, *The Modernity of Witchcraft*.

14. Verger, "Grandeur et décadence du culte Ìyámi òsòròngà (ma mère la sorcière) chez les Yoruba," 141–243; Washington, *Our Mothers, Our Powers, Our Text*, 14–17.

15. Dunglas, "Contribution à l'histoire du Moyen-Dahomey," vol. I, 35.

16. He also traces the origins of Kétu to Ọyọ-Ile rather than Ile-Ifẹ in the process. Adediran, *Frontier States of Western Yorùbáland*, 74–80.

17. Moulero, "Essai historique sur la ville de Kétou: Le Roi Andé," 4; Dunglas, "Contribution à l'histoire du Moyen-Dahomey," vol. I, 63–64; Parrinder, *The Story of Ketu*, 25. Crowther may provide a description on an engraving on the Kétu palace gate depicting a Kétu victory over Dahomey "by the third king from the present one." Parrinder takes it to be a reference to Dahomey's attack on Iwoye during the reign of Akibiowu (c. 1780–1795), but the gory description of "Ketu victorious warriors standing in the piles of decapitated heads and their wives carrying some of the heads strung together in a triumphal march about the streets" sounds more like the violent victory that King Ande (c. 1760–1780) was said to have won over Da-

homey. Crowther, January 8, 1853, in "Account of a Journey to Ketu," Church Missionary Society (CMS), CA2/031/128.

18. Archibald Dalzel, British governor at Cape Coast Castle (Ghana) and supporter of the slave trade, wrote of a Dahomey victory over the town itself, whereas Kétu and Dahomey traditions emphasize not only the Dahomey attack on the outlying village of Iwoye (said to be the birthplace of the mother of Alákétu Akibiowu himself), but also the coincidence of two extraordinary events: the appearance of a fatally wounded elephant who collapsed between the two armies and the occasion of a solar eclipse. The dead elephant was thought to presage the demise of one of the kings. The solar eclipse was said in Kétu traditions to be evidence of the power of the king of Kétu. Dalzel, *The History of Dahomy*, 200–01; Dunglas, "Contribution à l'histoire du Moyen-Dahomey," vol. I, 69–70; Parrinder, *The Story of Ketu*, 34–35. For the story of the connection to Afro-Brazilian Candomblé through the kidnapped princess Otampê Ojarô, see Lima, "O conceito de "Nação" nos Candomblés da Bahia," 83–86, and chapter 7 below. In fact, there were no solar eclipses recorded in West Africa in 1789, but there was one on June 4, 1788. See "The NASA Eclipse Website: Solar Eclipse Explorer for Africa," http://eclipse.gsfc.nasa .gov/JSEX/JSEX-AF.html (accessed June 15, 2009). Given that King Kpengla of Dahomey died in 1789 during a time of political unrest, partly symbolized by the rumor that he died of smallpox, the earlier solar eclipse and the image of the elephant may have been incorporated into the oral histories of the battle in both Dahomey and Kétu. On the symbolism of smallpox in death of Dahomey kings, see Bay, *Wives of the Leopard*, 155–59.

19. Parrinder, *The Story of Ketu*, 76.

20. Iroko and Igue, *Les villes Yoruba du Dahomey*, 14–16. The Akaba Idena doorway was restored and declared a historical site by UNESCO.

21. For similar examples in other Yoruba towns, see Peel, *Ijeshas and Nigerians*; Barber, *I Could Speak until Tomorrow*, 50–62; Watson, " 'Ibadan-A Model of Historical Facts,'" 5–26.

22. Camille Elegbede, interview with the author, November 2, 1998, in the Ajapasu Kekere Compound, which claims origins among the Baatonu/Bariba; Jeanne Akanro and Vicencia Ode, interview with the author, December 9, 1998, in Gbudu Compound, which also traces the founders hometown among the Baatonu/Bariba; Camille Fagbohun and Pascal Fagbohun, interview with the author, January 15, 1999, in Mejioṣu Compound, where residents claim origins in Sabe (Savé); Maimounatou Soumanou, Nanfissatou Saliou, interview with the author, January 26, 1999, in the Ajati Compound in the Muslim quarter of Masafe, where people also trace their origins to Sabe; Felix Odjoawo, interview with the author, December 5, 1998, in Ojuare Compound, where people link their founder to the Tapa region. Lloyd, "The Yoruba Lineage," 241; Fagbite, "Sens des Mutations Socio-Economiques à Kétu," 52–56; Adediran, *Frontier States of Western Yorùbáland*, 184–85.

23. Goddard, "Town-Farm Relationship in Yorubaland," 21–29. In 1853, CMS missionary Samuel Crowther pegged Ijaka Oke as the eastern boundary of the Kétu kingdom. The village was twenty-four miles east of Kétu's town center and was a few miles away from outlying villages linked to Abẹokuta.

24. Bascom, "Urbanization Among the Yoruba," 446–54; Wheatley, "Significance of Traditional Yoruba Urbanism," 393–423; Lloyd, "The Yoruba: An Urban People?"; Law, "Towards a History of Urbanization in Pre-colonial Yorubaland."

25. Nanfissatou Saliou, interview with the author, January 26, 1999. The distant ancestor whose name was forgotten in this case traveled from Savé with his wife.

26. Raymond Fashain, interview with the author, November 11, 1998.

27. Alhaja Nanfissatou Saliou and Maimounatou Soumanou, interview with the author,

January 26, 1999; Salamantou Osseni, interview with the author, March 1, 1999; Berry, *Fathers Work for Their Sons*, 47n197.

28. McCabe, "Histories of Errancy," 46–49.

29. Adedoyin Olouye and Fatoke Casimir Elegbede, interview with the author, December 17, 1998.

30. Mamadou Imoru, interview with the author, January 28, 1999.

31. La Pin, "Story, Medium, and Masque," 30–35.

32. CMS, CA2/031/128, Reverend Samuel Crowther, Account of Journey to Kétu, January 16, 1853.

33. Archives Nationales du Bénin (ANB), 1E11 3-1, "Rapport sur la mission accomplie dans la region Kétou-Savé du 18 janvier au 20 février 1894," 3 mars, 1894.

34. Crowther, November 21 and November 22, 1852, in "Journal of Samuel Crowther for the quarter ending December 1852," CMS CA 2 031–034, Reel 61, Yale University Divinity Library (YUL), New Haven, Conn.

35. YUL, CMS CA 2 031–034, Reel 61, Reverend Samuel Crowther, August 23, 1846, in "Journal of Samuel Crowther ending September 25, 1846." When he first mentioned the Alá-kétu in his diary, Crowther referred to him as a "chief."

36. Asai may have been the Esa Kétu, a royal minister charged with welcoming visitors. CMS, CA2/031/128, Reverend Samuel Crowther, January 8, January 10, and January 15, 1853, in "Account of a Journey to Kétu, January 5–19, 1853."

37. ANB, 1E11 3-1, "Rapport sur la mission accomplie dans la region Kétou-Savé du 18 janvier au 20 février 1894," 3 mars, 1894.

38. The five royal families are Alapini, Magbo, Aro, Mefu, and Meṣa, and the most recent Alákétu (kings) named from each family have been: Aladé Ìfẹ́(Aro), Adétútù (Magbo), Adewori (Alapini), Odemufekun (Mefu), Onyegen (Mesha).

39. ANB, 1E11 3-1, "Rapport sur la mission accomplie dans la region Kétou-Savé du 18 janvier au 20 février 1894," 3 mars, 1894; Pied, "De Porto-Novo à Oyo, février–mars 1891," 265.

40. The term "oral historian" is Susan Geiger's; Miller uses the term "oral narrator." Miller, "Introduction: Listening for the African Past," 5–6; Geiger, "What's So Feminist about Women's Oral History?" 180n6.

41. R. P. Thomas Moulero was ordained in 1928. Paul Ignace Faly, also of Kétu, was ordained in 1949. Asiwaju, *Western Yorubaland under European Rule 1889–1945*, 242.

42. Ibid., 33n11; Drewal, "Thomas Moulero: Historian of Gèlèdé," *The University of African Art Press*, 2008, 4, http://www.universityofafricanart.org/Image/Text/drewal%20moulero.pdf (accessed August 13, 2009); Drewal and Drewal, *Gẹ̀lẹ̀dẹ́: Art and Female Power among the Yoruba*; Olinto, *The Water House*, 210.

43. The manuscript for Dunglas's article is located at the former Institut de la Recherche Appliqué du Dahomey (IRAD). Edouard Dunglas, "Légendes et Histoire du Royaume-Kétou," typescript, n.d. British missionary and religious scholar Geoffrey Parrinder worked with Dunglas during his research, publishing an English version based on his collaboration with Dunglas. Even though Parrinder claimed to have done his own additional research to produce an original work, since it is so close to Dunglas's version, it will not be analyzed in detail here. Parrinder's text is footnoted where relevant. Parrinder, *The Story of Ketu*, 3. For a recent French translation of Parrinder's book, see Parrinder, *Les Vicissitudes de l'histoire de Kétou*.

44. Moulero, "Essai historique," vol. 9, 7.

45. Iroko, "Les personnes agées n'ont jamais eu en Afrique le monopole de la tradition."

46. Dunglas, "Contribution à l'histoire du Moyen-Dahomey," vol. I, 11–15.

47. Moulero, "Essai historique sur la ville de Kétou," vol. 9, 7n1; Moulero, "Essai historique sur la ville de Kétou: Le Roi Adiro (suite)," 3; Moulero wrote that it was "difficult to discern between legend and the historical," in Moulero, "Essai historique sur la ville de Kétou: Les travaux des premiers rois," 4.

48. Quayson, Strategic Transformations in Nigerian Writings, 40.

49. Dunglas, "Contribution à l'histoire du Moyen-Dahomey," vol. I, 37.

50. Ibid., 60–61, 64, 100–101. Dunglas also collected songs in the Gbe language of Dahomey. For example, see Dunglas, "Contribution à l'histoire du Moyen-Dahomey," vol. II, 114, 118.

51. Moulero, "Les rois de Kétou," 7–8.

52. Dunglas, "Contribution à l'histoire du Moyen-Dahomey," vol. I, 59.

53. Cohen, Rulers of Empire; Harrison writes of earlier scholar-administrators and their engagement with West African Islam in Harrison, France and Islam in West Africa, 1860–1960, 97–117.

54. Dunglas did not mention Moulero in his acknowledgments. Parrinder claimed that they consulted Moulero's work together. Dunglas, "Contribution à l'histoire du Moyen-Dahomey," vol. II, 11–15; Parrinder, The Story of Ketu, 3.

55. La Pin, "Story, Medium, and Masque," 144–45.

56. Moulero, "Conquête de Kétou," 61; Dunglas, "La Première attaque," 7–19.

57. Vansina, Oral Tradition, 112. Emphasis mine.

58. Beidelman, "Myth, Legend and Oral History," 74–97; Miller, "Introduction: Listening for the African Past," 5–6; Cooper, "Oral Sources and the Challenge of African History," 191–215.

59. White, Miescher, and Cohen, "Introduction: Voices, Words, and African History," 1–27.

60. Moulero, "Essai historique sur la ville de Kétou," 7.

61. Dunglas, "Contribution à l'histoire du Moyen-Dahomey," vol. I, 13. Geoffrey Parrinder wrote his English version of Kétu history to keep it from becoming lost to an English readership. Parrinder, The Story of Ketu, 3.

62. White, Miescher, and Cohen, "Introduction: Voices, Words, and African History," 2, 11–12.

63. Barber, I Could Speak until Tomorrow, 58.

64. La Pin, "Story, Medium, and Masque," 20.

2. How Kings Lost Their Mothers

1. Johnson, History of the Yorubas from the Earliest Times, 63; Kaplan, "Iyoba, the Queen Mother of Benin," 72–102; Hanson, "Queen Mothers and Good Government in Buganda," 219–36.

2. Law, The Oyo Empire, c.1600–c.1836, 37–43.

3. Ibid., 43–44.

4. Willem Bosman, a Dutch trader stationed at Ouidah in the late 1690s, does not mention Ọyọ by name but describes their well-known use of a cavalry. Willem Bosman, "A new and accurate description of the coast of Guinea, divided into the Gold, the Slave, and the Ivory Coasts." Eighteenth Century Collections Online. Gale. Wesleyan University, http://find.galegroup.com/ecco/infomark.do?&contentSet=ECCOArticles&type=multipage&tabID=To01&prodId=ECCO&docId=CW101007353&source=gale&userGroupName=31841&version=1.0&docLevel=FASCIMILE (accessed July 2, 2009); Pruneau de Pommegorge, Description de la Nigritie, 235–36; Adams, Remarks on the Country Extending from Cape Palmas to the River Congo, 222.

5. Johnson, *History of the Yorubas from the Earliest Times,* 63.

6. Ibid., 59–60, 62, 65–66, 76.

7. Ibid., 64.

8. Clapperton, *Hugh Clapperton into the Interior of Africa,* 159–60.

9. Johnson, *History of the Yorubas from the Earliest Times,* 66. In contrast, the Oni Ọjà in Kétu was a eunuch the king was never allowed to see, an interdiction that led to the death of one Kétu king who was tricked into meeting the Oni Ọjà on market day. Dunglas, "Contribution à l'histoire du Moyen-Dahomey," vol.I, 57–58; Parrinder, *The Story of Ketu,* 44.

10. Drewal and Drewal, *Gẹ̀lẹ̀dẹ́: Art and Female Power among the Yoruba,* 10–11.

11. Johnson, *History of the Yorubas from the Earliest Times,* 65–66.

12. Matory, *Sex and the Empire That Is No More,* 9.

13. Ibid., 10.

14. Johnson, *History of the Yorubas from the Earliest Times,* 63, 66.

15. Parrinder, *The Story of Ketu,* 11.

16. Matory, *Sex and the Empire That Is No More,* 79.

17. Johnson, *History of the Yorubas from the Earliest Times,* 66.

18. Ibid., 56.

19. Clapperton, *Hugh Clapperton into the Interior of Africa,* 107.

20. Awẹ, "Iyalode Efunsetan Aniwura (Owner of Gold)"; Matory, *Sex and the Empire That Is No More,* 18–20.

21. Law, *Oyo Empire, c.1600–c.1836,* 245–99; Apter, *Black Critics and Kings,* 36.

22. Ogunyẹmi, *Africa Wo/Man Palava,* 45–46, 48, 60.

23. Bay, *Wives of the Leopard,* 48. Suzanne Blier provides the translation of Aligbonon's name (which she spells Aligbonu) and gives alternative versions and interpretations of the origins of the Dahomey kingdom. Blier, "The Path of the Leopard," 401–402, 402n41.

24. Bay, *Wives of the Leopard,* 52.

25. Many Europeans visited Ouidah and Dahomey during the eighteenth century, but only in the twentieth century did European writers hear that Na Geze helped her father defeat Ouidah in 1727 by obtaining the missing parts for the guns used by her father's army. She had, as the story goes, treated the king of Ouidah and his leading ministers to ample food and drink the day before the attack and ordered her servants to wet the stores of Ouidah gunpowder to render it ineffective. Ibid., 59–60.

26. Ibid., 74–76.

27. Ibid., 76. On placeholders in Dahomey more generally, see Blier, "Path of the Leopard," 391.

28. Snelgrave, *A New Account of Some Parts of Guinea,* 34.

29. Ibid., 38–39; Bay, *Wives of the Leopard,* 11, 353.

30. Snelgrave, *A New Account of Some Parts of Guinea,* 97–106.

31. Akinjogbin, *Dahomey and Its Neighbours,* 77–80; Law, "Slave-Raiders and Middlemen," 45–68.

32. Snelgrave, *A New Account of Some Parts of Guinea,* 12–25; Harms, *The Diligent,* 199–221.

33. Snelgrave, *A New Account of Some Parts of Guinea,* 61–63.

34. Ibid., 130; Norris, *Memoirs of the Reign of Bossa Ahádee,* 27, 54.

35. Bay, *Wives of the Leopard,* 111–17.

36. Ibid., 92–96.

37. Ibid., 91.

38. Pruneau de Pommegorge, *Description de la Nigritie,* 172–73.

39. Norris, *Memoirs of the Reign of Bossa Ahádee,* 40–48, 107–108. Robin Law and Edna

Bay examine the implications of the Tegan's actions, in Norris's uncorroborated account, for the emergence of the Yovogan. Law, "The Slave-Trader as Historian," 229–30; Bay, *Wives of the Leopard*, 108–109.

40. Bay, *Wives of the Leopard*, 152.

41. Dalzel, *The History of Dahomy*, 82, 175–76.

42. Pires, *Crônica de uma embaixada*, 59, 84, 93–94; Bay, *Wives of the Leopard*, 67, 151.

43. Bay, *Wives of the Leopard*, 74, 78–84, 162.

44. Between 1616 and 1863, 1,534,827 enslaved Africans embarked ships from ports in the Bight of Benin, with 1,333,739 of them disembarking, mainly in the Americas (about 700 went to Europe and just over 1,200 are listed as "other"). "Voyages: The Trans-Atlantic Slave Trade Database," http:www.slavevoyages.org, http://slavevoyages.org/tast/database/search .faces?yearFrom=1514&yearTo=1866&mjbyptimp=60500 (accessed June 9, 2009).

45. The actual number of ships providing information on the sex and age of slave captives is small, less than 13 percent, so age and gender ratios are reconstructed based on historical data available. Eltis, "Construction of the Trans-Atlantic Database" (accessed on June 9, 2009). For the gender ratios for the Bight of Benin for the eighteenth-century Atlantic slave trade, the majority of the information comes from ships that took slaves to the Caribbean rather than Brazil, where the vast majority of slaves from this region—almost 60 percent—landed. Also see Eltis and Engerman, "Was the Slave Trade Dominated by Men?" 237–57.

46. Most of the limited data on sex ratios in the eighteenth century refers to ships that sold slaves in the Caribbean. "Voyages: The Trans-Atlantic Slave Trade Database," http:// slavevoyages.org/tast/database/search.faces?yearFrom=1701&yearTo=1800&mjbyptimp= 60500To (accessed June 9, 2009).

47. Paul Lovejoy suggests that women who were enslaved and sent to the Americas from the Bight of Benin region in the nineteenth century tended to be Yoruba-speaking and from nearer the coast because they were more likely to be pawned for debts. Women and girls who were pawns garnered a larger profit when sold to slave traders if the debt was not paid. Lovejoy, "The Yoruba Factor in the Trans-Atlantic Slave Trade," 49–50.

48. Bay, *Wives of the Leopard*, 143.

49. Ibid., 199–200.

50. Snelgrave, *A New Account of Some Parts of Guinea*, 50–51.

51. Pruneau de Pommegorge, *Description de la Nigritie*, 165; Norris, *Memoirs of the Reign of Bossa Ahádee*, 88–89, 99.

52. Norris, *Memoirs of the Reign of Bossa Ahádee*, 99, 101–102, 108.

53. Ibid., 110–11.

54. Bay, *Wives of the Leopard*, 65–66.

55. Clapperton, *Hugh Clapperton into the Interior of Africa*, 153.

56. Norris, *Memoirs of the Reign of Bossa Ahádee*, 50–51.

57. Dalzel, *History of Dahomy*, 211.

58. Pires, *Crônica de uma embaixada*, 70–71.

59. Norris, *Memoirs of the Reign of Bossa Ahádee*, 128–29; Dalzel, *The History of Dahomy*, 204–05, 222–23; Bay, *Wives of the Leopard*, 160–61.

60. D'Almeida-Topor, *Les Amazones*; Law, "The 'Amazons' of Dahomey," 245–60; Bay, *Wives of the Leopard*, 136–39, 207.

61. Forbes, *Dahomey and the Dahomans*, 66; Bay, *Wives of the Leopard*, 208.

62. Bay, *Wives of the Leopard*, 240–41; Herskovits, *Dahomey*, 111.

63. Bay, *Wives of the Leopard*, 15, 72.

64. Herskovits, *Dahomey*, 111.

65. Burton, *A Mission to Gelele*, 211; Forbes, *Dahomey and the Dahomans*, 238; Bay, "The Royal Women of Abomey," 281–88; Bay, *Wives of the Leopard*, 243–44.

66. For a general discussion of the potential power of sisters in extended families, see Sacks, *Sisters and Wives*; Bay, *Wives of the Leopard*, 244–47.

67. Bay, *Wives of the Leopard*, 271–72.

68. Gollmer, August 16, 1859, in "Missionary Tour to the Ketu Country," CMS, 043/132.

3. Giving Away Kétu's Secret

1. Clapperton, *Hugh Clapperton into the Interior of Africa*, 144.

2. Imam Alhaji Nassirou Raji, interview with the author, February 23, 1999; Alhaji Machoudi, interview with the author, December 2, 1998. In the short pamphlet produced to celebrate the centennial in 1994 of Kétu's rebuilding after the war with Dahomey, Sofo is named simply as the first imam of Kétu, and the engaging story of Sofo's many wives is omitted. Odjo, "A la découverte de Kétou," 11.

3. Peel, *Religious Encounter and the Making of the Yoruba*, 187–90.

4. Matory describes *ifá* divination and Islam as in a "mutually constituting dialogue." Matory, "Rival Empires," 496.

5. Islam arrived on the African continent and was diffused through West Africa, particularly in the Mali empire far northwest of Yoruba towns, at least by the fourteenth century. It may have been as early as the latter sixteenth century when Muslim practices from Mali reached Yoruba populations, though conversion to Islam in West Africa occurred most rapidly and extensively during the nineteenth and twentieth centuries. Peel, *Religious Encounter*, 115–16.

6. Matory, "Rival Empires," 496; Owomoyela, *Yoruba Proverbs*, 468–69.

7. Imam Alhaji Nassirou Raji, interview with the author, February 23, 1999. "Kanike" is specifically associated with Hausa speakers from the region of Kanuri. Gbadamosi, *The Growth of Islam among the Yoruba*, 25; also see reference to Kaniki in Ouidah in Marty, *Études sur l'Islam au Dahomey*, 108.

8. Adediran, "Islam and Political Crises in Kétu," 7.

9. The Kanike represent one or two of approximately twenty Muslim lineages that occupy Masafe and Yawomi quarters. People view Ile Laku ("big house") compound in Masafe as the home of the actual descendants of Sofo or the Kanike. Alhaji Lawani Kifuli, interview with the author, December 3 and 4, 1998. Masafe Owa also may be an offshoot of Ile Laku. One Muslim man noted that though people say that Muslims are foreigners, the only *àlejò ọba* (strangers of the ruler) were at Ile Laku. Interview with the author. Name of interviewee has been omitted.

10. For a reference to the Kétu Muslim quarter and its mosque in the nineteenth century, see Church Missionary Society Archives (CMS), CA2 031/128, Samuel J. Crowther, "Account of a Journey to Kétu," January 15, 1853. The Muslim quarters in Yoruba towns are often known as *sabo*, understood to be a shortened version of the Hausa phrase *sabon gari*, meaning "new town." Cohen, *Custom and Politics in Urban Africa*, 9. The other common name for Muslim neighborhoods in West Africa is *zongo*. Cohen notes that the Hausa word *zango* refers to cattle markets in Western Nigeria, in contrast to the term *sabo*, which is used to refer to living areas of Muslim strangers. Hausa Muslims in Ghana live in neighborhoods called *zongo*, and the Muslim part of Cotonou, Bénin, is also known as the Zongo. Cohen, *Custom and Politics in Urban Africa*, 224n6; Schildkrout, *People of the Zongo*, 67.

11. Ivor Wilks discusses this relationship between Muslim migrants and their hosts as part

of a "Suwarian" tradition, prevalent in areas linked to the former Mali and Songhay empires. Wilks, "The Transmission of Islamic Learning in the Western Sudan," 162–97.

12. Many of the towns and villages in the region visited by Captain Hugh Clapperton in the 1820s were later destroyed by war. Thomas Bowen to Brother Taylor, July 1st or 10th, 1851. Letter taken from Home and Foreign Mission Journal of February 1852, Southern Baptist Historical Library and Archives (SBHLA), Microfilm (MF) 2040-1.

13. Gollmer, *Charles Andrew Gollmer*, 148.

14. Sanders, "The Hamitic Hypothesis," 521–32.

15. Thomas Bowen to (Brother) Rev. J. B. Taylor, November 21, 1851, SBLHA, MF 2040-1.

16. Thomas Bowen to (Brother) Rev. J. B. Taylor, November 13, 1859, SBLHA, MF 2040-2.

17. McKenzie, "Samuel Crowther's Attitude to Other Faiths during the Early Period," 6.

18. Crowther, January 9, 1853, in "Account of Journey to Ketu," CMS, CA2/031/128.

19. This would have been the five-day market as opposed to the daily or more local regional market held on different days. Crowther, January 11, 1853, in "Account of Journey to Ketu," CMS, CA2/031/128.

20. Ali vacated his quarters for Crowther during Crowther's visit. Crowther, January 7 and January 12, 1853, in "My Journey to Ketu," CMS, 021/1-24. Biodun Adediran interprets the displacement of Ali as an insult that encouraged anti-Christian sentiment among the Muslim populations, Adediran, "Islam and Political Crises in Kétu," 11; Crowther, January 16, 1853, in "My Journey to Ketu," CMS, 021/1-24.

21. James Barber, April 3, 1853, in "My Journey to Ketu," CMS, 021/1-24.

22. James Barber, June 25, 1853, in "James Barber's Second Journey to Ketu," CMS, 021/1-24; Adediran, "The Ketu Mission, 1853–1859," 89–104.

23. Gollmer, August 15, 1859, in "Missionary Tour to the Ketu Country," CMS, 043/132. The fresh drinking water was originally delivered to Gollmer on a Sunday and he at first wanted to refuse it altogether but then agreed to accept it on another day to avoid "disturb[ing] [his] friendly relations" with the Muslim man. Similar incidents had occurred during previous visits by missionaries. When the Alákétu Adebia wished to send gifts to Crowther on a Sunday, Crowther advised that no work could be done on that day, and the royal ministers opted to give the gifts on another day. Crowther, January 9, 1853, in "My Journey to Ketu," CMS, 021/1-24. During his second vision to Kétu, Barber completely refused a gift sent to him by the newly named Alákétu because it was delivered on a Sunday. Barber, June 26, 1853, in "My Journey to Ketu," CMS, 021/1-24.

24. Gollmer, August 18, 1859, in "Missionary Tour to the Ketu Country," CMS, 043/132.

25. The factions that emerged after Alákétu Adebia's death continued to clash during the reign of the subsequent king, Alákétu Adiro Olumaja, perhaps explaining why he fled to an outlying village of Kétu. Moulero, "Essai historique sur la ville de Kétou: Le Roi Adiro (suite)," 4.

26. Adediran, "The Ketu Mission," 89–104. Authors have argued that African communities viewed Islam and Christianity as additions to existing indigenous religious pantheons. Peel, "The Pastor and the Babalawo," 338–69.

27. James Barber, June 24, 1853, in "James Barber's Second Journey to Ketu," CMS, 021/1-24.

28. Moulero, "Essai historique sur la ville de Kétou," 4.

29. Dunglas, "Contribution à l'histoire du Moyen-Dahomey," vol. II, 97–99.

30. Arigba's name remained an honorary title in Kétu; people remember another infamous man named Arigba in the 1920s or 1930s whose own story may have merged with that of the nineteenth-century figure. Alákétu Adétútù also granted the title to a wealthy, influential Muslim man, the former husband of my research assistant.

31. Dunglas reports that Pakoyi was also a "Minister of Muslim Affairs" in Kétu, with the

title "Olumale" (leader of Muslims). Dunglas, "Contribution à l'histoire du Moyen-Dahomey," vol. II, 149; Moulero, "Conquête de Kétou," 62.

32. Moulero, "Conquête de Kétou," 62; Dunglas, "Contribution à l'histoire du Moyen-Dahomey," vol. II, 135–43.

33. Bibliothèque Nationale de Bénin (BNB), UOD 203-III, "Les Deux Guerres de Kétou 1882 et 1884 ou 1884–1886 et Conquête de Kétou par Glélé et Conquête d'Abomey par la France—d'après un témoin oculaire," Undated typescript, 14–15.

34. Interviews with the author. Names of the interviewees have been omitted. The Muslim community in Agbome in the early twentieth century consisted primarily of Kétu descendants and former Kétu slaves. Archives Nationales du Senegal (ANS) 8G 14, Cercle d'Abomey au Gouverneur du Dahomey, 6 août 1907. Maupoil, "Contribution à l'étude de l'origine musulmane," 94. Maupoil found that the house of Arepa's descendants was in ruin by the 1930s. Residents had deserted it after 1892. The fate of the descendants of Arepa's many "wives" remains unclear.

35. Alhaja Safouratou Mama, interview with the author, October 5, 2006.

36. Lloyd, "Agnatic and Cognatic Descent among the Yoruba," 484–500.

37. Interview with the author. Name of interviewee has been omitted.

38. Interview with the author. Name of interviewee has been omitted.

39. Thomas Bowen to (Brother) Rev. J. B. Taylor, November 21, 1851, SBLHA, MF 2040-1.

40. Adegnika and Djossa, "Les Premières heures d'évangélisation à Kétou," 26.

41. Assétou Ayouba is identified by name, along with a photograph, in (BNB), UOD 203-III, "Les Deux Guerres de Kétou;" Moulero, "Conquête de Kétou," 64–67.

42. Morton-Williams, "A Yoruba Woman Remembers Servitude," 102–17.

43. On the expanded industry of women in the nineteenth-century Dahomey palace, see Bay, *Wives of the Leopard*, 210–13.

44. Bowen, *Adventures and Missionary Labours*, 149.

45. Edna Bay, "Servitude and Success in the Palace of Dahomey," 145, 200–209.

46. Bowen, *Adventures and Missionary Labours*, 148.

47. Miers and Kopytoff, "Slavery as an Institution of Marginality," 18–20; Orlando Patterson, *Slavery and Social Death*.

48. Crowther, January 15, 1853, in "Account of a Journey to Ketu," CMS, CA2/031/128.

49. Crowther, January 16, 1853, in "Account of a Journey to Ketu," CMS, CA2/031/128.

50. Crowther, January 11, 1853, in "Account of a Journey to Ketu," CMS, CA2/031/128.

51. Crowther, January 16, 1853, in "Account of a Journey to Ketu," CMS, CA2/031/128.

52. Ajayi, *Christian Missions in Nigeria 1841–1891*, 106–108, 245–53; Ayandele, *Missionary Impact in Modern Nigeria, 1842–1914*, 201–202, 206, 210–16. Crowther pronounced harshly against polygyny as part of the Lambeth Conference in 1888.

53. Ajayi, "Samuel Ajayi Crowther of Oyo," 293–94, 299, 302–303.

54. Ibid., 305–306n45; Samuel Crowther, August 21, 1846, journal for the quarter ending September 25, 1846, CMS CA 2 031–034, copy at Yale University Divinity Library Film Ms109.

55. James Barber, April 3, 1853, in "My Journey to Ketu," CMS, 021/1–24.

56. Barber, June 26, 1853, in "James Barber's Second Journey to Ketu," CMS, 021/1–24.

57. Moulero, "Essai historique sur la ville de Kétou," 3–5. It is possible that the story of the favorite wife and her curse upon Kétu is an embellishment used to explain the calamity that befell Kétu a few years later.

58. Gollmer, *Charles Andrew Gollmer*, 180.

59. Charles Andrew Gollmer, August 12, 1859, in "Missionary Tour to the Ketu Country, Journal Extracts for the half year ending September 2, 1859," CMS, 043/132.

60. Gollmer, August 12, 1859, "Missionary Tour to the Ketu Country," CMS, 043/132.

61. Gollmer, August 15, 1859, in "Missionary Tour to the Ketu Country," CMS, 043/132.

62. Gollmer, August 16–17, 1859, in "Missionary Tour to the Ketu Country," CMS, 043/132.

63. Gollmer, August 16, 1859, in "Missionary Tour to the Ketu Country," CMS, 043/132.

64. Aublet, *La Guerre au Dahomey 1888–1893*, 334; Bay, *Wives of the Leopard*, 297–98.

65. Moulero, "Conquête de Kétou," 67; Bay, *Wives of the Leopard*, 304–305. While it is unclear if the woman was Behanzin's biological mother or a "public mother," the act and symbolism of the sacrifice demonstrates profound despair.

66. Garcia, *Le Royaume du Dahomé face*, 249–54.

67. Hazoumé, "Tata Ajachê soupo ma ha awouinyan," *La Reconnaissance Africaine* 1 (1925): 7–9; Hazoumé, "Tata Ajachê soupo ma ha awouinyan," *La Reconnaissance Africaine* 2 (1925): 7–8; Hazoumé, "Tata Ajachê soupo ma ha awouinyan," *La Reconnaissance Africaine* 3 (1925): 7–8.

68. Athanase Allayé, interview with the author, September 23, 2006.

69. Deogratias Odelui, former mayor, interview with the author, January 14, 1999.

70. ANB, 1E14 1–4, "Rapport Politique—Ouidah," January 1904; Vicencia Ode, interview with the author, December 9, 1998.

71. Archives du Ministère des Affaires Etrangères (AMAE), Chargé du Portugal à Paris sur la répatriation des Dahoméens, 4 août, 1898, New Series, Dahomey 67 (1896–1911); ANB, 1E11 1, Témoin d'un ancien esclave de Kétou à São Tomé, 8 avril 1900.

72. Pellet, "Au Dahomey de Porto-Novo à Kétou," 561–63; Pellet, "Au Dahomey de Porto-Novo à Kétou," 573–76. Pellet later made a speech in 1901 in which he rejected the idea of mass liberation of slaves in West Africa. Pellet, "Rapport de Mgr. Pellet," 5.

4. "Where women really matter"

1. One of the earliest examples of French women formally serving in the French administration comes from Morocco a couple of years later, when French women were recruited as arts educators for Moroccan women; see Irbouh, *Art in the Service of Colonialism*. In Algeria, wives of colonial administrators, such as French feminist Hubertine Auclert at the turn of the century and writer Marie Bugéja after World War I, wrote politicized tracts about French colonial policy. See, for example, Clancy-Smith, "Islam, Gender, and Identities in the Making of French Algeria," 167–72; Eichner, "*La Citoyenne* in the World," 63–84; Bowlan, "Civilizing Gender Relations in Algeria," 175–92. For African women as colonial agents in British colonial West Africa, see Day, "The Female Chiefs of the Mende, 1885–1977"; Day, "Nyarroh of Bandasuma, 1885–1914," 415–37. After the war, there would be women French colonial officials in French West Africa, such as Denise Moran Savineau, discussed below in chapter 5. In their introduction to their volume on African colonial intermediaries and employees, Benjamin Lawrance, Emily Osborn, and Richard Roberts note the limited analysis of women and gender in their compilation. Lawrance, Osborn, and Roberts, "African Intermediaries and the 'Bargain' of Collaboration," 26–28.

2. ANB, 1E11 2–3, Bertheux, "Rapport sur situation politique de la partie orientale Zagnanado, Kétou-Hollis-Adja-Ouéré," 22 mai 1911.

3. Nago is the term used in Dahomey to describe Yoruba speakers. ANB, 1E 11 1–5, "Transmission d'un rapport et d'un dossier annexe en Commission permanente du conseil de Gouvernement rélatifs au rattachement du canton de Kétou à la circonscription provisoire de Pobé," Lieutenant-Gouverneur du Dahomey à Gouverneur de l'Afrique Occidentale Française (AOF), 17 octobre 1915.

4. "Royal wife" is not the equivalent of "queen" in the French sense of the word.

5. Institut pour la Recherche Appliqué du Dahomey (IRAD), Document du Porto-Novo 20, Cercle de Pobé-Kétou. Anonymous and undated document describing the 1910s, attributed to Edouard Dunglas, though he was an administrator in Kétu decades later.

6. ANB, 1E 11 3–1, Lieutenant H. Aubé, "Rapport sur la mission accomplie dans la region Kétou-Savé du 18 janvier au 20 février 1894," 3 mars 1894.

7. Parrinder, *The Story of Ketu*, 66.

8. Babatunde Oroufila, interview with the author, June 24, 1997; Iyalode Basilia Abero, interview with the author, July 16, 1997; Soumanou Ganiou and Kelani Guiwa, interview with the author, January 29, 1999.

9. In previous publications, she is referred to as Ida Alaba, with her title preceding her name. The French often called her Queen Ida but during my interviews people always called her Alaba Ida.

10. Conklin, *A Mission to Civilize*, 113.

11. The unsigned and undated document housed at IRAD, Document of Porto-Novo 20, refers to her as *chef du canton* (head of district). The IRAD document also suggests that she was consulted on the performance of village heads. Asiwaju writes that Alaba was the head of the district, but based on interviews rather than on French colonial documents. Asiwaju, "The Alaketu of Ketu," 145. The following document from 1915 clearly states that Onyegen was *chef du canton*, Centre des Archives Outre-Mer (CAOM), 14 Mi 837, "Demande de rattachement du Canton de Kétou au Cercle Provisoire du Pobé," Lieutenant-Gouverneur du Dahomey à Gouverneur Général de l'AOF, 17 octobre 1915.

12. Babatunde Oroufila, interview with the author, June 24, 1997.

13. Bénin, Direction des Archives Nationales, "Rapport du tournée," 86.

14. Drewal, "Symbols of Possession," 15, 17; IRAD, Document of Porto-Novo 20; Pierre Idowu Ladele, interview with the author, September 30, 2006.

15. ANB, 1E 20 2–3, "Rapport Mensuel, Cercle de Zagnanado," janvier 1906. Administrative circles were akin to a province.

16. ANB, 1E 11 2–4, "Rapport sur l'incident du village de Digne," 11 novembre 1912.

17. IRAD, Document of Porto-Novo 20. Several villages listed have other men who served as head or "chief" of the village. For the full list of villages put under jurisdiction including Ilikimu, Issélou, Idigne, Ilahé, Ilara, and Ọbatẹdo, see CAOM, 14 Mi 837, "Rattachement du Canton de Kétou au Cercle de Pobé," 13 juillet 1915.

18. ANB, 1E 11 2–4, "Telegramme Officiel," 12 avril 1911.

19. ANB, 1E 11 2–4, "Cercle de Zagnanado, Interrogatoire de Fagbité," 22 avril 1911.

20. ANB, 1E 11 1–5, "Retour de l' Ex-Queen Ida," Le Capitaine Malnous de l'Infanterie Commandant le Cercle à Gouverneur du Dahomey, 17 mai 1918.

21. Asiwaju, *Western Yorubaland under European Rule 1889–1945*, 149n17; Soule Brouaima, interview with the author, December 10, 1998.

22. ANS, 2G10 22, "Situation politique et administrative, 1909," 21 mars 1910. The highest office in each West African colony actually was lieutenant governor; the head of the entire French West Africa federation of colonies was governor general.

23. People referred to the educated African interpreter as *òyìnbó* or as "white man" or as "European" because of his status. ANB, 1E 11 2–3, Lieutenant-Gouverneur p.i. à Governeur Général de l'AOF, 24 mai 1911.

24. IRAD, Document of Porto-Novo 20.

25. ANB, 1E20 4-2, "Situation politique, Cercle de Zagnanado, juin 1908."

26. ANB, 1E11 2-3, Bertheux, "Rapport sur la situation politique de la partie orientale Zagnanado, Kétou-Hollis-Adja-Ouéré," 22 mai 1911.

27. Bénin, Direction des Archives Nationales, "Rapport du tournée," 84.

28. Ibid., 85.

29. ANB, 1E 11 2-4, "Rapport sur l'incident du village de Digne," 11 novembre 1912.

30. On several occasions, before he became incapacitated and was replaced by assistant chiefs, Alákétu Onyegen requested the assistance of guards or other personnel to collect taxes. ANB, 1 E11 1-2 "L'Administrateur Juillet St. Lager (Cercle de Zagnanado) à Lieutenant-Governeur du Dahomey," 21 février 1905 and 18 août 1905.

31. ANB, 1E 11 1, "Rapport sur le recrutement dans le canton de Kétou," 13 juillet 1915.

32. CAOM, 14 Mi 837, "Le Chef de Poste Auxiliaire Barretto à l'Administrateur du Cercle," 2 août 1915.

33. CAOM, 14 Mi 837, "Telegramme Officiel," 7 septembre 1915.

34. ANB, 1E11 2–3, "Rapport concernant le règlement à Kétou, des incidents signalés par l'Administrateur du Cercle à Gouverneur de la Colonie," 21 septembre 1915.

35. On the practice of suicide among weakened Yoruba kings, see Johnson, *History of the Yorubas from the Earliest Times,* 168–77.

36. ANB, 1E11 1–5, "Rapport du Tournée," 29 septembre 1915.

37. CAOM, 14 Mi 837, "Demande de Rattachement du Canton de Kétou au Cercle Provisire du Pobé," Lieutenant-Gouverneur du Dahomey a Gouverneur Général de l'AOF, 17 octobre 1915. In an earlier version of the report, the French official refers to Onyegen as the king. CAOM 14 Mi 837, "Rapport concernant le règlement à Kétou, des incidents signalés par l'Administrateur du Cercle à M. le Gouverneur de la Colonie," 21 or 29 septembre 1915. At one point, the local French official refers to Abimbọla as the "chef de Kétou," but the meaning is unclear. CAOM, 14 Mi 837, L'Administrateur du Cercle à M. le Lieutenant-Gouverneur du Dahomey en tournée, 15 septembre 1915.

38. Crowther, January 11, 1853, in "Account of a Journey to Ketu," CMS, CA2/031/128; Gollmer, August 15, 1859, in "Missionary Tour to the Ketu Country," CMS, 043/132.

39. Soule Brouaima, interview with the author, December 10, 1998.

40. Salamantou Osseni, interview with the author, March 1, 1999.

41. Céline Idowu, Boyoko Iko, and Sikiratou Idowu, interview with the author, March 1, 1999; Adebayo Adegbite and Adeniran Alabi Fagbohun, interview with the author, March 7, 1999.

42. Celine Idowu, Boyoko Iko, and Sikiratou Idowu, interview with the author, March 1, 1999.

43. Lloyd, "Sacred Kingship and Government among the Yoruba," 221–37.

44. Benjamin Oyewusi, interview with the author, November 27 and 30, 1998; Asiwaju, "The Alaketu of Ketu," 146.

45. Iya Afobaje Salamantou Egunlope Brouaima, interview with the author, November 2 and 26, 1998.

46. Asiwaju, *Western Yorubaland under European Rule 1889–1945,* 271–72.

47. Palau Marti, *Le Roi-Dieu au Bénin,* 59.

48. ANB, 1E 11 1–5, "Destitution de la Reine Ida de Kétou," Le Capitaine Commandant de Cercle de Holli-Kétou, 2 mars 1918.

49. ANB, 1E 11 1–5, "Retour de l' Ex-Queen Ida," Le Capitaine Malnous de l'Infanterie Commandant le Cercle à Gouverneur du Dahomey, 17 mai 1918; Saoudatou Moussa, interview with the author, February 19, 1999.

50. Parrinder reports that she died in 1938 in Irocogny, a village outside of Kétu's central town. Parrinder, *The Story of Ketu,* 66.

51. Mamadou Imoru, interview with the author, January 28, 1999.

52. Celine Idowu, Boyoko Iko, and Sikiratou Idowu, interview with the author, March 1, 1999.

53. Barber, "Going too Far in Okuku," 71–83.

54. Isola, *Efunsetan Aniwura, Iyalode Ibadan and Tinuubu, Iyalode Egba,* 6.

55. Awẹ, "Iyalode Efunsetan Aniwura," 57.

56. Achebe, *Farmers, Traders, Warriors, and Kings,* 197–217.

57. Barber, "How Man Makes God," 724–45; Barnes, "The Many Faces of Ogun," 8.

58. ANB, 1E 11 2–4, "Rapport sur l'incident du villlage de Digne," 11 novembre 1912.

59. Bachirou Babatunde Olofindji, interview with the author, May 8, 1999, Indigne; Souberou Inita and Idji Inita, interview with the author, Ilikimu, May 8, 1999.

60. Alaba Ida waged most of her failed recruitment drives in the small Gbe-speaking villages near Kétu or the eastern Yoruba villages under Yá Ṣègén's jurisdiction, avoiding the central town or heartland of the kingdom.

61. Asiwaju, *Western Yorubaland under European Rule 1889–1945,* 94; Alhaji Lawani Kifuli, interview with the author, December 3 and 4, 1998.

62. IRAD, Document du Porto-Novo 20. Ondo is an *òrìṣà* who possesses or "mounts" his priests, who were described as males in accounts from the 1950s and 1970s. The priesthood may have changed over the years, or Yá Ṣègén's title may have been unique to Ọbatẹdo. Verger, "Trance and Convention in Nago-Yoruba Spirit Mediumship," 50–66; Drewal, "Symbols of Possession," 15–24.

63. Iya Libara Catherine Oyewole Adebiyi, interview with the author, July 15, 1997.

64. Accampo, "Gender, Social Policy and the Formation of the Third Republic," 1–27.

65. Scott, *Only Paradoxes to Offer,* 11.

66. Even in Gorée, Saint Louis, Dakar, and Rufisque—the Four Communes of Senegal first established in 1848, in which resident Africans technically enjoyed rights as citizens—French and mixed-raced communities initially dominated local politics until political alliances that included Western-educated Africans and Muslims coalesced in the election of African deputy Blaise Diagne in 1916. Nevertheless, throughout the colonial period, most African residents of the Four Communes remained restricted in their political power and influence in relation to the French administration. See Robinson, *Paths of Accommodation,* 97–139.

67. Cohen, *The French Encounter with Africans.*

68. William Ponty, "Circulaire sur la politique indigene," 22 septembre 1909, *Journal Officiel du Dahomey.*

69. I borrow the term "new men" from Conklin, *A Mission to Civilize,* 113.

70. Alice Conklin criticizes scholarship that implies that France simply wanted to change Africans into Frenchmen. Ibid., 73–74.

71. William Ponty, "Session de l'ouverture du Conseil de Gouvernement de l'Afrique Occidentale Française, 14 December 1908," *Journal Officiel du Dahomey.*

72. Gouverneur Général Ponty à Lieutenant-Gouverneur Dahomey, 12 avril 1908, *Journal Officiel du Dahomey.*

73. CAOM, 574/1, "Rapport politique du 4ème trimestre," Gouverneur Général AOF à Ministre des Colonies, 9 mars 1914.

74. Conklin, *A Mission to Civilize,* 176–78.

75. François Clozel, "Discours au Conseil du Gouvernement de l'Afrique Occidentale Française, 29 novembre 1915," *Journal Officiel du Dahomey.*

76. CAOM, 574/1, François Clozel à Gabriel Angoulvant, 13 juin, 1916; CAOM, 574/1, Gabriel Angoulvant à Ministre des Colonies, 8 mars 1917. From June to December 1916, Gabriel Angoulvant, infamous for his brutal "pacification" campaign in Côte d'Ivoire, served as Clozel's acting governor general. He was asked to keep an eye on Noufflard's handling of the events in Da-

homey. Noufflard himself was eventually dismissed because of his handling of the upstarts in the Ohori region.

77. CAOM, 574/3, "Rapport Politique, 2ème trimester 1917," Gouverneur Général Fourn à Ministre des Colonies, 13 juillet 1917.

78. Governor General Joost Van Vollenhoven, "Circulaire au sujet des chefs indigènes," 15 août 1917, *Journal Officiel du Dahomey.*

79. CAOM, 574/3, "Rapport politique 3ème trimester 1917," Lieutenant Général Fourn à Gouverneur Général AOF, 29 octobre 1917.

80. Accampo, "Gender, Social Policy and the Formation of the Third Republic," 1–27; Grayzel, *Women's Identities at War.*

81. Roberts, *Civilization without Sexes.*

82. McBride, "Divorce and the Republican Family," 72; Schafer, *Children in Moral Danger,* chapter 2; Childers, *Fathers, Families, and the State in France.*

83. CAOM, 14 Miom 1078, 17G 61, Governeur Général Joost Van Vollenhoven à Ministre des Colonies, 20 décembre 1917.

84. For a different discussion of European fears of emasculation in the Belgian Congo, see Hunt, *A Colonial Lexicon,* 156–57.

85. ANS, 2G 25/21, "Rapport Politique Annual, 1925"; Conklin, *A Mission to Civilize,* 217.

5. "Without family . . . there is no true colonization"

1. Le Roy, "La désorganisation de la famille Africaine," 17.

2. Following the printout of the survey in the issue of the French Antislavery Society's journal on March 31, 1910, it also notes that the questionnaire was reproduced in the magazine *Dépêche colonial,* "promising excellent publicity." Anonymous, "Enquête colonial sur l'organisation de la famille," 23.

3. Pellet, "Rapport de Mgr. Pellet," 5.

4. Le Roy, "La désorganisation de la famille Africaine," 13.

5. ANS, Vicaire Apostolique Louis Dartois à Monseigneur Legros, Directeur Générale de la Société Antiesclavagiste de la France, October 15, 1904; Dartois, "Le Village Saint-Lazare à Zagnanado, Dahomey," 139–40.

6. The reprint of the survey is anonymous but it follows an article by Mgr. Le Roy titled, "Le relèvement de la famille en Afrique" (Uplifting the African Family) and is introduced by Le Myre de Vilers, president of the French Antislavery Society. Anonymous, "Enquête colonial sur l'organisation de la famille," 20, 22, 23.

7. Father Vallée wrote another report on Kétu published in the French Antislavery Society's journal in 1908. Delafosse and Poutrin, *Enquête coloniale,* xxii, xxiv, xxvii. Studies by Delafosse and Poutrin are added to the edited results from the survey but do not fit with the survey material. The actual editors of the 1930 publication are anonymous.

8. Ibid., 181–82.

9. Ibid., 183.

10. Vallée, "Village de Liberté de St. Augustin," 217.

11. Delafosse and Poutrin, *Enquête coloniale,* 184.

12. Ibid., 186.

13. Ibid., 189–90.

14. Vacharet, "Le village de liberté," 392–93; Vallée, "Village de liberté de St. Augustin," 217–20.

15. Delafosse and Poutrin, *Enquête coloniale,* 190.

16. I use pseudonyms for the couple and their child. The court case appears in ANB, 1M169 20.

17. Administrator Duboscq arrived at his post on October 21, 1912, and had worked with Alaba Ida and Yá Ṣègén before they were removed from their positions. Though he had been stationed in the region for three years, Duboscq's lack of knowledge of marriage practices in Zagnanado and in Kétu suggests that the responses to the French Antislavery Society, including descriptions of Zagnanado and Abomey, presumably completed five years earlier, were never seen or retained by the French colonial administration but traveled instead through missionary circles.

18. ANB, 1M169 20, Questionnaire sur le mariage selon la coutume de Zagnanado (Agony), Réponses par Guendehou, Chef du Canton de Cove et Premier Assesseur du Tribunal, 5 juin 1915. Guendehou was responding to a question about whether separation constituted the dissolution of a marriage. The first part of his answer was "No, marriage was not dissolved based upon that fact."

19. ANB, 1M169 20, Lieutenant-Governeur à l'Administrateur du Cercle, 1 juin 1915. It is unclear where the lieutenant governor was getting his information on marriage in Abomey and Savé (Sabe) when he did not have the same type of information for Kétu. ANB, 1M169 20, Questionnaire sur le mariage selon la coutume de Zagnanado (Agony), Réponses par Avoundela, Président du Tribunal de la Subdivision de Zagnanado, 6 juin 1915. Avoundela and Guendehou distinguished between *ha dido* marriage in Abomey that applied only to women descended from the ruling lineage. These women freely could enter liaisons with men and maintain control over any children that resulted from that marriage.

20. ANB, 1M169 20, Questionnaire addressée à Adekambi sur la coutume indigène, 6 juin 1915. For an explanation for the use of the term "Nago" for Yoruba speakers in Dahomey, see Law, "Ethnicity and the Slave Trade," 212–15.

21. ANB, 1M169 20, Questionnaire addressée à Adekambi sur la coutume indigène, 6 juin 1915. The Catholic priest, based in Zagnanado, suggested religion was a motive, accusing the French colonial administration of siding with Muslims over Catholics. But Adekambi rarely evoked his Muslim identity, submitted to local practices to marry Adogbonu, and sent his children to Catholic school. ANB, 1M169 20, L'Administrateur à Lieutenant-Gouverneur du Dahomey, 15 mai 1915.

22. ANB, 1M169 20, L'Administrateur à Lieutenant-Gouverneur du Dahomey, 8 juin 1915.

23. ANB, 1M169 20, Réponses par Avoundela et Guendehou, 5–6 juin 1915. Ponty, *Justice indigéne*; Cachard, *The French Civil Code*, 10; Smith, *Feminism and the Third Republic*, 179–81.

24. Johnson, *History of the Yorubas from the Earliest Times*, 116.

25. Ibid., 7, 26.

26. Ajisafe, *The Laws and Customs of the Yoruba People*, 56.

27. Ibid., 62.

28. Ibid., 56, 58.

29. Ibid., 51–52.

30. Ibid., 2, 19–20, 48.

31. Ibid., 6.

32. Fadipe, *The Sociology of the Yoruba*, 317.

33. Ibid., 80, 85.

34. Ibid., 114–16.

35. For interpretation of *igiyar arme* as "thread/ties of marriage," see Cooper, *Marriage in Maradi*, 10. *Arme* or *aure* is marriage while *igiya* is "thread or rope." The Arabic term for marriage is *nikah*. *Sàráà* is derived from the Arabic term *sadaqa*, meaning almsgiving. Some Yo-

rùbá Muslims in Kétu claimed marriage by sàráà as better than "selling away their daughters." Fadipe, *The Sociology of the Yoruba*, 67. Kétu residents who were not Muslim sometimes derided the practice of sàráà as "giving daughters away." Women in the Hausa Muslim community in Maradi, Niger, found marriage by sàráà degrading. Cooper, *Marriage in Maradi*, 98.

36. Fadipe, *The Sociology of the Yoruba*, 91–92; Mann, *Marrying Well*, 43; Judith Byfield, "Women, Marriage, and Divorce," 35–38.

37. Le Roy, "La désorganisation de la famille Africaine," 12; Schneider, *Quality and Quantity*, 37–41; Accampo, "Integrating Women into the Teaching of French History," 278; Cole, "'There Are Only Good Mothers,'" 640–41.

38. Zola, *Fruitfulness*, 471–81.

39. Conklin, *A Mission to Civilize*, 68–70; Sacré-Cœur, *La Femme Noire*, 233.

40. Schneider, *Quality and Quantity*, 36.

41. *Journal Officiel Lois et Décrets* (9 décembre 1924), 10803 as quoted in Ibid., 141–42. In Dakar, headquarters of French West Africa, social hygiene policies had been reinvigorated a few years earlier with the founding of a new training school for African doctors and midwives in 1918, a maternity hospital in Dakar in 1919, and an Office of Social Hygiene in 1921. Conklin, *A Mission to Civilize*, 221.

42. Gouverneur Général Carde aux Lieutenant-Gouverneurs de l'AOF, 15 février 1926 as quoted in Sacré-Cœur, *La Femme Noire*, 233.

43. CAOM, AFFPOL 3063, Inspecteur, 2eme Classe Haranger, Chef d'Inspection, Mission de Dahomey à Ministre des Colonies, Paris, 19 juin 1929.

44. Abbatucci, "La Maternité en Afrique Noire," 106.

45. Thomas, *The French Empire between the Wars*, 165.

46. For similar concerns and policies to combat depopulation and fertility in Europe and Africa, see Nancy Rose Hunt's study of Belgian colonialism in the Belgian Congo, Hunt, *A Colonial Lexicon*, 243–46.

47. Brévié, "Circulaire sur la codification des coutumes indigènes, 75, 77–78.

48. Maupoil, "L'Etude des coutumes juridiques de L'AOF," 13–14.

49. Betts, *Assimilation and Association in French Colonial Theory*; Conklin, *A Mission to Civilize*, 203–11.

50. In his circular on the codification of indigenous customs, Governor General Brévié lists the studies done to date, noting that they were "fragmentary." Brévié, "Circulaire sur la codification des coutumes indigènes, 72–75.

51. *Coutumier du Dahomey*. Bernard Maupoil, former French administrator and scholar of divination in Dahomey, introduced the collection in 1939, blaming the delay on the large task given to an understaffed administration and the antiquated format of the questionnaire. Maupoil, "L'Etude des coutumes juridiques de L'AOF," 37–38.

52. Kétu was not mentioned specifically as a source of the information in the 1933 publication, though a questionnaire for the broader region was completed. In the 1939 version, the discussion of the Yoruba was limited to areas south of Kétu. *Coutumier*, 30, 39.

53. Ibid., 12–13.

54. Ibid., 37.

55. Ibid., 57.

56. Governor General Brévié, "Extraits des Instructions données par le Gouverneur Général en date du 8 Mars 1932 pour l'application du décret du 3 décembre 1931 réorganisant la justice indigene en AOF," as quoted in Sacré-Cœur, *La Femme Noire*, 266.

57. Governor General de Coppet, "Circulaire au sujet des mariages indigènes," 7 mai 1937, as quoted in ibid., 270–71.

58. Lydon, "Women, Children and the Popular Front's Mission," 179.

59. Northwestern University Library (NWU), Denise Moran Savineau, "La Famille en A.O.F: Condition de la Femme" (1938), 1.

60. Ibid., 26.

61. Ibid., 216.

62. Ibid., 218–20.

63. Sacré-Cœur, *The House Stands Firm,* vii–x. She served as a member of the Academy of Sciences Overseas, the Superior Council of Overseas Social Affairs, and the Superior Council of Overseas Sociological Research, and she was known in French administrative circles. Georges Hardy, honorary director of the Ecole Coloniale (Colonial School) that trained French administrators, wrote the introduction to her first book.

64. Sacré-Cœur, *La Femme Noire,* 15–18.

65. Ibid., 236–37.

66. Ibid., 244.

67. Sacré-Cœur, *The House Stands Firm,* 224, 231.

68. The image of the nuclear, middle-class family was an idealized norm that did not capture the experiences of all American and European women across time and place. The classic white American feminist text is Friedan, *The Feminine Mystique.*

69. In contrast to the "first wave" of American feminism that began in the nineteenth century and focused on voting rights, the "second wave" of the 1960s emphasized "sisterhood." When American feminism, in the 1980s, began to acknowledge actively an American women's experience informed by race, class, and sexuality, it was seen as a new "third wave" that called into question earlier white feminist writings, even though black, Latina, Asian, working-class, and Native American women had been organizing around and theorizing about womanhood(s) for decades. bell hooks, "Sisterhood: Political Solidarity between Women," 396–411, originally published in hooks, *Feminist Theory: From Margin to Theory;* White, "Black Feminist Interventions," 25–80; Thompson, "Multiracial Feminism," 336–60; Maclean, *Freedom Is Not Enough,* 117–55.

70. Hall, "Feminism and Feminist History," 1–40; Midgley, *Gender and Imperialism.* For case studies in India and the Sudan respectively, see Burton, *Burdens of History;* and Janice Boddy, *Civilizing Women.*

71. Offen, "Body Politics," 138–59; Eichner, "*La Citoyenne* in the World," 64.

72. Céline Idowu, interview with the author, March 30, 2000. In her study of Yoruba concepts of menstruation and fertility, Elisha Renne documents similar language of nostalgia for past practices and condemnation for modern-day attitudes. Renne, "'Cleaning the Inside,'" 197.

73. Seidou Sadikou, interview with the author, April 5, 2000; Alhaji Akeju Moussouloumi, interview with the author, April 4, 2000.

74. I tried to estimate time period based the on the reigns of different Alákétu. Thus, the woman here claimed to have "known" Alákétu Onyegen (1894–1918) and that her daughter was married during the time of Alákétu Odemufekun (1918–1936). Interview with the author. Name of interviewee omitted.

75. Interview with the author. Name of interviewee omitted.

76. See chapter 3 above.

77. Interviews with the author. Names of interviewees are omitted.

78. Interview with the author. Name of interviewee omitted.

79. Interview with the author. Name of interviewee omitted.

80. Many people in Kétu, including ministers at the king's palace, identified Koyato in the Verger photograph that I showed them in October 2006, but no one was willing to discuss her

òrìṣà (deity). Their reticence was understandable; the deity in question was probably the potent Nana Buku, said to control birth and death. Thompson, *Flash of the Spirit*, 68–71; Drewal and Drewal, *Gẹ̀lẹ̀dẹ́: Art and Female Power among the Yoruba*, 166, 170; Washington, *Our Mothers, Our Powers, Our Texts*, 63–64.

81. Interview with the author. Name of interviewee omitted.

82. Peel, *Religious Encounter and the Making of the Yoruba*, 234–36.

83. Mann, *Marrying Well*, 77–91.

84. Interview with the author. Name of interviewee omitted.

85. Schneider, *Quality and Quantity*, 209–16.

86. Offen, "Body Politics," 138–59; Conklin, "Redefining 'Frenchness,'" 65–83.

87. Conklin, *A Mission to Civilize*, 220–21, 224.

6. "The Opening of the Eyes"

1. Some people claimed that Alhaji Moussa Laurent began *fàyàwó* (pulling chest to ground; cross-border trade) in the 1920s or 1930s, but his own children and one of the women he married in the 1930s said that he took up *fàyàwó* in the 1940s. Prior to that time he was a weaver. Alhaji Taofik Moussa, interview with the author, May 18, 2000.

2. Peel, "Ọlaju: A Yoruba Concept of Development," 139–65. Peel also tends to translate the term as "enlightenment" to recognize the association made with the arrival of missionaries in the nineteenth century.

3. ANB, 1E11 2, "Rapport sur la situation politique, Cercle Ouéré-Kétou-Hollis," 7 décembre, 1894. *Aloufa* is the French adaptation of the Yoruba *àlùfáà* or *alfa* meaning "Muslim cleric." The French were using the word *aloufa* in these early documents in the same way that they used the term *marabout* throughout Africa. Triaud, "Introduction," 11–29.

4. ANB, 1E11 2(2), "Rapport politique," 30 octobre–30 novembre 1894. Protectorat d'Agony-Ouéré-Kétou à Directeur d'Affaires Politiques, 22 juillet 1895; ANB, 1E11 2(2), "Rapport sur la situation politique du Cercle Ouéré-Kétou-Holli," 10 mai–10 juin 1895; ANB, 1E20 3(2), "Rapport de l'administrateur des colonies à M. Lieutenant-Gouveneur," 10 janvier 1906.

5. ANS, 2G1 36, "Rapport Politique," 19 décembre 1901. Liotard's report concerns the entire border from the coast to Kétu and makes a special notation about Sakété. Sakété lies about halfway between Kétu and Porto-Novo, on the coast.

6. ANB, 1E11 2(1), "Lettre du Résident au Gouverneur," 6–7 février 1898; ANB, 1M 37(13), "Affaire Soumanou," 9 mai 1916. This particular case involved an array of Muslim and non-Muslim local and Lagos traders trying to smuggle ivory.

7. Alhaji Lawani Kifuli, interview with the author, May 21, 2000; Ìyá Libara Cathérine Adebiyi, interview with the author, May 24, 2000. Local, regional trade in these types of products continued through the rest of the colonial period.

8. ANB, 1E11 2(3), "Rapport du tournée," 29 septembre 1915; ANS, S10, Douanes No. 1052, 26 octobre 1917; ANS, S10, "Lettre du Chef des Douanes," 26 mai 1917; Journal Official de l'Afrique Occidentale Française (JOAOF), Arrêté portant suppression du bureau des Douanes d'Irocogny (Dahomey), 25 février 1935. A second post was supposed to open at Iga, south of Kétu, but as late as 1917 it was still not created.

9. Madeleine Adekambi, interview with the author, May 12, 2000.

10. Mondjannagni, "Quelques aspects historiques, économiques, and politiques," 34–35. One interviewee exclaimed that if a person could carry palm oil nuts the long, treacherous distance to the coast just once, that person would be rich. Salamantou Imoru, interview with the author, April 26, 2000.

11. ANS, S10, "La Création des Douanes à la frontière du Dahomey," 7 mars 1914. Customs offices were created at Irocogny, Jabata, and three other sites. The man noted the existence of customs officials during this period but they primarily stayed in Jabata in the Savé region.

12. Benjamin Oyewusi, interview with the author, April 10, 2000.

13. Pascal Fagbohun, interview with the author, April 7, 2000; Sani Salami, interview with the author, April 22, 2000.

14. Benjamin Oyewusi, interview with the author, April 10, 2000.

15. Alhaja Safouratou Mama, research assistant, personal communication, October 2006. Alhaji Moussa Mama died in 1988 after a debilitating illness; years later, elderly people's eyes gleamed at the sight of his adult daughter Alhaja Safouratou Mama, my research assistant. They would honor Alhaji Moussa Laurent's memory by citing the nickname of his father, a renowned hunter and maker of medicine.

16. Benjamin Oyewusi, interview with the author, April 10, 2000.

17. Those who continued to farm would work in *fàyàwọ́* during the dry season only. Those who worked in *fàyàwọ́* all year round noted that during the rainy season, one could move goods with more ease because the customs agents did not come out or could not operate their bikes or motorcycles as well in the rain. Patrice Ajibade, interview with the author, April 12, 2000.

18. Alhaji Taofik Moussa, interview with the author, May 18, 2000.

19. Ayodele Félicité Fagbohun, interview with the author, May 4, 2000; Ìyá Libara Cathérine Oyewole Adebiyi, interview with the author, April 20, 2000.

20. Ayodele Félicité Fagbohun, interview with the author, May 4, 2000; Subedatou Mouritala, interview with the author, April 25, 2000.

21. These court cases were discovered in the now defunct subprefecture of Kétu. With decentralization, Kétu has its own mayor and budget, and I was told that the older documents were no longer part of their holdings; it is unclear where these assorted documents would have been sent. Only fifteen cases appeared in the records for 1963 and 1964, eight of them involving bridewealth disputes, referred to as "dowry reimbursement" (*remboursement de dot*). Such a small, isolated number of examples cannot suggest definitive patterns for these types of cases.

22. Archives de la Sous-Prefecture de Kétou (ASPK), V.A. vs. A.O. (1963). Full names of parties are omitted.

23. ASPK, C.I. vs. I.A. (1964).

24. ASPK, O.O. vs. I.A. (1964).

25. Iroko and Igue, *Les villes Yoruba du Dahomey*, 5. Benjamin Oyewusi, interview with the author, April 10, 2000.

26. Seidou Amala apparently traveled to Mecca several years before Alhaji Moussa Laurent and Saha and died en route. People claim that Saha returned with Seidou Amala's baggage. Alhaji Shouaibou Chekoni, interview with the author, April 3, 1999. By the 1950s the French colonial government was organizing and overseeing Air France flights from West Africa to Mecca. ANB, 4E9 3, "Pilgrimage à la Mecque," 7 juin 1951. The document noted the requirement, fees, and paperwork required of Muslim pilgrims.

27. Gbadamosi, *The Growth of Islam among the Yoruba*, 5. Gbadamosi claims Kétu was a center for Islamic learning but does not cite any sources.

28. ANB, 1E20 4, "Rapport Politique, Cercle de Zagnanado," juin 1914.

29. Alhaji Lawani Kifuli, interview with the author, April 13, 2000.

30. Imam Alhaji Nassirou Raji, interview with the author, April 23, 1999.

31. Marty, *Études sur l'Islam au Dahomey*, 139–40. ANS, Série J, 1904. Reference to the qur'anic school may concern a man named Ogouansi with twenty-two students. This may be

the same Alayansi mentioned by the imam as his first teacher. Magaji is a name/title associated with the Hausa language. Kétu residents also pointed to the possible existence of schools that existed sometime in the 1920s under the guidance of men named Amadu, Mamah, and Lawani. Other schools were headed by Seidou Amala, Saha, Abudu Azziz, Atiku, Mamadou Lawal, Mamadou Aruna Arepa (Lawani Guiwa), and perhaps Abibu and Abubakar. Alhaji Lawani Kifuli, interview with the author, December 16, 1998; Alhaji Shouaibou Chekoni, interview with the author, April 3, 1999.

32. The simplified pronunciation is known as *amúkálàmù* or *amukala* (we bring pen). There is an equivalent of this practice in Hausa areas to the north, but that pronunciation and writing style known as *ajami* became a popular medium for a range of literary arts in Hausa communities. Alhaji Lawani Kifuli, interview with the author, December 14 and 16, 1998. Since that time, some Kétu *àlùfáà* (scholars) have learned Arabic in various parts of Nigeria and other areas of Bénin Republic. However, *amúkálàmù* remains the popular style of instruction in all schools in Kétu except for one.

33. A woman named Aminatou may have served as Ìyá Sunna during the 1920s and 1930. She was followed by Sefiatou, and Rucayatou of Iṣaare. Imam Alhaji Nassirou Raji, interview with the author, February 3, 1999; Seinabu Bakary, interview with the author, February 18, 1999.

34. The association between Islam and *ọlàjú* in Kétu contrasts with the Peel's characterization of that relationship in Ileṣa. Peel, "Ọlaju: A Yoruba Concept of Development," 153.

35. Childers, *Fathers, Families, and the State in France.*

36. Pedersen, *Family, Dependence, and the Origins of the Welfare State,* 224–288.

37. Ibid., 357–58.

38. Under the Fourth Republic, the French-controlled Caribbean islands of Martinique and Guadeloupe, the South American colony of Guyana, and the island of Reunion off the coast of East Africa became full departments equal to those in mainland France, while West African colonies became Overseas Territories with limited representation in the French National Assembly. In other reactions to the reorganization of the French empire, Vietnam declared independence in 1945, triggering a war with the French that lasted until 1954. Cameroon, the former German colony administered by France and Britain after World War I, tried to become a Trust Territory of the United Nations in order to gain independence.

39. Cooper, *Decolonization and African Society,* 281–85.

40. Ibid., 287. Grand Conseil, *Bulletin* No. 12, session de 6 novembre 1941, 15–36 as quoted in Cooper, *Decolonization and African Society,* 556n27.

41. Cooper, *Decolonization and African Society,* 315–21.

42. Grivot, *Réactions Dahoméennes,* 7, 11–12.

43. Ibid., 171.

44. Ibid., 96, 102–103, 107; France. Afrique Occidentale Française, *Conférence Africaine Française Brazzaville,* 35.

45. Ibid., 19, 30.

46. Ibid., 33–34.

47. A little more than 10 percent of the delegates came from the colonies, some renamed "departments," others "territories."

48. Glélé, *Naissance d'un Etat noir,* 71–73; Manning, *Francophone Sub-Saharan Africa,* 139–41.

49. Grivot, *Réactions Dahoméennes,* 81.

50. On anticolonial protest in Dahomey during World War I, see Garcia, "Les mouvements de résistance au Dahomey."

51. Jules Brévié, "Circulaire sur les chefs indigènes," 28 septembre 1932, cited and translated in Hargreaves, *France and West Africa,* 219–20.

52. Reste, *Le Dahomey,* cited in Cornevin, *Histoire du Dahomey,* 425–46.

53. Desanti, *Du Danhome,* 97, cited in Cornevin, *Histoire du Dahomey,* 426–27.

54. CAOM, AFFPOL 576/14, Gouverneur Général de l'AOF à Ministre des Colonies sur les chefs indigènes au Dahomey, 2 juillet 1935.

55. Asiwaju writes that Bankole Okanleke, long recognized as a village chief by the French administration, had insinuated himself into the position as canton chief after Alákétu Odemufekun's death in 1936, trying to capture the crown, only to see Alákétu Adewori named instead. Asiwaju connects Adewori's official installation—which he dates to 1947—to Okanleke's untimely death in a fire. Asiwaju, *Western Yorubaland under European Rule 1889–1945,* 94. When I interviewed people specifically about Adewori's status as Alákétu or canton chief, they invariably said that he had been king and canton chief beginning in 1937. Asiwaju, "The Alaketu of Ketu," 146–47. On the continuous problems with the Ohori (Hollidje) region that led to the creation of the Cercle Holli-Kétou in the 1910s and its dissolution in 1933; see CAOM, 14 Miom 2157, "Rapport d'Inspection du Cercle de Holli-Kétou," 13 mars 1933. At that time, Hollidje became part of the circle of Porto-Novo and Kétu was absorbed into the circle of Abomey. On the creation of a Kétu subdivision within the circle of Abomey, see CAOM 14 Miom 2155, "Arrêté portant ouverture la création de la subdivision de Kétou dans le Cercle d'Abomey," 30 avril 1947.

56. CAOM, 14 Miom 2721, "Revue trimestrielle pour le premier trimestre, 1949." The French official writes derisively of these "traditional" kings as *roitelets* (kinglets). But as the official head of the canton after 1947, the king of Kétu was recognized as head of a group of geographically and ethnically related villages and as an agent of the French administration with a salary and secretary. Cornevin, *Histoire du Dahomey,* 425–26.

57. Asiwaju, *Western Yorubaland under European Rule 1889–1945,* 111n91.

58. Asiwaju, "The Alaketu of Ketu," 154–55.

59. Glélé, *Naissance d'un Etat noir,* 92.

60. Ibid., 100–106, 139–42.

61. Camille Elegbede, October 7, 2007; Anani Abimbola, October 5, 2007; Antonin Iko Alayé, October 6, 2007; Gérard Adechinan, October 2007, interviews with Athanase Alayé; Manning, *Slavery, Colonialism, and Economic Growth in Dahomey,* 277–78.

62. Chafer, *The End of Empire in French West Africa,* 131–33; Staniland, "The Three-Party System in Dahomey," 310.

63. Anignikin, "La régionalisation de la lutte anti-impérialiste," 251.

64. The candidate was Camille Elegbede, a schoolteacher since retired, who has helped scholars who have worked in Kétu, including myself, with his knowledge of local history. Camille Elegbede, October 7, 2007; Anani Abimbola, October 5, 2007; Antonin Iko Alayé, October 6, 2007; Gérard Adechinan, October 2007, interviews with Athanase Alayé; Decalo, *Historical Dictionary of Benin,* 216.

65. Glélé, *Naissance d'un Etat noir,* 304, 310–11.

7. Mothers and Fathers of an Atlantic World

1. Nago is used as a general term for Yoruba in Brazil. Robin Law argues that the term Nago may have originally referred only to the western Yoruba in West African usage and that the later generic use of Nago for Yoruba, especially in French-controlled Dahomey, reflected feedback from Brazilians who returned to West Africa. Law, "Ethnicity and the Slave Trade," 212–215.

2. For an exception, see a case study of a Brazilian Candomblé house headed by a man in Matory, *Black Atlantic Religion,* 224–66.

3. Ibid., 285.

4. NWU Africana Library, Lorenzo D. Turner Papers, Africana Manuscripts 23, Box 40, Folder 5, "Our Recollections of Lagos," Martiniano do Bonfim and Anna M. Santos, n.d. The term *agudá* is a local term for Brazilians who returned to West Africa during the eighteenth and nineteenth centuries. On *agudá* culture and history in West Africa, see Yai, "The Identity, Contributions, and Ideology of the Aguda," 72–82; Guran, *Agudás*.

5. Matory, *Black Atlantic Religion*, 115–48.

6. Matory, "The English Professors of Brazil," 79.

7. Landes, *The City of Women*, 28.

8. Ibid., 27–28.

9. Pierson, *Negroes in Brazil*, 242–43, 272.

10. Nina Rodrigues, *L'Animisme Fétichiste de Nègres de Bahia*.

11. Ramos, "The Negro in Brazil," 522.

12. Pierson, *Negroes in Brazil*, 321–25, 336–39.

13. Landes, *The City of Women*, 26–27.

14. Berlin, "From Creole to African," 251–88; Mann and Bay, "Shifting Paradigms in the Study of the African Diaspora," 3–21; Lindsay, "'To Return to the Bosom of their Fatherland,'" 22–50; Matory, "The English Professors of Brazil," 72–103; Turner, "Some Contacts of Brazilian Ex-Slaves," 55–67.

15. Turner, "Some Contacts of Brazilian Ex-Slaves," 60–62; NWU, Africana Manuscripts 6 35/6, Melville Herskovits Papers, Lorenzo Turner to Melville Herskovits, February 4, 1941.

16. Gershenhorn, *Melville J. Herskovits and the Racial Politics of Knowledge*, 92.

17. Herskovits, *Acculturation*, 10.

18. Herskovits, *The Myth of the Negro Past*, 15, 34.

19. Hollanda, *Pierre Verger: Mensageiro*.

20. Jean Pierre Meunier, "Le Biguine à Paris: Migration et Mutation d'une Musique Métisse de la Caraïbe," at http://svr1.cg971.fr/lameca/dossiers/biguine_paris/index.htm (accessed April 17, 2007).

21. Métraux and Verger, *Le pied à l'étrier*, 56.

22. NWU, Herskovits Papers, 6 35/6, Box 42, Folder 3, Pierre Verger to Melville Herskovits, December 25, 1948.

23. Nóbrega and Echeverria, *Verger: Um retrato em preto e branco*, 171–73, 178–79. For another interpretation of Mãe Senhora and Pierre Verger's relationship, see Alberto, "Terms of Inclusion," 256–80.

24. Pierre Verger, *Orishas: Les dieux Yoruba*, 28.

25. NWU, Herskovits Papers, 6 35/6, Box 42, Folder 3, Pierre Verger to Melville Herskovits, February 8, 1949.

26. NWU, Herskovits Papers, 6 35/6, Box 50, Folder 27, Pierre Verger to Melville Herskovits, January 29, 1950.

27. Lühning, "Pierre Fatumbi Verger e sua obra," 318, 330.

28. Métraux and Verger, *Le pied à l'étrier*, 62.

29. Fundação Pierre Verger (FPV), 1–B 352 (I), Pierre Verger to Roger Bastide, April 16, 1953.

30. Johnson, *History of the Yorubas from the Earliest Times*, 78, 133, 379, 551. On a different interpretation of the origin of the title Aṣipa in New Ọyọ, see Goddard, "Ago that Become Oyo," 209.

31. Santos, *Ancestralidade Africana no Brasil Mestre Didi*, 67–69; Verger, *Flux et Reflux*, 632.

32. The water house of the title also was an actual well built by members of the da Rocha family with whom Olinto claimed a maternal link. Mba, "Literature as a Source of Nigerian

History," 356–57; Tallman, "The Ethnographic Novel," 14. Olinto is also known by the name Antônio Olinto Marques da Rocha.

33. Olinto, *Brasilieros na Africa,* 165–66; Olinto, *The Water House,* 54–69.

34. Olinto, *The Water House,* 398–99; Olinto, *The Glass Throne.*

35. Carneiro, "The Structure of African Cults in Bahia," 272; Nina Rodrigues, *L'Animisme Fétichiste de Nègres de Bahia*; Querino, *Costumes Africanos no Brasil*; Carneiro, *Candomblés da Bahia*; Bastide, *The African Religions of Brazil.* Matory counters the academic focus on Kétu Candomblé with his study of a Jeje house.

36. Carneiro, *Candomblés da Bahia,* 61. Based on interviews he conducted in Bahia and in Dahomey in the 1960s, Brazilian anthropologist Vivaldo da Costa Lima concluded that Iyá Kalá and Iyá Nassô were honorific titles for the same person and that Iyá Nassô was a title for the female Şango priest of the king of Ọyọ. Lima, "O conceito de 'Nação' nos Candomblés da Bahia," 80–82.

37. Johnson, *History of the Yorubas from the Earliest Times,* 64. Because of the reference to the Ọyọ title and other religious forms, Matory argues that an Ọyọ rather than specifically Kétu influence prevailed in the three famous Candomblé houses, otherwise identified with Kétu. Matory, *Black Atlantic Religion,* 121–22.

38. Schomburg Center for Research in Black Culture (SC), Melville Herskovits Papers, Box 22, Folder 135; Box 19, Folder 119. In Yoruba, the phrase would appear as *mojúbà.*

39. Pierre Verger asserted that two women, Iyanaso Akala (or Iyanasso Oka) and Iyaluso Danadana, founded the Candomblé house. Verger, *Orishas: Les dieux Yorouba,* 27–28. He also wrote that the Yoruba name of Engenho Velho was Iya Omi Ase Aira Intile.

40. Carneiro, *Candomblés da Bahia,* 63.

41. Her own parents were Gurunci, associated with a distant region of Burkina Faso. Sodré and de Lima, *Um vento sagrado,* 26.

42. Lima, "O conceito de 'Nação' nos Candomblés da Bahia," 83–86. The late eighteenth-century attack by Dahomey is described in Dalzel, *The History of Dahomy,* 202, and Dunglas, "Contribution à l'histoire du Moyen-Dahomey," vol. I, 68–70. Also see chapter 1 above. Renato da Silveira has recently tried to trace both the founder of Alaketo and the founders of Engenho Velho to this Dahomey attack. Silveira, "Sobre a Fundação do Terreiro do Alaketo," 345–79.

43. Harding, *A Refuge in Thunder,* 100–101.

44. Dzidzienyo, "The African Connection," 142–43. Dzidzienyo cites an article that describes Olga do Alaketo as a "pawn of the powerful"; after attending two arts festivals in West Africa in 1966 and 1977, she was invited to prepare a special meal for the Brazilian president.

45. Matory, *Black Atlantic Religion,* 241–42.

46. de Beauvoir, *Force of Circumstance,* 516–20, 524; Butler, *Freedoms Given, Freedoms Won*; Harding, *A Refuge in Thunder.* For a critique, see Matory, "Gendered Agendas," 409–39.

47. Robertson, "Africa into the Americas?" 9–21. For an Afrocentrist position and a critique, see Collins, *Black Feminist Thought*; and White, "Black Feminist Interventions," 132–50.

48. Matory, *Black Atlantic Religion,* 190–92.

49. Pierson, *Negroes in Brazil,* 285. Pierson also implied that the women priests were a new phenomenon.

50. Herskovits and Herskovits, "The Negroes of Brazil," 265.

51. Harding, *Refuge in Thunder,* 70–71.

52. Matory, *Black Atlantic Religion,* 35.

53. FPV, Nigeria Correspondance, 1-B 394, Alaafin Adeyemi to Madame Senhora, Iyanaso, August 14, 1952.

54. Hollanda, *Pierre Verger: Mensageiro.*

55. Freyre, *The Masters and the Slaves*, 278–79.

56. Siegel, *Uneven Encounters*, 206–34; Alberto, "Terms of Inclusion," 106–107. I am grateful to Marc Hertzman for bringing both of these texts to my attention.

57. Andrews, *Blacks and Whites in São Paulo, Brazil*, 215–16; Matory, *Black Atlantic Religion*, 202–203. Mãe Senhora's son Mestre Didi describes her acceptance speech in 1965 upon receiving the title, in Santos, *Ancestralidade Africana*, 102. Also see Alberto, "Para Africano Ver," 94.

58. Landes, *The City of Women*, 82–83.

59. Clécio Max, "Mãe Stella.": at http://povodosanto.blogspot.com/2008/02/se-ns-no -preservarmos-natureza-viva.html (accessed July 13, 2009). The term *aconchego* was translated as "maternal comfort and kindness" in a translation of the article on a website for Ilê Axé Opô Afonjá at http://www.geocities.com/ileohunlailai/page12af.html (accessed October 8, 2007; site now discontinued.) Matory translates *aconchego* ("maternal comfort and kindness") as "snuggly embrace." Matory, *Black Atlantic Religion*, 205.

60. Faria, *A Cidade das Mulheres* [*City of Women*]. Mãe Stella's lighthearted allusion to sexual relationships within the Candomblé temple is interesting considering Landes and Carneiro's discussion of a lesbian priestess in the 1930s and Matory's reference to lesbian priestesses heading Candomblé houses in more recent years, Landes, *The City of Women*, 46–47; Matory, *Black Atlantic Religion*, 213–14.

61. Paulina Alberto argues that by engaging with the Black Mother image and the concept of a special relationship between West Africa and Brazil, Mãe Senhora and others like Romana de Conceição also helped bolster the myth of Brazil's "racial democracy" during the pivotal period of the 1960s when Brazil reinstated democracy and tried to carve out a new foreign policy that engaged with a newly independent Africa. Alberto, "Para Africano Ver," 101–108. Matory argues that terms like "queen" and "lady" place black Brazilians outside of the national Brazilian identity as a republic and a democracy. Matory, *Black Atlantic Religion*, 27–28, 203. Royalist terms do not simply refer to a glorious African past. Black queens and ladies remind us that in an Atlantic world, especially in the Americas, women of color did not come easily by titles of respect and dignity. In Olinto's *The Water House*, Mariana Silva achieves success as an entrepreneur, trader, and property owner, but only realized what she had achieved when a man addresses her as "Sinha" (lady) rather than "Yaya" (black woman/girl). Olinto, *Water House*, 137.

62. Verger, *Orishas: Les dieux Yorouba*, passim; da Cunha and Verger, *Da senzala ao Sobrado*.

63. FPV, Photography Library, Roi Adewori, Ketou, Dahomey, 1948–1979, number 6234; Fundação Pierre Verger, Photography Library, Candomblé Opô Afonjá, Salvador, Brazil, 1948–1967, number 27593; Alex Baradel, personal communication with author, August 2006.

64. Joseph, "Black Mothers and Daughters," 92.

Epilogue

1. Idji, "1884–1994: Cent ans déjà!" 7.

2. Bierschenk and de Sardan, "Powers in the Village," 151, 155; Camille Elegbede, October 7, 2007; Anani Abimbola, October 5, 2007; Antonin Iko Alayé, October 6, 2007; Gérard Adechinan, October 2007, interviews with Athanase Alayé.

3. Nwajiaku, "The National Conferences in Benin and Togo Revisited," 429.

4. I could not determine the precise dates of the trip, but given that the National Conference occurred in January and February of 1990, it is unlikely that the trip could have been arranged any earlier or at the same time.

5. Dzidzienyo, "The African Connection," 139–40; Alberto, "Para Africano Ver," 78–117.

6. UNESCO, "The Slave Route Project," http://unesdoc.unesco.org/images/0015/001511/151178e.pdf (accessed June 3, 2008); Aruajo, "Political Uses and Memories of Slavery in the Republic of Benin," Institute of Historical Research, http://www.history.ac.uk/ihr/Focus/Slavery/articles/araujo.html (accessed April 3, 2007). The Ghana declaration was made in 1995.

7. See chapter 7 above.

8. Adrien Adeniyi Adeoti, interview with the author, October 2, 2006. The full name of the Argentinian organization is Ilé Àṣe Oṣun Doyo, Instituto de Investigación y la Difusión de las Culturas Negras, http://www.doyo.com.ar/frame.htm.

9. Hollanda, *Pierre Verger: Mensageiro.*

10. Jules Adesina, interview with the author, September 21, 2006; Fidèle Olude, interview with the author, September 24, 2006.

11. Adrien Adegnika, interview with the author, October 4, 2006.

12. Odjo, *La revue du centénaire,* 55–56. Several men were featured in individualized photographs including a former schoolteacher named Paul Fadairo, Alákétu Adewori, and three recently appointed kings in villages that had been part of the Kétu kingdom in the nineteenth century.

13. Alákétu Aladé Ìfẹ́'s ministers, interview with the author, September 19, 2006.

14. Ìyálóde Basilia Abero, interview with the author, July 16, 1997; Ìyá Libara Cathérine Oyewole Adebiyi, interview with the author, July 15, 1999.

15. Alhaji Moussadikou Soumaila, interview with the author, September 24, 2006.

16. Odjo, *La revue du centénaire,* 55–56; Alákétu Aladé Ìfẹ́, interview with the author, September 19, 2006.

17. Ìyá Afọbajẹ Salamantou Egunlope Brouaima, interviews with the author, November 2 and 26, 1988; Drewal and Mason, *Beads, Body, and Soul.*

18. This problem became painfully clear in my interview with Fidèle Olude on September 24, 2006, when he constantly mixed the names and titles of women he listed as Ìyá Libara, Ìyá Ọba, and Afin Ọba Obìnrin during the reigns of Alákétu Onyegen, Alákétu Odemufekun, and even Alákétu Adewori.

19. Jules Adesina, interview with the author, September 21, 2006; Fidèle Olude, interview with the author, September 24, 2006. Edna Bay shows that by the nineteenth century some princesses in Dahomey were taking on roles as *ahosi* ("wives" of the king). Bay, *Wives of the Leopard,* 248.

20. Blair, *Abeokuta Intelligence Report,* 25–26. That the women spoke openly of their political decline raises another set of questions worthy of systematic research.

21. Denzer, "Yoruba Women," 10–11.

22. Ìyálóde Basilia Abero, interview with the author, July 16, 1997. Some of her associates at the time were Ọtún Ìyálóde and Osì Ìyálóde, her assistants to the "right" and the "left."

23. Gbe speakers in the Kétu region are referred to as Mahi, rather than Fon, the more common term for Gbe speakers in Bénin Republic.

24. Mayor Lucie Sessinou Tidjani, interview with the author, October 6, 2006.

25. Gouvernement du Bénin, "Message du Maire: La 3eme Femme Maire du Bénin s'installe," http://www.gouv.bj/communes/oueme_plateau/ketou/message.php (accessed April 30, 2007; site now discontinued).

26. Mayor Lucie Sessinou Tidjani, interview with the author, October 6, 2006.

27. "La Commune de Kétou," http://www.ketou.bj/index.php (accessed July 16, 2009). Athanase Alayé, personal communication with the author, August 19, 2009. It was suggested that there was controversy and dissension around Mayor Tidjani's re-election bid. Doctor Salami Saliou Osseni assumed the office of mayor in Kétu in May 2009.

28. Scott, *Gender and the Politics of History,* 200.

29. Laqueur, *Making Sex*; Fausto-Sterling, *Sexing the Body*.

30. Lindsay and Miescher, "Introduction: Men and Masculinities," 1–29.

31. Hunt, "Introduction," 1–15; Allman, Geiger, and Musise, "Women in African Colonial Histories," 3, 10.

32. For example, Molara Ogundipe-Leslie developed the term "stiwanism" from her acronym STIWA (Social Transformation Including Women in Africa). She writes, "'STIWA' allows me to discuss the needs of African women today in the tradition of the spaces and strategies provided in our indigenous cultures. . . . Women have to participate as co-partners in social transformation." Ogundipe-Leslie, "Stiwanism," 229–30. Chikwenye Ogunyẹmi differentiates between her own definition of "African womanism" and Alice Walker's "womanism" by emphasizing "African women's inclusive, mother-centered ideology, with its focus on caring—families, communal, national, and international. . . . Other oppressive sites include totalitarianism, militarism, ethnicism, (post)colonialism, poverty, racism, and religious fundamentalism." Ogunyẹmi, *Africa Wo/Man Palava*, 114. Obioma Nnaemeka elaborates on her own term for African feminism, "negofeminism," as "feminism of negotiation" and "no *ego* feminism." She finds the art of negotiation integral to Igbo and many other African cultures and also critiques "the *ego* trip that engenders feminist arrogance, imperialism, and power struggles." Nnaemeka, "Foreword: Locating Feminisms/Feminists," 12. Nnaemeka first introduced the concept of "negofeminism" in Nnaemeka, "Feminism, Rebellious Women, and Cultural Boundaries," 80–113. For an overview of African feminism(s), especially in literature, see Arndt, *The Dynamics of African Feminism*, 27–70.

33. Imam, Sow, and Mama, *Engendering the African Social Sciences*, 6.

34. Kemp et al., "The Dawn of a New Day," 131–62; Miles, "North American Feminisms/Global Feminisms," 172.

Essay on Sources and Methodology

1. Bloch, *The Historian's Craft*, 63.

2. For example, see Geiger, "What's So Feminist about Women's Oral History?" 169–82; Cooper, "Oral Sources and the Challenge of African History," 191–215. For a critique of the lack of actual interpretation of African oral sources, see White, *Speaking with Vampires*, 43–50.

3. I thank Misty Bastian for the use of the term "middle way" to describe my analysis.

4. Félix Odjoawo, interview with the author, December 5, 1998.

Bibliography

Archives and Manuscript Collections

Bénin

Archives de la Sous-Préfecture du Kétou, Kétou
Archives Nationales du Bénin, Porto-Novo
    1E11, Rapports Politiques et Correspondances (Cercle de Holli-Kétou)
    1E14, Rapports Politiques et Correspondances
    1E20, Rapport Politiques et Correspondances (Cercle de Zagnanado)
    4E9, Affaires musulmanes
Bibliothèque National du Bénin, Porto-Novo
Institut de Recherche Appliquée du Dahomey, Porto-Novo

Brazil

Fundação Pierre Verger, Salvador
    1–B 348 (II), Gilbert Louget
    1–B 352, Roger Bastide
    1–B 394, Nigeria Correspondance

France

Archives de la Société des Missions Africaines, Lyon
Archives de la Ministère des Affaires Etrangères, Paris
    New Series, Dahomey 67 (1896–1911)
Centre des Archives Outre-Mer, Aix-en-Provence, (now Archives Nationales d'Outre-Mer)
    14 Mi 837, Affaires Politiques, Administratives et musulmanes Dahomey 1886–1920
    14 Mi 1078, Affaires politiques, Afrique Occidentale Française 1895–1920
    14 Miom 2155, Situations territoriale de Hollidje 1934–1948
    14 Miom 2157, Porto-Novo et Affaires Politiques 1934–1947
    14 Miom 2721, Rapport Politiques, Dahomey 1947–1953, 1957
    Fonds Modernes (FM) 574, Affaires Politiques Dahomey
    Fonds Modernes (FM) 576, Affaires Politiques Dahomey

Great Britain

Archives of the Church Missionary Society, University of Birmingham, Birmingham
    CA2 031/128, Samuel J. Crowther

CMS, 021/1–24, James Barber
CMS, 043/132, Charles Gollmer

Senegal

Archives Nationales du Sénégal, Archives de l'Afrique Occidentale Française, Dakar
2G, Rapport periodiques 1895–1940
8G, Affaires Politiques, Administratives et musulmanes Dahomey 1886–1920
Série S, Douanes et Impots, 1822–1920
Institut Fondamentale d'Afrique Noire, Dakar

United States

Northwestern University Library Archives, Melville J. Herskovits Library of African Studies,
Evanston, Illinois
Melville J. Herskovits Papers
Lorenzo D. Turner Papers
Denise Moran Savineau, "La Famille en A.O.F: Condition de la Femme," 1938.
Schomburg Center for Research in Black Culture, New York, New York
Melville J. Herskovits Papers
Southern Baptist Historical Library and Archive, Nashville, Tennessee
Microfilm (MF) 2040–1 and 2040–2, Thomas J. Bowen Papers, 1846–1876
Yale University Divinity Library, New Haven, Connecticut
CMS CA 2 031–034, Ms109, Samuel J. Crowther

Published Materials

Abbatucci, Dr. Séverin. "La Maternité en Afrique Noire." *Revue d'hygiène et de Médicine Préventive* 54, no. 2 (Feb. 1932).
Accampo, Elinor A. "Gender, Social Policy and the Formation of the Third Republic: An Introduction " In *Gender and the Politics of Social Reform in France, 1870–1914,* ed. Elinor A. Accampo, Rachel G. Fuchs, and Mary Lynn Stewart, 1–27. Baltimore and London: Johns Hopkins University Press, 1995.
———. "Integrating Women into the Teaching of French History, 1789 to the Present." *French Historical Studies* 27, no. 2 (Spring 2004): 267–92.
Achebe, Nwando. *Farmers, Traders, Warriors, and Kings: Female Power and Authority in Northern Igboland, 1900–1960.* Portsmouth, N.H.: Heinemann, 2005.
Acholonu, Catherine. *Motherism: The Afrocentric Alternative to Feminism.* Owerri, Nigeria: Afa Publications, 1995.
Adams, John. *Remarks on the Country Extending from Cape Palmas to the River Congo: Including Observations on the Manners and Customs of the Inhabitants.* 1822. Reprint, London: Frank Cass, 1966.
Adediran, Biodun. *The Frontier States of Western Yorùbáland: Circa 1600–1889: State Formation and Political Growth in an Ethnic Frontier Zone.* Ibadan, Nigeria: IFRA, 1994.
———. "Islam and Political Crises in Kétu: A Case-Study of the Role of Muslims in a Nineteenth Century Yoruba Polity." *Ife Journal of Religions* III (1982–1989): 3–18.
———. "The Ketu Mission, 1853–1859: An Abortive Experiment by the CMS in the Western Yorubaland." *Journal des Africanistes* 56, no. 1 (1986): 89–104.
Adegnika, Adrien, and Marcellin Djossa. "Les Premières heures d'évangélisation à Kétou: Faits

Inédits." In *Centenaire de la paroisse: Consécration de l'Eglise Sainte Thérèse d'Avila, Kétou, samedi 18 octobre 1997*, 26–27. Cotonou, Bénin: Graphitec, n.d.

Ajayi, J. F. Ade. *Christian Missions in Nigeria 1841–1891: The Making of a New Elite*. Evanston, Ill.: Northwestern University Press, 1965.

———. "Samuel Ajayi Crowther of Oyo." In *Africa Remembered: Narratives by West Africans from the Era of the Slave Trade*, ed. Philip Curtin, 289–316. Madison: University of Wisconsin Press, 1967.

Ajisafe, A. K. *The Laws and Customs of the Yoruba People*. London: Routledge, 1924.

Akinjogbin, I. A. *Dahomey and Its Neighbours, 1708–1818*. Cambridge: Cambridge University Press, 1967.

Alberto, Paulina Laura. "Para Africano Ver: African-Bahian Exchanges in the Reinvention of Brazil's Racial Democracy, 1961–63." *Luso-Brazilian Review* 45, no. 1 (2008): 78–117.

———. "Terms of Inclusion: Black Activism and the Cultural Conditions for Citizenship in a Multi-Racial Brazil, 1920–1982." Ph.D. dissertation, University of Pennsylvania, 2005.

Allman, Jean, Susan Geiger, and Nakanyike Musise. "Women in African Colonial Histories." In *Women in African Colonial Histories*, ed. Jean Allman, Susan Geiger, and Nakanyike Musise, 1–15. Bloomington: Indiana University Press, 2002.

Amadiume, Ife. *Male Daughters, Female Husbands: Gender and Sex in an African Society*. London: Zed Books, 1987.

———. *Re-Inventing Africa: Matriarchy, Religion, and Culture*. London and New York: Zed Books, 1997.

Andrews, George Reid. *Blacks and Whites in São Paulo, Brazil, 1888–1988*. Madison: University of Wisconsin Press, 1991.

Anignikin, Sylvain. "La Régionalisation de la lutte anti-impérialiste: Une Contribution de la jeunesse Béninoise à la dynamique de la nation en Afrique." In *Les Jeunes en Afrique: La Politique et la Ville*, ed. Hélène d'Almeida-Topor et al., 247–58. Paris: Editions L'Harmattan, 1992.

Anonymous. "Enquête colonial sur l'organisation de la famille, les fiançailles et le mariage chez les indigènes des colonies Françaises d'Afrique." *L'Afrique Libre: Revue de L'Anti-esclavagisme et des Questions Sociales* 4, no. 1 (31 mars 1910): 19–23.

Apter, Andrew. *Black Critics and Kings: The Hermeneutics of Power in Yoruba Society*. Chicago: University of Chicago Press, 1992.

Arendell, Terry. "Conceiving and Investigating Motherhood: The Decade's Scholarship." *Journal of Marriage and the Family* 62, no. 4 (November 2000): 1192–1207.

Arndt, Susan. *The Dynamics of African Feminism: Defining and Classifying African-Feminist Literatures*. Trenton, N.J.: Africa World Press, 2002.

Araujo, Ana Lucia. "Political Uses and Memories of Slavery in the Republic of Benin." Institute of Historical Research, http://www.history.ac.uk/ihr/Focus/Slavery/articles/araujo.html.

Asiwaju, A. I. "The Alaketu of Ketu and the Onimeko of Meko: The Changing Status of Two Yoruba Rulers under French and British Rule." In *West African Chiefs: Their Changing Status under Colonial Rule in Africa*, ed. Michael Crowder and Obaro Ikime, 134–60. New York: Africana Publishing, 1970.

———. *Western Yorubaland under European Rule 1889–1945: A Comparative Analysis of French and British Colonialism*. Atlantic Highlands, N.J.: Humanities Press, 1976.

Aublet, Edouard Edmond. *La Guerre Au Dahomey 1888–1893, 1893–1894: d'après les documents officiels*. Paris: Berger-Levrault, 1894.

Awẹ, Bọnanlẹ. "Iyalode Efunsetan Aniwura (Owner of Gold)." In *Nigerian Women in Historical Perspective*, ed. Bọnanlẹ Awẹ, 57–71. Lagos and Ibadan, Nigeria: Sankore/Bookcraft, 1992.

Ayandele, E. A. *Missionary Impact in Modern Nigeria, 1842–1914: A Political and Social Analysis.* London: Longman, 1966.

Bailyn, Bernard. "The Idea of Atlantic History." *Itinerario* 20, no. 1 (1996): 19–41.

Barber, Karin. "Going Too Far in Okuku: Some Ideas About Gender, Excess, and Political Power." In *Gender and Identity in Africa,* ed. Mechthild Reh and Gudrun Ludwar-Ene, 71–83. Hamburg, Germany: Lit, 1995.

——. "How Man Makes God: Yoruba Attitudes toward the Orisa." *Africa* 51, no. 3 (1981): 724–45.

——. *I Could Speak until Tomorrow:* Oriki, *Women and the Past in a Yoruba Town.* Washington, D.C.: Smithsonian, 1991.

Barnes, Sandra. "The Many Faces of Ogun: Introduction to the First Edition." In *Africa's Ogun: Old World and New,* ed. Sandra Barnes, 1–26. Bloomington: Indiana University Press, 1997.

Bascom, William. "Urbanization among the Yoruba." *American Journal of Sociology* 60, no. 5 (1955): 446–54.

Bastian, Misty. "'Vultures of the Marketplace': Southeastern Nigerian Women and Discourses of the Ogu Umunwaanyi (Women's War) of 1929." In *Women in African Colonial Histories,* ed. Jean Allman, Susan Geiger, and Nakanyike Musise, 260–81. Bloomington: Indiana University Press, 2002.

Bastide, Roger. *The African Religions of Brazil: Toward a Sociology of the Interpenetration of Cultures.* Translated by Helen Sebba. Baltimore: Johns Hopkins University Press, 1978.

Bay, Edna. "The Royal Women of Abomey." Ph.D. dissertation, Boston University, 1977.

——. "Servitude and Success in the Palace of Dahomey." In *Women and Slavery in Africa,* ed. Claire Robinson and Martin Klein, 340–67. Madison: University of Wisconsin Press, 1983.

——. *Wives of the Leopard: Gender, Politics, and Culture in the Kingdom of Dahomey.* Charlottesville: University of Virginia Press, 1998.

Beidelman, Thomas O. "Myth, Legend and Oral History: A Kaguru Traditional Text." *Anthropos* 65, no. 1 (1970): 74–97.

Benin. Direction des Archives Nationales. "Rapport du Tournée dans le Cercle De Zagnanado (Holli-Kétou)." *Mémoire du Bénin* 1 (1993): 82–87.

Berlin, Ira. "From Creole to African: Atlantic Creoles and the Origins of African-American in Mainland North America." *William and Mary Quarterly* 53, no. 2 (1996): 251–88.

Berry, Sara. *Fathers Work for Their Sons.* Berkeley: University of California Press, 1985.

Betts, Raymond. *Assimilation and Association in French Colonial Theory, 1890–1914.* New York and London: Columbia University Press, 1961.

Bierschenk, Thomas, and Jean-Pierre Olivier de Sardan. "Powers in the Village: Rural Benin between Democratisation and Decentralisation." *Africa* 73, no. 2 (2003): 145–73.

Blair, Major J. H. *Abeokuta Intelligence Report.* 1937. Reprint, Abeokuta: n.p., 2002.

Blier, Suzanne Preston. "The Path of the Leopard: Motherhood and Majesty in Early Danhome." *Journal of African History* 36, no. 3 (1995): 391–417.

Bloch, Marc. *The Historian's Craft.* Translated by Peter Putnam. New York: Alfred A. Knopf, 1953.

Boddy, Janice. *Civilizing Women: British Crusades in Colonial Sudan.* Princeton, N.J., and Oxford: Princeton University Press, 2007.

Bosman, Willem. "A New and Accurate Description of the Coast of Guinea, Divided into the Gold, the Slave, and the Ivory Coasts." London: printed for James Knapton, and Dan. Midwinter, 1705, *Eighteenth Century Collections Online.* Gale. Wesleyan University, http://find.galegroup.com/ecco/infomark.do?&contentSet=ECCOArticles&type=multipage

&tabID=T001&prodId=ECCO&docId=CW101007353&source=gale&userGroupName
=31841&version=1.0&docLevel=FASCIMILE.

Bowen, Thomas J. *Adventures and Missionary Labours in Several Countries in the Interior of Africa, from 1849 to 1856.* 1857. Reprint, London: Frank Cass, 1968.

Bowlan, Jeanne. "Civilizing Gender Relations in Algeria: The Paradoxical Case of Marie Bugèja, 1919–39." In *Domesticating the Empire: Race, Gender, and Family Life in French and Dutch Colonialism,* ed. Julia Clancy-Smith and Frances Gouda, 175–92. Charlottesville and London: University of Virginia Press, 1998.

Brévié, Jules. "Circulaire sur la codification des coutumes indigènes, 19 mars 1931." In *La Justice Indigène en Afrique Occidentale Française.* Gorée: Imprimerie du Gouvernement Général, 1932.

Burton, Antoinette. *Burdens of History: British Feminists, Indian Women, and Imperial Culture, 1865–1915.* Chapel Hill and London: University of North Carolina Press, 1994.

Burton, Richard. *A Mission to Gelele, King of Dahome.* Edited by C. W. Newbury. New York: Praeger, 1966.

Butler, Kim D. *Freedoms Given, Freedoms Won: Afro-Brazilians in Post-abolition São Paulo and Salvador.* New Brunswick, N.J.: Rutgers University Press, 1998.

Byfield, Judith. "Women, Marriage, and Divorce and the Emerging Colonial State in Abeokuta (Nigeria) 1892–1904." In *"Wicked" Women and the Reconfiguration of Gender in Africa,* ed. Dorothy Hodgson and Sheryl McGurdy, 27–46. Portsmouth, N.H.: Heinemann, 2001.

Cachard, Henry. *The French Civil Code.* Rev. ed. Paris: LeCram Press, 1930.

Carneiro, Edison. *Candomblés da Bahia.* 3d ed. Rio de Janeiro: Conquista, 1961.

———. "The Structure of African Cults in Bahia." *The Journal of American Folklore* 53, no. 210 (1940): 271–78.

Chafer, Tony. *The End of Empire in French West Africa: France's Successful Decolonization?* Oxford: Berg, 2002.

Childers, Kristen Stromberg. *Fathers, Families, and the State in France, 1914–1945.* Ithaca, N.Y. Cornell University Press, 2003.

Clancy-Smith, Julia. "Islam, Gender, and Identities in the Making of French Algeria, 1830–1962." In *Domesticating the Empire: Race, Gender, and Family Life in French and Dutch Colonialism,* ed. Julia Clancy-Smith and Frances Gouda, 154–74. Charlottesville: University of Virginia Press, 1998.

Clapperton, Hugh. *Hugh Clapperton into the Interior of Africa: Records of the Second Expedition 1825–1827.* Edited by Jamie Bruce-Lockhart and Paul E. Lovejoy. Leiden, Netherlands, and Boston: Brill, 2005.

Cohen, Abner. *Custom and Politics in Urban Africa: A Study of Hausa Migrants in Yoruba Towns.* Berkeley: University of California Press, 1969.

Cohen, William B. *The French Encounter with Africans: White Response to Blacks, 1530–1880.* Bloomington: Indiana University Press, 1980.

———. *Rulers of Empire: The French Colonial Service in Africa.* Stanford, Calif.: Hoover Institution Press, 1971.

Cole, Joshua H. "'There Are Only Good Mothers': The Ideological Work of Women's Fertility in France before World War I." *French Historical Studies* 19, no. 3 (Spring 1996): 639–72.

Collins, Patricia Hill. *Black Feminist Thought: Knowledge, Consciousness, and the Politics of Empowerment.* New York and London: Routledge, 1991.

Comaroff, Jean, and John Comaroff, eds. *Modernity and Its Malcontents: Ritual and Power in Postcolonial Africa.* Chicago and London: University of Chicago Press, 1993.

Commune de Kétou. "La Commune De Kétou." http://www.ketou.bj/index.php.

Conklin, Alice L. *A Mission to Civilize: The Republican Idea of Empire in France and West Africa, 1895–1930*. Stanford, Calif.: Stanford University Press, 1997.

———. "Redefining 'Frenchness': Citizenship, Race Regeneration, and Imperial Motherhood in France and West Africa, 1914–1940." In *Domesticating the Empire: Race, Gender, and Family Life in French and Dutch Colonialism*, ed. Julia Clancy-Smith and Frances Gouda, 65–83. Charlottesville: University of Virginia Press, 1998.

Cooper, Barbara. *Marriage in Maradi: Gender and Culture in a Hausa Society in Niger, 1900–1989*. Portsmouth, N.H.: Heinemann, 1997.

———. "Oral Sources and the Challenge of African History." In *Writing African History*, ed. John Edward Philips, 191–215. Rochester, N.Y.: University of Rochester Press, 2005.

Cooper, Frederick. *Decolonization and African Society: The Labor Question in French and British Africa*. Cambridge: Cambridge University Press, 1996.

Cooper, Frederick, and Ann Laura Stoler. *Tensions of Empire: Colonial Cultures in a Bourgeois World*. Berkeley: University of California Press, 1997.

Cornevin, Robert. *Histoire du Dahomey*. Paris: Berger-Levrault, 1962.

da Cunha, Marianno Carneiro, and Pierre Verger. *Da Senzala ao Sobrado: Arquitetura Brasileira na Nigéria e na República Popular Do Benim* [From Slave Quarters to Town Houses: Brazilian Architecture in Nigeria and the People's Republic of Benin]. São Paulo: Nobel: Editions USP, 1985.

Dahomey. *Coutumier du Dahomey*. Porto-Novo: Imprimerie du Gouvernement, 1933.

———. *Journal Officiel du Dahomey 1894–1960*.

d'Almeida-Topor, Hélène. *Les Amazones*. Paris: Rochevigne, 1984.

Dalzel, Archibald. *The History of Dahomy, an Inland Kingdom of Africa*. 1793. Reprint, London: Frank Cass, 1967.

Dartois, Vicaire Apostolique Louis. "Le Village Saint-Lazare à Zagnanado, Dahomey." *Société Antiesclavagiste de France* (1905): 135–40.

Day, Lynda Rose. "The Female Chiefs of the Mende, 1885–1977: Tracing the Evolution of an Indigenous Political Institution." Ph.D. dissertation, University of Wisconsin–Madison, 1988.

———. "Nyarroh of Bandasuma, 1885–1914: A Re-Interpretation of Female Chieftaincy in Sierra Leone." *Journal of African History* 48 (2007): 415–37.

de Beauvoir, Simone. *Force of Circumstance*. Translated by Richard Howard. Reprint, New York: G. P. Putnam's Sons, 1965.

Decalo, Samuel. *Historical Dictionary of Benin*. 2d ed. Metuchen, N.J.: Scarecrow Press, 1987.

Delafosse, Maurice, and Dr. Léon Poutrin. *Enquête coloniale dans l'Afrique française occidentale et équatoriale, sur l'organisation de la famille indigène, les fiançailles, le mariage*. Paris: Sociétés d'Editions Géographiques, Maritimes et Coloniales, 1930.

Denzer, Laray. "Yoruba Women: A Historiographical Study." *International Journal of African Historical Studies* 27, no. 1 (1994): 1–39.

Diop, Cheikh Anta. *Cultural Unity of Black Africa: The Domains of Patriarchy and Matriarchy in Classical Antiquity*. Chicago: Third World Press, 1978.

Drewal, Henry John, and Margaret Thompson Drewal. *Gẹlẹdẹ: Art and Female Power among the Yoruba*. Bloomington: Indiana University Press, 1983.

Drewal, Henry John, and John Mason. *Beads, Body, and Soul: Art and Light in the Yoruba Universe*. Los Angeles: Fowler Museum of Cultural History, 1997.

Drewal, Margaret Thompson. "Symbols of Possession: A Study of Movement and Regalia in an Anago-Yoruba Ceremony." *Dance Research Journal* 7, no. 2 (1975): 15–24.

Dunglas, Edouard. "Contribution à l'histoire du Moyen-Dahomey (Royaume d'Abomey, de Kétou et de Ouidah)." *Etudes Dahoméennes* 19, vol. 1 (1957): 7–185.

———. "Contribution à l'histoire du Moyen-Dahomey (Royaume d'Abomey, de Kétou et de Ouidah)." *Etudes Dahoméennes* 20, vol. 2 (1957): 3–152.

———. "La Première attaque des Dahoméens contre Abẹokuta (3 mars 1951)." *Etudes Dahoméennes* 1 (1948): 7–19.

Dzidzienyo, Anani. "The African Connection and the Afro-Brazilian Condition." In *Race, Class and Power in Brazil*, ed. Pierre-Michel Fontaine, 135–53. Los Angeles: Center for Afro-American Studies UCLA, 1985.

Eichner, Carolyn J. "*La Citoyenne* in the World: Hubertine Auclert and Feminist Imperialism." *French Historical Studies* 32, no. 1 (Winter 2009): 63–84.

Eller, Cynthia. *The Myth of Matriarchal Prehistory: Why an Invented Past Won't Give Women a Future*. Boston: Beacon Press, 2000.

Eltis, David. "Construction of the Trans-Atlantic Database: Sources and Methods." http://www.slavevoyages.org/tast/database/methodology-16.faces.

———. "The Diaspora of Yoruba Speakers: Dimensions and Implications." In *The Yoruba Diaspora in the Atlantic World*, ed. Toyin Falola and Matt D. Childs, 17–39. Bloomington: Indiana University Press, 2004.

Eltis, David, and Stanley L. Engerman. "Was the Slave Trade Dominated by Men?" *Journal of Interdisciplinary History* 23, no. 2 (1992): 237–57.

———. "Fluctuations in Sex and Age Ratios in the Transatlantic Slave Trade, 1663–1864." *The Economic History Review*, New Series, 46, no. 2 (1993): 308–23.

Fadipe, N. A. *The Sociology of the Yoruba*. Edited by Francis Okedeji and Oladejo Okedeji. Ibadan, Nigeria: University of Ibadan Press, 1970.

Fagbite, Thomas. "Sens Des Mutations Socio-Economiques à Kétu." Mémoire de Maîtrise, Université du Bénin, 1983.

Faria, Lázaro. *A Cidade Das Mulheres* [City of Women]. Bahia, Brazil: Casa de Cinema da Bahia, 2005. DVD.

Fausto-Sterling, Anne. *Sexing the Body: Gender Politics and the Construction of Sexuality*. New York: Basic Books, 2000.

Forbes, Frederick E. *Dahomey and the Dahomans: Being the Journals of Two Missions to the King of Dahomey and Residence at His Capital in the Year 1849 and 1850*. Vol. 2. 1851. Reprint, London: Frank Cass, 1966.

France. Afrique Occidentale Française. *Conférence Africaine Française Brazzaville, 30 janvier 1944–8 février 1944*. Paris: Ministère des Colonies, 1945.

———. *La justice indigène en Afrique Occidentale Française*. Gorée: Imprimerie du Gouvernement Général, 1932.

Freyre, Gilberto. *The Masters and the Slaves*. Translated by Samuel Putnam. 1933. Reprint, Los Angeles: University of California Press, 1986.

Friedan, Betty. *The Feminine Mystique*. 1963. Reprint, New York: W. W. Norton, 1997.

Games, Alison. "Atlantic History: Definitions, Challenges, and Opportunities." *American Historical Review* 111, no. 3 (June 2006): 741–57.

Garcia, Luc. "Les Mouvements de résistance au Dahomey (1914–1917)." *Cahiers d'études africaines* 10, no. 37 (1970): 144–78.

———. *Le Royaume du Dahomé face à la pénétration coloniale*. Paris: Karthala, 1998.

Garrard, Timothy. "Myth and Metrology: The Early Trans-Saharan Trade." *Journal of African History* 23, no. 4 (1982): 443–61.

Gbadamosi, T. G. O. *The Growth of Islam among the Yoruba, 1841–1908.* Atlantic Highlands, N.J.: Humanities Press, 1978.

Geiger, Susan. "What's So Feminist about Women's Oral History?" *Journal of Women's History* 2, no. 1 (Spring 1990): 169–82.

Gershenhorn, Jerry. *Melville J. Herskovits and the Racial Politics of Knowledge.* Lincoln: University of Nebraska Press, 2004.

Geschiere, Peter. *The Modernity of Witchcraft: Politics and the Occult in Postcolonial Africa.* Translated by Peter Geschiere and Janet Roitman. Charlottesville: University of Virginia Press, 1997.

Gilroy, Paul. *The Black Atlantic: Modernity and Double Consciousness.* Cambridge, Mass.: Harvard University Press, 1993.

Glélé, Maurice. *Naissance d'un état noir: L'évolution politique et constitutionelle du Dahomey.* Paris: Librairie générale de droit et de jurisprudence, 1969.

Goddard, S. "Town-Farm Relationship in Yorubaland: A Case Study from Oyo." *Africa* 35, no. 1 (1965): 21–29.

———. "Ago That Become Oyo: An Essay in Yoruba Historical Geography." *The Geographical Journal* 137, no. 2 (1971): 207–11.

Gollmer, Charles Henry Vidal. *Charles Andrew Gollmer: His Life and Missionary Labours in West Africa, Compiled from His Journals and the Church Missionary Society's Publications.* 2d ed. London: Hodder and Stoughton, 1889.

Gouvernement du Bénin. "Message du Maire: La 3eme femme Maire du Bénin s'installe." http://www.gouv.bj/communes/oueme_plateau/ketou/message.php. Site now discontinued.

Grayzel, Susan R. *Women's Identities at War: Gender, Motherhood and Politics in Britain and France During the First World War.* Chapel Hill and London: University of North Carolina Press, 1999.

Griswold, Robert L. "Introduction to the Special Issue on Fatherhood." *Journal of Family History* 24, no. 3 (1999): 251–54.

Grivot, Réné. *Réactions Dahoméennes.* Paris: Editions Berger-Levrault, 1954.

Guran, Milton. *Agudás: Os "Brasileiros" do Benim.* Rio de Janeiro: Editora Nova Fronteira, 1999.

Guyer, Jane I. *Marginal Gains: Monetary Transactions in Atlantic Africa.* Chicago: University of Chicago Press, 2004.

Hall, Catherine. "Feminism and Feminist History." In *White, Male, and Middle Class: Explorations in Feminism and History,* ed. Catherine Hall, 1–40. New York: Routledge, 1992.

Hanson, Holly. "Queen Mothers and Good Government in Buganda: The Loss of Women's Political Power in Nineteenth-Century East Africa." In *Women in African Colonial Histories,* ed. Jean Allman, Susan Geiger, and Nakanyike Musise, 219–36. Bloomington: Indiana University Press, 2002.

Harding, Rachel E. *A Refuge in Thunder: Candomblé and Alternative Spaces of Blackness.* Bloomington: Indiana University Press, 2000.

Hargreaves, John D., ed. *France and West Africa: An Anthology of Historical Documents.* London: MacMillan, 1969.

Harms, Robert. *The Diligent: A Voyage through the Worlds of the Slave Trade.* New York: Basic Books, 2002.

Harrison, Christopher. *France and Islam in West Africa, 1860–1960.* Cambridge and New York: Cambridge University Press, 1988.

Hazoumé, Paul. "Tata Ajachê soupo ma ha awouinyan." *La Reconnaissance Africaine* 1 (1925): 7–9.

———. "Tata Ajachê soupo ma ha awouinyan." *La Reconnaissance Africaine* 2 (1925): 7–8.

———. "Tata Ajachê soupo ma ha awouinyan." *La Reconnaissance Africaine* 3 (1925): 7–8.

Henderson, Helen K. "Onitsha Woman: The Traditional Context for Political Power." In *Queens, Queen Mothers, Priestesses, and Power: Case Studies in African Gender,* ed. Flora E. S. Kaplan, 215–43. New York: New York Academy of the Sciences, 1997.

Henige, David. *Oral Historiography.* Oxford: Clarendon Press, 1982.

Herskovits, Melville J. *Acculturation: A Study in Culture Contact.* New York: J. J. Augustin, 1938.

———. *Dahomey: An Ancient West African Kingdom.* Vol. 1. New York: J. J. Augustin, 1938.

———. *The Myth of the Negro Past.* New York: London Harper & Brothers, 1941.

Herskovits, Melville, and Frances Herskovits. "The Negroes of Brazil." *Yale Review* 42 (Autumn 1942): 263–79.

Higginbotham, Evelyn Brooks. "African-American Women's History and the Metalanguage of Race." *Signs* 17, no. 2 (Winter 1992): 251–74.

Hollanda, Luiz Buarque de. *Pierre Verger: Mensageiro entre dois mundos.* Brazil and New York: Latin American Video Archives, 1998. VHS.

hooks, bell. *Feminist Theory: From Margin to Center.* Boston: South End Press, 1984.

———. "Sisterhood: Political Solidarity between Women." In *Dangerous Liaisons: Gender, Nation, and Postcolonial Perspectives,* ed. Anne McClintock, Aamir Mufti, and Ella Shohat, 396–411. Minneapolis: University of Minnesota Press, 1997.

Hunt, Nancy Rose. *A Colonial Lexicon: Of Birth Ritual, Medicalization, and Mobility in the Congo.* Durham, N.C., and London: Duke University Press, 1999.

———. "Introduction." In *Gendered Colonialisms in African History,* ed. Nancy Rose Hunt, Tessie R. Liu, and Jean Quataert, 1–15. Williston, Vt.: Blackwell, 1996.

Idji, Kolawole. "1884–1994: Cent ans déjà!" In *La revue du centenaire de la renaissance de Kétou,* ed. Sourou Odjo. n.p.: Golden Press, 1994.

Ifeka-Moller, Caroline. "Female Militancy and Colonial Revolt: The Women's War of 1929, Eastern Nigeria." In *Perceiving Women,* ed. Shirley Ardener, 127–57. London: Malaby Press, 1975.

Imam, Ayesha, Fatou Sow, and Amina Mama, eds. *Engendering the African Social Sciences.* Dakar, Senegal: CODESRIA, 1997.

Irbouh, Hamid. *Art in the Service of Colonialism: French Art Education in Morocco, 1912–1956.* London: Tauris Academic Studies, 2005.

Iroko, Félix. "Les personnes agées n'ont jamais eu en Afrique le monopole de la tradition." *Afrique Histoire* (n.d.), http://www.oozebap.org/text/historiaoral-fr.htm.

Iroko, Félix, and Ogunsola John Igue. *Les villes Yoruba du Dahomey: L'exemple de Kétou.* Ibadan, Nigeria: 1974.

Isola, Akinwumi. *Efunsetan Aniwura, Iyalode Ibadan and Tinuubu, Iyalode Egba: Two Yoruba Historical Dramas.* Translated by Pamela J. Olubunmi Smith. Trenton, N.J.: Africa World Press, 2004.

James, Stanlie M. "Mothering: A Possible Black Feminist Link to Social Transformation?" In *Theorizing Black Feminisms: The Visionary Pragmatism of Black Women,* ed. Stanlie M. James and Abena Busia, 45–56. London: Routledge, 1993.

Jetter, Alexis, Annelise Orleck, and Diana Taylor, eds. *The Politics of Motherhood: Activist Voices from Left to Right.* Hanover, N.H.: University Press of New England, 1997.

Johnson, Rev. Samuel. *History of the Yorubas from the Earliest Times to the Beginning of the British Protectorate.* Edited by Obadiah Johnson. Reprint ed. Lagos, Nigeria: C.S.S. Bookshops, 1921.

Joseph, Gloria I. "Black Mothers and Daughters: Their Roles and Functions in American Society." In *Common Differences: Conflicts in Black and White Feminist Perspectives*, ed. Gloria I. Joseph and Jill Lewis, 75–126. Boston: South End Press, 1982.

Kaplan, Flora. "*Iyoba*, the Queen Mother of Benin: Images and Ambiguity in Gender and Sex Roles in Court Art." In *Queens, Queen Mothers, Priestesses and Power: Case Studies in African Gender*, ed. Flora Kaplan, 72–102. New York: New York Academy of Sciences, 1997.

Kemp, Amanda, Nozizwe Madlala, Asha Moodley, and Elaine Salo. "The Dawn of a New Day: Redefining South African Feminism." In *The Challenge of Local Feminisms: Women's Movements in Global Perspective*, ed. Amrita Basu, 131–62. Boulder, Colo., and Oxford: Westview Press, 1995.

Koven, Seth, and Sonya Michel. "Introduction: 'Mother Worlds.'" In *Mothers of a New World: Maternalist Politics and the Origins of Welfare States*, ed. Seth Koven and Sonya Michel, 1–42. New York: Routledge, 1993.

Landes, Ruth. *The City of Women*. 1947. Reprint, Albuquerque: First University of New Mexico Press, 1994.

La Pin, Deirdre. "Story, Medium, and Masque: The Idea and Art of Yoruba Storytelling." Ph.D. dissertation, University of Wisconsin–Madison, 1977.

Laqueur, Thomas. *Making Sex: Body and Gender from the Greeks to Freud*. Boston: Harvard University Press, 1992.

Law, Robin. "The 'Amazons' of Dahomey." *Paideuma* 39 (1993): 245–60.

——. "Ethnicity and the Slave Trade: 'Lucumi' and 'Nago' as Ethnonyms in West Africa." *History in Africa* 24 (1997): 205–19.

——. "Local Amateur Scholarship and the Construction of Yoruba Ethnicity, 1880–1914." In *Ethnicity in Africa: Roots, Meanings and Implications*, ed. Louise de la Gorgendière, Kenneth King, and Sarah Vaughn, 55–90. Edinburgh: Centre for African Studies, University of Edinburgh, 1996.

——. *The Oyo Empire, c.1600–c.1836: A West African Imperialism in the Era of the Atlantic Slave Trade*. Oxford: Clarendon Press, 1977.

——. "Slave-Raiders and Middlemen, Monopolists and Free-Traders: The Supply of Slaves for the Atlantic Trade in Dahomey, c.1715–1850." *Journal of African History* 30, no. 1 (1988): 45–68.

——. "The Slave-Trader as Historian: Robert Norris and the History of Dahomey." *History in Africa* 16 (1989): 219–35.

——. "Towards a History of Urbanization in Pre-Colonial Yorubaland." Proceedings of a seminar held in the Centre of African Studies, University of Edinburgh, 1977.

Lawrance, Benjamin N., Emily Lynn Osborn, and Richard L. Roberts, "African Intermediaries and the 'Bargain' of Collaboration." In *Intermediaries, Interpreters, and Clerks: African Employees and the Making of the Colonial Africa*, ed. Benjamin N. Lawrance, Emily Lynn Osborn, and Richard L. Roberts, 3–34. Madison: University of Wisconsin Press, 2006.

Le Roy, Mgr. Alexandre. "La désorganisation de la famille africaine: La cause, la remède." *Société Antiesclavagiste de France* 30 (June 1902): 12–23.

Lima, Vivaldo da Costa. "O conceito de 'Nação' nos Candomblés da Bahia." *Afro-Asia* 12 (1976): 65–90.

Lindsay, Lisa. "'To Return to the Bosom of Their Fatherland': Brazilian Immigrants in Nineteenth-Century Lagos." *Slavery and Abolition* 15, no. 1 (1994): 22–50.

Lindsay, Lisa, and Stephan F. Miescher. "Introduction: Men and Masculinities in Modern African History." In *Men and Masculinities in Modern Africa*, 1–29. Portsmouth, N.H.: Heinemann, 2003.

Lloyd, P. C. "Agnatic and Cognatic Descent among the Yoruba." *Man* New Series 1, no. 4 (1966): 484–500.

———. "Sacred Kingship and Government among the Yoruba." *Africa* 30, no. 3 (1960): 221–37.

———. "The Yoruba: An Urban People?" In *Urban Anthropology: Cross-Cultural Studies of Urbanization*, ed. A. Southall, 107–23. New York: Oxford University Press, 1973.

———. "The Yoruba Lineage." *Africa* 25, no. 3 (1955): 235–51.

Lovejoy, Paul. "The Yoruba Factor in the Trans-Atlantic Slave Trade." In *The Yoruba Diaspora in the Atlantic World*, ed. Toyin Falola and Matt D. Childs, 40–55. Bloomington: Indiana University Press, 2004.

Lühning, Angela. "Pierre Fatumbi Verger e sua obra." *Afro-Asia* 21–22 (1998–1999): 315–64.

Lydon, Ghislaine. "Women, Children and the Popular Front's Mission of Inquiry in French West Africa." In *French Colonial Empire and the Popular Front*, ed. Tony Chafer and Amanda Sackur, 170–87. London: MacMillan Press, 1999.

MacLean, Nancy. *Freedom Is Not Enough: The Opening of the American Workplace*. Cambridge, Mass.: Harvard University Press, 2006.

Mann, Kristin. *Marrying Well: Marriage, Status and Social Change among the Educated Elite in Colonial Lagos*. Cambridge: Cambridge University Press, 1985.

Mann, Kristin, and Edna G. Bay. "Shifting Paradigms in the Study of the African Diaspora and of Atlantic History and Culture." In *Rethinking the African Diaspora: The Making of a Black Atlantic World in the Bight of Benin and Brazil*, ed. Kristin Mann and Edna G. Bay, 3–21. London: Frank Cass, 2001.

Manning, Patrick. *Francophone Sub-Saharan Africa, 1880–1985*. Cambridge: Cambridge University Press, 1988.

———. *Slavery, Colonialism, and Economic Growth in Dahomey, 1640–1960*. Cambridge: Cambridge University Press, 1982.

Marty, Paul. *Études sur l'Islam au Dahomey: Le bas Dahomey, le haut Dahomey*. Paris: Ernest Leroux, 1926.

Matory, J. Lorand. *Black Atlantic Religion: Tradition, Transnationalism, and Matriarchy in the Afro-Brazilian Candomblé*. Princeton, N.J.: Princeton University Press, 2005.

———. "The English Professors of Brazil: On the Diasporic Roots of the Yorùbá Nation." *Comparative Studies in Society and History* 41, no. 1 (1999): 72–103.

———. "Gendered Agendas: The Secrets Scholars Keep About Yorùbá-Atlantic Religion." *Gender & History* 15, no. 3 (2003): 409–39.

———. "Rival Empires: Islam and the Religions of Spirit Possession among the Oyo-Yoruba." *American Ethnologist* 21, no. 3 (1994): 495–515.

———. *Sex and the Empire That Is No More: Gender and the Politics of Metaphor in Oyo Yoruba Religion*. 2d ed. New York: Berghahn, 1997.

Maupoil, Bernard. "Contribution à l'étude de l'origine musulmane de la géomancie dans le Bas-Dahomey." Thèse complémentaire pour le Doctorat, 1945.

———. "L'étude des coutumes juridiques de l'AOF." In *Coutumiers Juridiques de l'Afrique Occidentale Française: Mauritanie, Niger, Côte d'Ivoire, Dahomey, Guinée Française*, 1–53. Government publication of French West Africa. Paris: Librairie Larose, 1939.

Max, Clécio. "Mãe Stella: 'Se nós não preservamos a natureza viva, termina tudo.'" *A Tarde*, April 30, 1995. http://povodosanto.blogspot.com/2008/02/se-ns-no-preservamps-natureza-viva .html./

Mba, Nina. "Literature as a Source of Nigerian History: Case Study of *The Water House* and the Brazilians in Lagos." In *History of the Peoples of Lagos State,* ed. Ade Adefuye, Babatunde Agiri, and Jide Osuntokun, 351–63. Lagos: Lantern Books, 1987.

McBride, Theresa. "Divorce and the Republican Family." In *Gender and the Politics of Social Reform in France, 1870–1914,* ed. Elinor A. Accampo, Rachel G. Fuchs, and Mary Lynn Stewart, 59–81. Baltimore and London: Johns Hopkins University Press, 1995.

McCabe, Douglas. "Histories of Errancy: Oral Yoruba *Àbíkú* Texts and Soyinka's 'Abiku.'" *Research in African Literatures* 33, no. 1 (Spring 2002): 45–74.

McKenzie, P. R. "Samuel Crowther's Attitude to Other Faiths during the Early Period." *Orita: Ibadan Journal of Religious Studies* V, no. I (June 1971): 3–17.

Métraux, Alfred, and Pierre Verger. *Le pied à l'étrier: Correspondance 12 Mars 1946–5 Avril 1963.* Edited by Jean-Pierre Le Bouler. Paris: Editions Jean-Michel Place, 1994.

Midgley, Clare, ed. *Gender and Imperialism.* Manchester: Manchester University Press, 1998.

Miers, Suzanne, and Igor Kopytoff. "Slavery as an Institution of Marginality." In *Slavery in Africa: Historical and Anthropological Perspectives,* ed. Suzanne Miers and Igor Kopytoff, 3–77. Madison: University of Wisconsin Press, 1977.

Miles, Angela. "North American Feminisms/Global Feminisms—Contradictory or Complementary?" In *Sisterhood, Feminisms and Power: From African to the Diaspora,* ed. Obioma Nnaemeka, 163–82. Trenton, N.J.: Africa World Press, 1998.

Miller, Joseph C. "Introduction: Listening for the African Past." In *The African Past Speaks: Essays on Oral Tradition and History,* ed. Joseph C. Miller, 1–59. Folkestone, England: Dawson; Hamden, Conn.: Archon, 1980.

Mondjannagni, A. "Quelques aspects historiques, économiques, and politiques de la frontière Nigeria-Dahomey." *Études Dahoméennes* New Series 1, no. 1 (1963–64): 17–59.

Morton-Williams, Peter. "A Yoruba Woman Remembers Servitude in a Palace of Dahomey, in the Reigns of Kings Glélé and Behanzin." *Africa* 63, no. 1 (1993): 102–17.

Moulero, Abbé Thomas. "Conquête de Kétou par Glélé et conquête d'Abomey par la France." *Études Dahoméennes* New Series 4 (May 1965): 61–68.

Moulero, Thomas. "Essai historique sur la ville de Kétou." *La Reconnaissance Africaine* 9 (1 janvier 1926): 7–8.

———. "Essai historique sur la ville de Kétou: Le Roi Adiro (suite)." *La Reconnaissance Africaine* 42 (1 septembre 1927): 3–4.

———. "Essai historique sur la ville de Kétou: Le Roi Andé." *La Reconnaissance Africaine* 31 (15 décembre 1926): 3–5.

———. "Essai historique sur la ville de Kétou: Les travaux des premiers rois." *La Reconnaissance Africaine* 20 (1 juillet 1926): 3–4.

———. "Les rois de Kétou." *La Reconnaissance Africaine* 12 (1 mars 1926): 7–8.

———. "Les rois de Kétou: Ordre de duccession et éducation du candidat au trône." *La Reconnaissance Africaine* 14 (1 avril 1926): 10–11.

Nina Rodrigues, Raymundo. *L'animisme fétichiste de Nègres de Bahia.* Bahia, Brazil: Reis & Comp., 1900.

Nnaemeka, Obioma. "Feminism, Rebellious Women, and Cultural Boundaries: Rereading Flora Nwapa and Her Compatriots." *Research in African Literatures* 26, no. 2 (1995): 80–113.

———. "Foreword: Locating Feminisms/Feminists." In Susan Arndt, *The Dynamics of African Feminism: Defining and Classifying African Feminist Literatures,* 9–15. Trenton, N.J.: Africa World Press, 2002.

———. "Introduction: Reading the Rainbow." In *Sisterhood, Feminisms and Power: From Africa to the Diaspora,* ed. Obioma Nnaemeka, 1–35. Trenton, N.J.: Africa World Press, 1998.

Nóbrega, Cida, and Regina Echeverria. *Verger: Um Retrato em preto e branco.* Salvador, Brazil: Corrupio, 2002.

Norris, Robert. *Memoirs of the Reign of Bossa Ahádee, King of Dahomy, an Inland Country of Guiney.* 1789. Reprint, London: Cass, 1968.

Nwajiaku, Kathryn. "The National Conferences in Benin and Togo Revisited." *Journal of Modern African Studies* 32, no. 3 (1994): 429–47.

Odjo, Sourou. "A la découverte de Kétou." In *La revue du centenaire de la renaissance de Kétou,* ed. Sourou Odjo, 9–15. N.p.: Golden Press, 1994.

———, ed. *La revue du centenaire de la renaissance de Kétou.* N.p.: Golden Press, 1994.

Offen, Karen. "Body Politics: Women, Work, and the Politics of Motherhood in France, 1920–1950." In *Maternity and Gender Policies: Women and the Rise of the European Welfare State, 1880s–1950s,* ed. Gisela Bock and Pat Thane, 138–59. New York: Routledge, 1991.

Ogundipe-Leslie, Molara. "Stiwanism: Feminism in an African Context." In *Recreating Ourselves: African Women and Critical Transformations,* 207–41.Trenton, N.J.: Africa World Press, 1994.

Ogunyẹmi, Chikwenye Okonjo. *Africa Wo/Man Palava: The Nigerian Novel by Women.* Chicago: University of Chicago Press, 1996.

Okonjo, Kamene. "The Dual-Sex Political System in Operation: Igbo Women and Community Politics in Midwestern Nigeria." In *Women in Africa: Studies in Social and Economic Change,* ed. Nancy J. Hafkin and Edna G. Bay, 45–58. Stanford, Calif.: Stanford University Press, 1976.

Olinto, Antônio. *Brasilieros na Africa.* Rio de Janeiro: Edições G.R.D., 1964.

———. *The Glass Throne.* Translated by Richard Chappell. London: Sel Press, 1995.

———. *The King of Ketu.* Translated by Richard Chappell. 1980. Reprint, London: Rex Collings, 1987.

———. *The Water House.* Translated by Dorothy Heapy. 1969. Reprint, New York: Carroll and Graf, 1985.

Owomoyela, Oyekan. *Yoruba Proverbs.* Lincoln and London: University of Nebraska Press, 2005.

Oyěwùmi, Oyèrónkẹ́. "Family Bonds/Conceptual Binds: African Notes on Feminist Epistemologies." *Signs* 25, no. 4 (2000): 1093–1098.

———. "Introduction: Feminism, Sisterhood, and Other Foreign Relations." In *African Women and Feminism: Reflecting on the Politics of Sisterhood,* ed. Oyèrónkẹ́ Oyěwùmi, 1–24. Trenton, N.J.: Africa World Press, 2003.

Palau Marti, Montserrat. *Le Roi-Dieu au Bénin.* Paris: Berger-Levrault, 1964.

Parrinder, E. Geoffrey. *The Story of Ketu: An Ancient African Kingdom.* Ibadan, Nigeria: Ibadan University Press, 1956.

———. *Les vicissitudes de l'histoire de Kétou.* Translated by Toussaint Soussouhountou. Cotonou, Bénin Republic: Les Editions du Flamboyant, 1997.

Patterson, Orlando. *Slavery and Social Death: A Comparative Study.* Cambridge, Mass.: Harvard University Press, 1982.

Pedersen, Susan. *Family, Dependence, and the Origins of the Welfare State: Britain and France, 1914–1945.* Cambridge: Cambridge University Press, 1993.

Peel, J. D. Y. *Ijeshas and Nigerians: The Incorporation of a Yoruba Kingdom 1890s–1970s.* Cambridge: Cambridge University Press, 1983.

———. "Ọlaju: A Yoruba Concept of Development." *Journal of Development Studies* 14, no. 2 (1977): 139–165.

———. "The Pastor and the Babalawo: The Interaction of Religions in Nineteenth-Century Yorubaland." *Africa* 60, no. 3 (1990): 338–69.

————. *Religious Encounter and the Making of the Yoruba.* Bloomington: Indiana University Press, 2000.

Pellet, Mgr. "Au Dahomey de Porto-Novo à Kétou." *Les Missions Catholiques* no. 1485 (19 novembre 1897): 561–63.

————. "Au Dahomey de Porto-Novo à Kétou." *Les Missions Catholiques* no. 1486 (26 novembre 1897): 573–76.

————. "Rapport de Mgr. Pellet-Vicaire Apostolique Du Bénin, présenté au Congrès Antiesclavagiste de Vienne." *Société Antiesclavagiste de France* 25 (mars 1901): 1–7.

Pied, Révérend Père. "De Porto-Novo à Oyo, févier–mars 1891." *Les Missions Catholiques,* no. 1199 (27 mai 1892): 260–67.

Pierson, Donald. *Negroes in Brazil: A Study of Race Contact at Bahia.* Chicago: University of Chicago Press, 1942.

Pires, Vicente Ferreira. *Crônica de uma embaixada Luso-Brasileira à Costa d'África em fins do século XVIII, incluindo o texto da viagem de África em o reino de Dahomé.* 1800. Reprint, Sao Paulo: Companhia Editora Nacional, 1957.

Ponty, William. *Justice indigène: Instructions aux administrateurs sur l'application du Décret du 16 août 1912 portant réorganisation de la justice en AOF.* Gorée, Senegal: Imprimerie du Gouvernement Général, 1913.

Pruneau de Pommegorge, Antoine. *Description de la Nigritie.* Amsterdam and Paris: Maradan, 1789.

Quayson, Ato. *Strategic Transformations in Nigerian Writings: Orality and History in the Work of Rev. Samuel Johnson, Amos Tutuola, Wole Soyinka, and Ben Okri.* Bloomington: Indiana University Press, 1997.

Querino, Manoel. *Costumes Africanos no Brasil.* 2d ed. 1938. Reprint, Recife, Brazil: Fundação Joaquim Nabuco-Editora Massangana, 1988.

Ramos, Arthur. "The Negro in Brazil." *The Journal of Negro Education* 10, no. 3 (July 1941): 515–23.

Renne, Elisha P. "'Cleaning the Inside' and the Regulation of Menstruation in Southwestern Nigeria." In *Regulating Menstruations: Beliefs, Practices, Interpretations,* ed. Etienne Van de Walle and Elisha P. Renne, 187–201. Chicago: University of Chicago Press, 2001.

Roberts, Mary Louise. *Civilization without Sexes: Reconstructing Gender in Postwar France, 1917–1927.* Chicago: University of Chicago Press, 1994.

Robertson, Claire. "Africa into the Americas? Slavery and Women, the Family, and the Gender Division of Labor." In *More Than Chattel: Black Women and Slavery in the Americas,* ed. David Barry Gaspar and Darlene Clark Hine, 3–40. Bloomington: Indiana University Press, 1996.

Robinson, David. *Paths of Accommodation: Muslim Societies and French Colonial Authorities in Senegal and Mauritania, 1880–1920.* Athens: Ohio University Press, 2000.

Sacks, Karen. *Sisters and Wives: The Past and Future of Sexual Equality.* Urbana: University of Illinois Press, 1982.

Sacré-Cœur, Soeur Marie-André du. *La Femme Noire en Afrique Occidentale.* Paris: Payot, 1939.

————. *The House Stands Firm: Family Life in Africa.* Translated by Alba I. Zizzamia. Milwaukee: Bruce Publishing Co., 1962.

Sanders, Edith. "The Hamitic Hypothesis: Its Origins and Function in Time Perspective." *Journal of African History* 10 (1969): 521–32.

Santos, Juana Elbein dos. *Ancestralidade Africana no Brasil Mestre Didi: 80 Anos.* Salvador, Brazil: SECNEB, 1997.

Schafer, Sylvia. *Children in Moral Danger and the Problem of Government in Third Republic France.* Princeton, N.J.: Princeton University Press, 1997.

Schildkrout, Enid. *People of the Zongo: The Transformation of Ethnic Identities in Ghana.* Cambridge: Cambridge University Press, 1978.

Schneider, William H. *Quality and Quantity: The Quest for Biological Regeneration in Twentieth-Century France.* Cambridge: Cambridge University Press, 1990.

Scott, Joan Wallach. *Gender and the Politics of History.* Rev. ed. New York: Columbia University Press, 1999.

———. *Only Paradoxes to Offer: French Feminists and the Rights of Man.* Cambridge, Mass.: Harvard University Press, 1996.

Siegel, Micol. *Uneven Encounters: Making Race and Nations in Brazil and the United States.* Durham, N.C.: Duke University Press, 2009.

Silveira, Renato da. "Sobre a fundação do terreiro do Alaketo." *Afro-Asia* 29/30 (2003): 345–79.

Smith, Paul. *Feminism and the Third Republic: Women's Political and Civil Rights in France, 1918–1945.* Oxford: Oxford University Press, 1996.

Snelgrave, William. *A New Account of Some Parts of Guinea and the Slave Trade.* 1734. Reprint, London: Frank Cass, 1971.

Snitow, Ann. "Feminism and Motherhood: An American Reading." *Feminist Review* 40 (1992): 33–51.

Sodrè, Muniz, and Luís Filipe de Lima. *Um vento sagrado: História de vida de um adivinho da tradição Nagô-Kêtu Brasileira.* Rio de Janeiro: Mauad, 1996.

Staniland, Martin. "The Three-Party System in Dahomey: I, 1946–56." *Journal of African History* 14, no. 2 (1973): 291–312.

Steady, Filomina Chioma. "African Feminism: A Worldwide Perspective." In *Women in Africa and the African Diaspora,* ed. Rosalyn Terborg-Penn, Sharon Harley, and Andrea Benton Rushing, 3–24. Washington, D.C.: Howard University Press, 1987.

———. "The Black Woman Cross-Culturally: An Overview." In *The Black Woman Cross-Culturally,* ed. Filomina Chioma Steady, 1–41. Cambridge, Mass.: Schenkman, 1981.

Stoeltje, Beverly J. "Asante Queen Mothers: A Study in Female Authority." In *Queens, Queen Mothers, Priestesses, and Power: Case Studies in African Gender,* ed. Flora E. S. Kaplan, 41–71. New York: New York Academy of the Sciences, 1997.

Sudarkasa, Niara. *The Strength of Our Mothers: African and African American Women and Families: Essays and Speeches.* Trenton, N.J.: Africa World Press, 1996.

———. *Where Women Work: A Study of Yoruba Women in the Marketplace and in the Home,* Anthropological Papers, No. 53. Ann Arbor: Museum of Anthropology, University of Michigan, 1973.

Sweet, James H. *Recreating Africa: Culture, Kinship and Religion in the African-Portuguese World, 1441–1770.* Chapel Hill: University of North Carolina Press, 2003.

Tallman, Janet. "The Ethnographic Novel: Finding the Insider's Voice." In *Between Anthropology and Literature,* ed. Rose De Angelis, 11–22. New York: Routledge, 2002.

Taylor, Diana. *Disappearing Acts: Spectacles of Gender and Nationalism in Argentina's "Dirty War."* Durham, N.C.: Duke University Press, 1997.

Thomas, Martin. *The French Empire between the Wars: Imperialism, Politics and Society.* Manchester: Palgrave, 2005.

Thompson, Becky. "Multiracial Feminism: Recasting the Chronology of Second Wave Feminism." *Feminist Studies* 28, no. 2 (Summer 2002): 336–60.

Thompson, Robert Farris. *Flash of the Spirit: African and Afro-American Art and Philosophy.* 1st ed. New York: Random House, 1983.

Triaud, Jean-Louis. "Introduction." In *Le temps des marabouts: Itinéraires et stratégies en Afrique Occidentale Française v. 1880–1960,* ed. David Robinson and Jean-Louis Triaud, 11–29. Paris: Karthala, 1997.

Turner, Lorenzo Dow. "Some Contacts of Brazilian Ex-Slaves with Nigeria, West Africa." *Journal of Negro History* 27, no. 1 (1942): 55–67.

United Nations Educational Scientific and Cultural Organization (UNESCO). "The Slave Route Project." http://unesdoc.unesco.org/images/0015/001511/151178e.pdf.

Vacharet, Ch. "Le village de liberté de Vilersville à Abomey (Dahomey)." *L'Afrique Libre-Revue de L'Antiesclavagisme et des questions sociales* 4ème Série, no. 15 (September 30, 1913): 391–93.

Vallée, J. "Village de liberté de St. Augustin à Kétou, Dahomey." *Société Antiesclavagiste de France* 55 (September 1908): 216–20.

Van Allen, Judith. "'Aba Riots' or 'Women's War': Ideology, Stratification, and the Invisibility of Women." In *Women in Africa: Studies in Social and Economic Change,* ed. Nancy Hafkin and Edna Bay, 59–85. Stanford, Calif.: Stanford University Press, 1976.

Vansina, Jan. *Oral Tradition: A Study in Historical Methodology.* Translated by H. M. Wright. 1961. Reprint, Chicago: Aldine Publishing Co., 1965.

Verger, Pierre. *Flux et Reflux de la traité des Nègres entre le Golfe de Bénin et Bahia de Todos os Santos, du XVIIe au XIXe siècle.* Paris: La Haye Mouton, 1968.

———. "Grandeur et décadence du culte Ìyámi Òsòròngà (Ma Mère La Sorcière) Chez Les Yoruba." *Journal de la Société des Africanistes* 35, no. 1 (1965): 141–243.

———. *Orishas: Les dieux Yorouba en Afrique et au Nouveau Monde.* Paris: A. M. Métailié, 1982.

———. "Trance and Convention in Nago-Yoruba Spirit Mediumship." In *Spirit Mediumship and Society in Africa,* ed. John Beattie and John Middleton, 50–66. New York: Africana Publishing Corp., 1969.

Walker, Cherryl. "Conceptualising Motherhood in Twentieth Century South Africa." *Journal of Southern African Studies* 21, no. 3 (1995): 417–37.

Washington, Teresa N. *Our Mothers, Our Powers, Our Texts: Manifestations of Àjé in Africana Literature.* Bloomington: Indiana University Press, 2005.

Watson, Ruth. "'Ibadan—A Model of Historical Facts': Militarism and Civic Culture in a Yoruba City." *Urban History* 26, no. 1 (1999): 5–26.

Wells, Julia. "Maternal Politics in Organizing Black South African Women: The Historical Lessons." In *Sisterhood, Feminisms, and Power: From Africa to the Diaspora,* ed. Obioma Nnaemeka, 251–62. Trenton, N.J.: Africa World Press, 1998.

Wheatley, Paul. "Significance of Traditional Yoruba Urbanism." *Comparative Studies of Society and History* 12 (1970): 393–423.

White, E. Frances. "Black Feminist Interventions." In *Dark Continent of Our Bodies: Black Feminism and the Politics of Respectability,* 25–80. Philadelphia: Temple University Press, 2001.

White, Luise. *Speaking with Vampires: Rumor and History in Colonial Africa.* Berkeley: University of California Press, 2000.

White, Luise, Stephan Miescher, and David William Cohen. "Introduction: Voices, Words, and African History." In *African Words, African Voices: Critical Practices in Oral History,* ed. Luise White, Stephan Miescher, and David William Cohen, 1–27. Bloomington: Indiana University Press, 2001.

Wilks, Ivor. "The Transmission of Islamic Learning in the Western Sudan." In *Literacy in African Societies,* ed. J. R. Goody, 162–97. Cambridge: Cambridge University Press, 1968.

Wolfe, Leslie R., and Jennifer Tucker. "Feminism Lives: Building a Multicultural Movement in the United States." In *The Challenge of Local Feminisms: Women's Movements in Global Perspective*, ed. Amrita Basu, 435–62. Boulder, Colo.: Westview Press, 1995.

Yai, Olabiyi Babalǫla. "The Identity, Contributions, and Ideology of the Aguda (Afro-Brazilians) on the Gulf of Benin: A Reinterpretation." In *Rethinking the African Diaspora: The Making of a Black Atlantic World in the Bight of Benin and Brazil*, ed. Kristin Mann and Edna G. Bay, 72–82. London: Frank Cass, 2001.

———. "Review of *Yoruba: Nine Centuries of African Art and Thought*." *African Arts* 25, no. 1 (1992): 20–29.

Young, Jason R. *Rituals of Resistance: African Atlantic Religion in the Kongo and the Lowcountry South in the Era of Slavery*. Baton Rouge: Louisiana State University Press, 2007.

Yusuf, Yisa Kehinde. "Contradictory Yoruba Proverbs About Women: Their Significance for Social Change." In *Nigerian Women in Social Change*, ed. Simi Afonja and Bisi Aina, 206–15. Ile-Ifę, Nigeria: Obafemi Awolowo University Press.

Zola, Emile. *Fruitfulness [Fécondité]*. Translated by Ernest Alfred Vizetelly. New York: Doubleday, 1900.

Interviews

Alákétu Aladé Ìfę́, September 19, 2006.

Ìyálóde Basilia Abero, July 16, 1997.

Adege Abeun, April 21, 2000.

Anani Abimbola, October 5, 2007. Interview conducted by Athanase Alayé.

Bakary Abudu, April 30, 2000.

Saliou Achirou, May 10, 2000.

Alhaji Ashafa Achirou, May 10, 2000.

Ìyá Libara Cathérine Oyewole Adebiyi, July 15, 1999, April 20, 2000.

Gérard Adechinan, October 2007. Interview conducted by Athanase Alayé.

Marguerite Adediran, April 13, 2000.

Adebayo Adegbite, March 7, 1999.

Blaise Adewori Adegbite, March 7, 1999.

Joseph Adewori Adegbite, March 7, 1999.

Jerome Adegute, March 30, 2000.

Madeleine Adekambi, May 12, 2000.

Osseni Adekambi, April 6, 2000.

Adrien Adeniyi Adeoti, October 2, 2006.

Jules Magbo Adetoku Adesina, April 9, 2000, September 21, 2006.

Ashani Adeyemi, April 3, 2000.

Adrien Adegnika, October 4, 2006.

Patrice Ajibade, April 12, 2000.

Jeanne Akanro, December 9, 1998, April 21, 2000.

Antonin Iko Alayé, October 6, 2007. Interview conducted by Athanase Alayé.

Athanase Alayé, September 23, 2006.

Ashiawou Amadou, April 28, 2000.

Karim Djibril Arepa, October 31, 1998.

Alhaji Bachirou Bakary, May 1, 2000.

Seinabu Bakary, February 18, 1999, May 8, 2000.

Ajoke Bankole, May 11, 2000.

Yaya Bello, May 2, 2000.
Ìyá Afɔbajɛ Salamantou Egunlope Brouaima, November 2 and November 26, 1998, April 17, 2000.
Soule Brouaima, December 10, 1998.
Celestine Buko, April 26, 2000.
Alhaji Shouaibou Chekoni, April 3, 1999.
Sholakunmi Dogba, April 26, 2000.
Souradjou Dugbe, April 27, 2000.
Camille Elegbede, November 2, 1998, October 7, 2007. Interview conducted by Athanase Alayé.
Egunlete Elegbede, September 22, 2006.
Fatoke Casimir Elegbede, December 17, 1998.
Marie Elegbede, April 26, 2000.
Ogundele Eleshude, April 3, 2000.
Adeniran Alabi Fagbohun, March 7, 1999, April 11, 2000.
Ayɔdele Felicite Fagbohun, May 4, 2000.
Camille Fagbohun, January 15, 1999.
Pascal Fagbohun, January 15, 1999, April 7, 2000.
Salami Fakeye, April 18, 2000.
Raymond Fashain, November 11, 1998, March 31, 2000.
Antoinette Fatoku, May 11, 2000.
Benoit Moulero Fayemi, March 30, 2000.
Soumanou Ganiou, January 29, 1999.
Kelani Guiwa, January 29, 1999.
Céline Idowu, March 1, 1999, March 30, 2000.
Sikiratou Idowu, March 1, 1999.
Boyoko Iko, March 1, 1999.
Mamadou Imoru, January 28, 1999.
Salamatou Imoru, April 26, 2000.
Souberou Inita, May 8, 1999.
Idji Inita, May 8, 1999.
Alhaji Lawani Kifuli, December 3, December 4, December 14, December 16, 1998, April 13, 2000.
Pierre Idowu Ladele, September 30, 2006.
Cathérine Laleye, March 31, 2000.
Alhaji Libari Ligali, May 9, 2000.
Alhaja Safouratou Mama, October 5, 2006.
Subedatou Mouritala, April 19 and April 25, 2000.
Moinatou Moussa, April 27, 2000.
Nimata Moussa, May 2, 2000.
Saoudatou Moussa, February 19, 1999.
Alhaji Taofik Moussa, May 18, 2000.
Alhaji Akeju Moussoulimi, April 4, 2000.
Vicencia Ode, December 9, 1998.
Mayor Deogratias Odeloui, January 14, 1999.
Marie Odeloui, April 3, 2000.
Félix Odjoawo, December 5, 1998.
Tabiatou Odubi, April 4, 2000.
Bachirou Babatunde Olofindji, May 8, 1999.
Ogundele Ogunleke, April 5, 2000.

Alaba Okanlawon, April 12, 2000.
Adedoyin Olouye, December 17, 1998.
Fidèle Olude, September 24, 2006.
Babatunde Oroufila, June 24, 1997.
Salamantou Osseni, March 1, 1999.
Marie Magdelene Oyede, May 12, 2000.
Benjamin Oyewusi, November 27 and November 30, 1998, April 10, 2000.
Imam Alhaji Nassirou Raji, February 3, April 23, 1999.
Seidou Sadikou, April 5, 2000.
Alhaja Nanfissatou Saliou, January 26, 1999, May 2, 2000.
Sani Salami, April 22, 2000.
Jarinatou Sanusi, May 2, 2000.
Al Haji Arouna Sikirou, May 9, 2000.
Alhaji Moussadikou Soumaila, September 24, 2006.
Alhaji Ganiou Soumanou, April 19, 2000.
Maimounatou Soumanou, January 26, 1999.
Alhaja Rafata Tairou, April 27, 2000.
Mayor Lucie Sessinou Tidjani, October 6, 2006.
Ramatou Yacubu, April 28, 2000.
Aissatou Yessoufou, April 13, 2000.

Index

LORELLE D. SEMLEY is Assistant Professor in the Department of History at Wesleyan University. Her work has been published in *Encyclopedia of Women and Islamic Cultures* and she is a contributor to *Crossing Memories: Slavery and African Diaspora* (forthcoming).